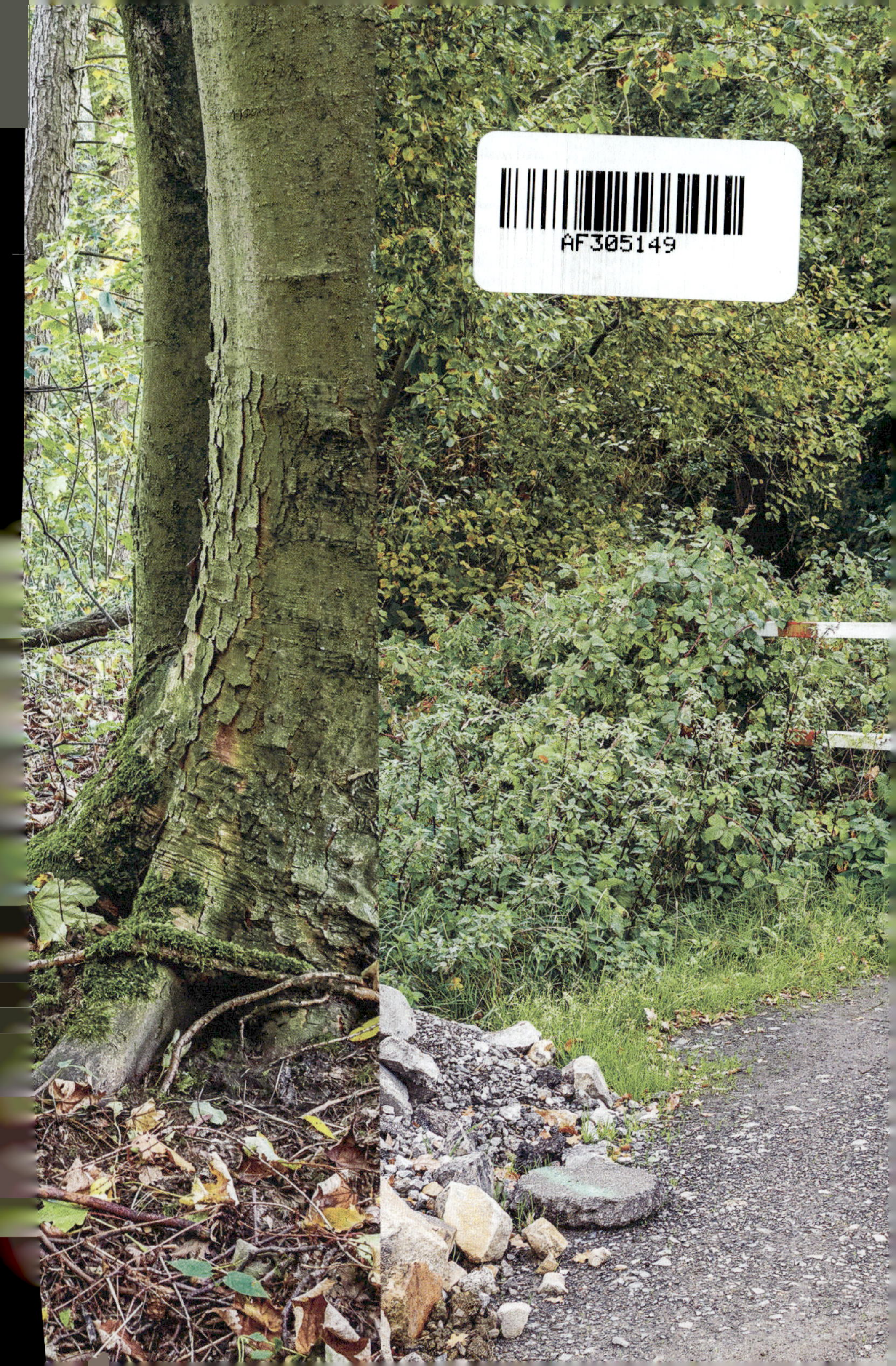
AF305149

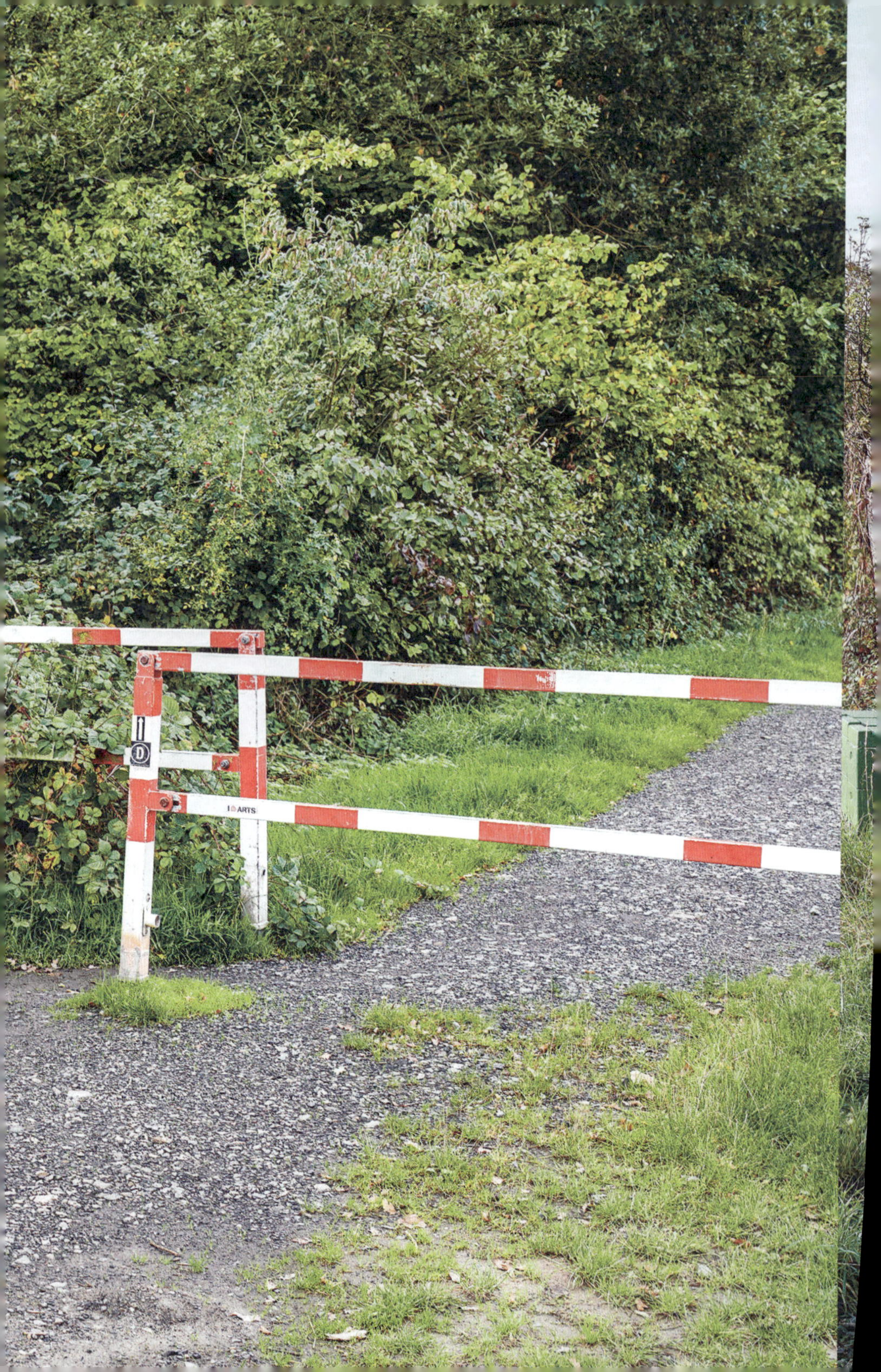

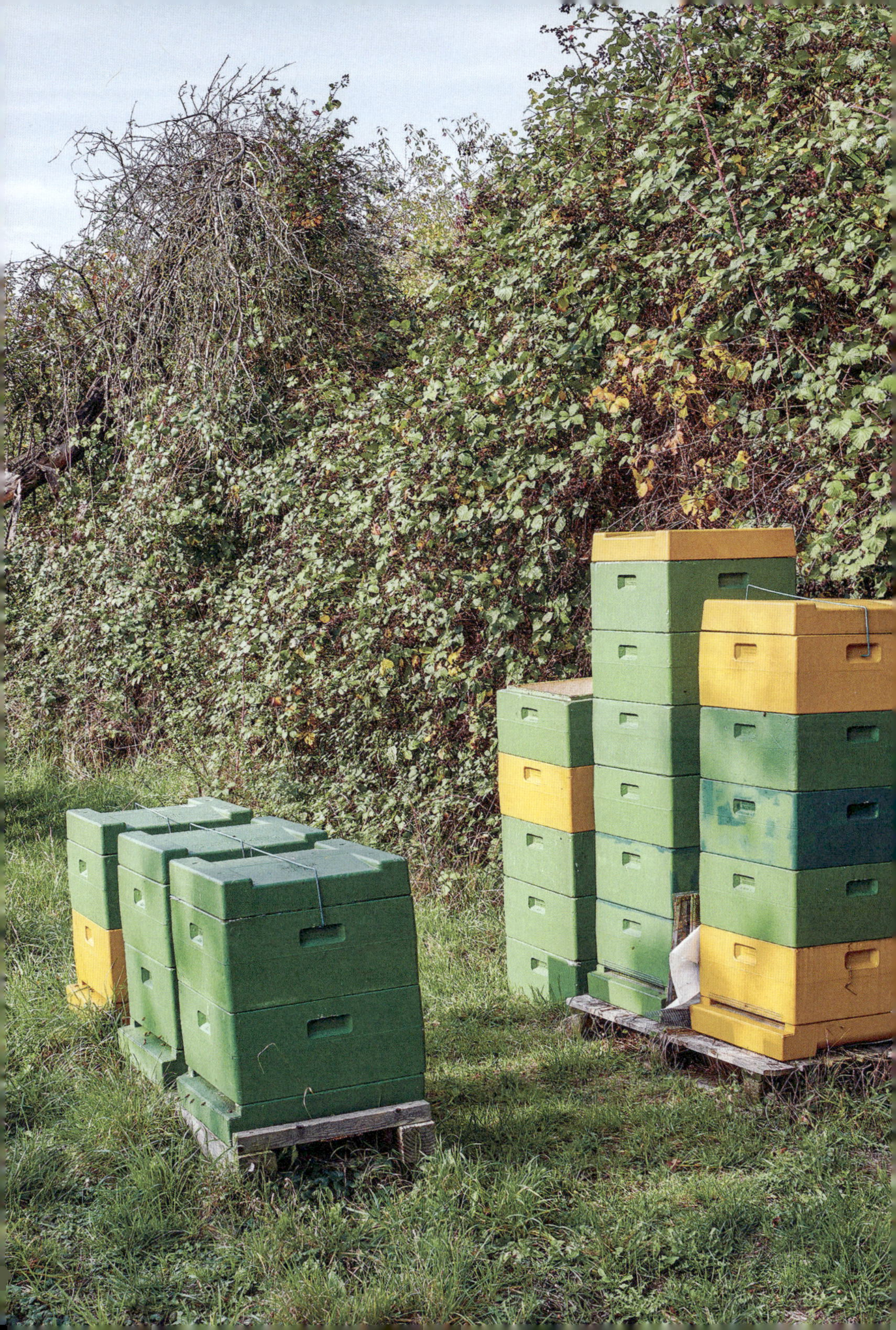

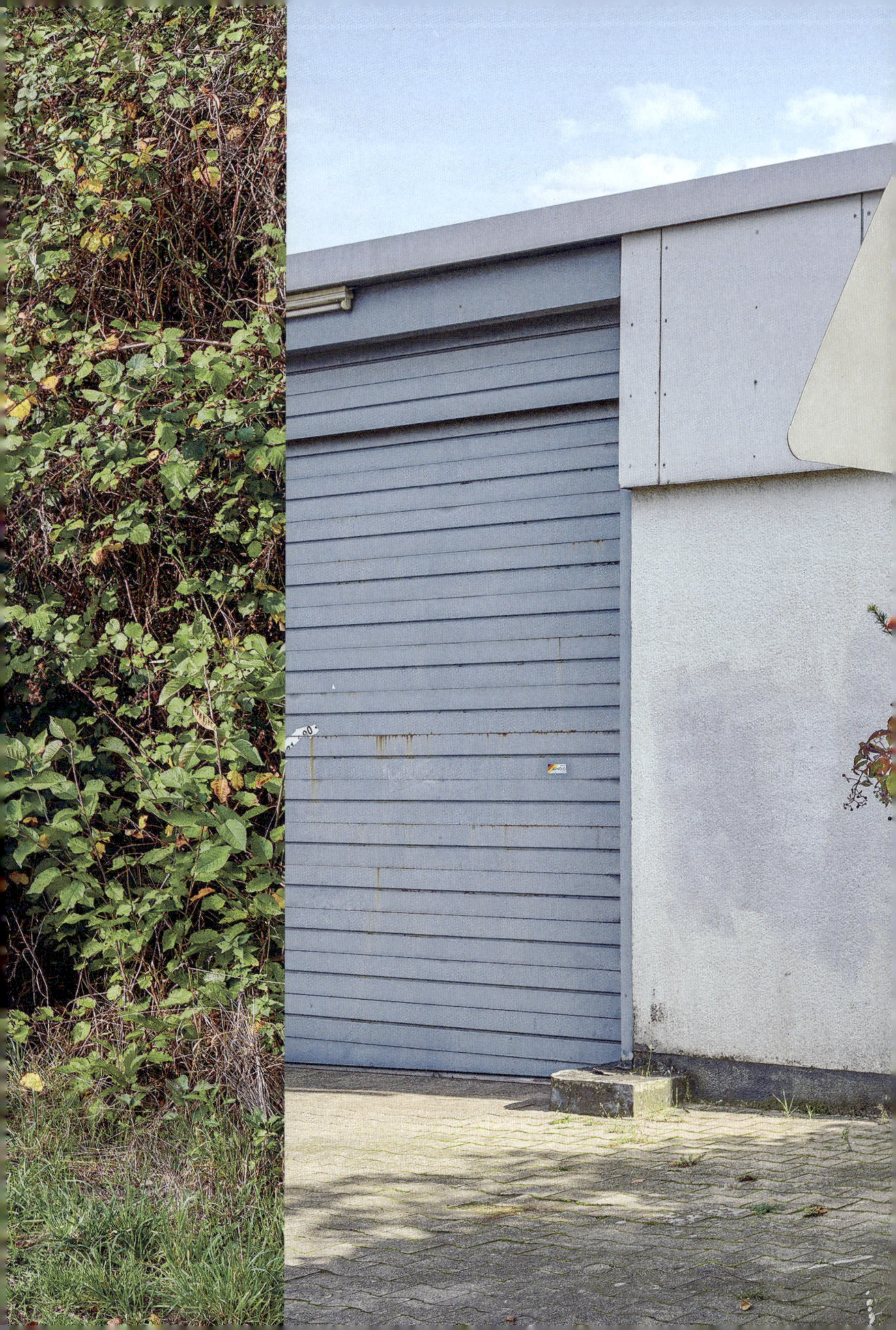

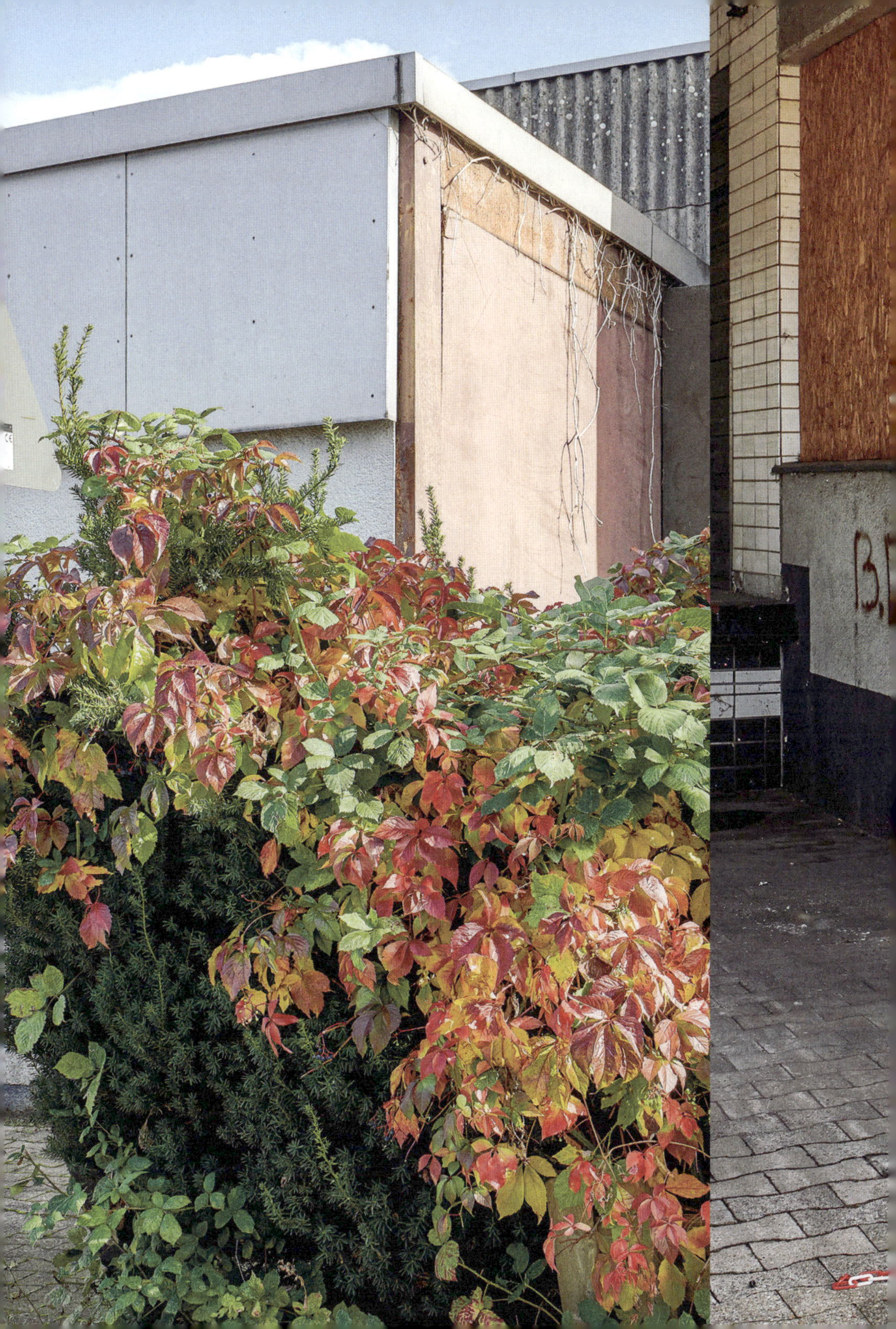

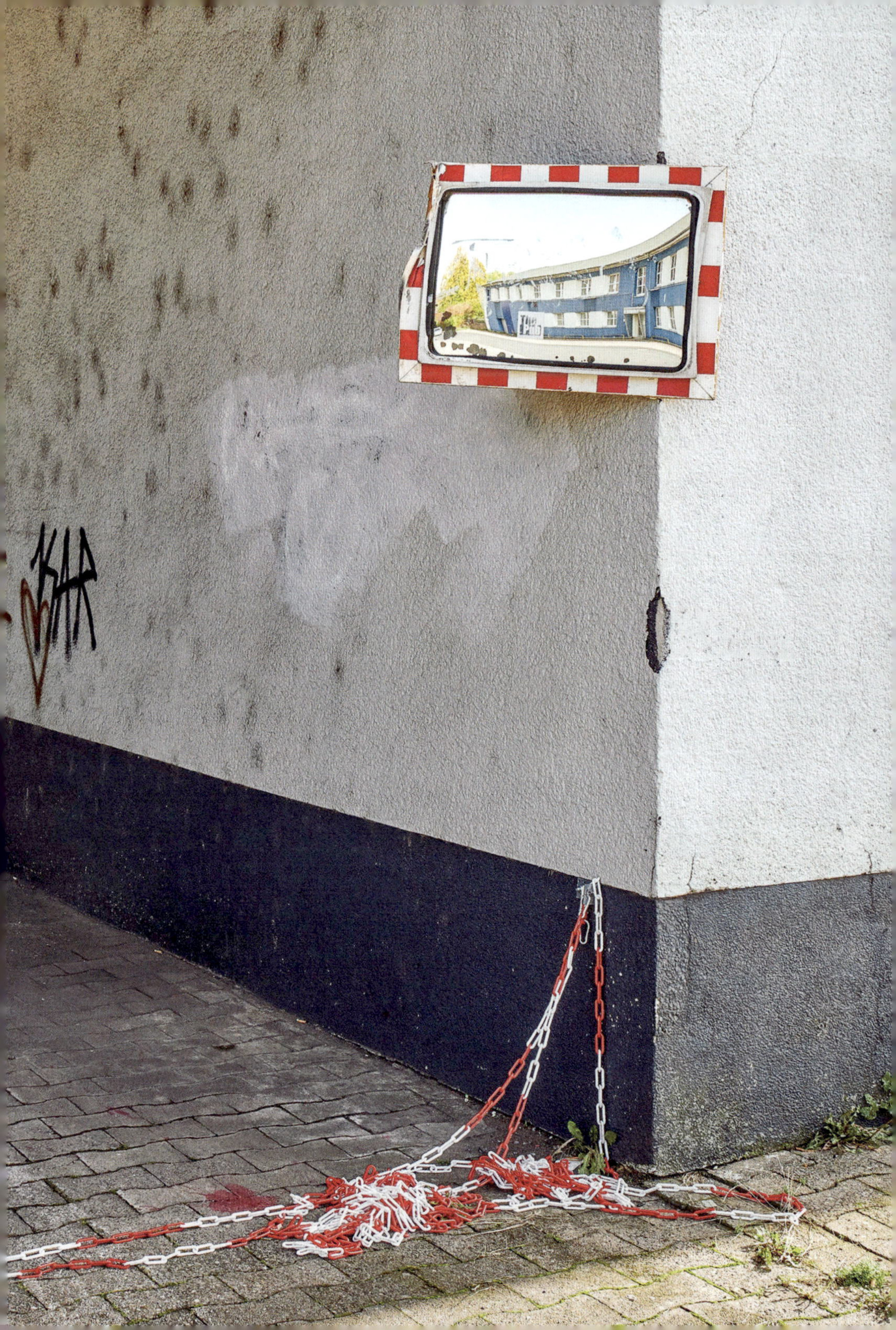

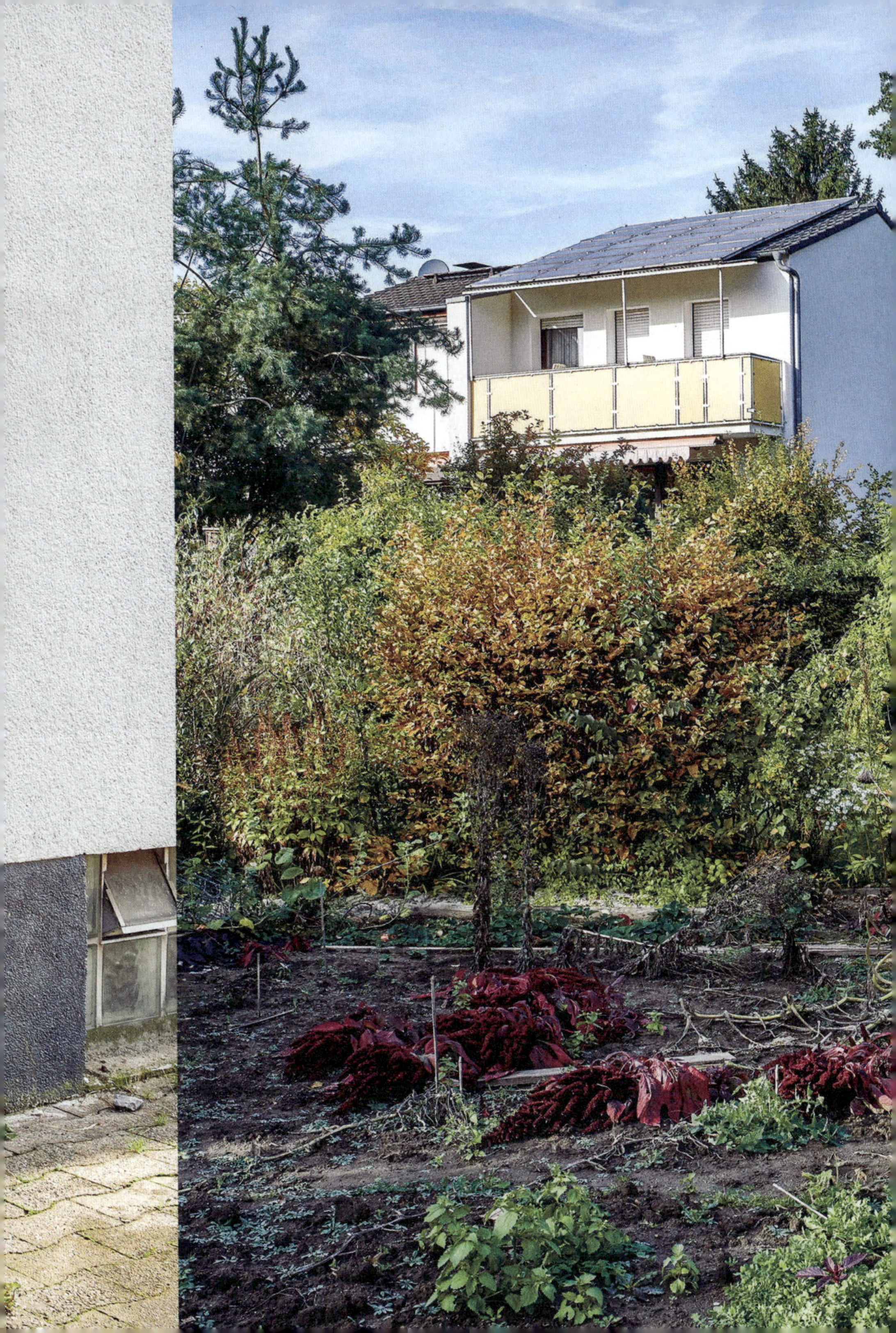

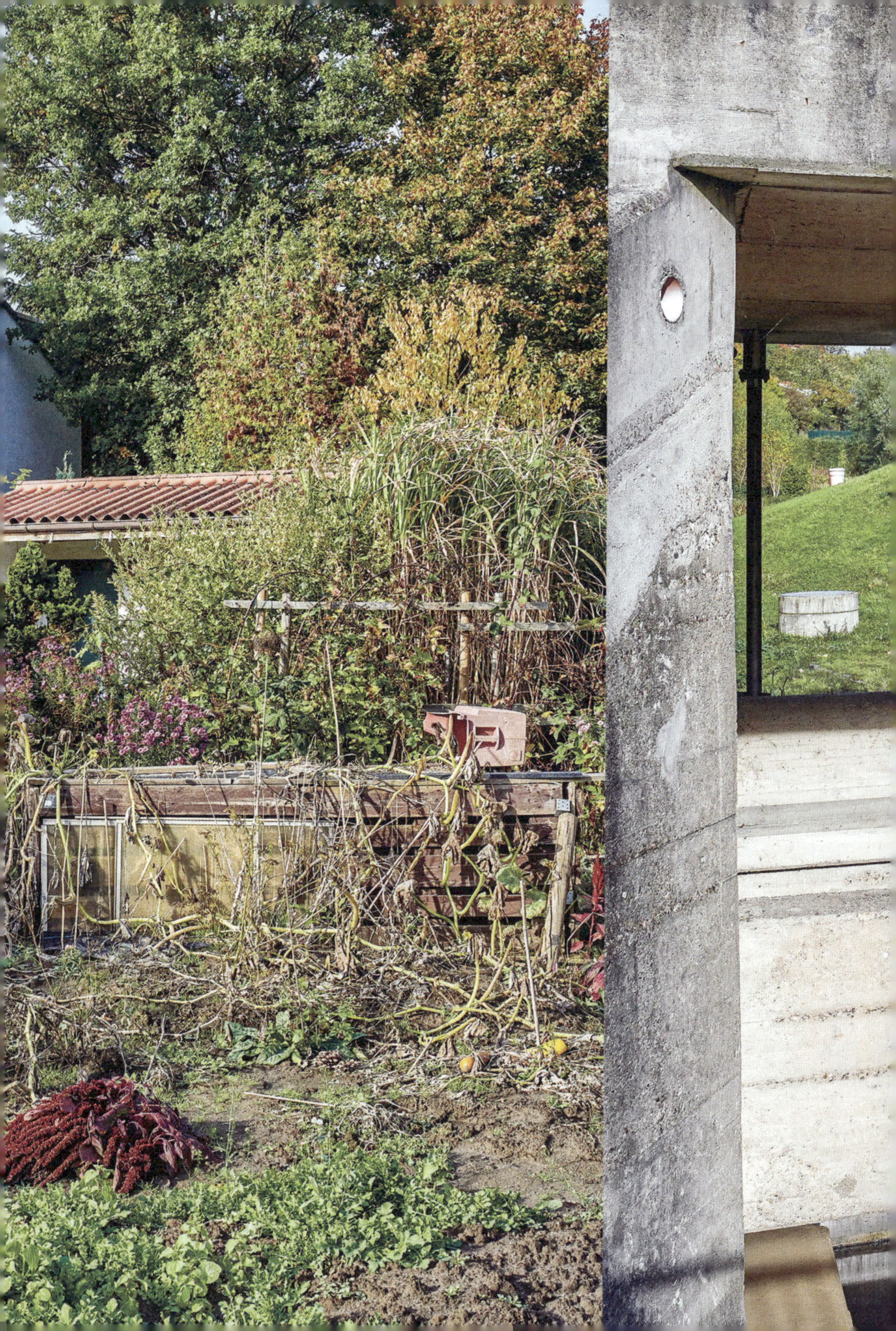

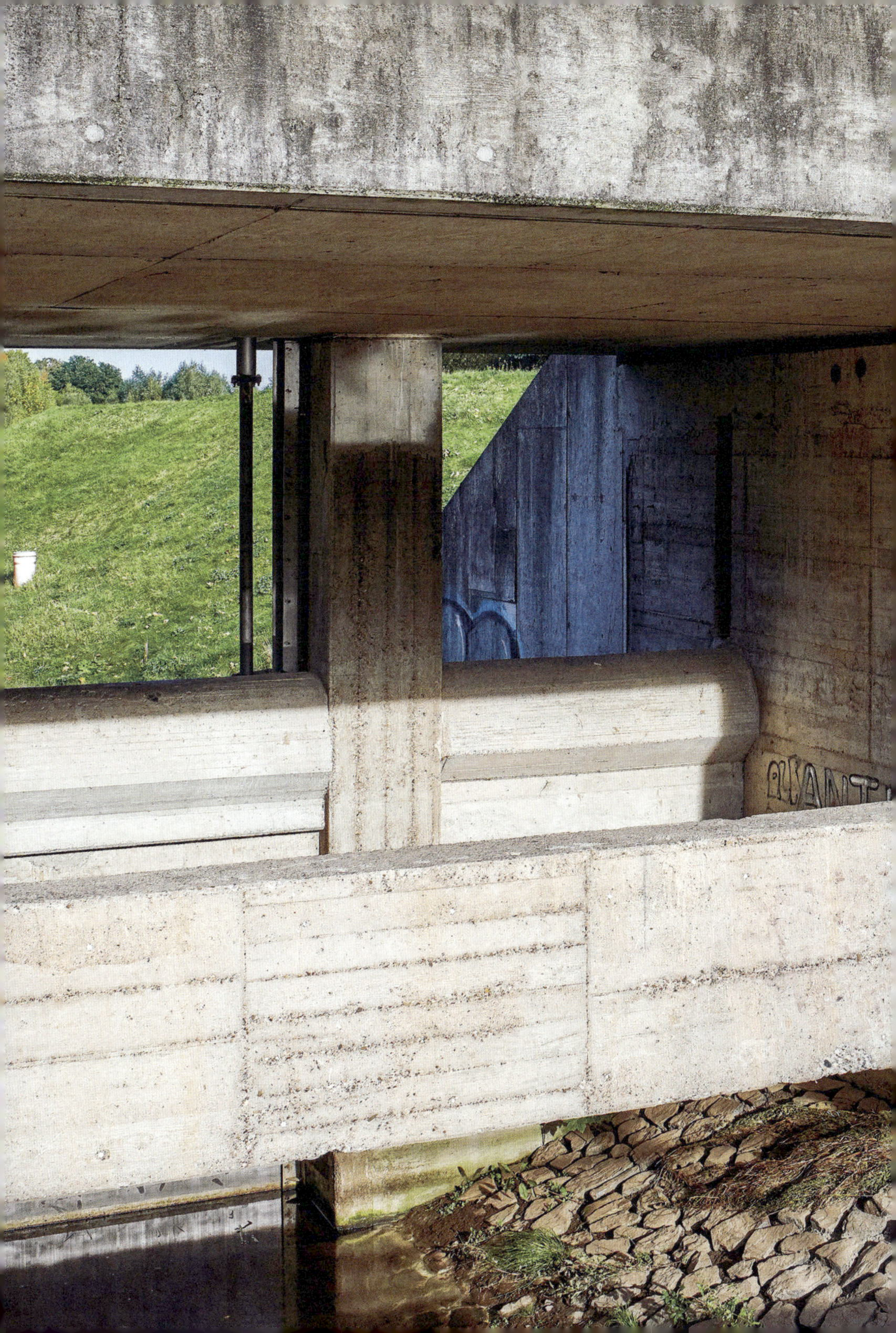

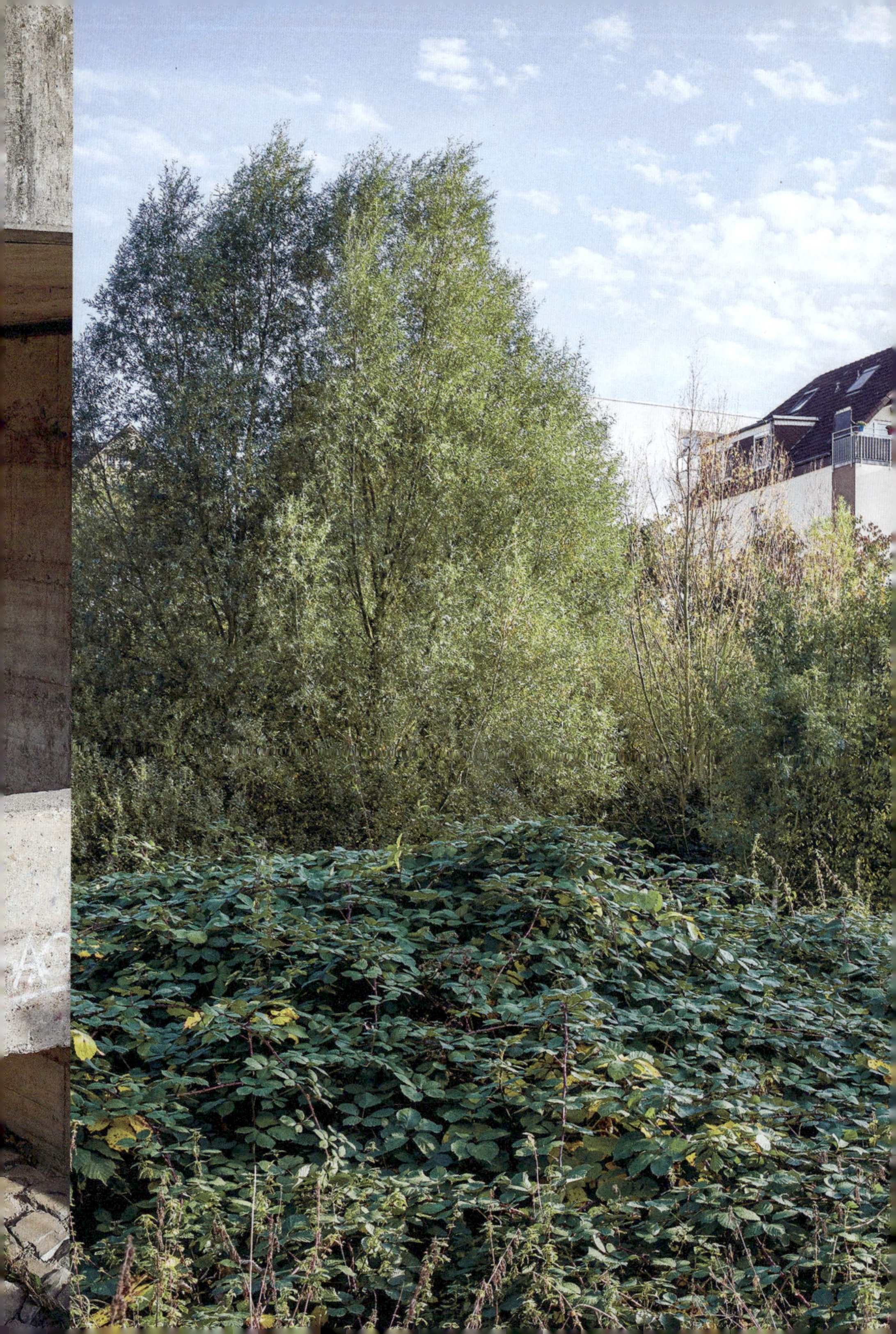

EMSCH ER KUNST WEG

Edited by Vera Battis-Reese, Karola Geiß-Netthöfel,
Uli Paetzel, Britta Peters

This collaboration project is being carried out by
Urbane Künste Ruhr, the Emschergenossenschaft
water board and the Regionalverband Ruhr, and
stands under the patronage of Ina Brandes,
Minister for Culture and Science of the Federal
State of North Rhine-Westphalia.

The Emscherkunstweg is supported by the
Ministry for Culture and Science of the Federal
State of North Rhine-Westphalia.

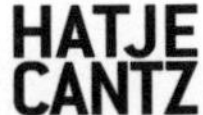
HATJE
CANTZ

CONTENTS

13

ART FOR
EVERYONE
AT ALL TIMES

«Art for everyone at all times!» is the adopted motto of
the Emscherkunstweg [Emscher Art Trail]. It is also a
promise that everyone who supports the project and fills
it with life upholds: the artists and collectives, Urbane
Künste Ruhr [Urban Arts Ruhr], the Emschergenossenschaft [Emscher Cooperative] water board and the
Regionalverband Ruhr [Regional Association Ruhr], as
the institutions responsible for the collaboration project's implementation; and of course you — the visitors
and viewers. Together, the twenty-four works of public
art currently included in the Emscherkunstweg form a
sculpture trail that runs along the banks of the Emscher
river, from its source in Holzwickede to its mouth in Dinslaken. They do indeed offer art for everyone at all times!
    As a growing — and now permanent — exhibition
of public art at the very heart of the Ruhr region, the
Emscherkunstweg provides a polyphonic artistic
response to one of the largest renaturation projects in
Europe and the industrial heritage that lies behind this.
In their outdoor locations, the artworks are accessible to
everyone at all times, and also free of charge: to cyclists
exploring more than a hundred kilometres of cycle paths
along the Emscher; to tourists and day trippers; and to
art enthusiasts from near and far. The site-specific art
projects invite all of us to engage with the history rooted
in the landscape of this region, and to reflect on the
major processes of structural change it is undergoing.
The artworks alter our view of the local environment and
at the same time contribute to its ongoing transformation.

15

Rarely are we able to have such a direct encounter with art, and rarely does an exhibition extend over such a wide area.

In 2010, the project *Emscherkunst* was initiated as a temporary exhibition to mark the European Capital of Culture RUHR.2010; in 2019, the decision was taken to develop the initiative into a permanent and sustainable sculpture trail. This publication traces the development of Emscherkunstweg from 2019 to the present day; in doing so, it raises important questions about the history of the site and addresses key issues of public art.

I was delighted to take on the patronage of this unique project. The quality and strength of the «common cause» of the Emscherkunstweg speak for themselves; this is underlined by the fact that it can already look back on thirteen successful years. I would like to extend sincere thanks to the cooperation partners for their unwavering commitment and support, as well as to the participating artists, without whose outstanding engagement the project could not have been realised.

Last but not least, I would like to encourage you all to explore and enjoy the Emscherkunstweg — it's well worth it! ←

INA BRANDES
Minister for Culture and Science
of the Federal State of
North Rhine-Westphalia

HOW FAR IS 100 KM?
A GREAT DEAL!

100 KM OF EMSCHER* * 84 km, to be exact
ADD UP TO ONE OF EUROPE'S LARGEST RENATURATION PROJECTS.

100 KM OF EMSCHER-WEG ADD UP TO A LOT OF DIFFERENT CYCLE TOURS.

100 KM OF EMSCHERKUNSTWEG ADD UP TO 24 SCULPTURES ALONG THE RIVER.

Flowing through the central Ruhr region from its source in Holzwickede to its newly created mouth in the Rhine, the Emscher river has borne witness to an eventful industrial history. Once Germany's dirtiest river — known locally as the «Köttelbecke», the dung stream — over the past thirty years the Emscher wastewater system has been restored into a near-natural river landscape. So far, three *Emscherkunst* exhibitions have accompanied this conversion process with a broad array of artistic approaches. In the meantime, artworks such as *Walkway and Tower* by Tadashi Kawamata, *Glückauf. Bergarbeiterproteste im Ruhrgebiet* [Good Luck. Miners' Protests in the Ruhr Region] by Silke Wagner or *Zauberlehrling* [Sorcerer's Apprentice] by Inges Idee have already achieved national acclaim as regional landmarks.

Since 2019, a permanent sculpture trail has been developed from this stock of works bordering the river. Three cooperation partners, the Emschergenossenschaft, as manager of the largest inter-city river conversion project in Europe, the Regionalverband Ruhr [Regional Association Ruhr], as developer of the central Emscher Landschaftspark in the midst of the Metropole Ruhr, and Urbane Künste Ruhr [Urban Arts Ruhr], as regional art producer, completed the Emscherkunstweg [Emscher Art Trail]. It is thanks to their commitment that today — along a fabulous stretch of one hundred kilometres — the region can boast a permanent and sustainable art project of its own. To this end, some of the already existing works have been overhauled in cooperation with the respective artists and new works added. The sculptures and installations created by Julius von Bismarck in collaboration with Marta Dyachenko, by David Jablonowski, Markus Jeschaunig, Sofía Táboas and Nicole Wermers continue the project's artistic exploration of this unique landscape at the heart of Europe's largest megalopolis.

The result is an artistic itinerary, a public collection of exciting works of contemporary art that, with few exceptions, is accessible to everyone at all times. Here, art lovers come to engage with specific works; cycling enthusiasts head for rewarding stopovers; people out walking encounter art en passant; dog-owners, pausing for a rest, take a seat on works intended for that purpose; and the sites are colonised by flora and fauna — as intended or in anarchic freedom. And in two of these installations you can even spend the night!

Our warmest thanks go to all the participating artists and those responsible for the previous exhibitions of *Emscherkunst,* without whose commitment such a broad-ranging collection of outstanding works could not have come about.

We also wish to thank Britta Peters, artistic director of Urbane Künste Ruhr, for her initiative in transforming the *Emscherkunst* project into the Emscherkunstweg.

Our thanks also go to the Emscherkunstweg team, made up of representatives of the three cooperation partners, which took care of the professional realisation of the five new productions, as well as

20

communication and public relations. We also wish to thank the many committed municipal administrations, committees and companies for their excellent collaboration.

Without the great non-material and financial commitment by the Federal State of North Rhine-Westphalia, such a project could not have been realised. Hence, particular thanks go to the Minister for Culture and Science of the Federal State of North Rhine-Westphalia and our patron, Ina Brandes.

Likewise, we also wish to thank Isabel Pfeiffer-Poensgen, who accompanied us as Minister and patron until 2022, and Reinhard Krämer from the Ministry of Culture and Science of the Federal State of North Rhine-Westphalia, a fellow campaigner from the very outset.

We are delighted to present the Emscher-kunstweg on the following pages and eager to learn what the future will bring for art in public spaces. ←

VERA BATTIS-REESE
Managing Director,
Kultur Ruhr GmbH/Urbane Künste Ruhr

KAROLA GEISS-NETTHOFEL
Regional Director,
Regionalverband Ruhr

ULI PAETZEL
Chairman of the Board,
Emschergenossenschaft

HERE TO STAY

FROM EMSCHERKUNST TO THE EMSCHER-KUNSTWEG

Britta Peters

23

I AM FOR AN ART THAT IS POLITICAL-EROTICAL-MYSTICAL, THAT DOES SOMETHING OTHER THAN SIT ON ITS ASS IN A MUSEUM.

Claes Oldenburg
1929—2022

In many regards, it seems natural to us that there were exhibitions of *Emscherkunst* [Emscher Art] in 2010, 2013 and 2016, and that there is an Emscherkunstweg [Emscher Art Trail] today. We simply enjoy it. But actually, the traditional notions of what art can be and is allowed to do first had to undergo major shifts and cross many boundaries before such a collaboration as ours — between Emschergenossenschaft, Regionalverband Ruhr and Urbane Künste Ruhr — could be conceivable.

Until the beginning of the 1950s, and even often long after that, public art was still exclusively understood as making a political statement in the form of statues, monuments and memorials and as an autonomous sculpture or as decorative art in architecture. It was not until the beginning of the 1970s that the first public art programmes emerged. Their funding was often decided by newly founded art commissions, and they explicitly included all areas of visual art, including temporary, performative and participatory approaches.[01] In contrast to the cult of the artistic genius and the approach that public art should serve a representative purpose, this extension of artistic vocabulary represented an opening to societal questions, while also a moving away from a narrow understanding of the physical artwork towards themes like process, collective authorship and interventions. Another issue that defined the discourse early on and primarily concerned artists was of the conditions of the public spaces, the decisions made in them and the existing (or lacking) opportunities for participation.

ART IN CONVERSION
An undertaking such as planning the *Emscherkunst* exhibitions was thus only conceivable after art — like the Emscher river — had been liberated from the limitations of traditional expectations, although before the year of the European Capital of Culture RUHR.2010, comparable projects had been realised for many decades with success. According to the wish of its many fathers and mothers, *Emscherkunst* was meant to get involved in and communicate the industrial landscape along the Emscher river as it was being converted into a cultural landscape through artistic projects. A process which began in the 1990s with the *International Building Exhibition (IBA) Emscher Park*. The proclaimed goal was to make the ongoing transformation of the Emscher area come alive for visitors. Jana Golombek has written an excellent analysis of the genesis of the corresponding narrative in «Hubs: The Emscherkunstweg as a New Layer of Industrial Culture».

When I became artistic director of Urbane Künste Ruhr in early 2018, the exhibition *Emscherkunst* had been held along the entire course of the river in altogether three stages spanning from Holzwickede near Dortmund to Dinslaken district near Duisburg. Expanding the network of cycle paths was progressing, and the Emscher river's remodelling was set to end soon in 2021. While Arwed Messmer's photo series «Emscher Walk» gives us a vivid picture of the landscapes on the banks of the Emscher in 2019 — arranged in the book from the source to the estuary — Agnes Sawer and Silke Wilts provide with their essay «The Emscher: A Black River Turns Blue» an insight into the history of the Emscher river and its remodelling. As soon as I took up my position, various people began to ask me how *Emscherkunst* might continue in the future — a question that was not easy to answer. What would it mean to plan another temporary exhibition along the Emscher? Where exactly would it take place, and were there still enough new thematic and geographic situations left for new projects, thus avoiding repetition? From my point of view as a curator, working with artists on new site- and context-specific works means giving them maximum creative freedom. This is the only way everyone can experience and perceive something different through art — something we have not already formulated, imagined or wished for. Claes Oldenburg's call for a political-erotical-mystical presence is a graphic and poignant description of this momentum.[02] Yet regardless of all the enthusiasm about the seemingly endless possibilities of contemporary art to address and convey complex issues and to collaborate with other fields of art, the promotion of the artistic ideas and the demands applied to the concrete projects should always be balanced. However, especially because so many things had already been tried conclusively at different locations in previous *Emscherkunst* exhibitions, I did not think it would be easy to guarantee this fundamental creative freedom.

BUILDING IN THE INVENTORY
After taking countless cycle tours along the Emscher with different groups of people, I was finally convinced by the quality of the already existing works — by Silke Wagner, atelier le balto, Tobias Rehberger and other renowned artists — to suggest to our cooperation partners that we should pursue the course of creating a permanent sculpture path. Instead of spending a lot of money and effort on a new exhibition, my plan was to secure the inventory of works in the sense of a public art collection both aesthetically as well as technically. Finally, I wanted to explicitly connect these works, some of which are far apart from each other, as the Emscherkunstweg, while gradually adding new installations. In this way, we would be able to create a sculpture trail that is about one hundred kilometres long that forms a connecting line in the region from east to west, and that complements the tall landmarks on the surrounding spoil tips, as a path that runs on level ground. An in-depth analysis of the relationship between these different landscape zones can be found in the essay «The New Green» by Thomas Hensolt and Stefanie Reichart.

My suggestion was not welcomed by everyone in the beginning, however. The aspect of sustainability was regarded as static, and the local press said it would dismantle the project instead of making it permanent. In the eyes of the critics, the model sculpture trail had a conservative image — something Martine van Kampen emphatically describes as the persistence and reliability of the permanent works in her essay «Epic Journeys Close to Home». Nonetheless, at the end of 2018, all parties involved were able to agree on this form of further development, and Marijke Lukowicz joined the team as an experienced and passionate curator with a focus on artistic revision. The title of her essay, «The Emscherkunstweg Is Alive: On Artistic Revision and the Programme of Events», indicates her programmatic approach in which she reveals what this somewhat technical term actually means and how the works along the Emscherkunstweg can be reactivated through performative events, conversations on site and online programmes.

THE FANTASTIC FIVE

In May 2021, we unveiled the first new work for the Emscherkunstweg, *Neustadt* [New Town] by Julius von Bismarck with Marta Dyachenko, on a stretch of green near the Alte Emscher (an arm of the Emscher river) in the Landscape Park Duisburg-Nord. Its twenty-three sculptures in a scale of 1:25 remind us of the different buildings and types of buildings that have been torn down in the Ruhr area since 2000. Instead of sites of industrial culture, *Neustadt* addresses the other side of the history of industrialisation: apartment buildings, churches, adult education centres and swimming pools. The work employs the same mechanism of memory as the globally popular phenomenon of miniature cities and country parks in order to explore not the established tourist attractions, but the changed criteria of beauty and utility that led to the buildings shown in *Neustadt* being demolished.

The artist David Jablonowski chose a different approach. In his installation *Public Hybrid,* he combined forms he created with a 3D printer out of recycled plastic with rocks that are millions of years old from a quarry in the town of Sprockhövel. The group of sculptures that was installed in an area directly next to the path in the Schüren district of Dortmund in November 2021 looks like a new kind of rock formation that nevertheless harmoniously blends with the existing landscape. It focusses on the history of extracting resources that has shaped the Ruhr area and adds plastic as a substance that now relies on the waste of previous types of plastic as a future-oriented raw material.

Nicole Wermer's *Emscher Folly,* located on the grounds of a functioning sewage plant in the Bruckhausen district of Duisburg, confronts Emscherkunstweg visitors with the realities of wastewater management and the mysterious scenario of roughly sixty bicycles that seem to have suddenly come to a halt and become welded together into a triangle shape with a steel framework. The contrast between the steel sculpture, with its many small parts — each bike was carefully chosen for its form and colour — and the surrounding industrial buildings could not be greater. Due to the materials used, the development of *Emscher Folly* was especially characterised by the fear of vandalism. In her essay «Vulnerability Is the Thing; the Thing Is Vulnerability», Jes Fernie has chosen this as the starting point for addressing the worries about destruction that always accompany public art. The installation, which for this reason was not completed until June 2022 after many years of planning, invites multiple different interpretations — for example, as a reference to the disappearance of the neighbouring fishing village of Alsum, or to the fact that where the mouth of the Emscher river meets the Rhine has been relocated three times now, each time towards the North.

We realised two further works after many years of planning: *Pool Lines* by Sofía Táboas and *Königsgrube* by Markus Jeschaunig. Sofía Táboas, a sculptor from Mexico, created her site-specific sculpture in the Schüren district of Dortmund. It is a rather low wall formation in the shape of two large triangles on which a dark green mosaic has been applied. Despite the work's formal austerity, it offers many poetic associations. It is part of a series of works by the artist in which the aesthetics of swimming pools are decisive and, as an imaginary pool from the past or the future, it directly refers to the Emscher river, which has been completely renatured along this stretch.

The past and future also define Markus Jeschaunig's installation *Königsgrube,* in which he transformed the former *Königsgrube* pumping station in the Röhlinghausen district of Herne into a hybrid landscape consisting of fragments of this demolished technical building and a newly planted flooded forest. He turned old pumping pipes into a fountain that runs on solar energy in which water either flows or drips into the basin, depending on how much energy has been generated. His work keeps the memory of the ground lowering and the pumping stations alive, which accompanied the above-ground Emscher canal as a technological structure, displaying a possible ecological use of the surrounding area that adheres to the principle of the sponge city.

A STRING OF PEARLS
FOR THE RUHR AREA
All of the sculptures that have been created along the extended banks of the Emscher since 2010 reflect the relationship between culture and nature in various forms. The five new works complement the already existing spectrum by adding new themes and different artistic approaches. As a rough and romantic trail on the former service routes along the old waste water canal, the Emscherkunstweg has a unique feature that counteracts the association of domestication that the term «sculpture trail» entails in an interesting way; neither the context of industrial history nor the semi-urban landscapes between the artworks can be ignored. Quite the opposite: the highly technological remodelling of the Emscher river and the renatured surroundings set the tone for the themes and the aesthetic basis for the development of the artistic works. They are an integral part of the overall composition.

Making the works permanent has, nonetheless, also opened the door to new ways of interpreting them, taking a little pressure off the landscape and the art in the future. With each fence that is torn down on the banks of the Emscher, the local population regains a small piece of the river and achieves a higher quality of life. The Emscherkunstweg is a true gem for the Ruhr area. ←

01 If we exclude different public art exhibition projects that took place before, like the project *Kultur für alle* [Culture for All] by Hilmar Hoffmann in Frankfurt that began in the 1960s, the Straßenkunst-Festival [Street Art Festival] in Hannover that began in 1970, and the Symposium Urbanum in Nuremberg in 1971, the first official municipal programme was established on the initiative of Volker Plagemann in Bremen in 1973. See, among others, Volker Plagemann, ed., *Kunst im öffentlichen Raum. Anstöße der 80er Jahre* (Cologne 1989).

02 The artist statement from Claes Oldenburg is from the catalogue for the exhibition *Environments, situations, spaces* in the Martha Jackson Gallery in 1961 → *walkerart. org/magazine/claes-olden-burg-i-am-for-an-art-1961.*

THE EMSCHER-KUNSTWEG IS ALIVE

ON ARTISTIC REVISION AND THE PROGRAMME OF EVENTS

Marijke Lukowicz

31

Perspektivisch gesehen, Spaghettieis
[In Perspective, Spaghetti Ice Cream]
Performance by Inga Krüger near the
new estuary in Dinslaken

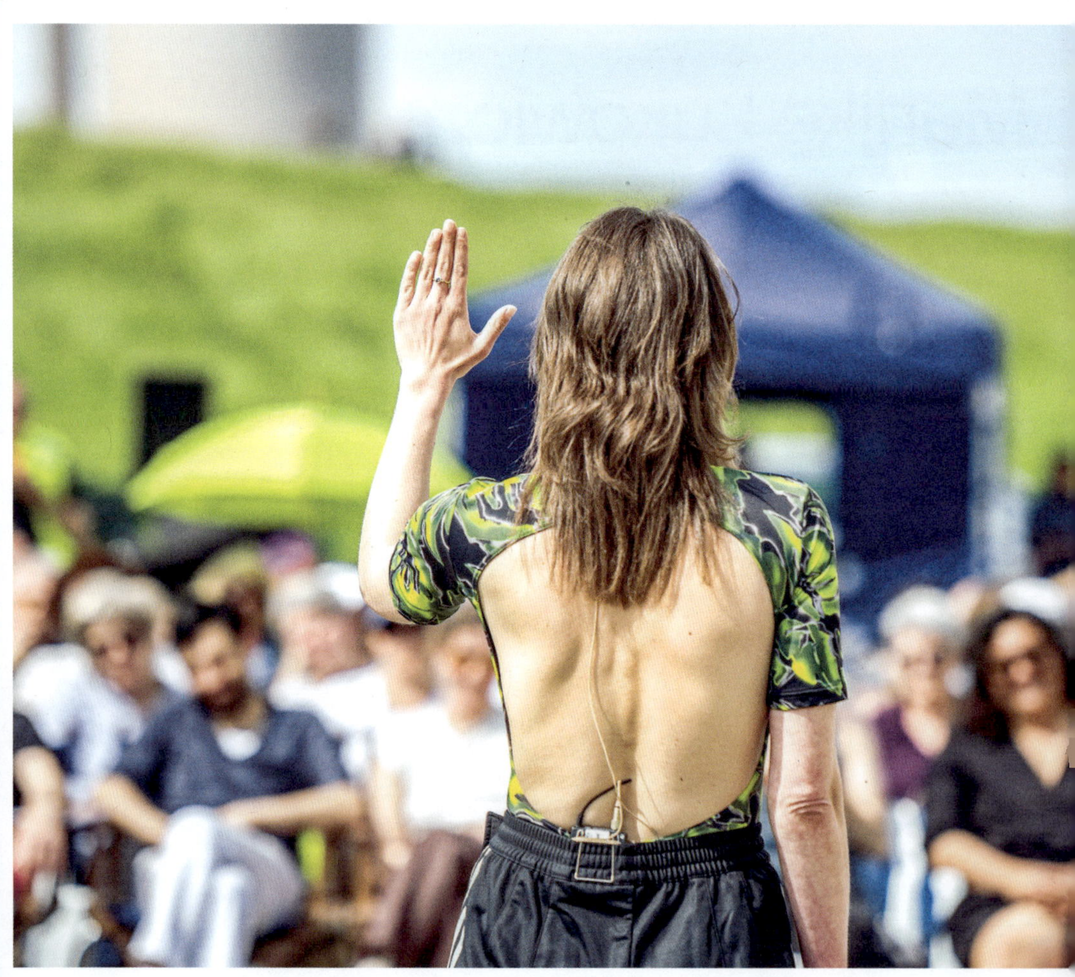

«Every generation has the right and the duty to hold its own discussions and make its own decisions about public art.» This is the view of the Deutsche Städtetag, the Association of German Cities, in its recommendations on public art.[01] Though this is primarily intended to mean that artefacts in public places which had originally been installed under certain political and representative commissioning regimes might subsequently be removed by later generations with more democratic views about representation, ultimately it also applies to ideas of what art is, which change according to time, context and an evolving curatorial praxis. Both are significant aspects of approaches to and debates about art in public spaces in its particular time.

While considering on a conceptual level how to maintain the *Emscherkunst* exhibits in the form of a permanent sculpture path, the Emscherkunstweg [Emscher Art Trail], this was a significant factor in addressing the issue of how to handle the existing inventory of artworks. The term «artistic revision» is an attempt to encapsulate the curatorial approach that emerged from these discussions and finds a deliberate technical echo in the context of the redevelopment of the Emscher. One objective envisaged in the establishment of the Emscherkunstweg between 2019 and 2023 as a lasting, sustainable art project for the region was to showcase existing artworks. These works had been created between 2010 and 2016 in association with the *Emscherkunst* exhibitions under the curatorial supervision of Florian Matzner.[02]

They are now presented in context and packaged together following a logical route along the Emscher. In addition, the artworks themselves and their contexts were subjected to critical scrutiny. This included the overall condition of the exhibits — for example, of the ten telescopes that originally made up Jeppe Hein's work *Connective Views,* which used unexpected effects to manipulate what could be seen of their surroundings, only a fraction still remained, and these were barely functional, so we decided to dismantle the work for curatorial reasons. However, we mainly looked at how the artworks now appeared in combination with spatial situations in the Emscher region, which had changed radically in the ten years after those works had been created. How had the environment changed? How were the artworks being perceived?

One example that is particularly emblematic is the installation *Kunstpause* [Art Break] by the collective atelier le balto from 2016. Here the artists included a form of »artistic revision« in the concept for maintaining the work right from the outset: once a year they visit the Ruhr region and check under the bridge Mallinckrodtbrücke in Dortmund-Huckarde to see how the hazelnut grove — an area previously used for offset planting — has grown while interacting with their architectural interventions in the form of wooden walkways and terraces. By 2021, when a half-pipe by the artist Roberto

Cuellar was constructed right alongside in collaboration with the Dortmund skateboard initiative, a substantial adaptation to these new spatial factors and perspectives and also the more expansive vegetation had become necessary, which was then carried out the following year.

We have also held discussions with many other artists, inviting them to visit their works again together with us and in some cases expand on or adjust their concepts. In the open-ended nature of these discussions it became apparent that artistic thinking in public spaces is consistent with an openness to change — indeed, it must be. Not only artworks might have changed after ten years and are never entirely complete in the fluid arena of outdoor public spaces: as they are often conceived in site-specific terms, they find themselves in a state of constant change in synchronicity, as it were, with their location. Places can change for reasons of urban or landscape planning, politics or bureaucracy. In particular, the formerly abandoned spaces and disused industrial sites along the once open Emscher sewer system have been redesignated in recent years. There were repeated discussions about potential new uses for the former Herne treatment plant between the Emscher and the Rhine-Herne canal that might transcend Silke Wagner's monumental wall mosaic *Glückauf. Bergarbeiterproteste im Ruhrgebiet* [Good Luck. Miners' Protests in the Ruhr Region]. In the course of these discussions the artist's attention was drawn to the low bungalow of the former administration building. An extension of her work followed, which repurposed the administrative building to display a newspaper on its walls. Here there are now large-scale posters of the protest newspaper that was distributed to visitors temporarily during the exhibition's original run in 2010. To achieve this, the entire building was covered in anthracite-coloured paint, consequently making a new sculptural intervention within the disused site.

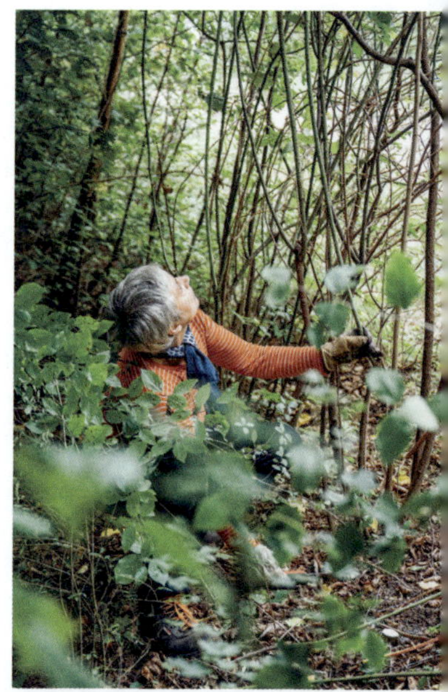

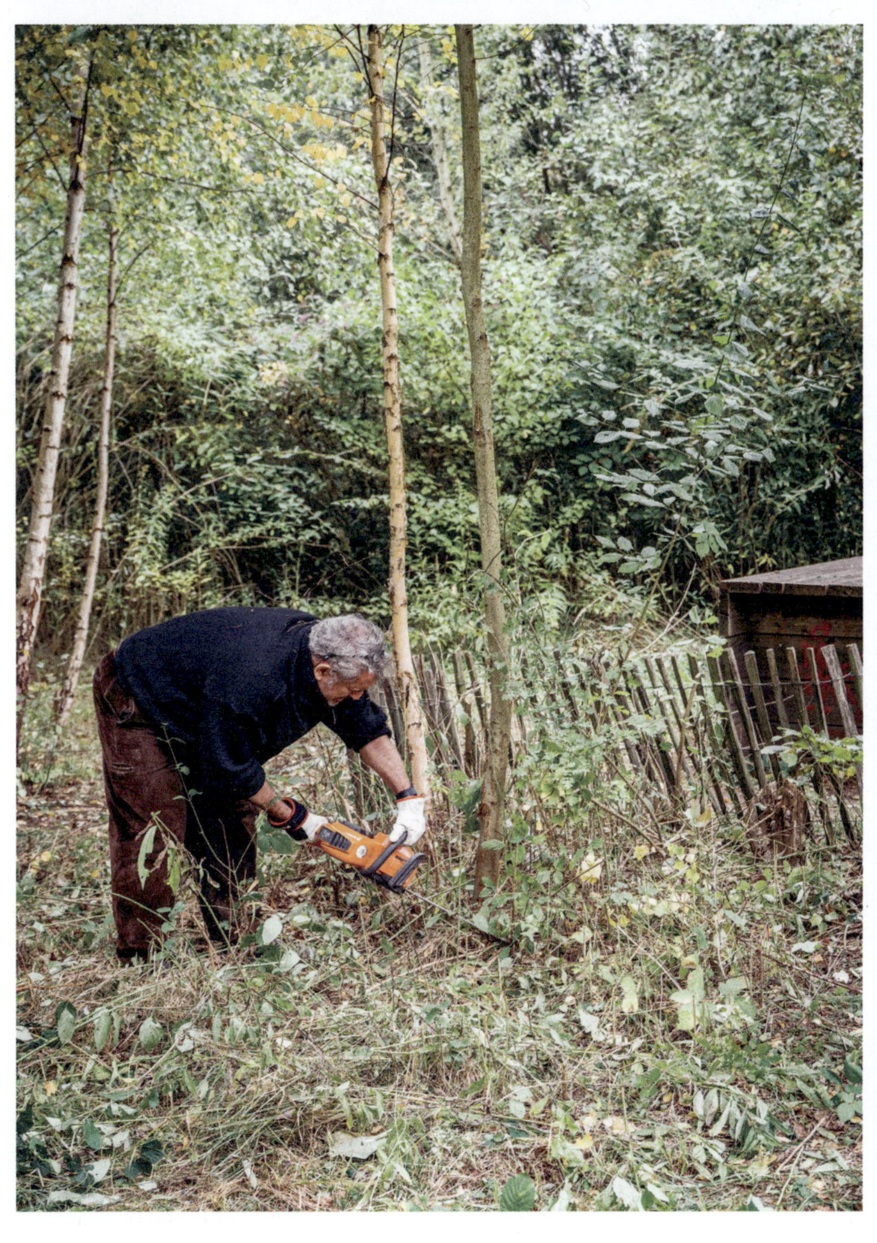

Artistic revision at *Kunstpause*:
Véronique Faucheur and Marc Pouzol at work

In the cases of two other artworks, their condition prompted formal and aesthetic adjustments. In 2019 the *Zauberlehrling* [Sorcerer's Apprentice] by Inges Idee had to be thoroughly overhauled when an inspection of the structure revealed significant defects. In order to overcome these, Inges Idee adapted the shape of the swaying electricity pylon, which led through collective discussion, to an entirely new colour scheme. Similarly, *Carbon Obelisk* by Rita McBride was also reworked in 2021. Changes to the material necessitated a new coating which, in consultation with the artist, was brighter and more clearly reflective.

Not all the works have undergone an «artistic revision», but it has been evident that the artists have been very pleased to enter into dialogue and to take the opportunity to look again at their works and maybe refresh them by adapting them. This curatorial method is possible with the Emscherkunstweg in that the artworks are still relatively «young» and there is therefore a good chance of entering a dialogue with the artists concerned. Fundamentally, however, this practice could also be transposed to civic or communal contexts and could be used, among other things, to counter criticisms of using public artworks as a form of «civic furniture» — especially when the process of «artistic revision» is made visible to the public.

At the Emscherkunstweg — albeit at times in greatly reduced form due to the COVID-19 pandemic — public discussions were held with artists and experts in order to provide a platform for debate about the artworks themselves and the issues that underlie them. Activating art works that otherwise stand «stoically» on the edge of the trail should also be facilitated through performative interventions. So, for example, as part of the series *Vor Ort* [On Site] a variety of mostly young artistic perspectives from the region were invited to react to the artworks and their respective locations. This was launched by Nicola Gördes and Stella Rossié with their performative intervention *Da geht bestimmt etwas schief* [Something Is Bound to Go Wrong] under the Mallinckrodtbrücke next to the work *Kunstpause* by atelier le balto. This location also fascinated Montserrat Gardò Castillo and Petr Hastik. Together with their dance collective, they devised the piece *BRUTOLOGY. The Built, the Unbuilt and the Unbuildable* in 2022. At the concert by Mülheim-based band Nasssau, Piet Oudolf's *Theater der Pflanzen* [Theatre of Plants] turned into a stage for experimental music on a fading summer evening. The series *Vor Ort* also resulted in cooperations with other groups who are active in public spaces such as Die Urbanisten [The Urbanists] from Dortmund, a skateboard initiative and the project Transurban from Cologne.[03]

Another audience development project are the newly established cycle tours. Conceived by Urbane Künste Ruhr [Urban Arts Ruhr] and run by the Emschergenossenschaft [Emscher Cooperative], guided cycle tours have taken place regularly during the summer

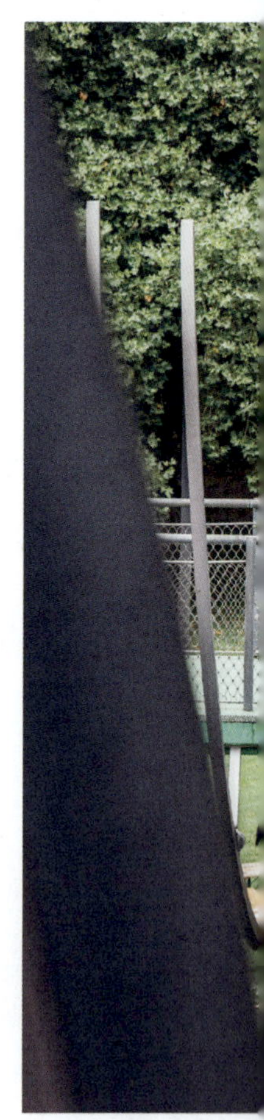

Tobias Rehberger on site for the tenth anniversary of *Slinky Springs to Fame*

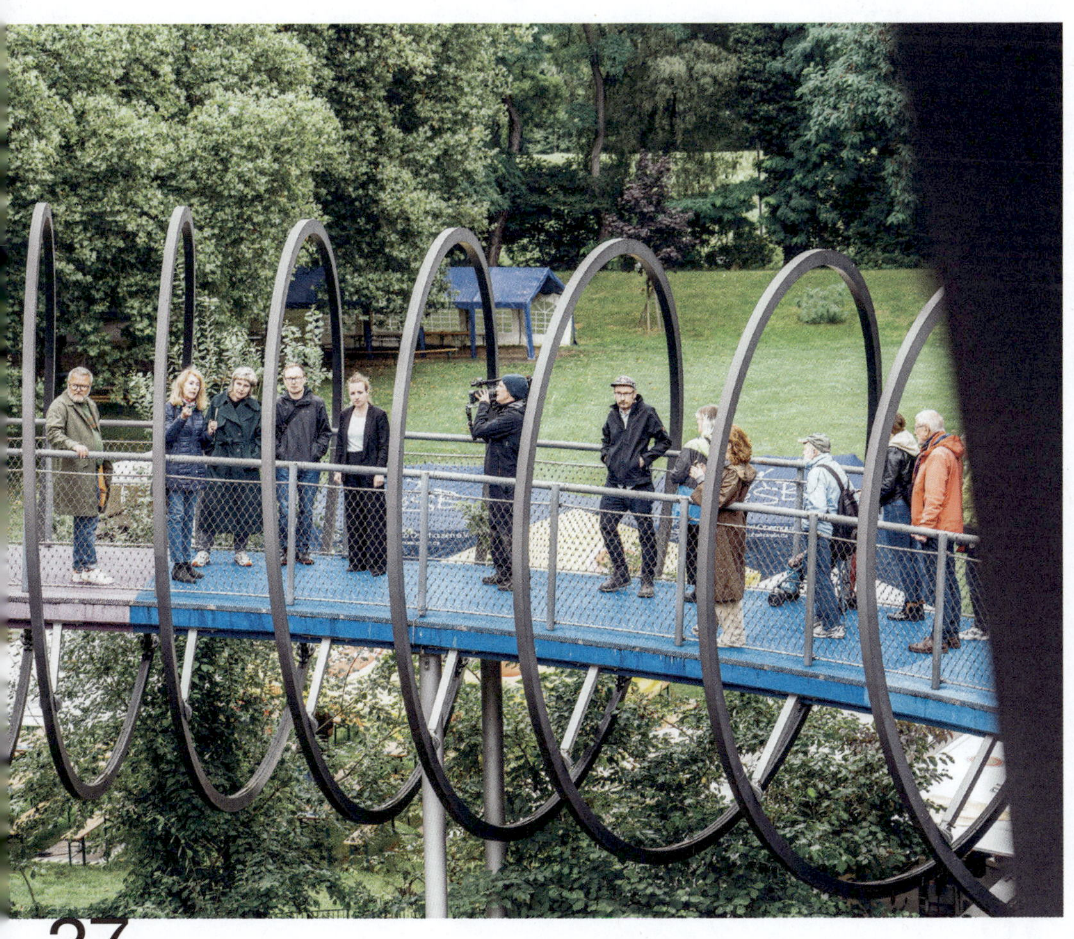

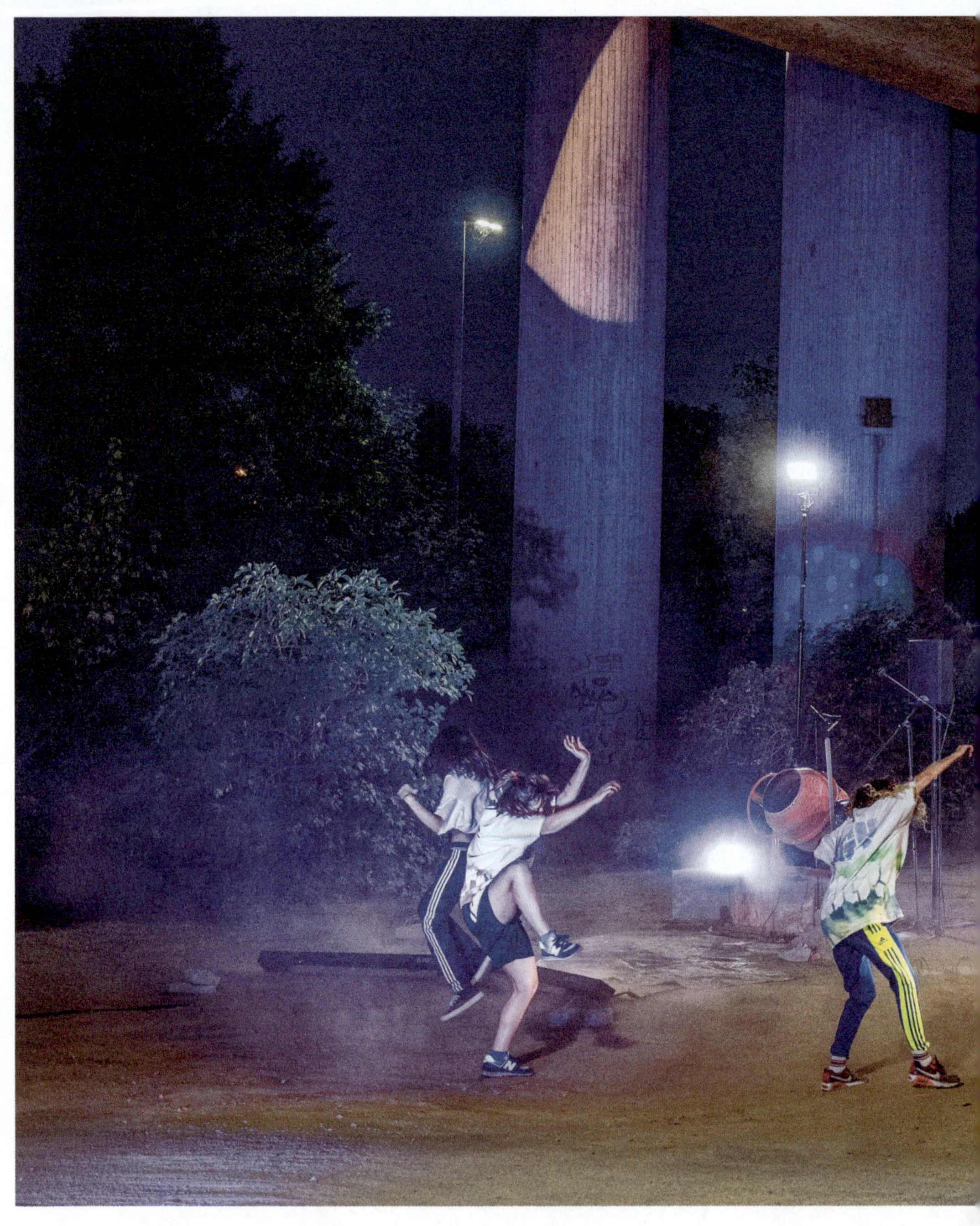

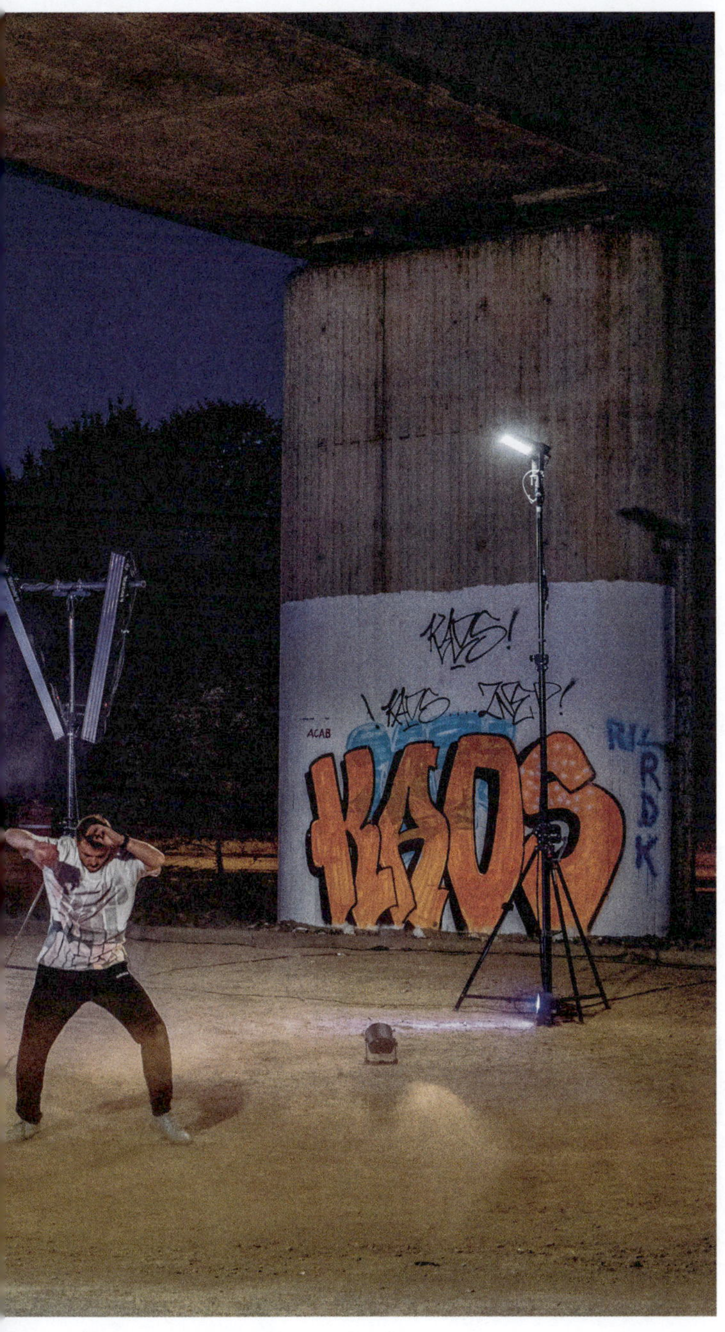

↑

Opening night: *BRUTOLOGY. The Built, the Unbuilt and the Unbuildable* by Montserrat Gardó Castillo and Petr Hastik under the Mallinckrodtbrücke in Dortmund

months since the end of 2019 — pandemic restrictions permitting. Between three and six artworks can be visited on a wide range of sections of the route. The guides explain not only the art but also how it is embedded in the changing landscape and the context of the redevelopment of the Emscher.

The COVID-19 pandemic took up a great deal of time in the previous phase of the Emscherkunstweg project. Although the artworks could be visited individually outdoors in the fresh air without any danger of infection at any time, events and audience development programmes were often only possible in very restricted forms. The Emscherkunstweg therefore expanded in the virtual space as an equally public place through the format *Emscherkunstweg: Online.* Within this framework, three new artistic productions were created for the website. The collective thisisinternet.de, made up of Lex Rütten and Jana Kerima Stolzer, as well as the two artists Ani Schulze and Alina Schmuch each created a video work based on the themes and specific features of the Emscherkunstweg. In the film *Pawāaraibu — filling the vacuum: Episode 1: pumps n' lungs* Lex Rütten and Jana Kerima Stolzer show a post-human image of the Ruhr region. Ani Schulze's work *Suffusion of Yellow* focusses, among other things, on the spiritual power of water in ritual cleansing, while the film *Badezimmerstudien: Episode 1: Die Besichtigung* [Bathroom Studies: Episode 1: The Viewing] by Alina Schmuch traces a connection between private bathrooms and the public, invisible infrastructure of the Emscher sewage.

The richly varied programme that supplements the permanent artworks of the Emscherkunstweg developed from the idea that enduring artworks in outdoor public spaces should not be regarded as static and self-enclosed. They are and remain part of an ever-new present, with which they should be brought into dialogue in order not to be confined to the role of unspeaking witnesses of the past. ←

→

Poetry for Future: Art oracle for all by the performance duo Meine Wunschdomain

01 «Kunst im öffentlichen Raum. Eine Handreichung», Deutscher Städtetag 2013, p. 4 → staedtetag. de/publikationen/ weiterepublikationen/ appellzumumgangmit- kunstimoeffentlichenraum (accessed 31 May 2023).

02 See *Emscherkunst 2010,* ed. Florian Matzner, Karl-Heinz Petzinka and Jochen Stemplewski, exh. cat. (Ostfildern, 2010); *Emscherkunst 2013,* ed. Florian Matzner, Lukas Crepaz, Karola Geiß-Netthöfel and Jochen Stemplewski, exh. cat. (Ostfildern, 2013); *Emscherkunst 2016,* ed. Florian Matzner, Lukas Crepaz, Karola Geiß- Netthöfel, Uli Paetzel, exh. cat. (Bielefeld/Berlin, 2016).

03 See *TRANSURBAN Residency Dortmund,* ed. Georg Barringhaus and Margrit Miebach (Cologne, 2021).

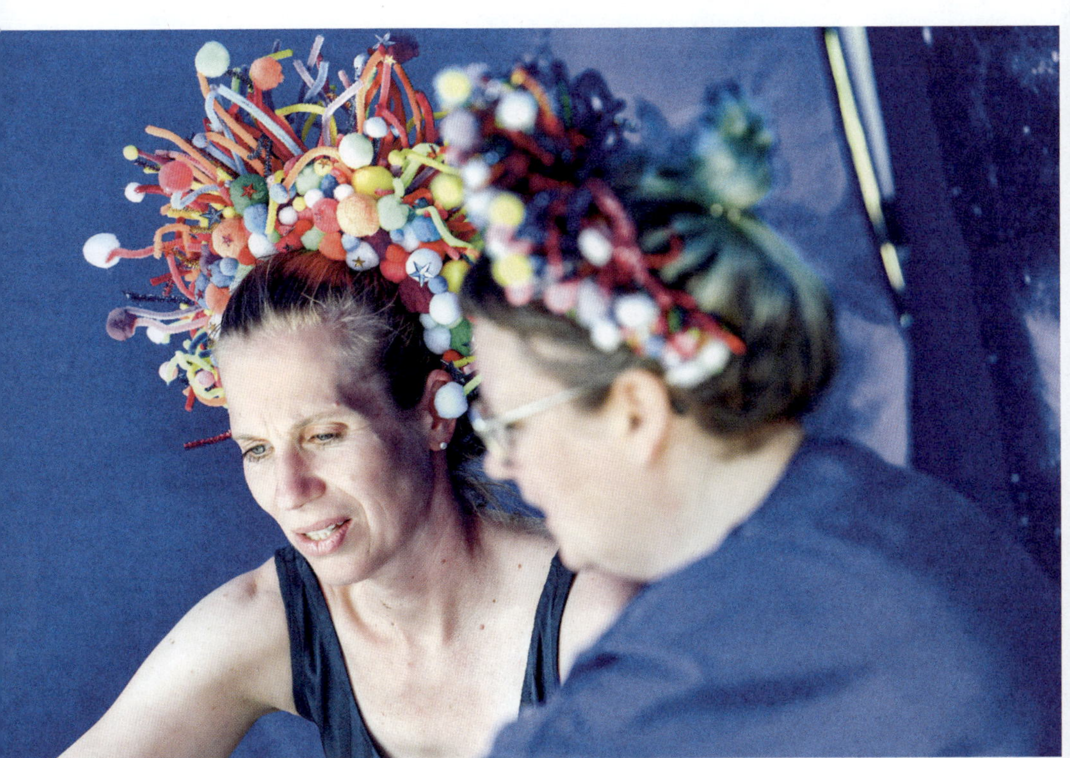

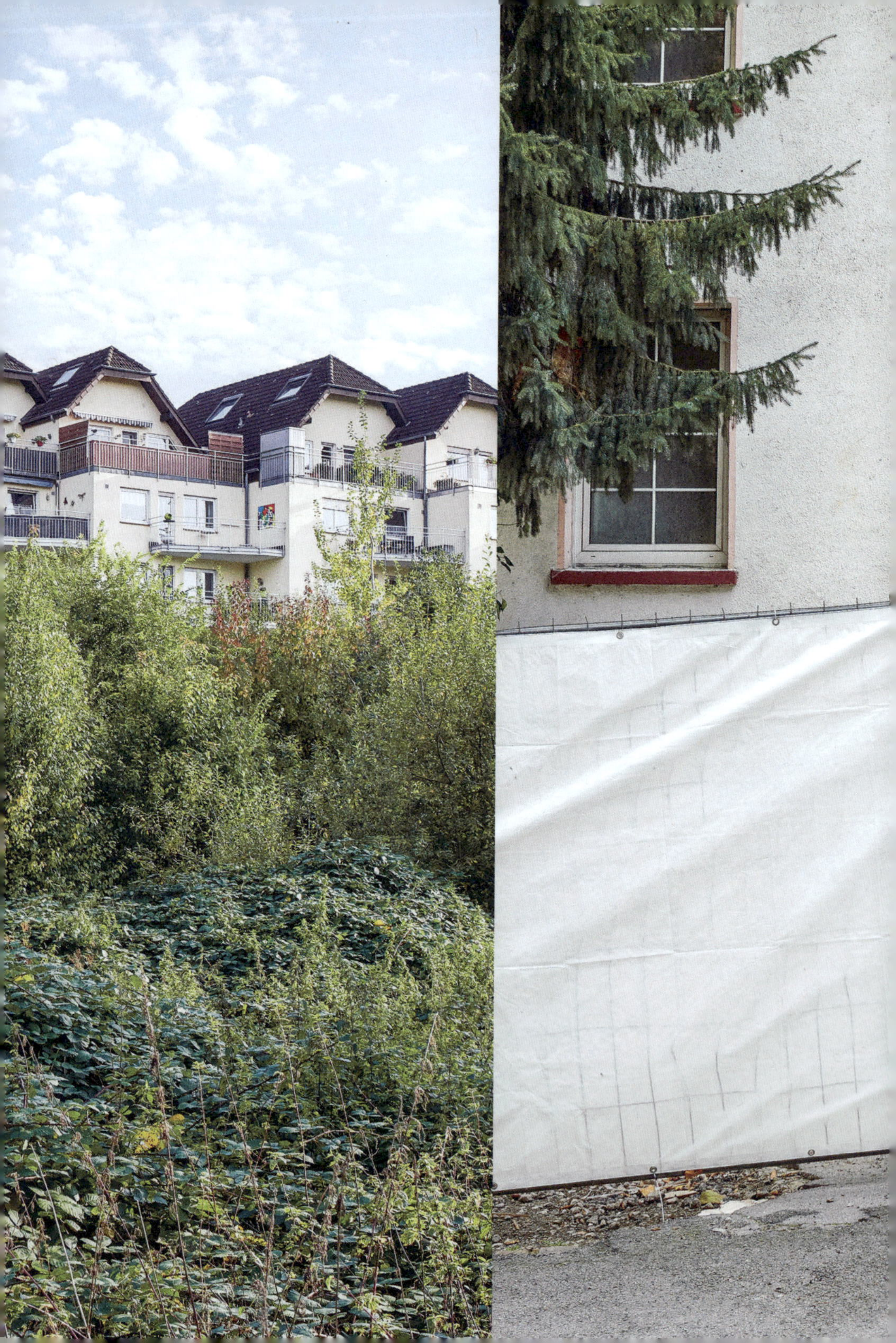

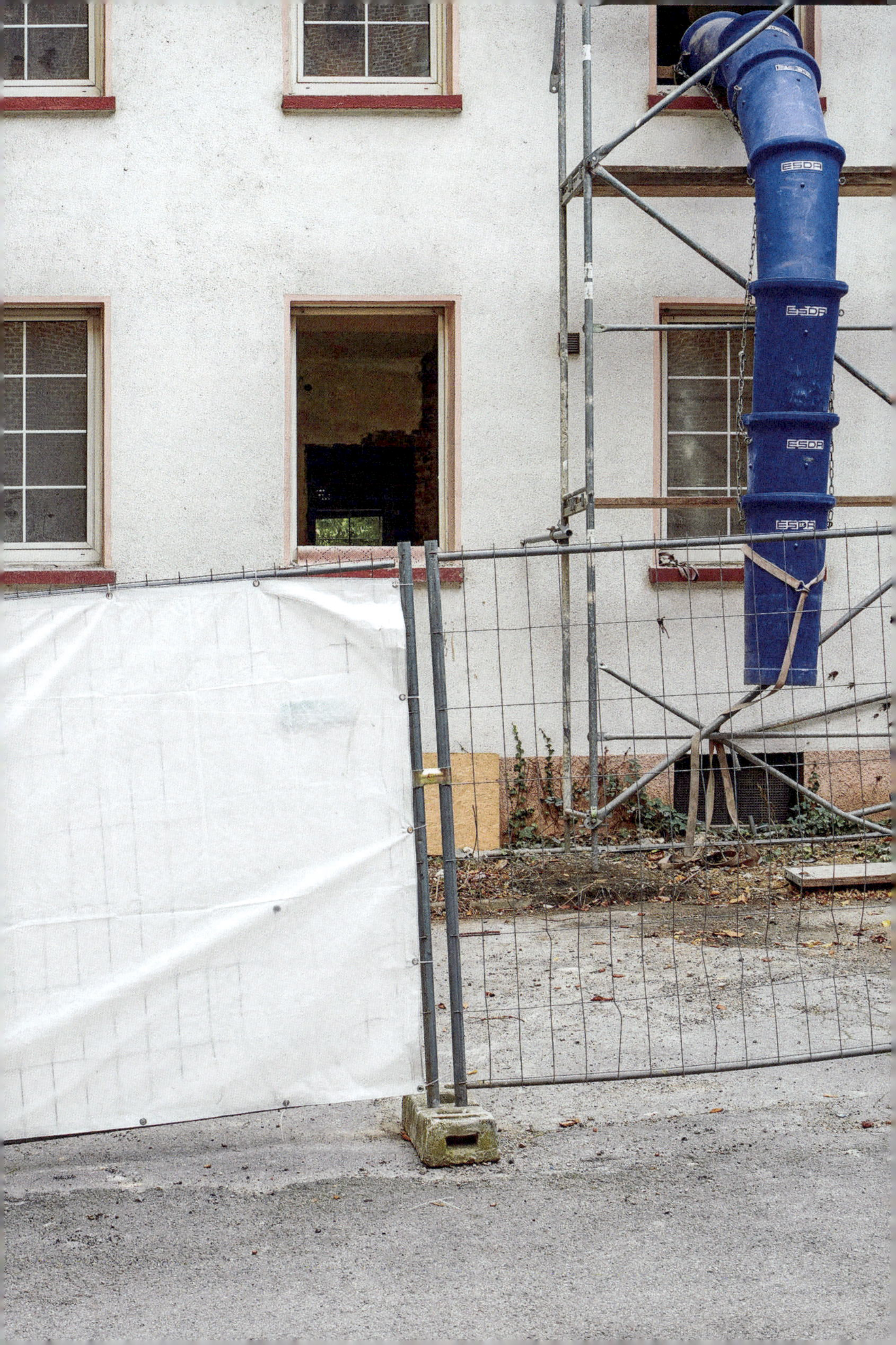

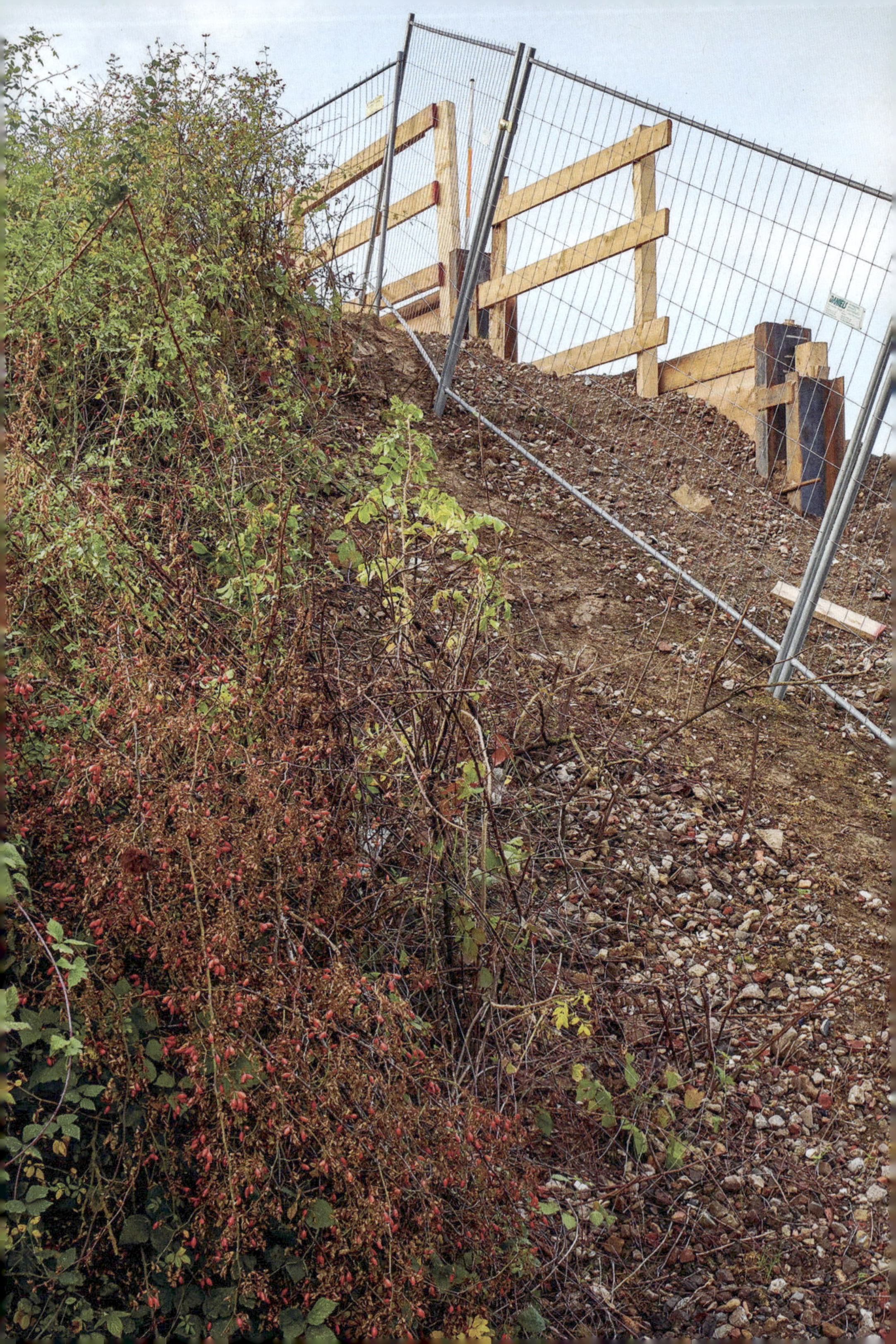

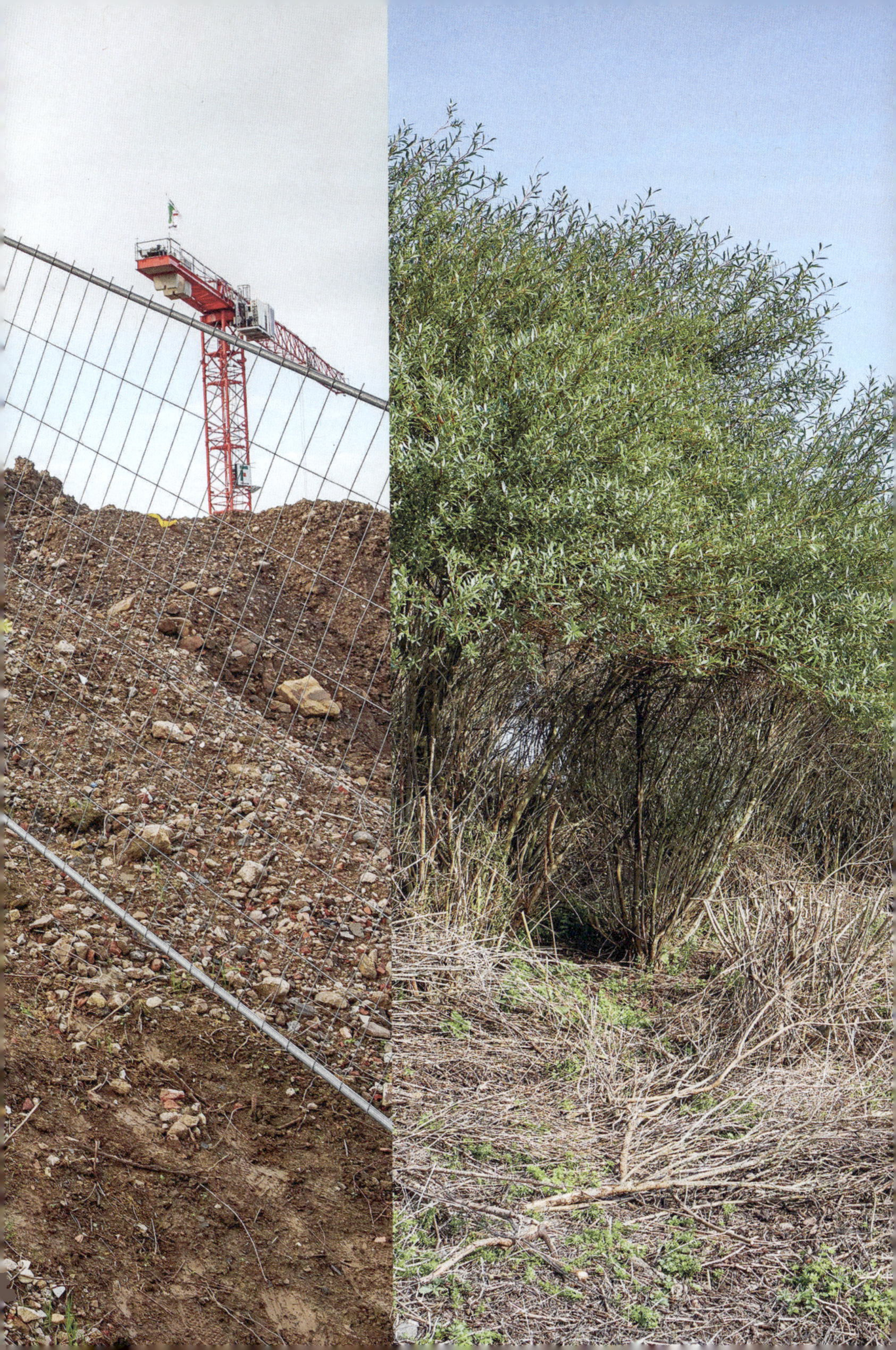

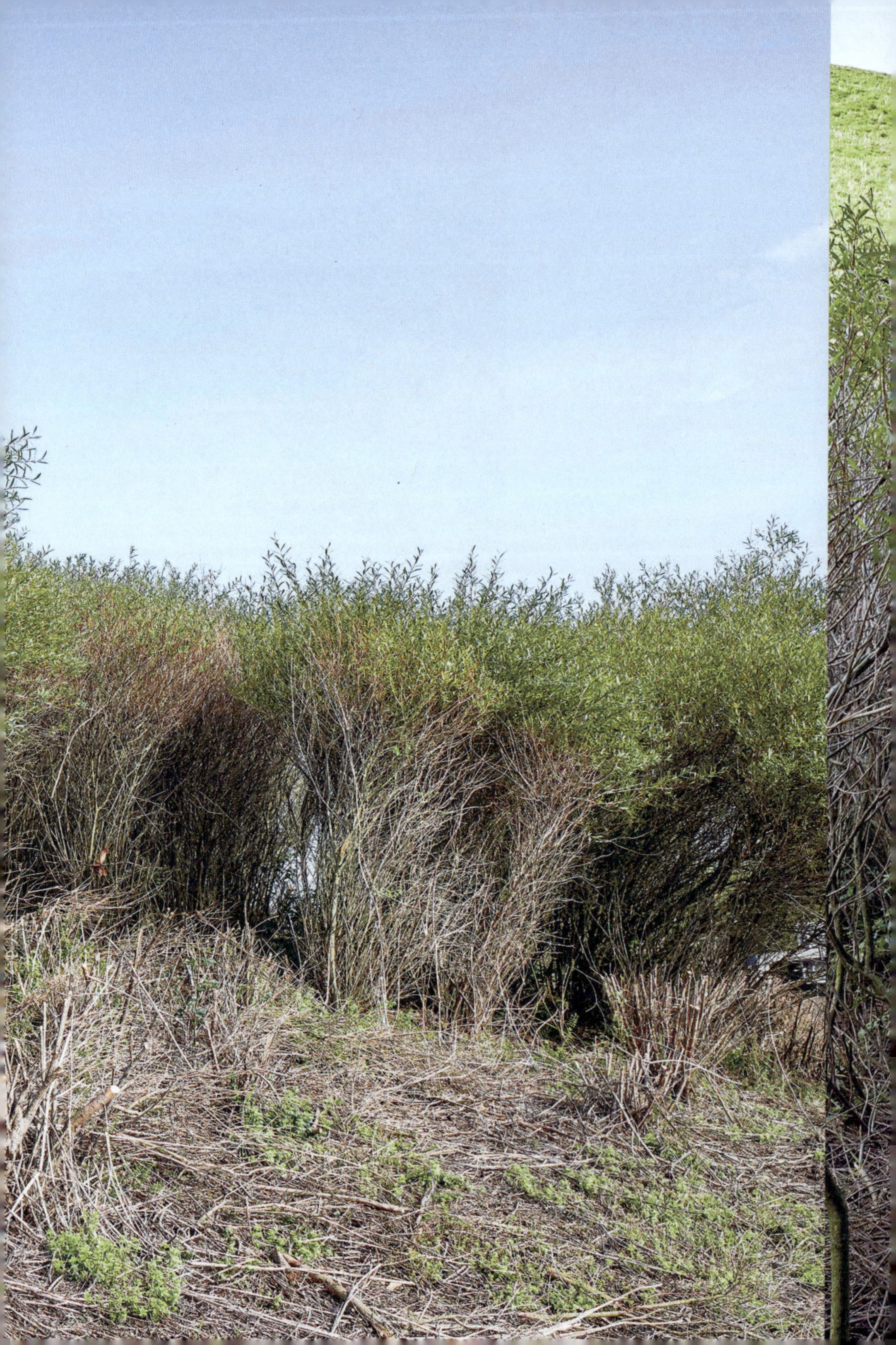

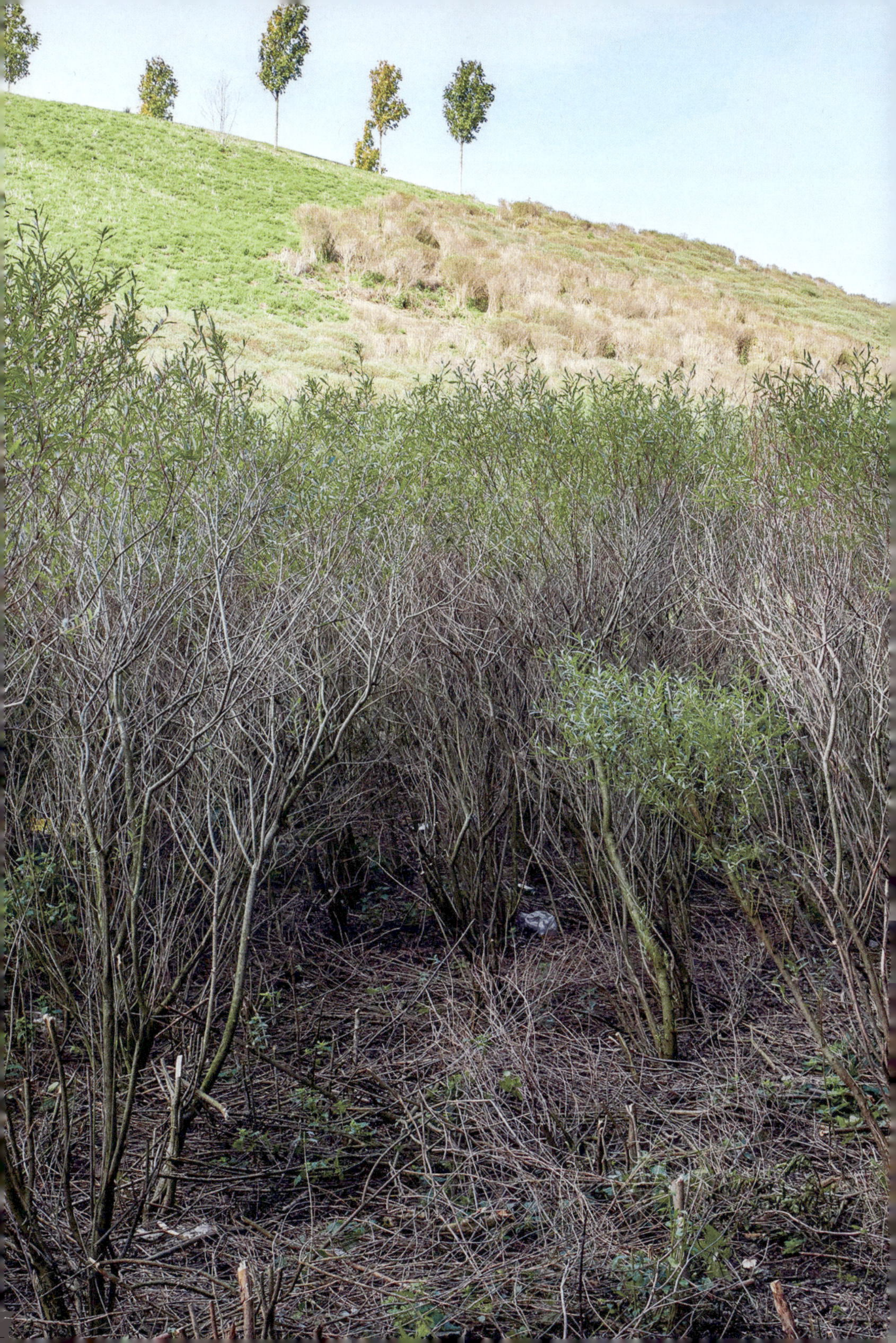

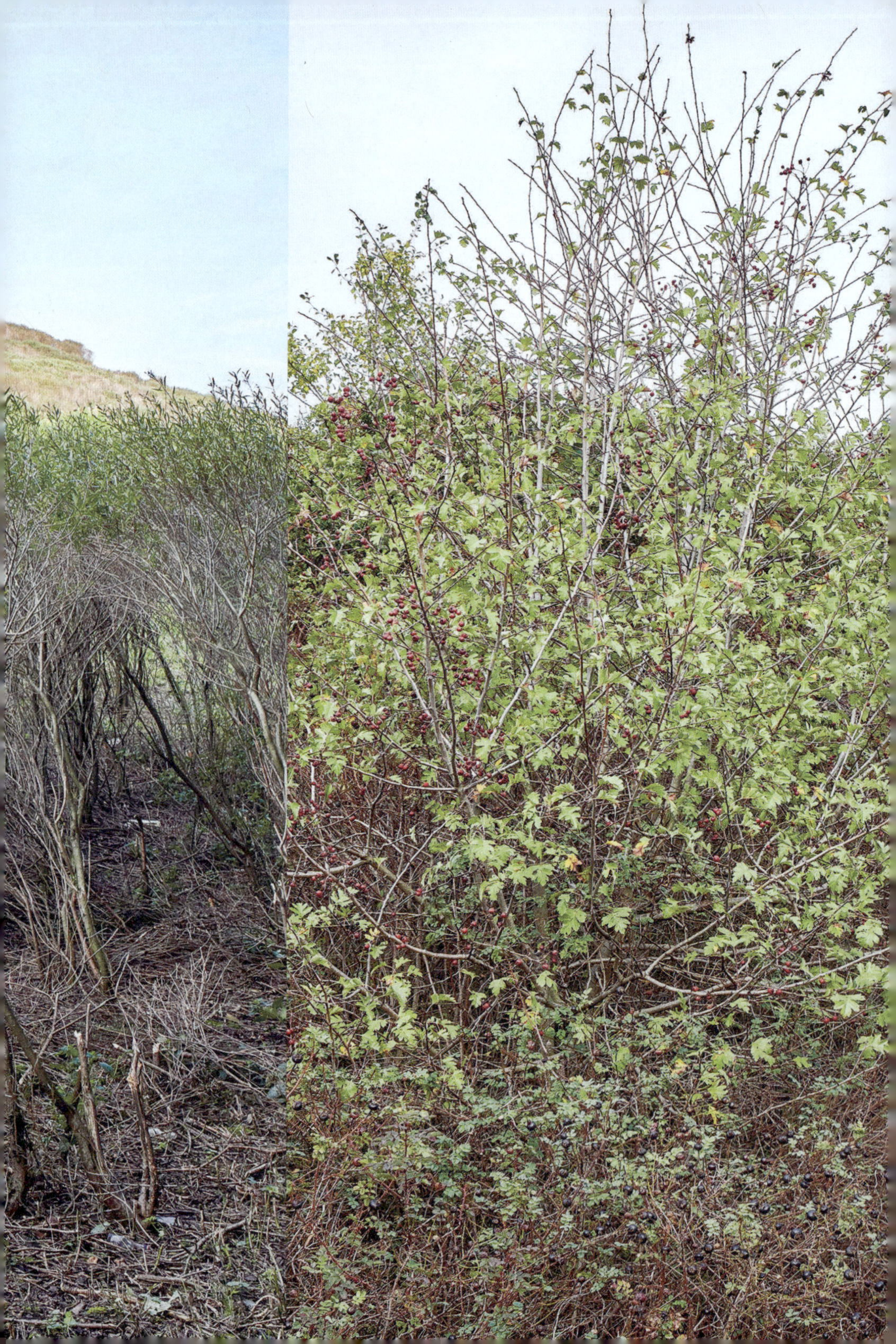

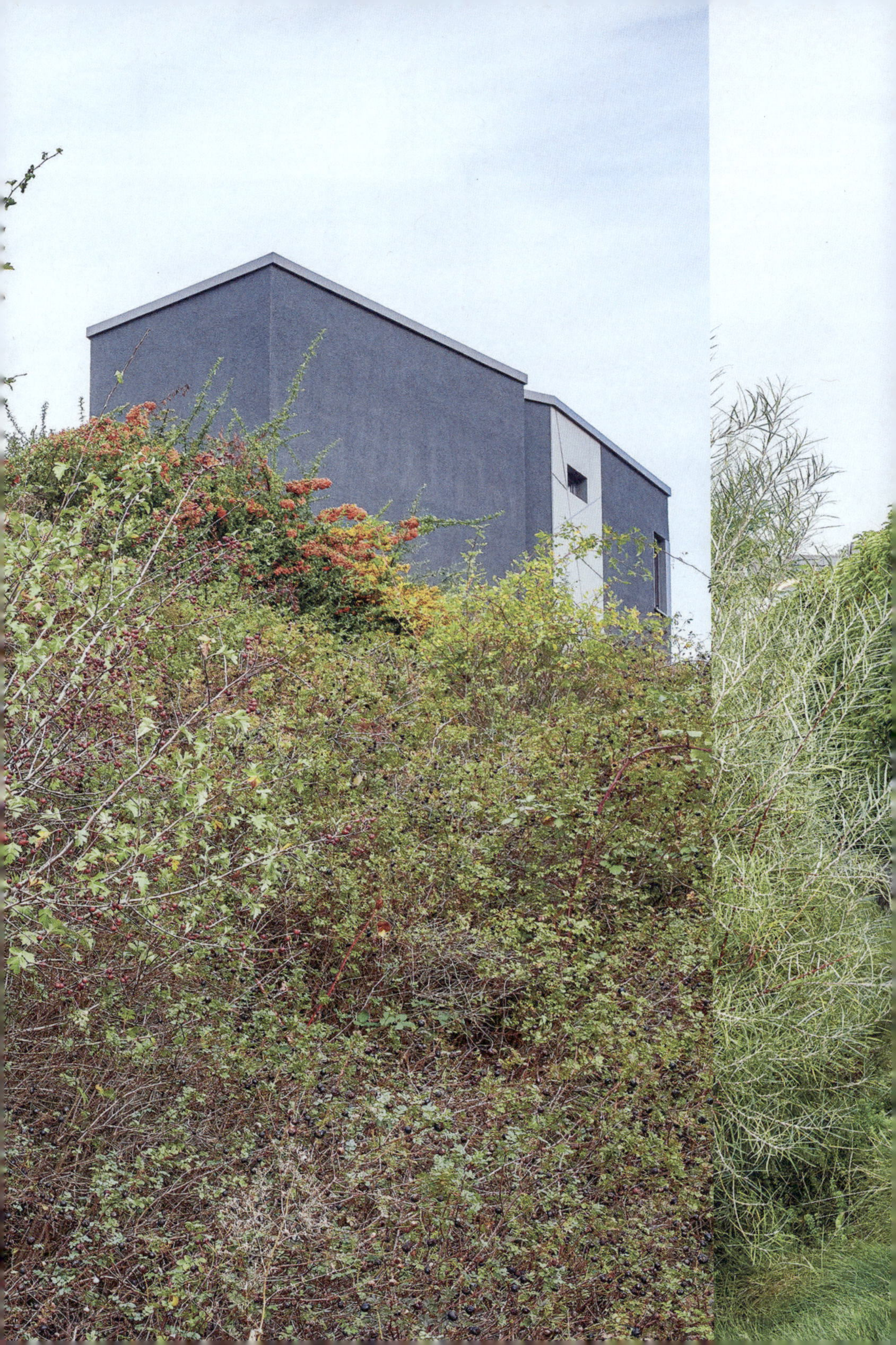

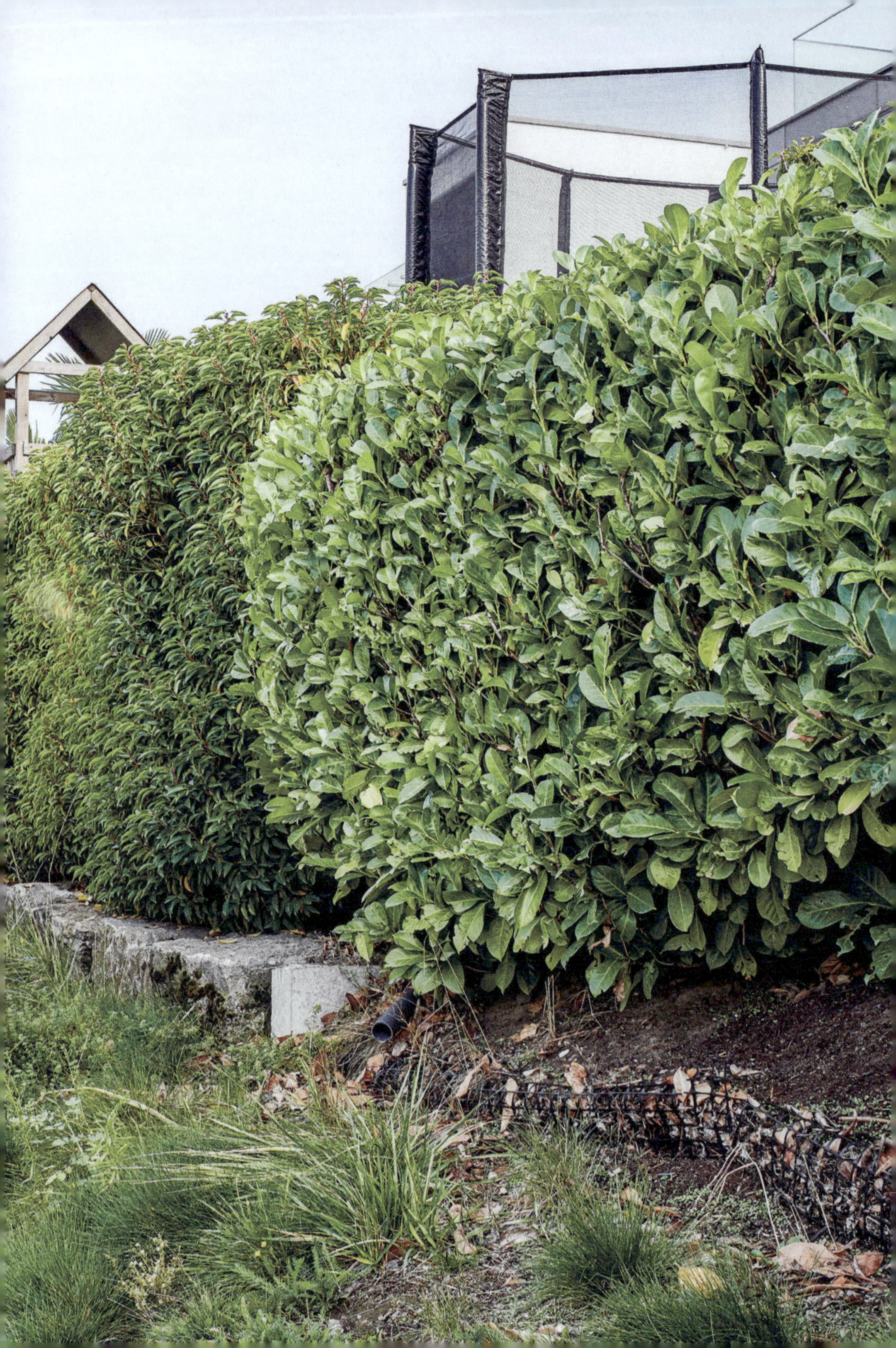

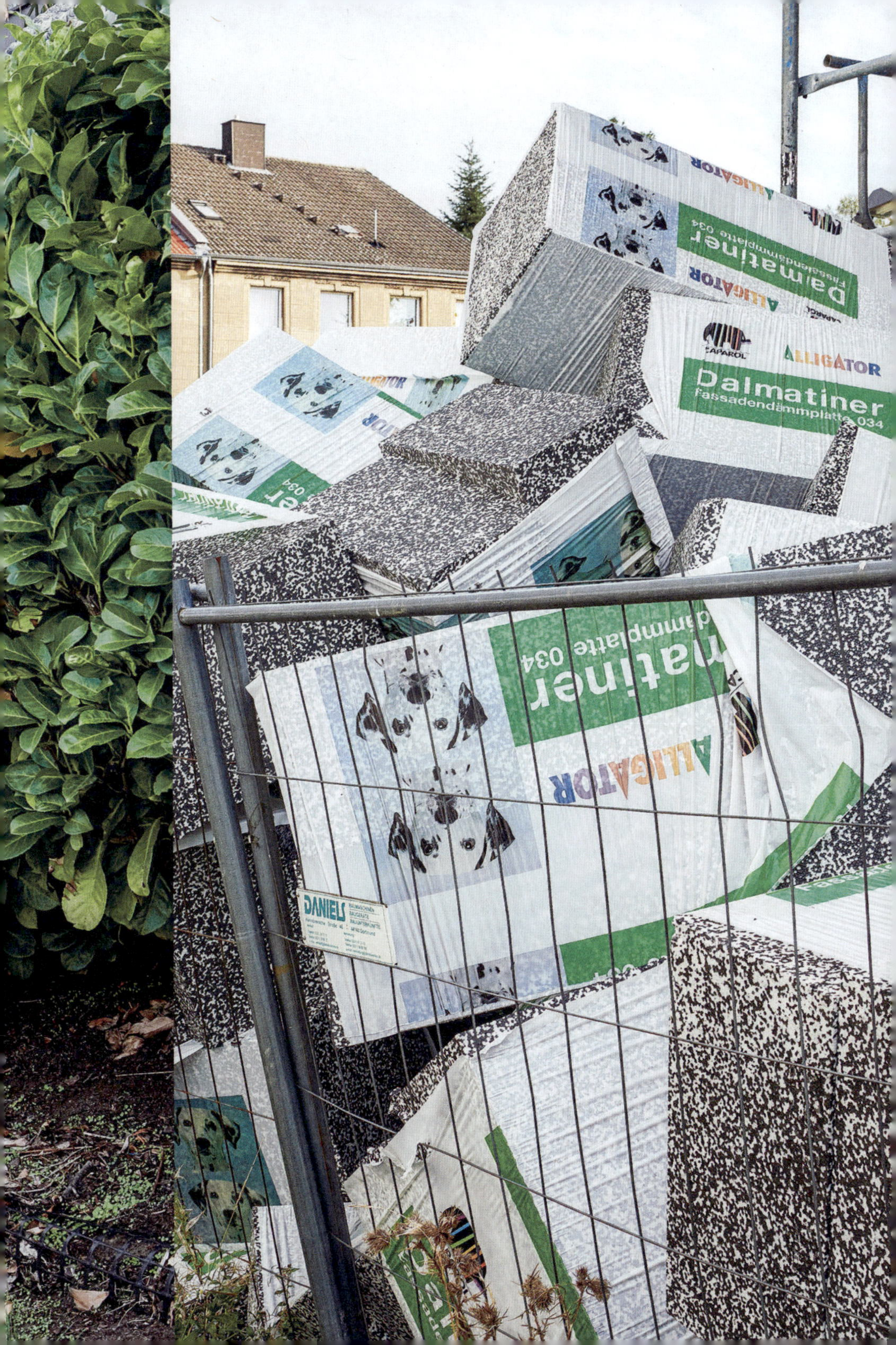

THE EMSCHER:
A BLACK RIVER
TURNS BLUE

Agnes Sawer
Silke Wilts

53

The Emscher river once used to snake its way idyllically through the rural landscape of the Ruhr region, through woodland and swamps, past meadows and fields. Yet, with the advent of industrialisation, this waterway, with its small, slowly flowing tributaries, which has its source in Holzwickede and joins the Rhine in Dinslaken, was visited by ecological collapse.

In the course of the nineteenth century, the once sparsely populated, arable landscape of the Ruhr region evolved into an industrial conurbation. In some places the population multiplied sixteen-fold within just five decades, causing the volume of effluent from the rapidly growing towns to increase and overwhelm the gently inclined rivers, including the sluggishly flowing Emscher river system. The land subsidence caused by mining finally brought the Emscher to a standstill, and the water that had been collected there then flooded the towns and cities with untreated sewage, resulting in cholera and typhoid epidemics.

Something had to change: the situation called for an overall masterplan for the region that would regulate wastewater disposal and treatment of effluent, and improve drainage and flood protection. In 1899, towns, municipalities, mining and industrial interests joined forces to found the Emschergenossenschaft [Emscher Cooperative] — Germany's first water management association — to remedy the dire ecological predicament. Since subsidence through mining would have repeatedly inflicted extremely severe damage on a subterranean sewer system, the Emschergenossenschaft decided to convert the existing watercourses into open sewage channels: accordingly, the previously meandering Emscher river and its tributaries were now straightened, shortened, deepened and lined as semi-trapezoid channels with concrete shell floors and side slabs to allow wastewater to be removed fast, flexibly and economically.

Thereafter, the Emscher coursed through the region in straight lines, conveying untreated effluent in open channels. The «Köttelbecke» [dung stream] — as the Emscher is also called in local slang — left a deep scar on the landscape of the Ruhr region.

CONVERSION
«The Emscher — black river forever» was the title of an essay by Gunther Annen, former managing director of the Emschergenossenschaft and Lippeverband waterboard, published in 1987 in the journal Forum Städte-Hygiene [Forum for Urban Hygiene]. Here, Annen describes how the Emscher might be transformed

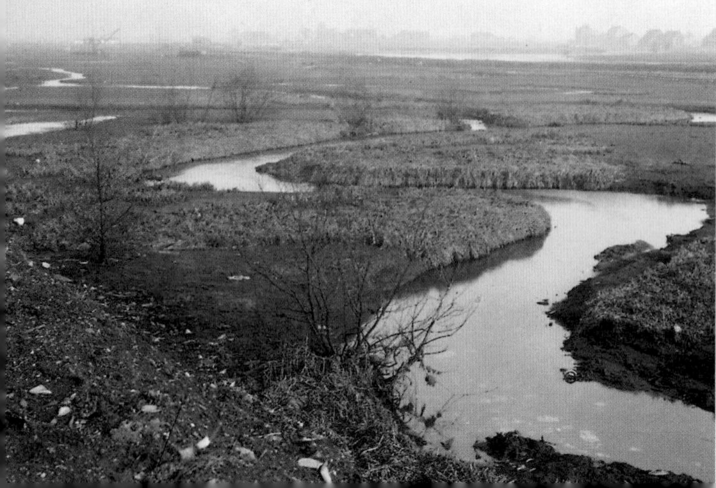

Emscher in Dortmund-Deusen, around 1900

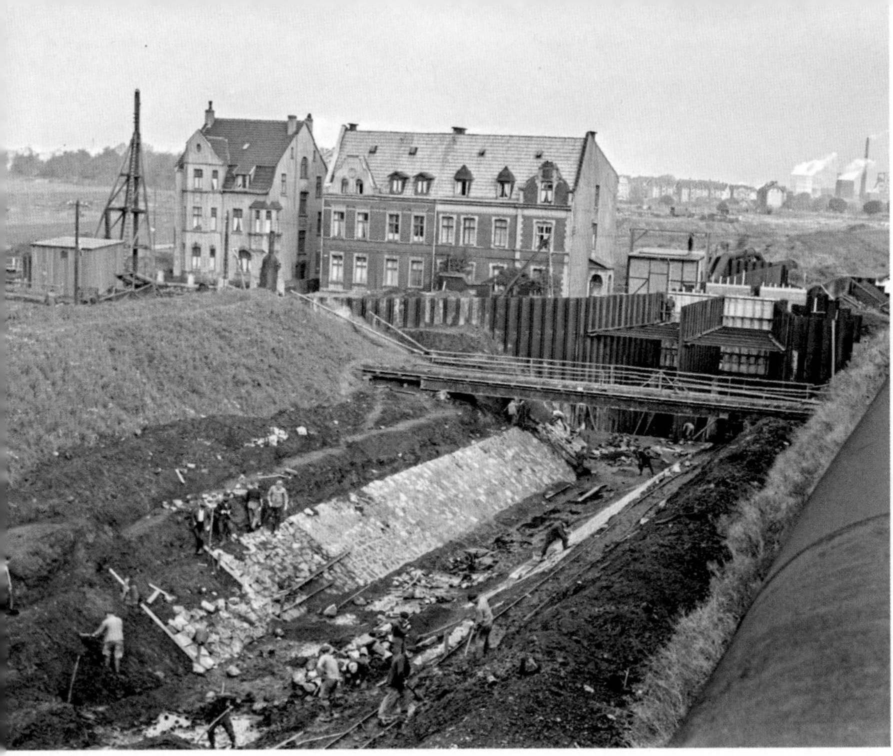

Huckarder Straße in
Dortmund, 1950

Emscher near
Nordstern Colliery, 1951

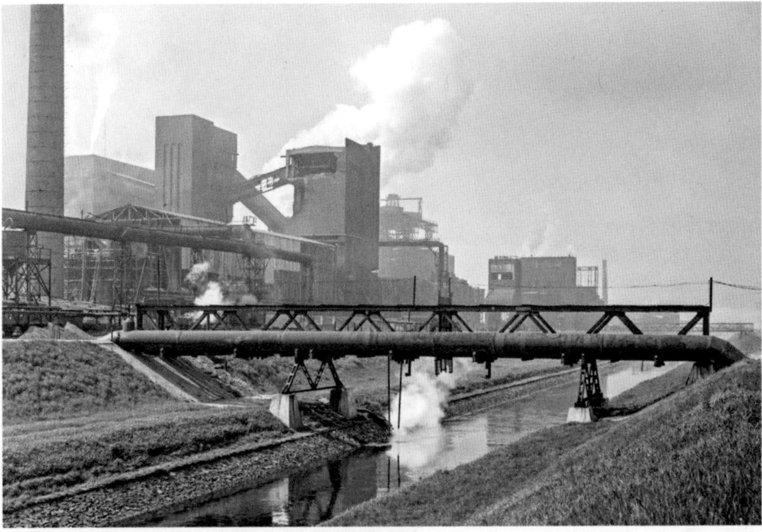

55

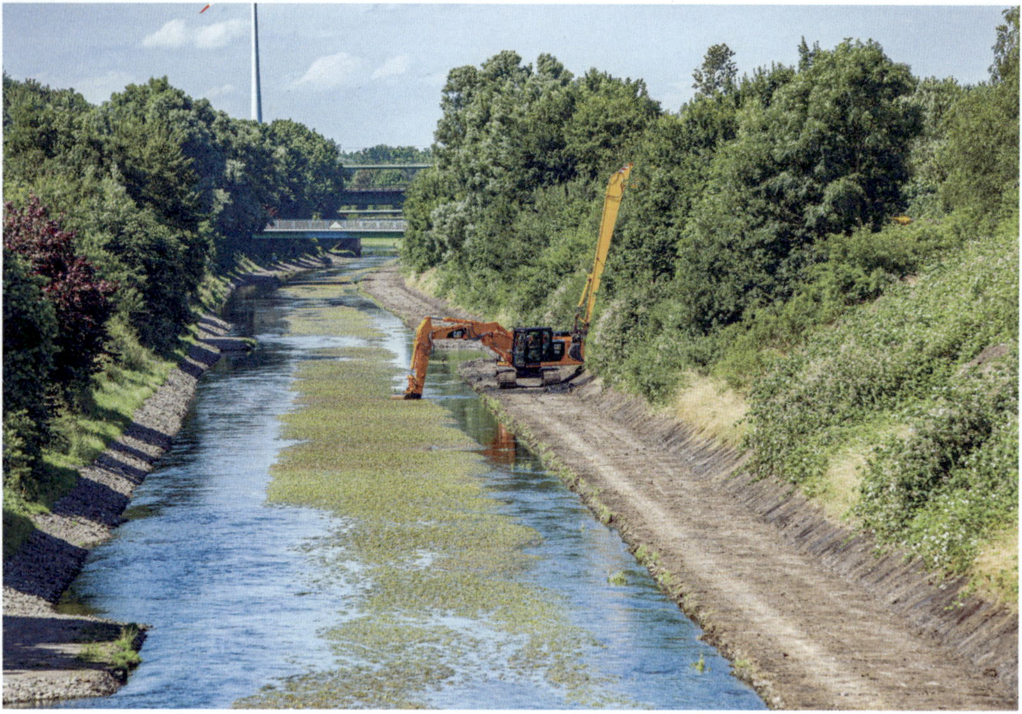

Emscher conversion in
Dortmund-Deusen

The renaturalised
Emscher in
Dortmund-Schönau

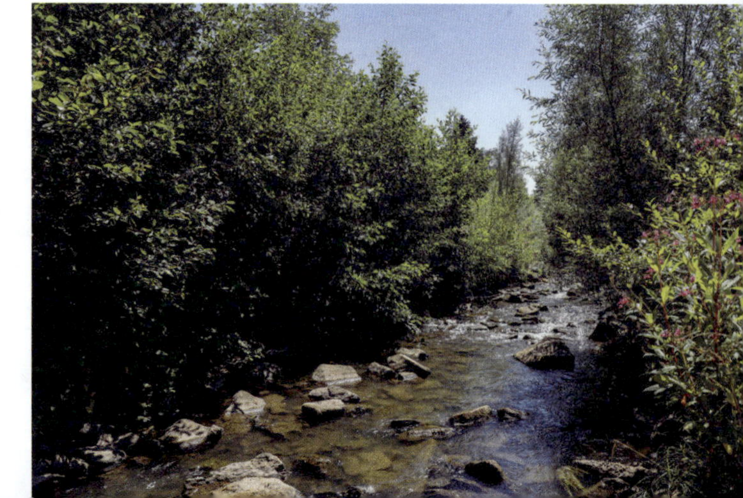

into an odour-free river. His suggested solution involved using the biological clarification plant in Dortmund-Deusen. Nonetheless, Annen also points out that by constructing preliminary treatment works we should not delude ourselves into assuming that the Emscher «could be transformed into a river with clear water. It will look better than it does today, but it will still be murky.» And, he adds, nor could fish be expected to thrive in this former «dung stream».[01]

But things turned out differently. When in the late 1980s the risk of land subsidence abated due to the relocation of coal mining further north, the idea of constructing an underground wastewater canal was implemented. So, in the early 1990s, the second transformation of the Emscher got underway. Since then, in an elaborate process, the river and its tributaries have gradually been emptied, first of wastewater, then stripped of their concrete shell lining, and restored to a near-natural condition.

To this end, the Emschergenossenschaft has built new, modern, large-scale sewage treatment plants and laid altogether 436 kilometres of new underground canals. The conversion was complete by the end of 2021.

Flora and fauna are gradually making a return to the Emscher, as can be seen in Dortmund. On this already renaturated stretch of the waterway we can already marvel at the effluent-free river and its green riparian zones. Where space allows, the once mechanically straightened rivers will in future not only be given new banks but also a more serpentine course. Increasingly, aquatic animals and fish are now again cavorting in these waters. Two years ago, one particular fish, the Emscher sculpin, was successfully reintroduced into the Borbeck Mühlenbach stream. The three-spined stickleback has been found in almost all renaturated sections of the river, while in the Emscher near Dortmund there have even been sightings of the indigenous brown trout.

The conversion of the Emscher river system is a technical challenge that calls for a great deal of engineering know-how. The centrepiece of this project is the fifty-one-kilometre Emscher Wastewater Canal (AKE), which runs from Dortmund's Deusen district to the Emscher mouth wastewater treatment plant in the city triangle between Dinslaken, Oberhausen and Duisburg. It receives wastewater from around 2.26 million inhabitants and considerable amounts of grey water from industry and commerce, conveying it to the Bottrop and Emscher mouth clarification plants. Work on the AKE was launched in September 2009. Step by step, from September 2018 onwards, the wastewater canal was gradually taken into operation. The conversion of the Emscher lasted until late 2021 — since then, the Emscher has only carried clarified water and rainwater. Over a period of some thirty years, the Emschergenossenschaft will be investing over five billion euros in the conversion of the river system.

THE FUTURE
The future of the Emscher region is blue-green, and the Emschergenossenschaft is supporting this development with a variety of projects that address issues related to nature and the environment, promoting an ecological improvement of our region. Not only does this make living alongside the Emscher increasingly attractive, but the participatory projects that have been conceived also encourage citizens to get actively involved

and to contribute to the shaping of our region. Together with various cooperative partners, the Emschergenossenschaft hosts projects and events at its farms in Holzwickede, Castrop-Rauxel/Dortmund, Bottrop and Dinslaken, as well as in various towns, where children and adults alike are invited to join in and contribute to this change. The topics on offer range from commitment to protecting wild bees to wine-growing in the region.

At Hof Emschermündung farm in Dinslaken the focus is on sustainability, for example, while at Hof Emscher-Auen farm in Castrop-Rauxel/Dortmund it is possible to experience the flora and fauna around the flood retention basin first-hand thanks to the hawk-training and leisure association Falken Bildungs- und Freizeitwerk Dortmund [Falcon Education and Leisure Centre], a cooperative partner of the Emschergenossenschaft. In «Blue Classrooms», small amphi-theatres set up by the Emschergenos-senschaft close to various waterways, school students can actively engage out-doors with the river as an ecosystem and experience the waterway at close quar-ters. These numerous projects enhance the quality of life in our region, while at the same time sensitising children and adults to the need for sustainable use of nature's resources.

Through the renaturation of the Emscher river system and the many projects initiated by the Emschergenos-senschaft in this context, the Ruhr region is improving apace and being sustainably reshaped. The cycle paths along the Emscher river already provide opportuni-ties for excursions, offering people in the area new forms of recreational activity and the means for pursuing a healthy lifestyle. The ecological improvement of the Emscher will further ameliorate our enjoyment of nature.

For the Emschergenossenschaft, art plays an important role in all these contexts. It functions as an intermediary between the Emscher and the people who can now experience the river in new ways as a result of its near-natural transformation. Nonetheless, it also aims to raise our perception and sharpen our awareness of environmental destruction and the problems associated with climate change. For this reason, the aim of the various projects initiated by the Emschergenossenschaft or realised in conjunction with its cooperation partners has always been to enable artistic ideas not only to foster new perspectives regarding the Emscher and the Ruhr region as a whole, but also to set impulses for ecological and sustainable action. ←

01 Gunther Annen, «Die Emscher — schwarzer Fluß auf immer?», *Forum Städte-Hygiene. Zeitschrift für Forschung und Technik in der Wasser-, Boden- und Luft-Hygiene*, 1987, July/August.

THE NEW GREEN

THE EMSCHERKUNSTWEG AS A SOURCE OF ARTISTIC ORIENTATION

Thomas Hensolt and Stefanie Reichart

Since many still have an image of the Ruhr as a grey industrial region in mind, visitors today are sometimes surprised by how green it actually is. While numerous historic headframes, blast furnaces and smokestacks attest to the existence of heavy industry, today mostly closed down, and mining, that era has been a thing of the past for some time now.

It is easy to lose an overview of the Ruhr region, with a surface area of more than 4,400 square kilometres and a population of 5.1 million living in fifty-three cities. Where municipalities flow into one another and blur, where wide train tracks, highways, canals and rivers do not serve as delimitations, but sometimes cut places down the middle, other forms of orientation are necessary. Hardly any other region in Germany has been shaped and altered by human hands as much as the Ruhr region. For this reason, not only are many points of orientation artificial; they have also been subjected to artistic treatment.

Beside the industrial structures, the slag stockpiles have now become a fixed component of the green leisure spaces in the Ruhr metropolitan area. They set striking accents and offer an opportunity to view the urban structure and the diverse landscape of the Ruhr region with a view from above. Where once church steeples and later blast furnaces and winding towers marked the towns of the Ruhr region like lighthouses, today artworks by prominent artists serve as so-called landmarks.

At the start of the nineteenth century, the landscape between the Rhine and Ruhr was largely flat or slightly hilly. Afterwards, for over two centuries the worthless material that was extracted from the depths as a by-product of mining and could not be used to build streets, refill strip mines or for landfills on the coast was piled up on slag heaps that grew and grew.

The highest artificial elevation, Halde Oberscholven in Gelsenkirchen, reaches a height of over 137 metres. This hill, which rose between 1966 and 1987, towers ninety metres over its surroundings with a surface area of thirty-eight hectares or more than fifty-three football pitches.

Beside the stone from mining, the remains from the steel industry, construction or war ruins was piled up on the more than 300 smaller and larger hills, usually directly near where the material was extracted. This ruthless mining and approach to nature was thus something the residents always had in view. This only changed in the 1950s: the eyesores were to be hidden, so the first slag stockpiles were greened.

But real progress was first made around thirty years later with the *Internationale Bauausstellung (IBA) Emscher Park* [International Building Exhibition Emscher Park]. These non-places were now not just supposed to be hidden, but transformed into places to experience nature, sites of leisure and recreation.

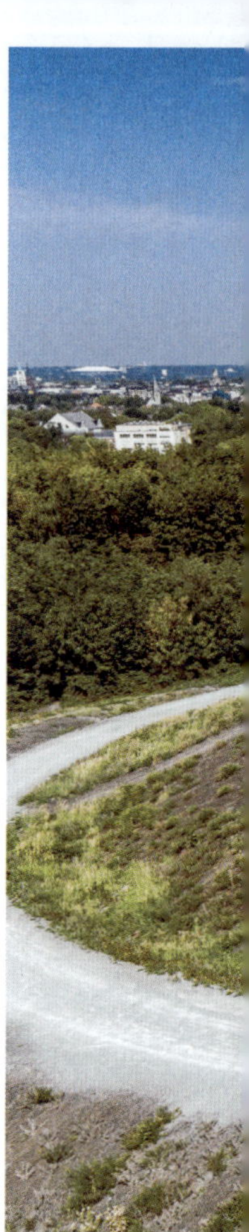

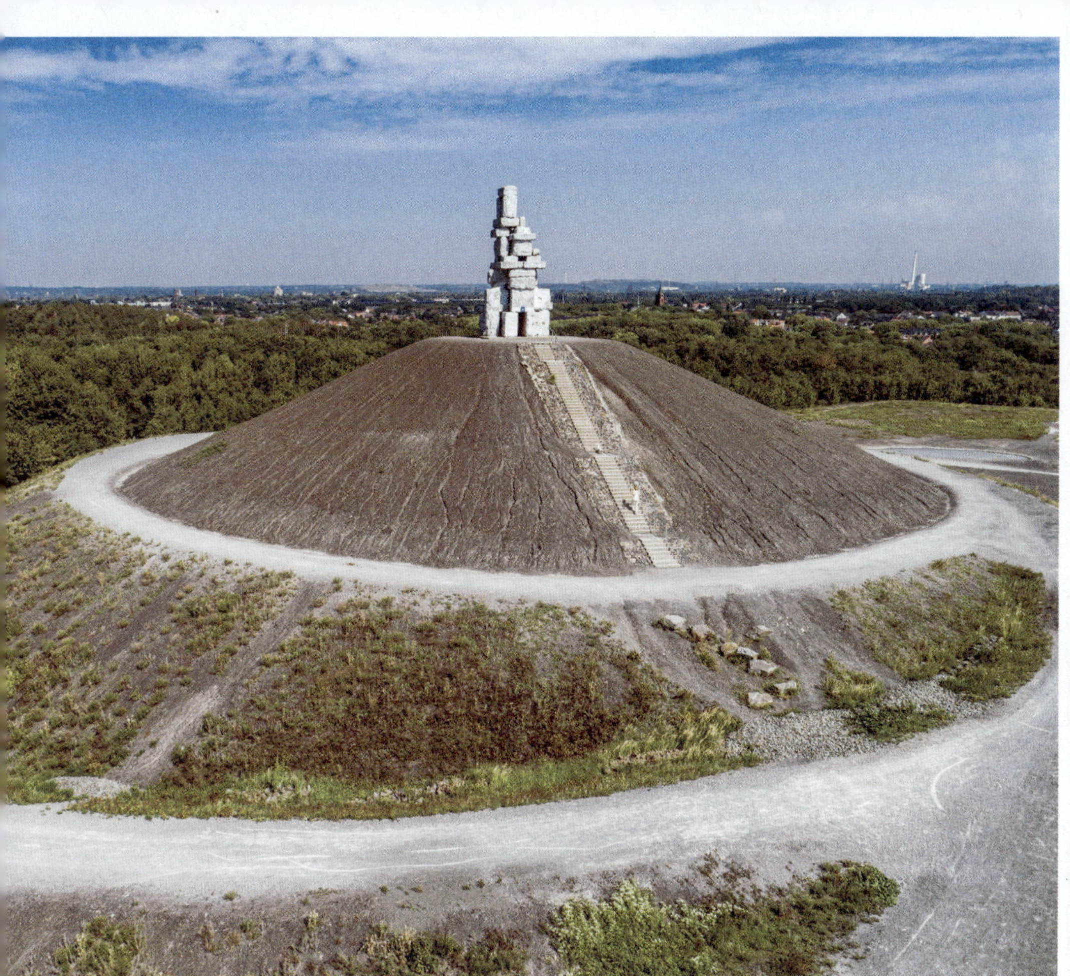

↑

Hermann Prigann's 1999 *Himmelstreppe*
[Stairway to Heaven] in Gelsenkirchen

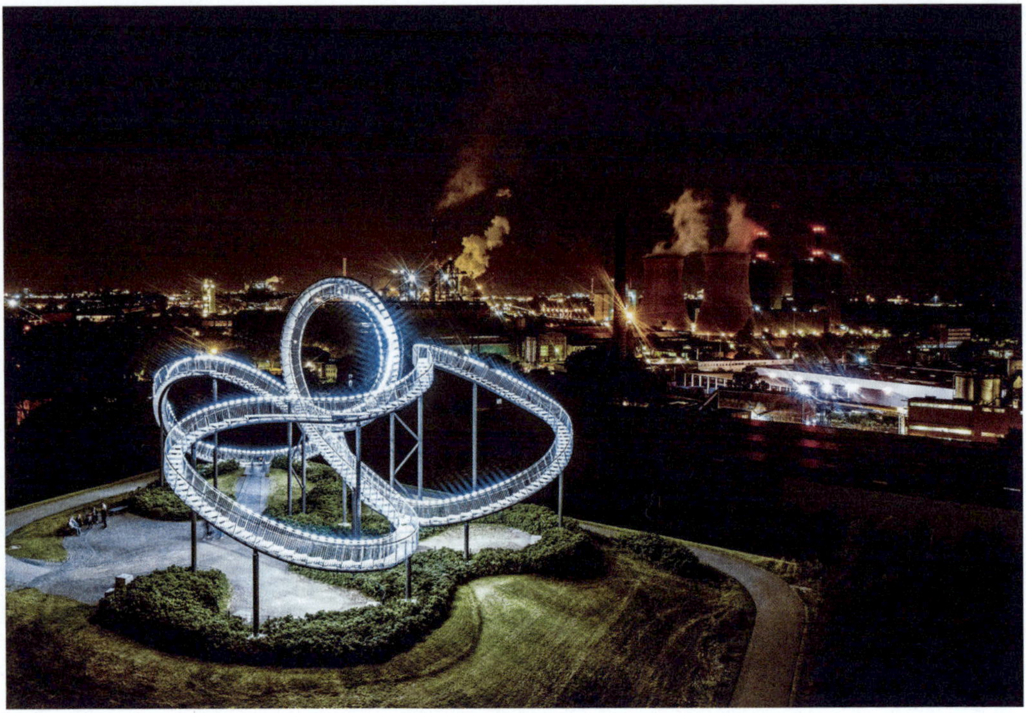

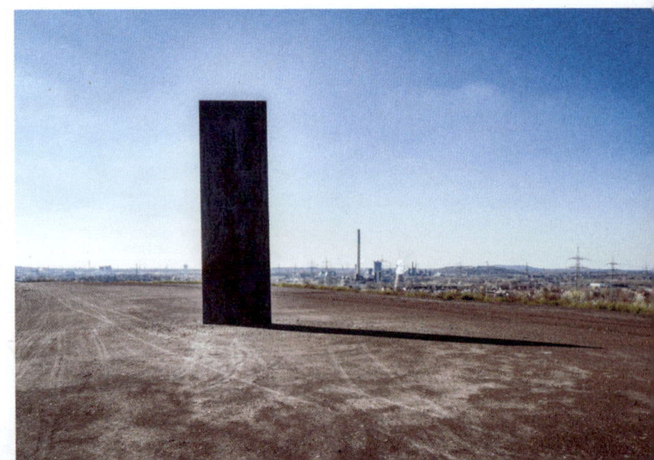

↑

Heike Mutter and Ulrich Genth's 2011 *Tiger & Turtle — Magic Mountain* in Duisburg

→

Richard Serra's 1998 *Bramme für das Ruhrgebiet* in Essen

Here, the fine arts played a central role: the first landmarks emerged as symbols for the transformation of the region visible from afar. Since then, a whole range of artworks have been placed on numerous stockpiles and vertically emphasise changes in the terrain of the Ruhr region caused by mining.

As site-specific works, they often refer to the region's industrial past, thematise the economic or social transformation or open exciting perspectives, as in the case of *Himmelstreppe* [Stairway to Heaven] by Hermann Prigann in Gelsenkirchen (1999). This work used construction components from a demolished Dortmund colliery to make a sculpture, visible from afar, that recalls archaic architectures. On the so-called Emscher Expressway, the A 42, it's then clear: we're in Gelsenkirchen. The same is true of the *Tetraeder* [Tetrahedron] (1995) in Bottrop or the *Horizontobservatorium* [Horizon Observatory] (2008) in Herten.

The work *Bramme für das Ruhrgebiet* [Slab for the Ruhr Area] by sculptor Richard Serra (1998) is famous far beyond the borders of the Ruhr region. With an apparent lightness, the untreated thirty-metre-high steel slab is inserted onto the plateau of Essen's Schurenbachhalde. The sixty-seven-tonne slab is inserted halfway into the ground, so that it can do without a foundation. What was once a source of controversy is now an icon of public art and a popular destination.

Only the former slag heap in Duisburg probably attracts more visitors. Here, Heike Mutter and Ulrich Genth have created with *Tiger & Turtle – Magic Mountain* (2011), which pays homage to modern leisure activities, a contrast to the long-past mentality of hard physical labour of the Ruhr region. On Heinrich-Hildebrand-Höhe towers a huge sculpture that imitates a roller coaster ride. But in this case — and here the past and the present encounter one another once again — the goal is only reached by way of your own physical effort, by foot instead of with a motor-driven car.

What began just before the turn of the century with *IBA Emscher Park* still continues today. Large intermunicipal transformation processes towards a green infrastructure are accompanied by artistic perspectives. The 1,500 public artworks in the Ruhr region provide orientation: they are part of the region's identity and a visible sign of transformation. For nearly two centuries, the entire infrastructure of the Ruhr region, with its rail lines, waterways and ultimately motorways, was oriented towards fulfilling the needs of industry. While local recreation sites were also created early on, like the five major parks in the area, they primarily served as green oases for the labour force to regenerate. It has only in recent years become an urgent challenge to provide sufficient green areas and paths, which is essential not just for the health of the local residents, but also for a sustainable ecology. This transformation was given an enormous boost in the 1990s: large landscape-architectural projects, like Emscher Landschaftspark with its slag stockpiles, were to open from the very start new perspectives with the techniques of the fine arts.

In the meantime, the Ruhr Regional Association has taken over forty-six slag heaps since the 1980s, greened them and developed them for local recreation and tourism, and twelve more will be added by 2035. Biodiversity hotspots and sites for renewable energies, slag heaps with recreational facilities and gastronomy will be created on an area of a good 2,300 hectares.

What began on the slag heaps was to continue in the area along the former Emscher wastewater canal. With the Emscher conversion, the Emschergenossenschaft [Emscher Cooperative] laid out cycle paths and the Emscher Art was created. With the transformation of the *Emscherkunst*-Festival into the permanent Emscherkunstweg [Emscher Art Trail], the vertical markings on the stockpiles became a horizontal cartography with artworks along the Emscher from east to west.

In contrast to their counterparts on the stockpiles, the artworks of the Emscherkunstweg are not always visible from a distance. They nestle subtly in formerly unwelcoming sites along the Emscher. Travelling from one to another, at best by bike, opens a long-neglected view of the Ruhr region from the perspective of a river. Nowhere can the exploitation of nature by the coal and steel industry be seen better than by looking at the impacts at eye level and directly before one's own door. As with the stockpiles, the artworks along the Emscher create a link to the history and geography of the Ruhr region. Artworks like the impressive *Monument for a Forgotten Future* (2010) by Olaf Nicolai, Douglas Gordon and Mogwai on the so-called Emscher Island, react to the shifting terrain, a landscape shaped by artificial canals and hydraulic engineering. A true-to-scale replica of a rock formation from Joshua Tree National Park takes the landscape shaped by humanity to absurd lengths. Other works refer to less well-known aspects, as for example *Neustadt* [New Town] by Julius von Bismarck with Marta Dyachenko (2021), which in a several-part installation explores the impacts of the structural transformation on the architecture of the cities of the Ruhr region.

These large, intermunicipal, sustainable projects are what will shape the image of the Ruhr region, now and in the future. They provide the former industrial sites a new function that caters to the needs of the residents and nature. Overarching art projects like the *IBA Emscher Park,* European Capital of Culture RUHR.2010 or the Emscherkunstweg are not only intended as local improvements. They are also projects that develop an attraction beyond the region, making the Ruhr more prominent on the international art map. The past and the future, industry and nature, art and culture: the region will continue to explore these subjects in upcoming projects such as *Manifesta 16 RUHR* or *IGA Metropole Ruhr 2027,* providing aesthetic resonance and (spatial) orientation using art. ←

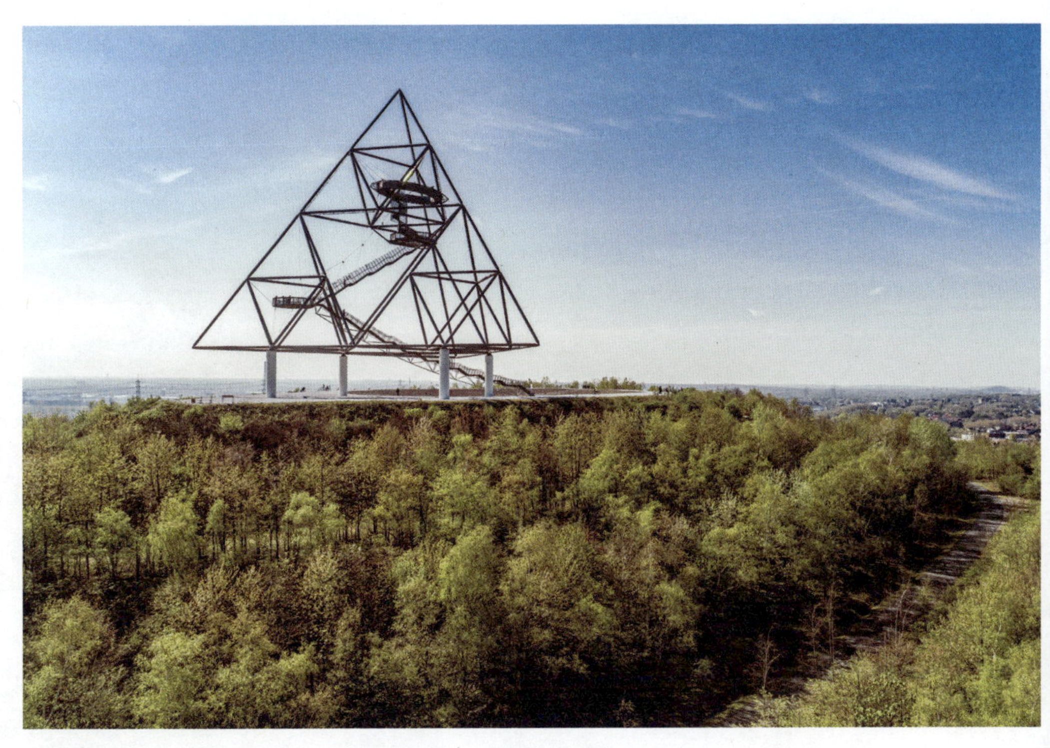

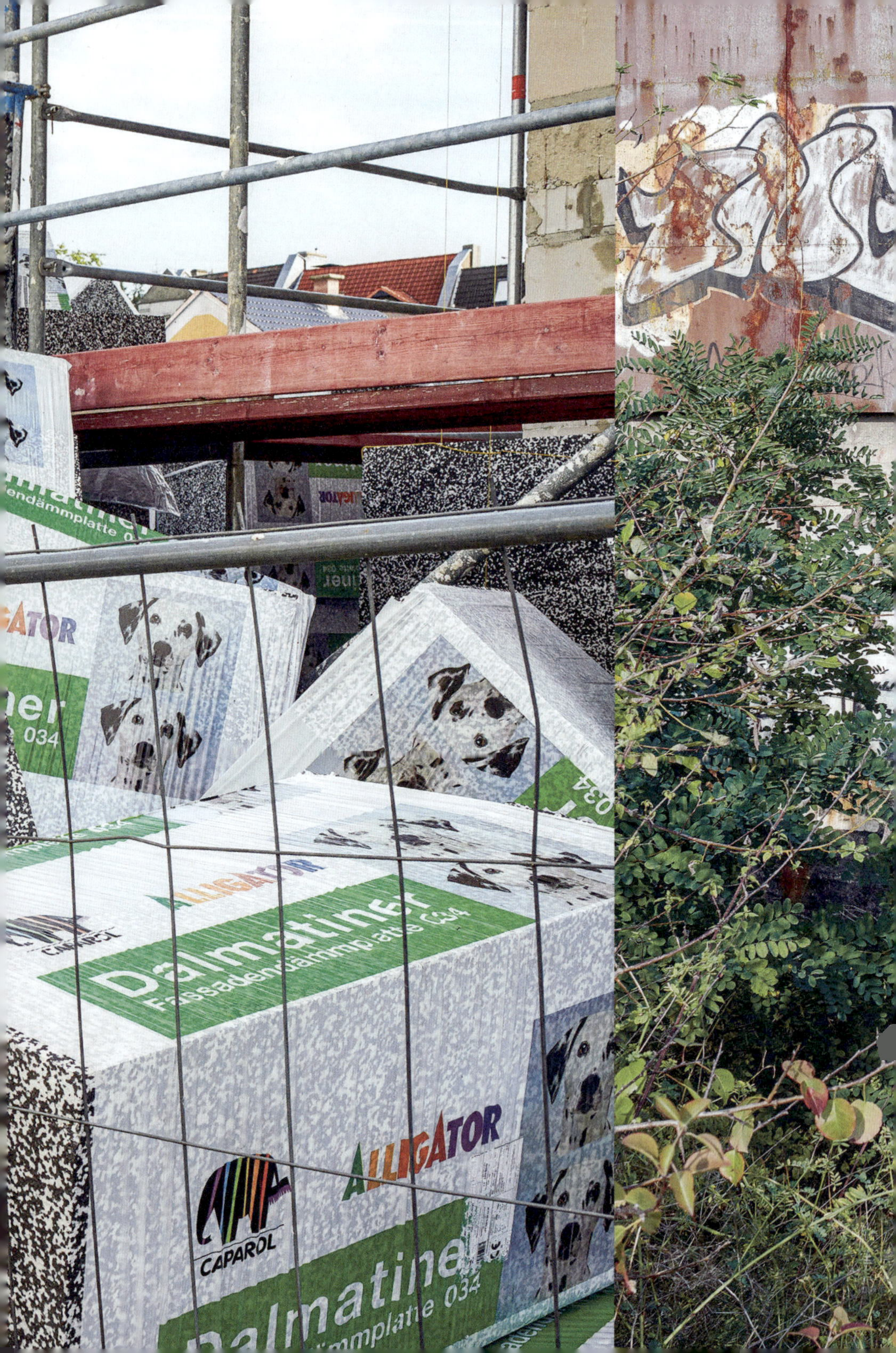

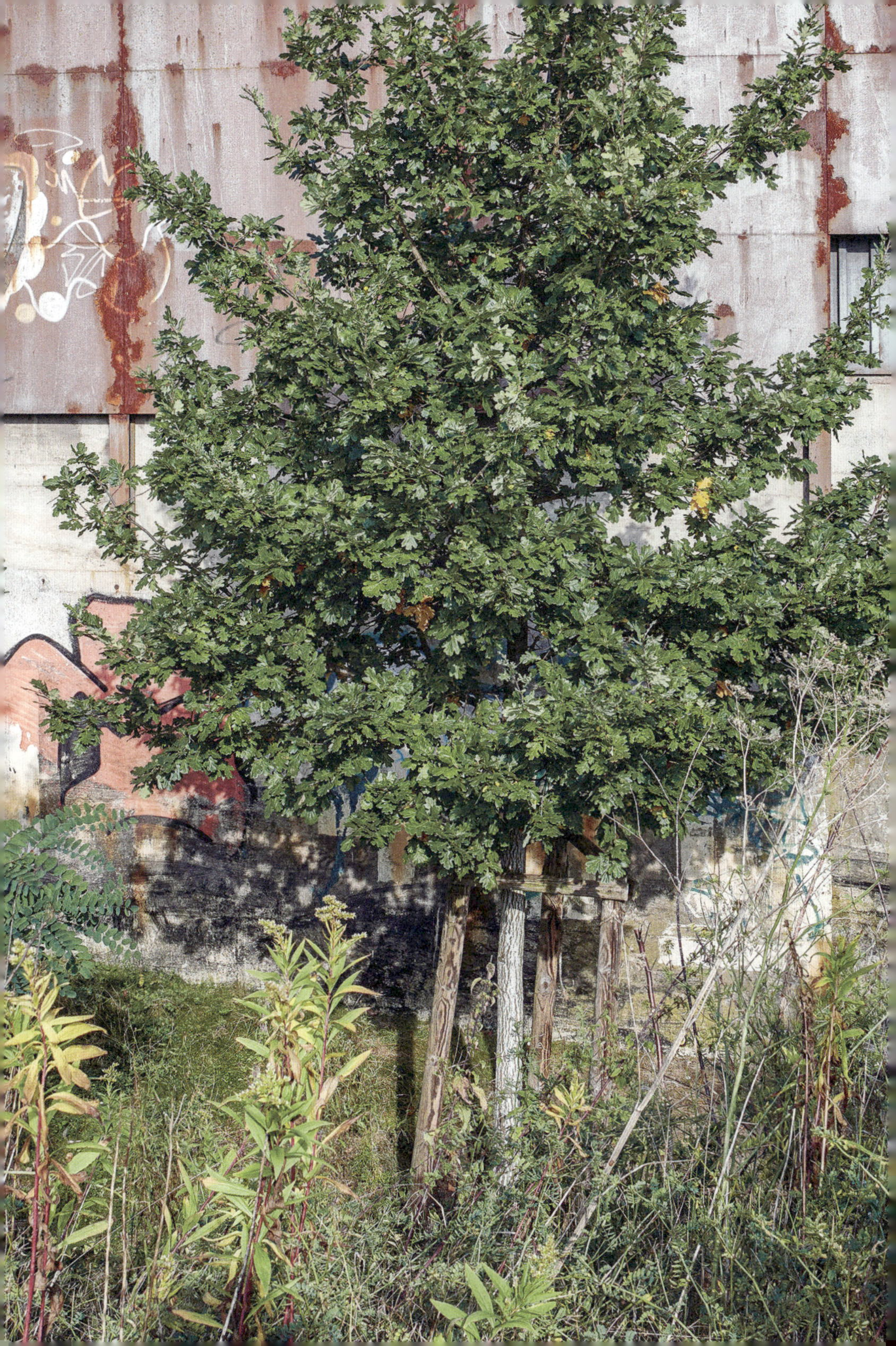

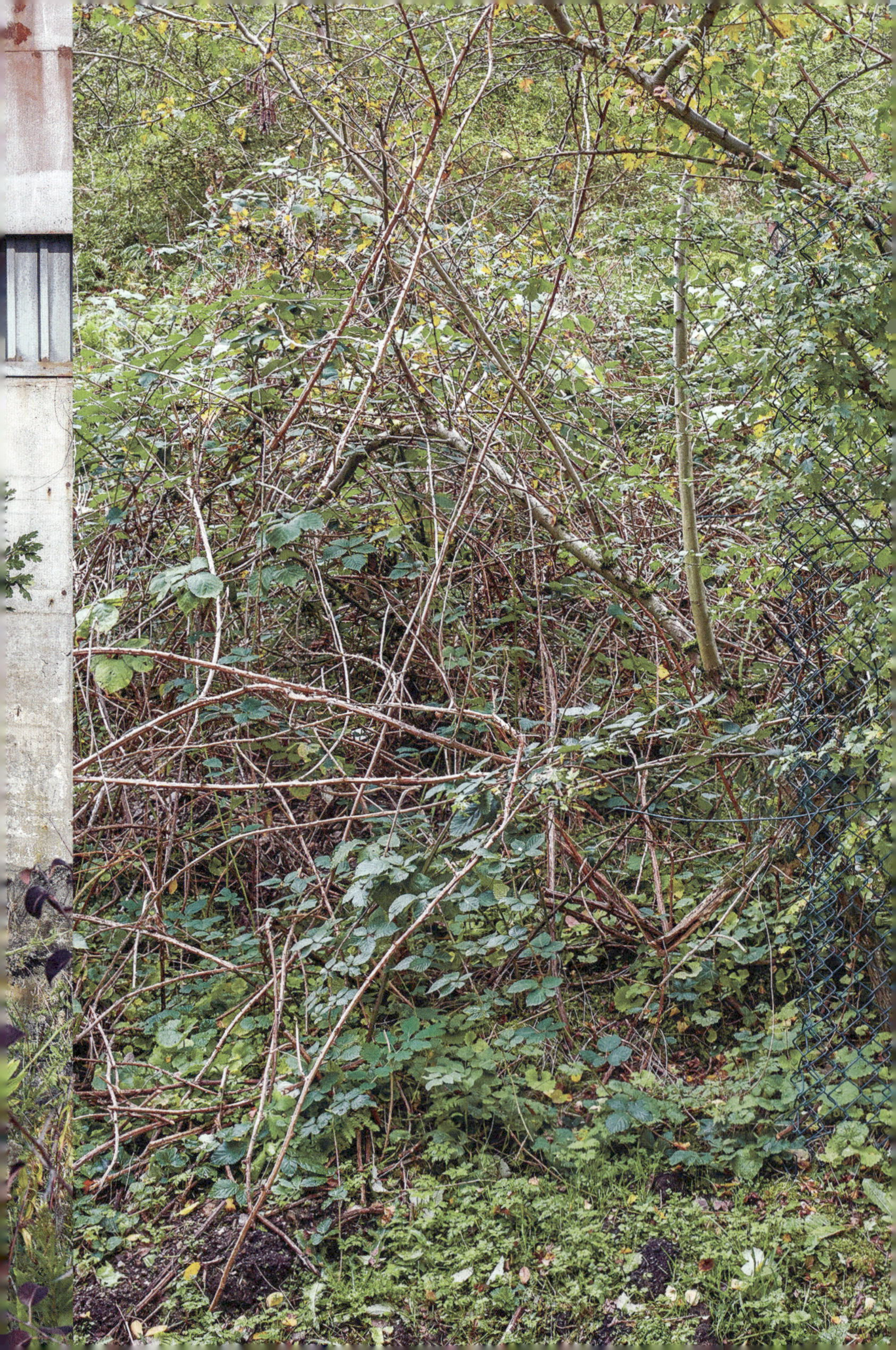

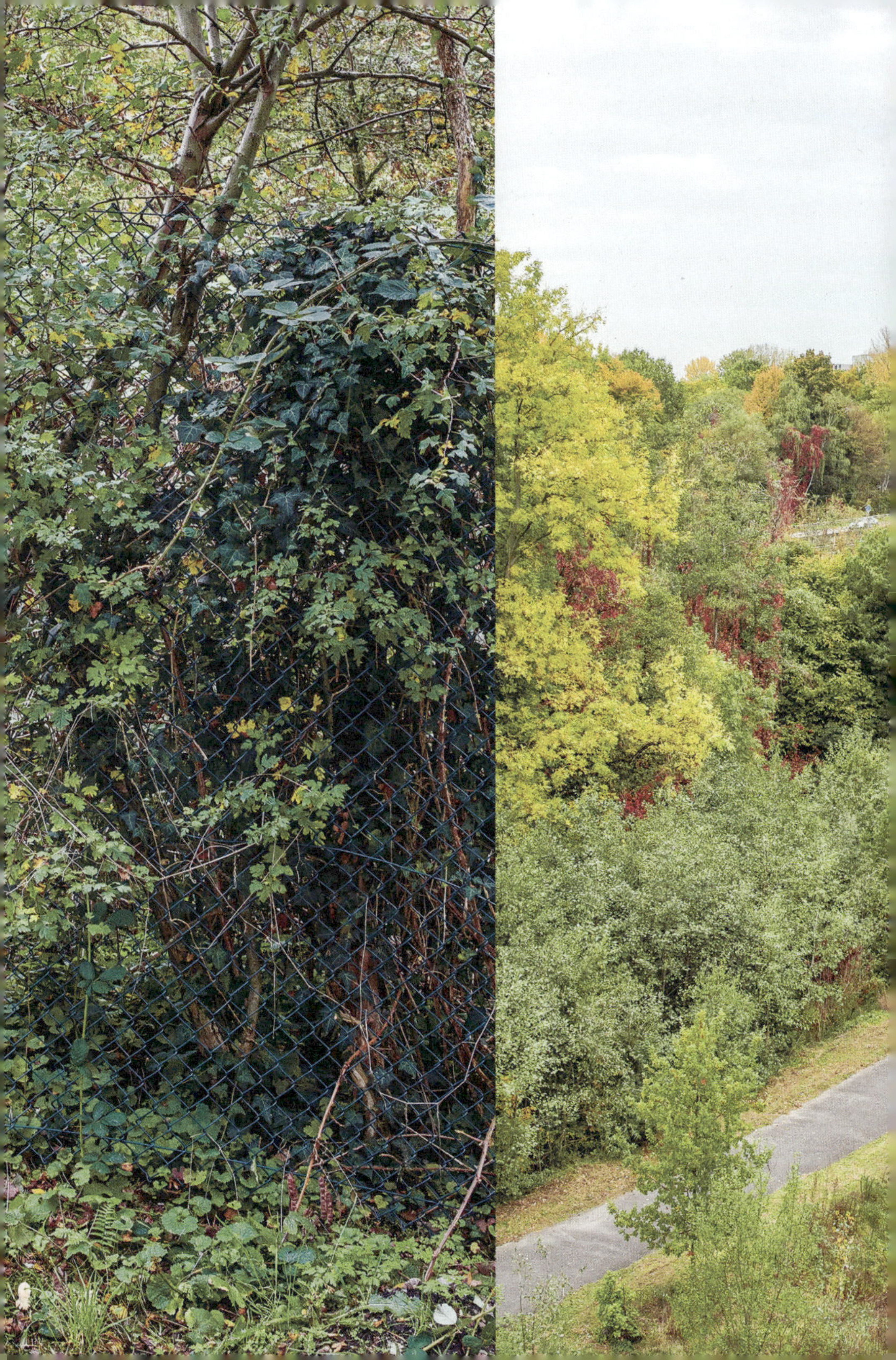

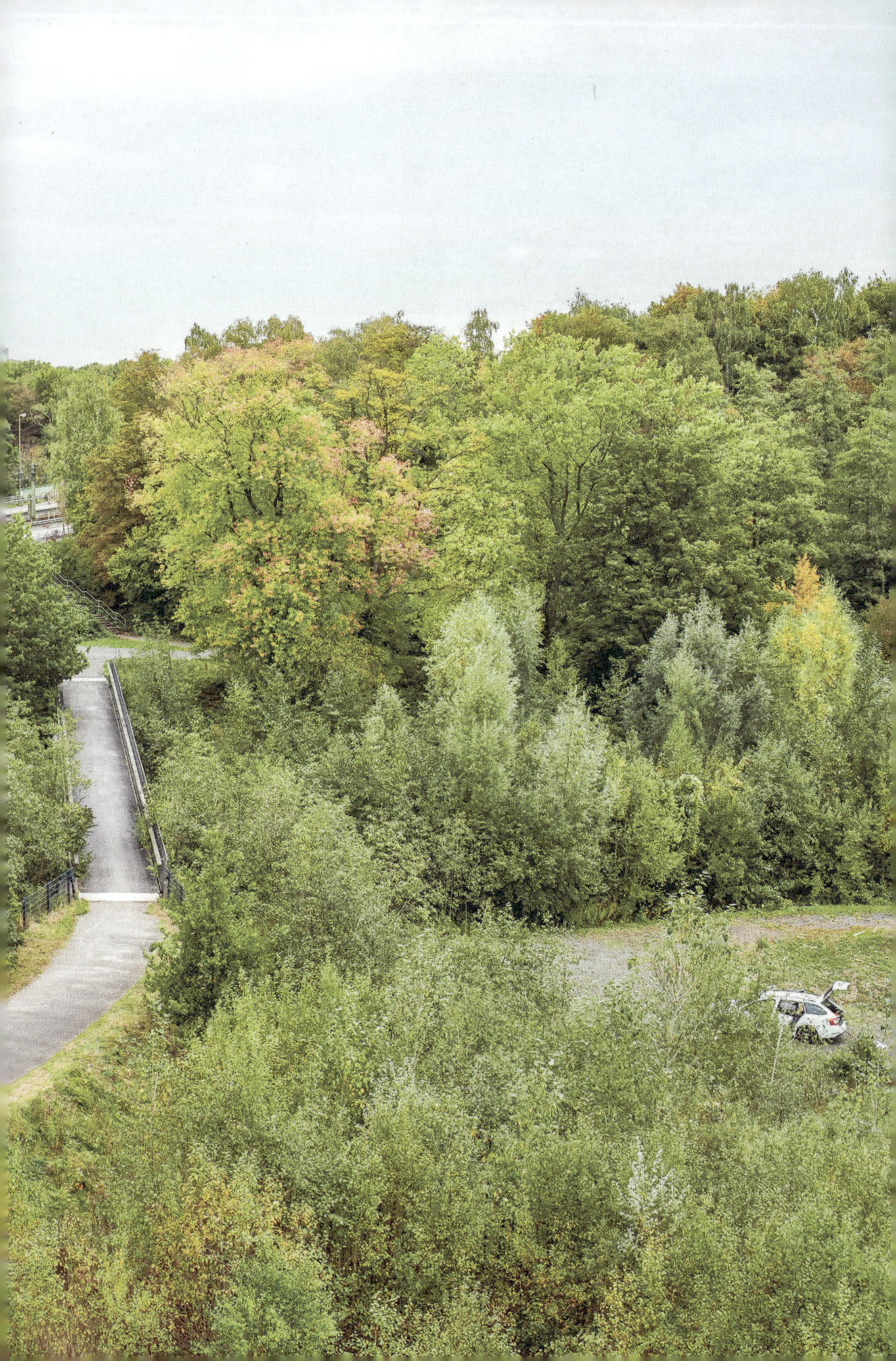

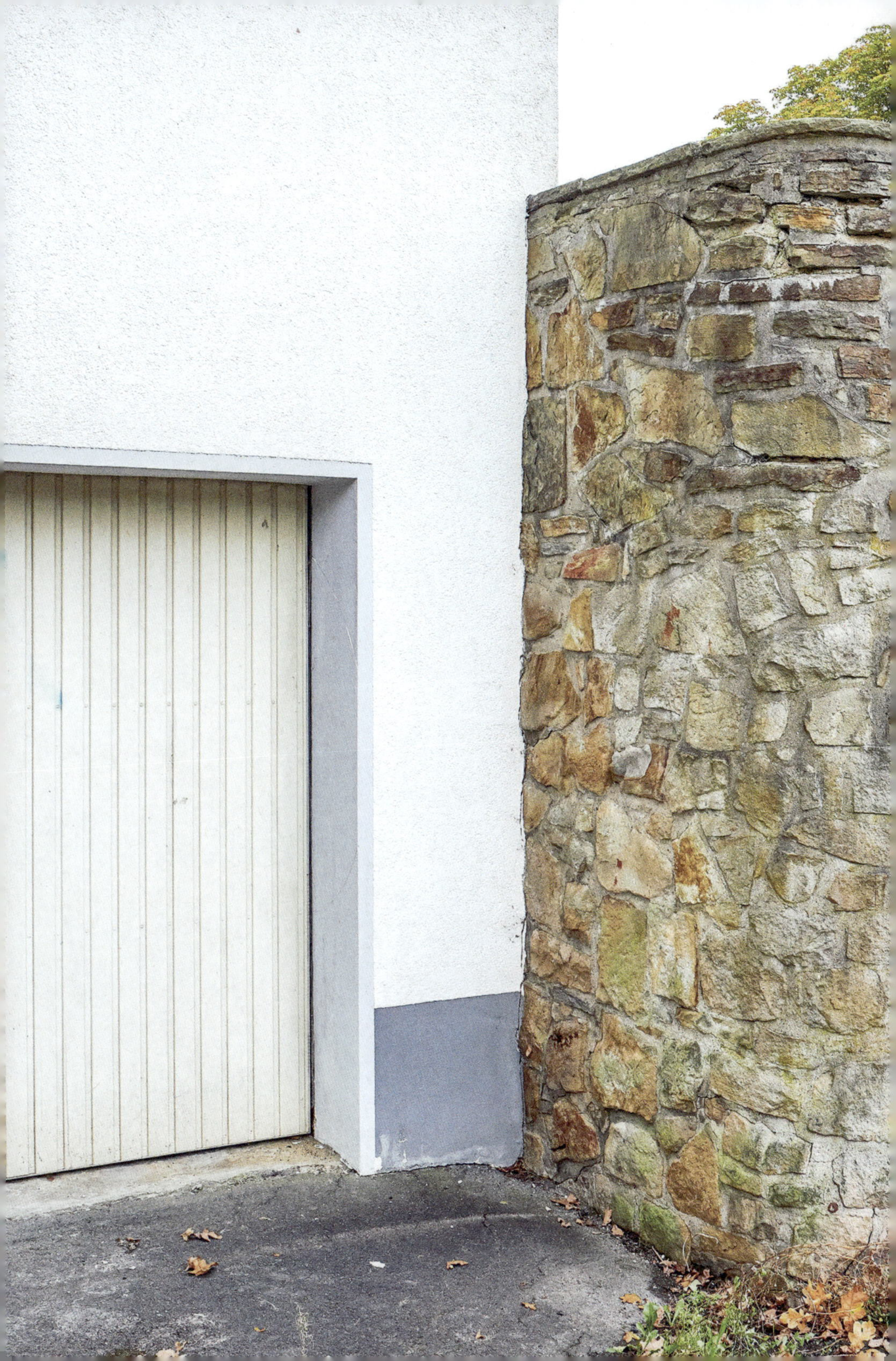

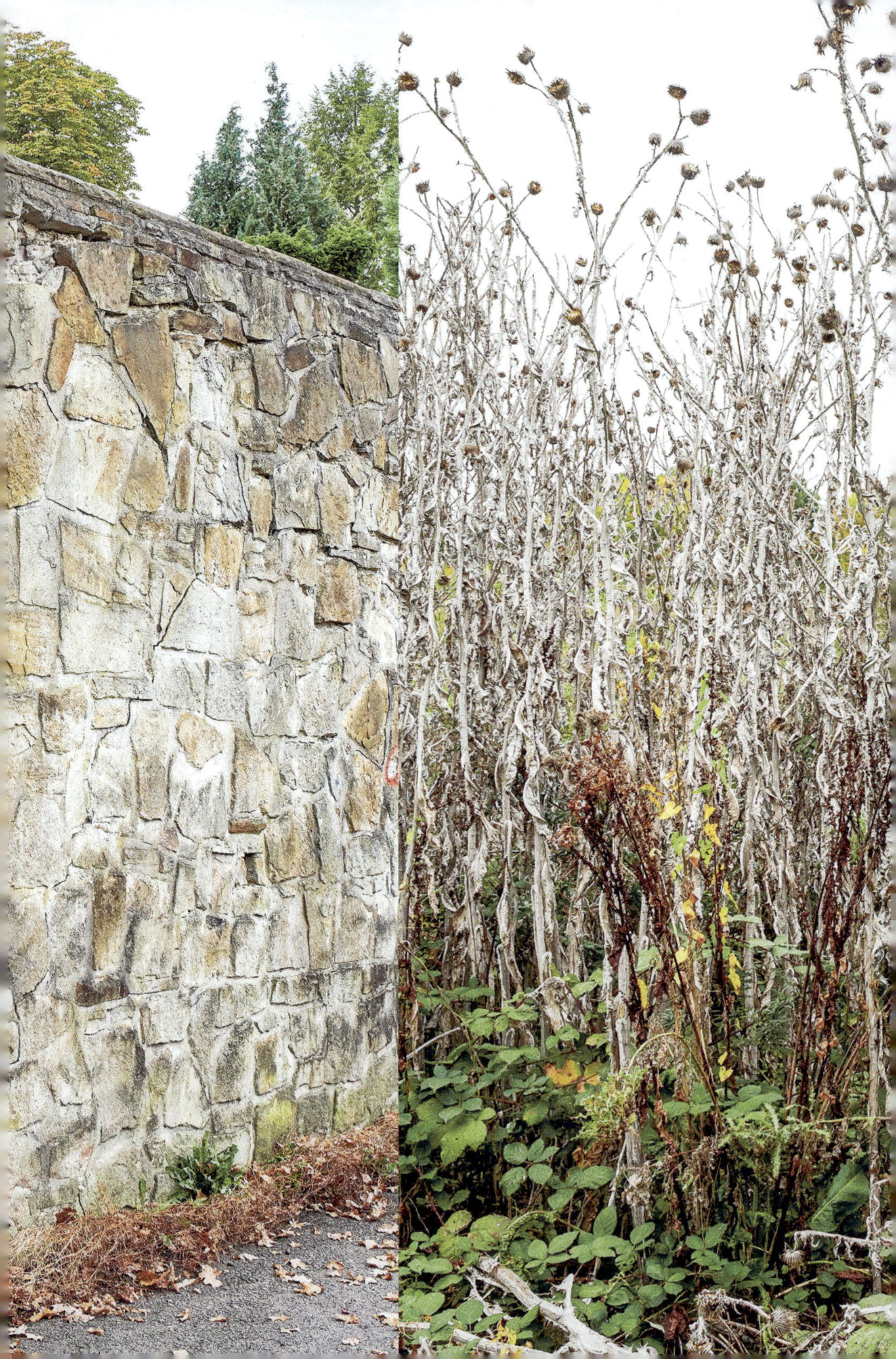

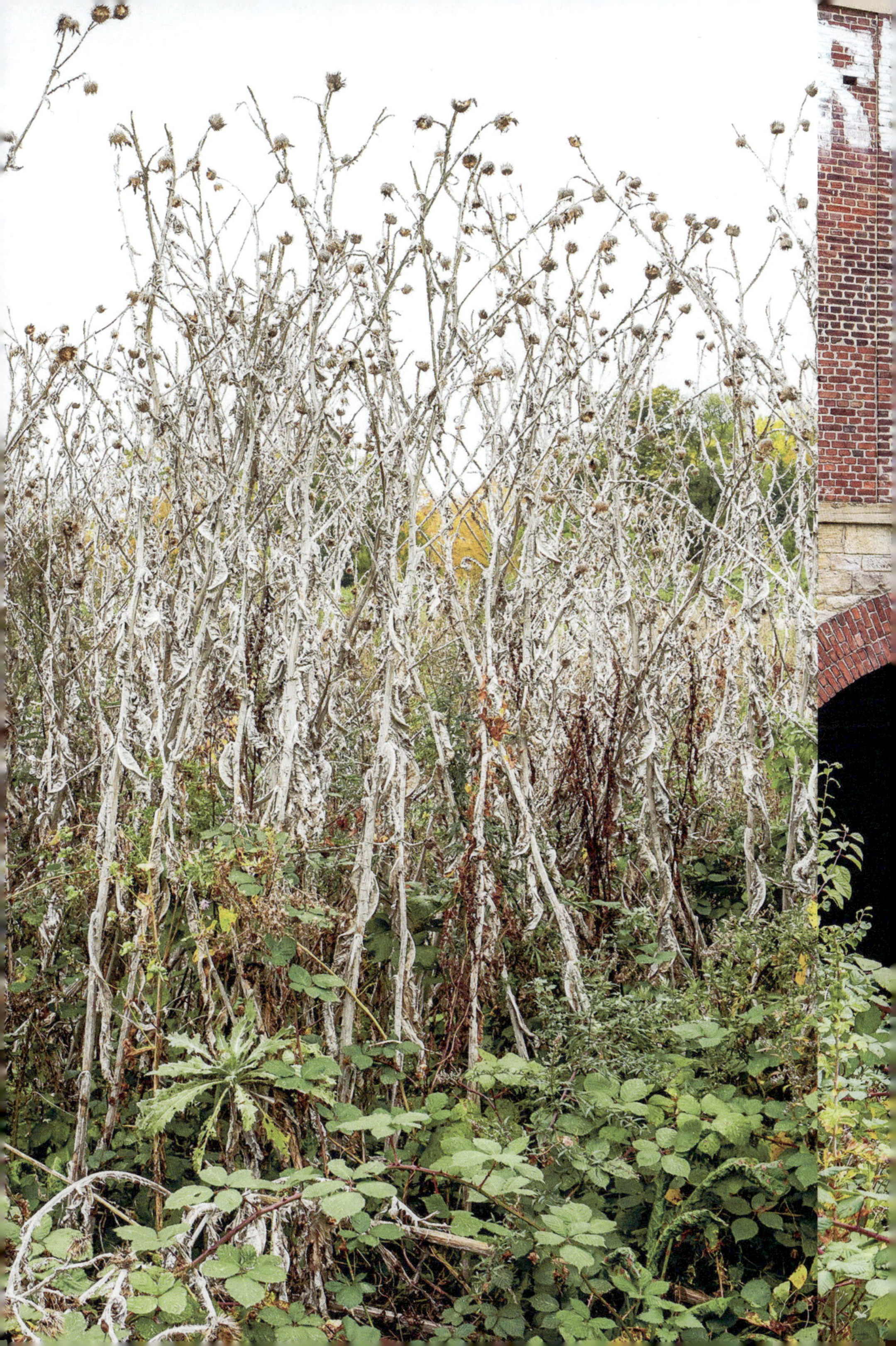

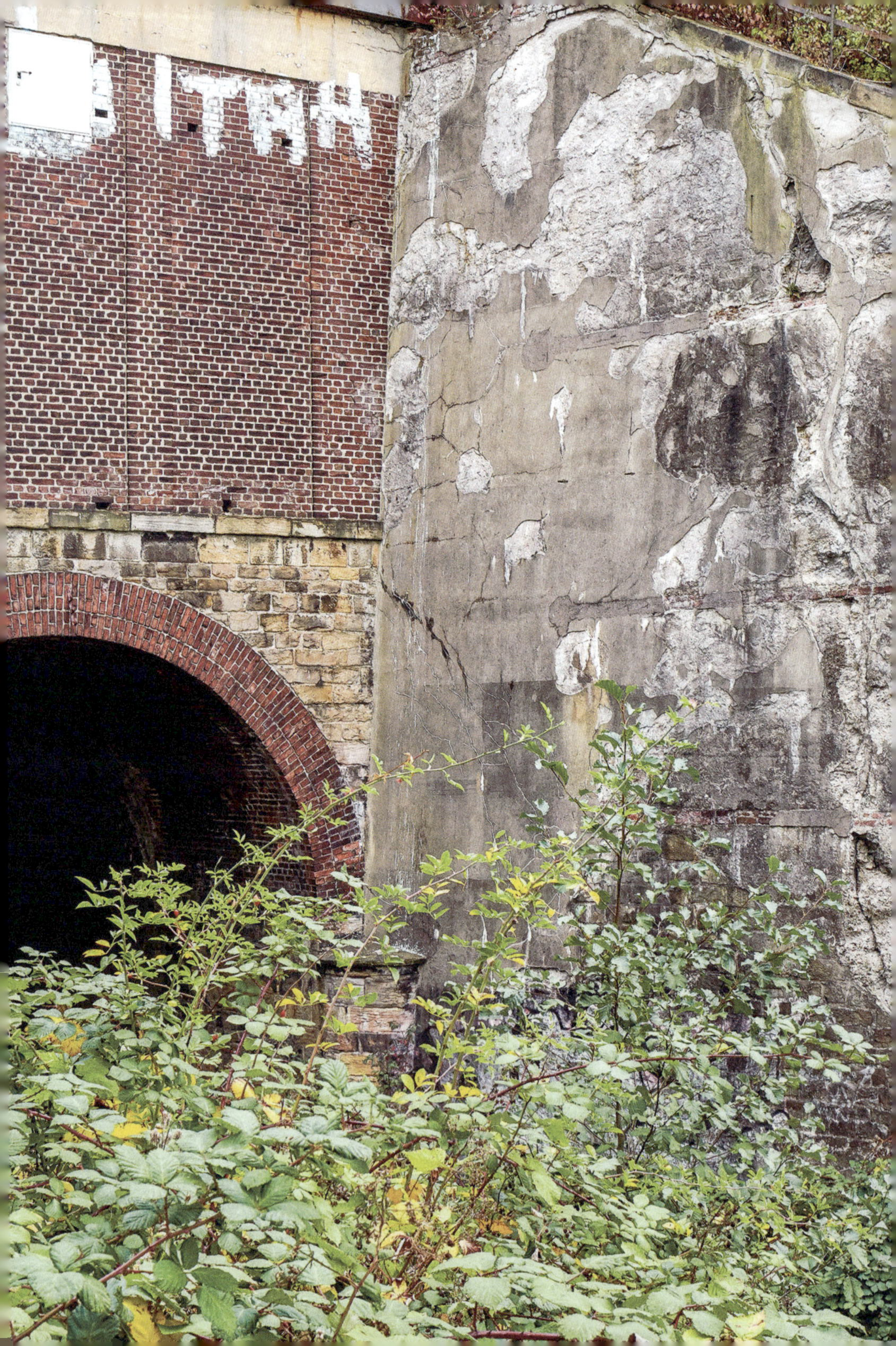

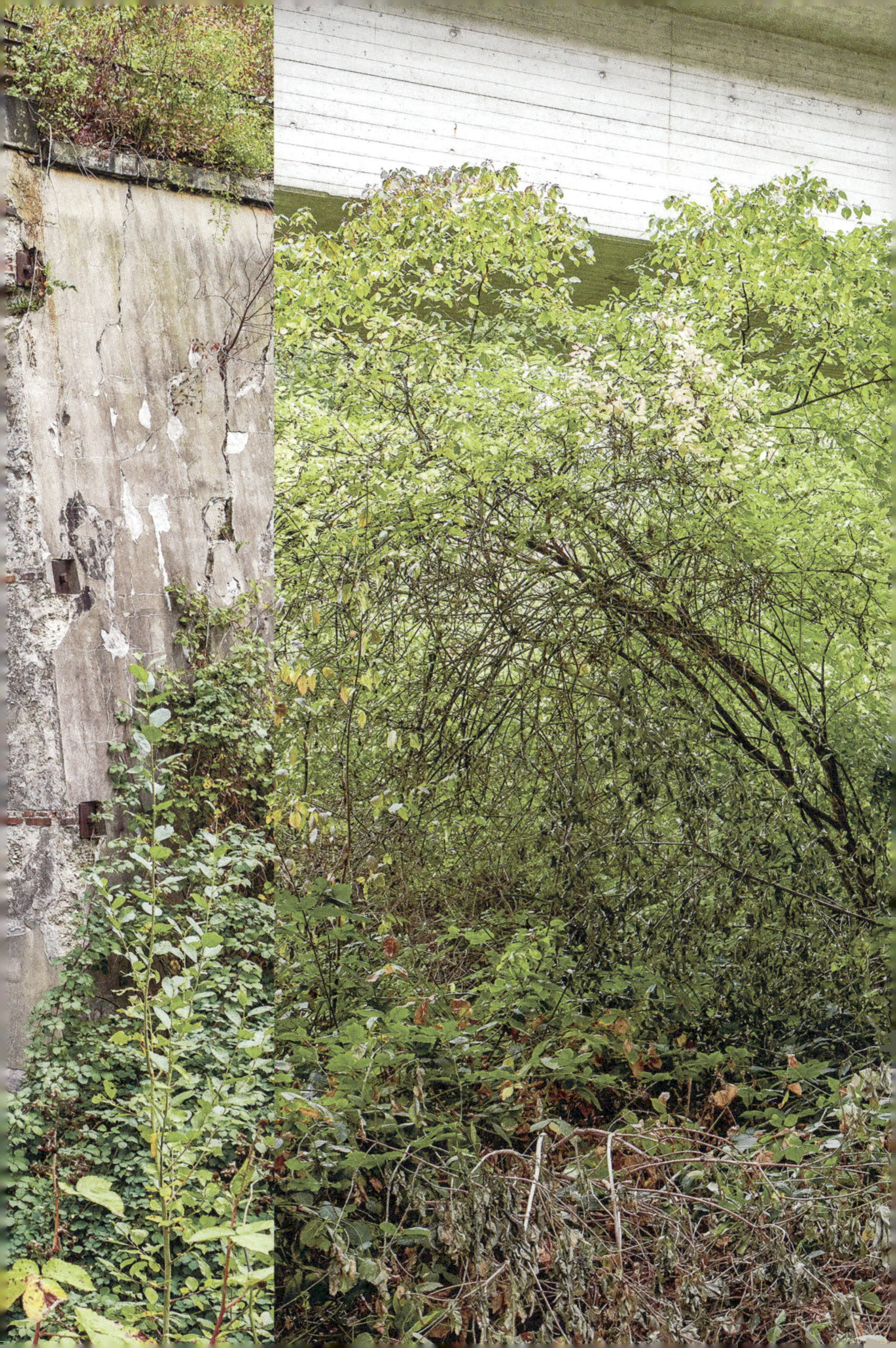

THE INSECT SOCIETIES (PART I)
Henrik Håkansson

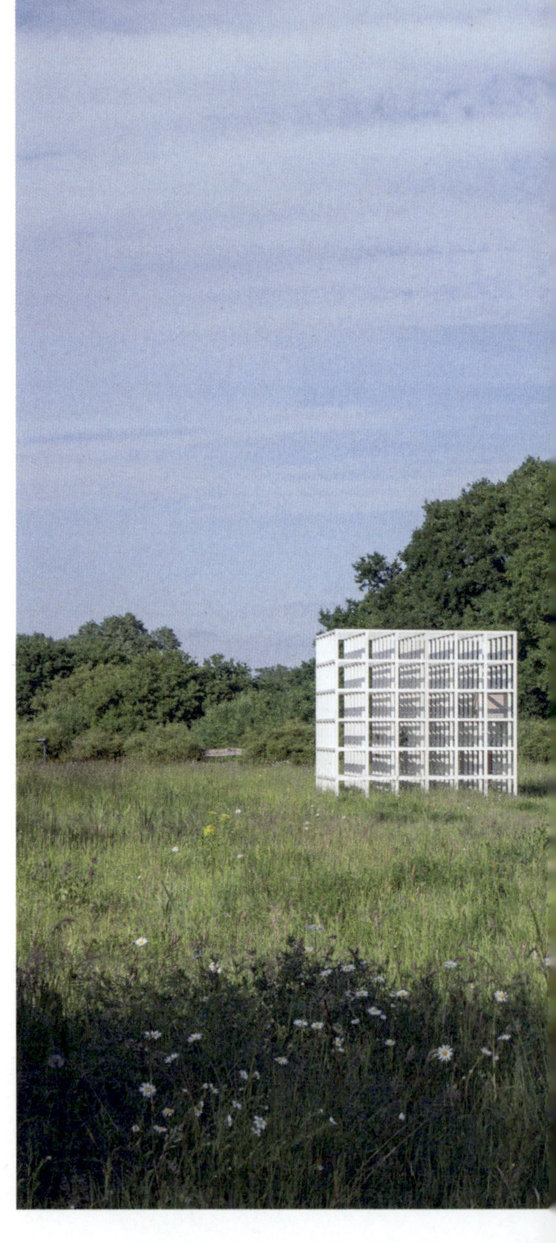

2016

MATERIAL
Wildflower field, two open cube
structures with 216 inner cubes,
wooden honey bee hives
(amount variable)
Dip-galvanised, powder-coated
steel pipes (6 cm, white), wood
Dimensions wildflower field:
2000 m^2
Dimensions steel cubes:
342 × 342 cm each
Dimensions bee hives:
50 × 50 cm each

ADDRESS
Emscherquellhof
Quellenstraße 2
59439 Holzwickede

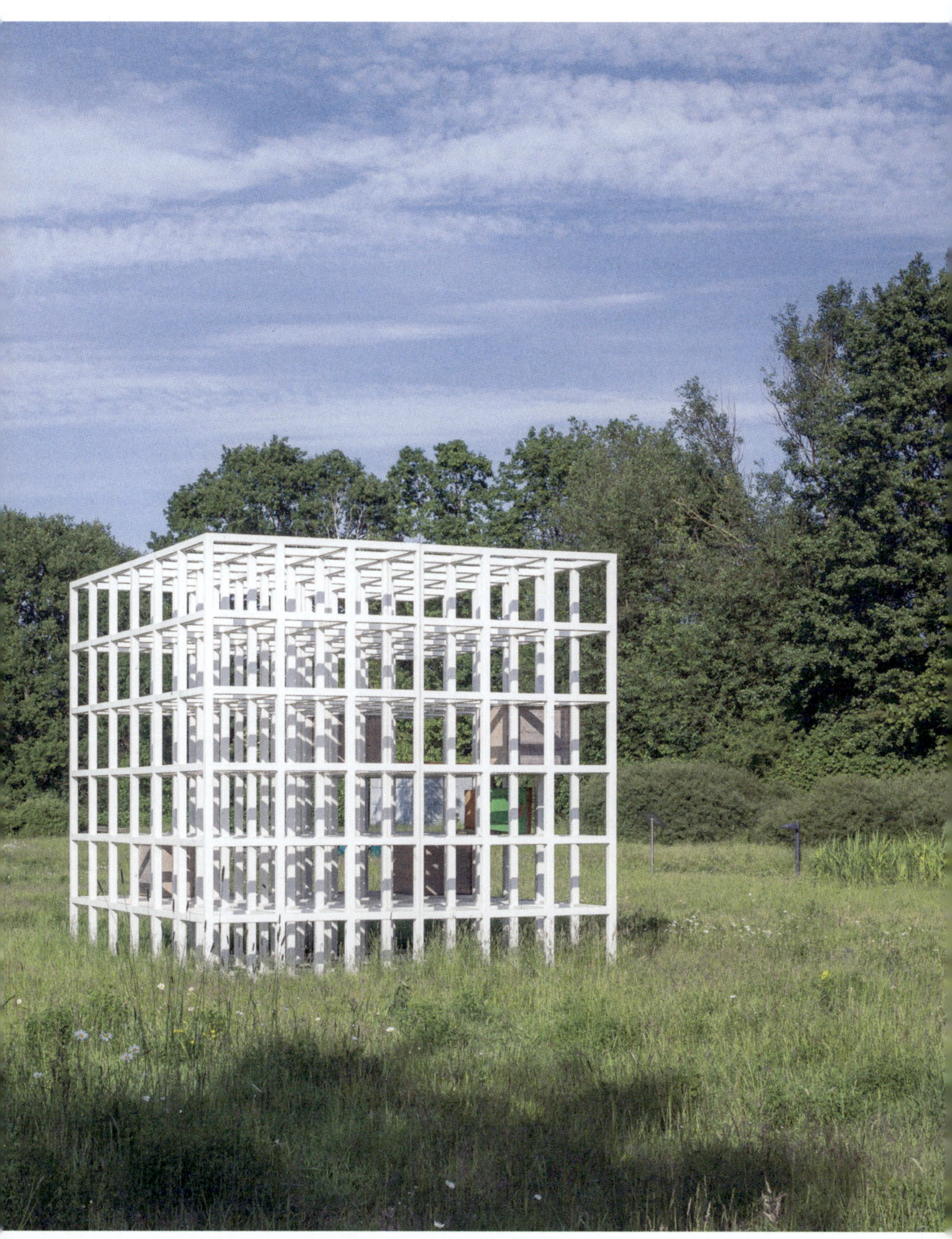

For the 2016 *Emscherkunst* exhibition Henrik Håkansson erected two cuboid edifices in a field behind the timber-frame farmhouse of the Emscherquellhof [Emscher source farm] in Holzwickede. The two minimalist sculptures are based on an open, grid-shaped structure of six-by-six cubes reminiscent of Sol LeWitt's iconic concept art of the 1960s: the basic element of his three-dimensional work was the modular structure of the cube which he generated in numerous variations to create a largely skeletal edifice. Håkansson enlarged the skeleton of cubes to create an edge length of almost three-and-a-half metres and erected it in the middle of nature. In contrast to the purely conceptual idea, the Swedish artist gave his object a function: the white cubes serve as a refuge for insects. In 2016, in collaboration with local apiarists, eight hollow spaces in each structure were furnished with wooden honey bee hives and wild bee houses. On the surrounding 2,000-square-metre-field, local varieties of wild flowers were sewn to give the bees sufficient sustenance. A frequent theme of Håkansson's artistic work is the precarious relationship between humanity and its environment, and how this is perceived. Humankind's exploitation of nature has had fatal consequences: among others, over many years ecologists have been observing the gradual extinction of bees. Bees guarantee the preservation of our ecosystem and make an indispensable contribution to biodiversity and to our food production. In contrast to honey bees, wild bees are solitary and often dependent on certain flowers, or have special needs regarding nesting sites. Hence, monocultures in agriculture, pesticides as well as climate change pose a threat especially to wild bees, which, unlike honey bees, are not looked after and fed by beekeepers.

With his colossal insect house in the middle of a flowering meadow, Håkansson gives, as it were, visual expression to the ecological vision for the new Emscher valley: to restore species diversity in flora and fauna. One aspect of the conversion of the Emscher river is the creation of a sustainable space for experience and relaxation which allows for balanced cohabitation with nature.

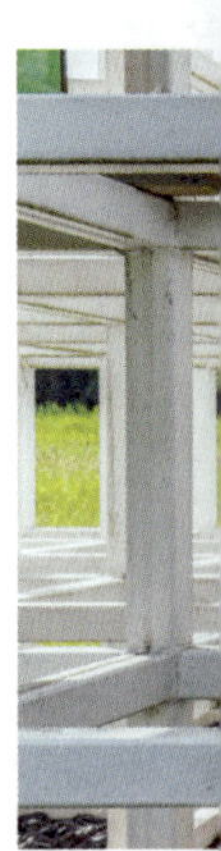

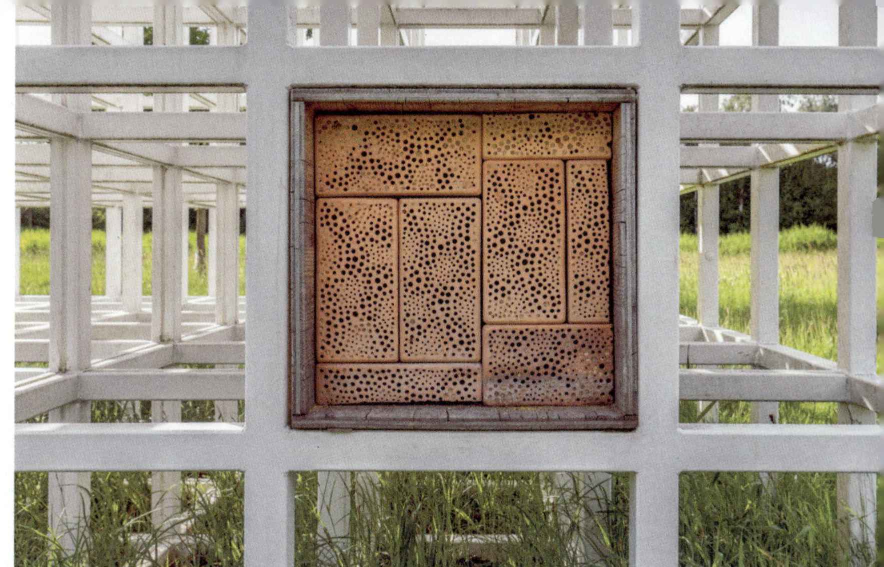

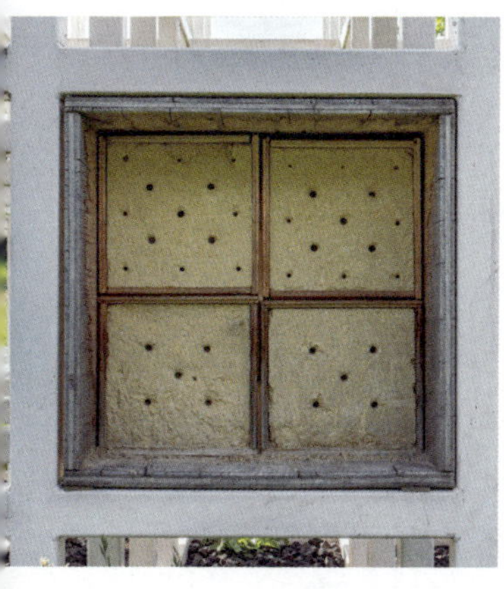

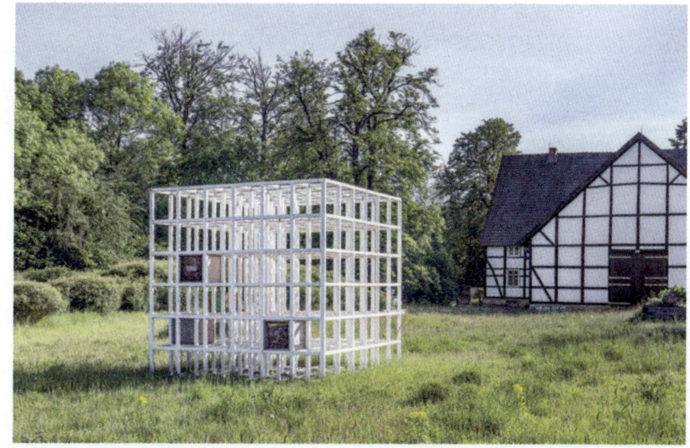

83

POOL LINES
Sofía Táboas

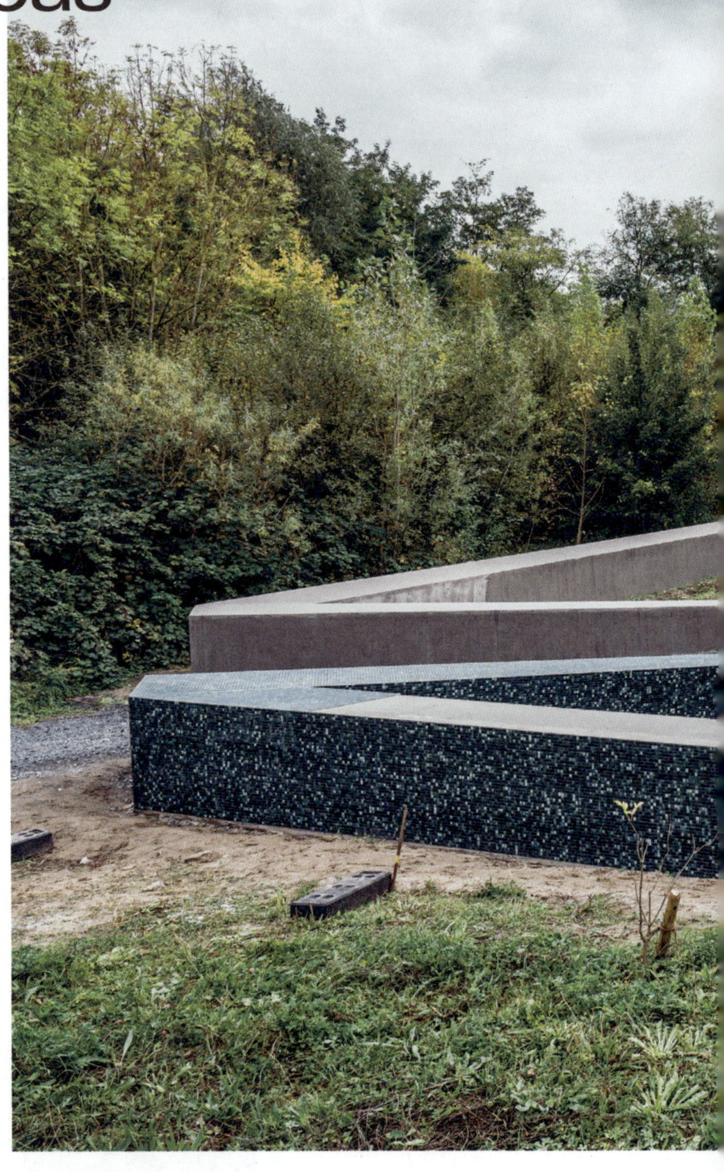

2023

MATERIAL
Concrete walls with
ceramic tile mosaic
Dimensions: 19 × 34 m

ADDRESS
Near Kleingartenanlage
im Massbruch
Grevelsbergstraße 120
44269 Dortmund

84

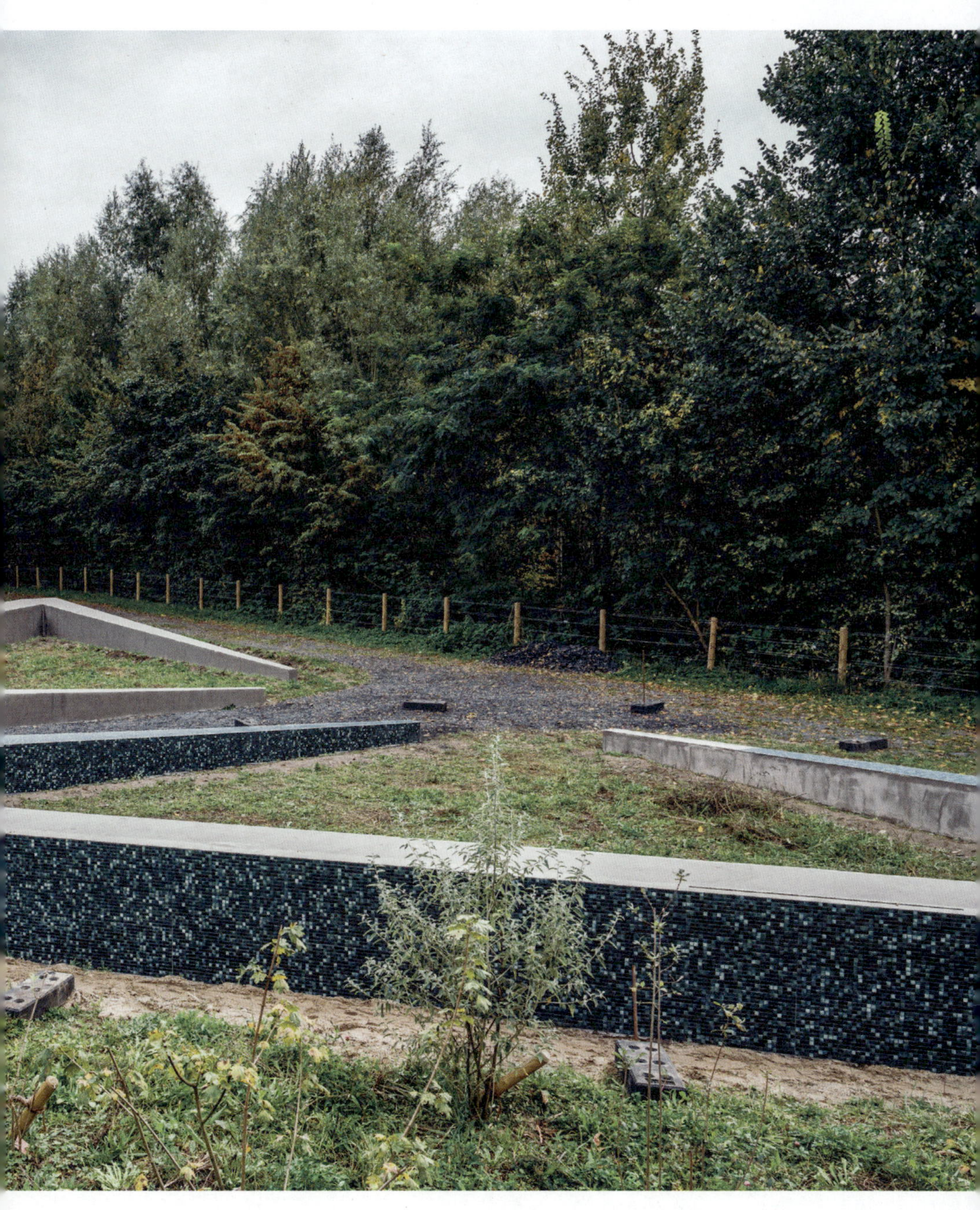

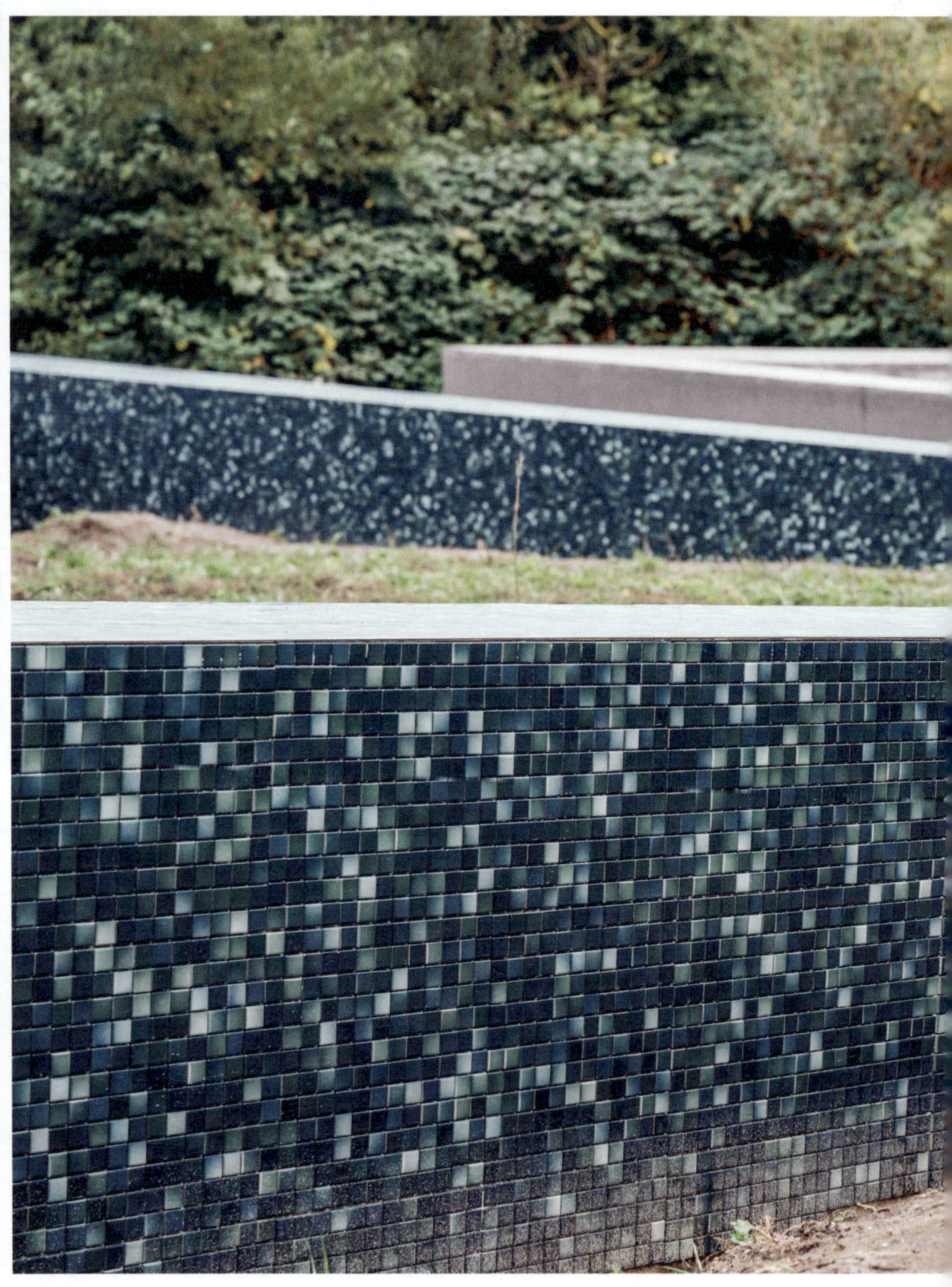

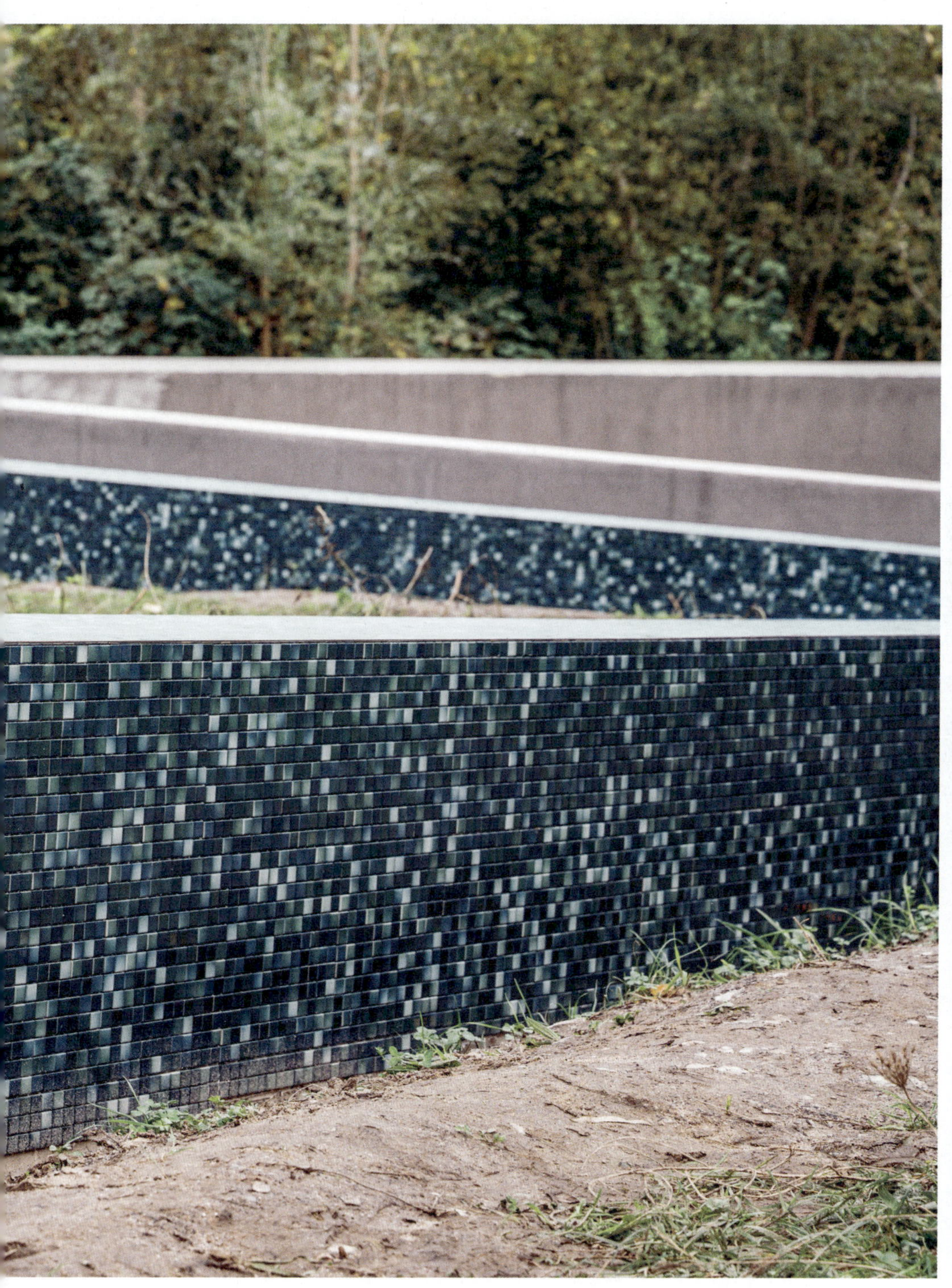

Two large triangles together constitute
a third triangular form. Their waist-high
walls are about one metre thick; they both
taper and flatten towards the ground. The
sculpture *Pool Lines* by Mexican artist
Sofía Táboas is clad with shimmering
green mosaic tiles. Are these the
archaeological remains of a swimming
pool from times when the Emscher
was still a meandering river? Have we
been projected into a mythical Bermuda
Triangle, bordered by a strictly geometric
greenstone mosaic? Or are these preparations for some future landing site?

Facing each other, both triangles
are open and encompass the section of
a meadow that lies between an industrial
estate and allotment gardens in the
Dortmund district of Schüren. In the background flows the Emscher, which along
this stretch has already been completely
renaturated. While blending into its surroundings, the sculpture's configuration
remains an alien body as attractive as it
is mysterious, a play between landscape
and architecture. The interior space
described by its walls is of the same
nature as the exterior space around it.
It both reflects and transforms the site of
the installation: the scarcely cultivated
green strip has become a garden
whose velvet green walls invite us to
linger a while.

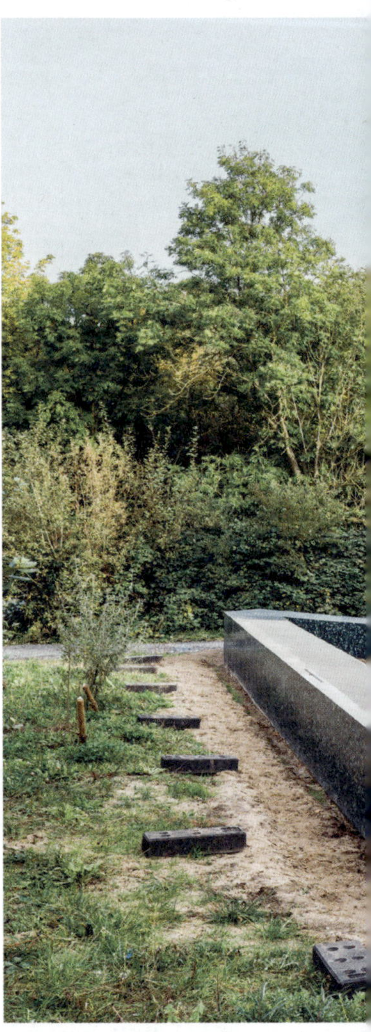

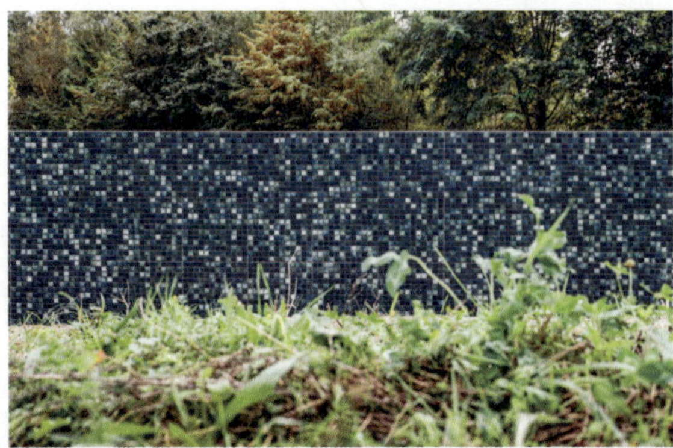

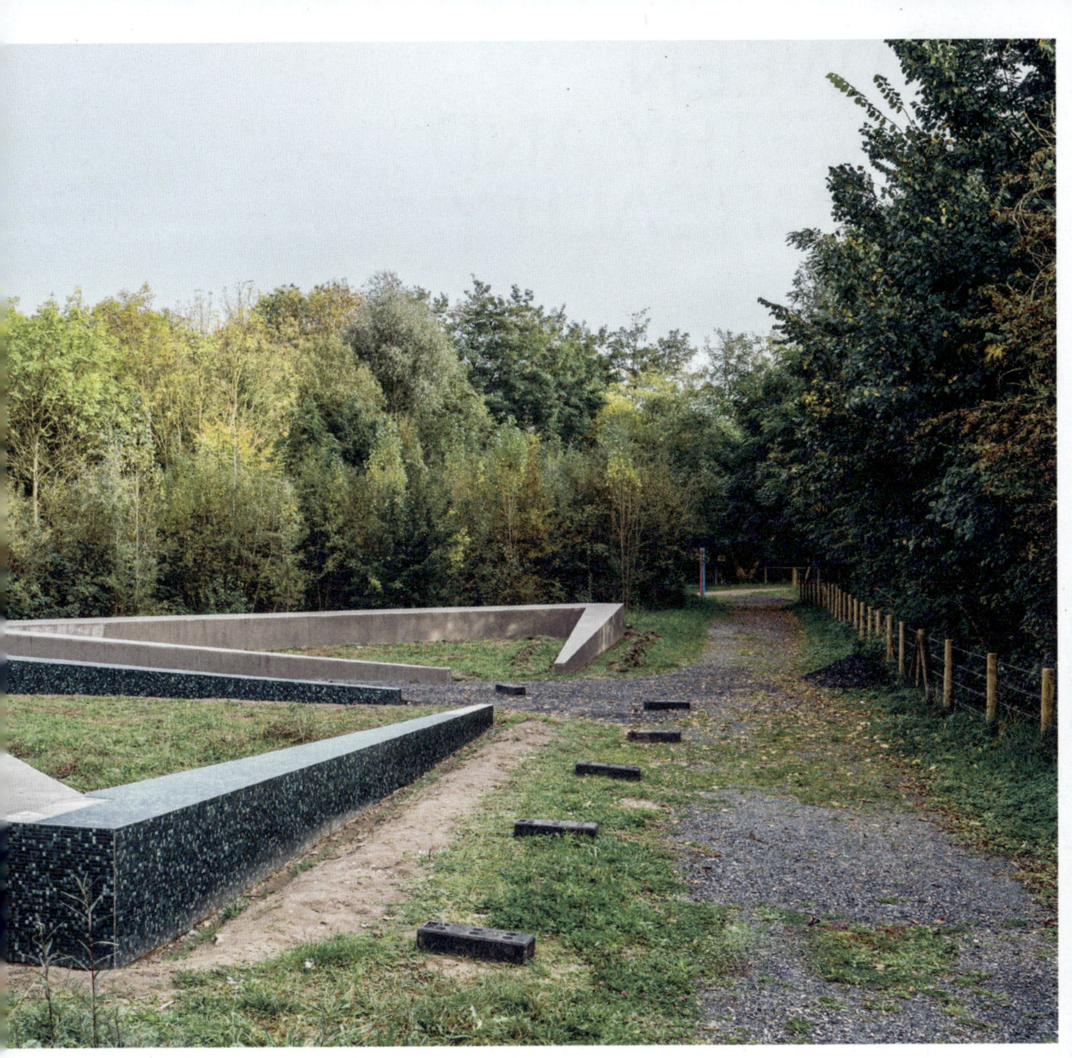

The artwork was still being set up
as this book was going to press.

BEETWEEN GEOMETRY AND CORPOREALITY

Juliane Duft
on *Pool Lines*
by Sofía Táboas

90

Between the trees a dark green structure shimmers. Further down the path to the Emscher river one can make out two enormous triangles of walls, each fifteen metres long and up to one metre thick. Like two mirrored counterparts, together they constitute an even larger triangular form. The corners pointing to each other are open, tapered and flatten towards the ground. This symmetrical constellation alongside the renaturated Emscher river in the Dortmund district of Schüren defines indeterminate spaces: it calls to mind baroque hedge mazes, but also mythical sites such as the Nazca Lines in Peru or the Bermuda Triangle. Equally, their gridded surfaces of small mosaic tiles are also reminiscent of elements typically found in horticulture like the water basins, fountains and pools of hotels or private estates. These tiled triangles do not hold water, but grasses and wild flowers. To some degree they resemble a pool that has been inverted or has subsided, emptying its contents into the ground — water that replenishes the plants.

Set between grey 1960s blocks of flats and allotments, the sculpture *Pool Lines* by the Mexican artist Sofía Táboas makes a strange appearance, like an edifice from another world, but also oddly familiar. It is invested with a timeless aesthetic evocative of retrospective associations, while also alluding to David Hockney's iconic paintings of Californian swimming pools as well as futuristic designs. Depending on your perspective, the sculpture feels either alluring or mysterious. In contrast to a baroque maze, it is impossible to get lost inside Táboas's lucid structure that is never more than waist-high — although both have in common that they represent cultivated, human-made nature. Each is a garden within a larger garden. Táboas's constellation is also reminiscent of works of Land Art such as Robert Smithson's celebrated *Spiral Jetty* (1969—70). Táboas's work is more landscape than object and relates specifically to the site and situation of the Emscher river conversion. However, unlike 1960s Land Art, it is not ephemeral but conceived as a permanent presence. With its resilient tiled surfaces, Táboas's sculpture is optimally shielded against wind and rain.

As a recurring aspect of her artistic work, here too Táboas is exploring the threshold between landscape and architecture — echoing Rosalind Krauss's postmodern definition of «sculpture in an expanded field», which in contemporary terms is considered to be neither landscape nor architecture. Through her art, Sofía Táboas explores the effect of architecture[01] on perception and the psyche. To do so, she transposes geometric architectural elements such as stained glass windows, doors, curtains, ladders and stairs, or folding screens into artificial, often dysfunctional situations, or uses them to create places that are open to new definition. As simple geometric fragments or serial repetitions, the architectural elements, both familiar and alien at the same time, suggest paradoxes in our living environment. In *Filtro Lama* [Mud Filter, 2011], for instance, double-walled windows become enclosed in vitro microcosms that allow bacteria and algae from Lake Xochimilco near Mexico City, which has been impacted by human intervention and climate change, to proliferate. Táboas's art investigates the interstices of social life; in her compilation of everyday fragments she scans the processes of seismographic change. Nature and architecture are not opposites in her work, but elements within a large fragile system — similar in this, perhaps, to Hans Haacke's early circulation pieces from the 1960s. The surroundings, the «outside», is explicitly incorporated through the openings of Táboas's triangular structures beside the Emscher. In this way, her sculpture reflects the larger garden, shaped by people: the neighbourhood, the city, the landscape of the Ruhr region and the course of the Emscher, which had once been turned into stone-bound architecture and is now being restored to a natural state, albeit a largely fictional one contrived by human agency.

Set in a strictly right-angled grid, the small «tesserae» (tiny tiles) that make up Táboas's mosaic form an almost smooth, shiny surface, a protective skin similar to the greenstone mosaics of Mexico's ancient cultures. The few surviving Toltec and Aztec mosaic artworks in the world, mostly masks and shields made of jade and turquoise, are among the most valuable examples of South American craftsmanship.[02] Many of these are currently in European museums; in Germany some were lost during World War II. According to their provenance, particularly the mosaic specimens held in Europe tell of the conquest of Mesoamerica by the «Conquistadores» and of their raids, but also of culture and language, as well as of the complex issues concerning the transmission of history.[03] What is certain, however, is that they were used for representing deities and as ritual objects, and that they have always been closely associated with natural forces governed by the gods that emanate from the heavens, the sea and the rivers. Yet Táboas's grid is industrially produced, made of ceramic tiles rather than natural stone, and hence also reminiscent of

architecture and Mexican wall mosaics of the 1950s and 1960s. The ancient greenstone mosaics in turn exerted a great influence on muralismo, a state-funded movement that began in 1921 in the wake of the Mexican Revolution. Echoing the country's Indigenous political tradition, murals in public places were intended to link Mexico's cultural heritage to the modernisation of the state. The artists were relatively free in their choice of motifs; motivated largely by their left-wing views, they conveyed scenes in a realistic style of Mexican history, especially of the Revolution and pre-Hispanic history to the predominantly illiterate population of the time. The wall mosaics were appreciated especially for their resilience. The outstanding works by the architect and painter Juan O'Gorman combine geometric abstraction with Mexican folklore.[04]

Accordingly, in this piece by Táboas, the small mosaic tiles unveil an entire cosmos of questions about humanity's relationship to its environment: spiritualism and rationality, craftsmanship and industry, indigenous conceptions of nature and imitations of nature. Her mosaic displays no motif as such, but varies slightly in colour from tile to tile, arranged as it is in a grid like the surrounding allotment gardens. The everyday, ephemeral materials of Arte Povera, the geometric abstraction of the European avant-garde, American Minimalism as well as Neoconcretismo and Tropicalismo are all embraced in Táboas's artistic work. Her geometric structures are borrowed from everyday life and are conceived as part of a complex reality, not unlike, say, the works of the Brazilian artist Hélio Oiticica from the 1960s. Here, grids and geometric bodies do not serve a rational purpose, but, like ghosts or pastiches of familiar places and objects, they play with memories and feelings — and provoke interactions with «actors» rather than «viewers». For Sofía Táboas, swimming pools are idyllic places of leisure and meeting places for people of diverse backgrounds. Since the early 2000s, she has frequently worked with the architecture of swimming pools. But she also occasionally creates mises-en-scène involving pyramids and signs of extraterrestrial forms of life. In this sense, the broad-tiled walls beside the Emscher are not only a visual reminder of sunbathing by the swimming pool, but in summer they also warm themselves in the sun and invite you to while your time away, to share a picnic or enjoy a break together. In our present-day world which is so obsessed with functionality, alongside a renaturated river liberated from its former function as a wastewater canal, Táboas has — not without a splash of humour — conceived a new, fluid space for plants and people based on her memory sketch of a pool: an environment whose use opens up between nature and culture, childhood idyll and melancholy, and allows for aimless idling and physical sensations. ←

01 See Rosalind Krauss, «Sculpture in the Expanded Field», *October* (Spring 1979): 30–44.

02 The Toltecs lived from around 800 to 1100 CE in what is now Mexico. The Aztecs regarded them as their forerunners since the culture that emanated from the city of *Tōllān* (Nahuatl for Tula) was considered the epitome of civilisation and craftsmanship. As a token of their veneration, they based their own turquoise mosaics on those of the Toltecs. See Karl A. Taube, «The Symbolism of Turquoise in Ancient Mesoamerica», in *Turquoise in Mexico and North America: Science, Conservation, Culture and Collections*, ed. J. C. H. King (London 2012), pp. 117—34, esp. p. 117.

03 It is unclear, for instance, where the green jade stones or the turquoise in the mosaics come from. On this, see, among others, Alyson M. Thibodeau, Leonardo López Luján, David J. Killick, Frances F. Berdan, Joaquin Ruiz, «Was Aztec and Mixtec turquoise mined in the American Southwest?», *Science Advances,* 13 June 2018, → science.org (last accessed 29 January 2023).

04 See Juan O'Gorman, *Unam Library* (Mexico City, 1943). The new library building was designed entirely by Juan O'Gorman. It combines strictly geometric, rationalist architecture with monumental representations of Mexican history, based stylistically on pre-Hispanic stone mosaics.

93

PUBLIC HYBRID
David Jablonowski

2021

MATERIAL
Ruhr sandstone,
3D printed
from recycled plastic

ADDRESS
Emscher-Weg,
near Adelenstraße
44269 Dortmund Schüren

94

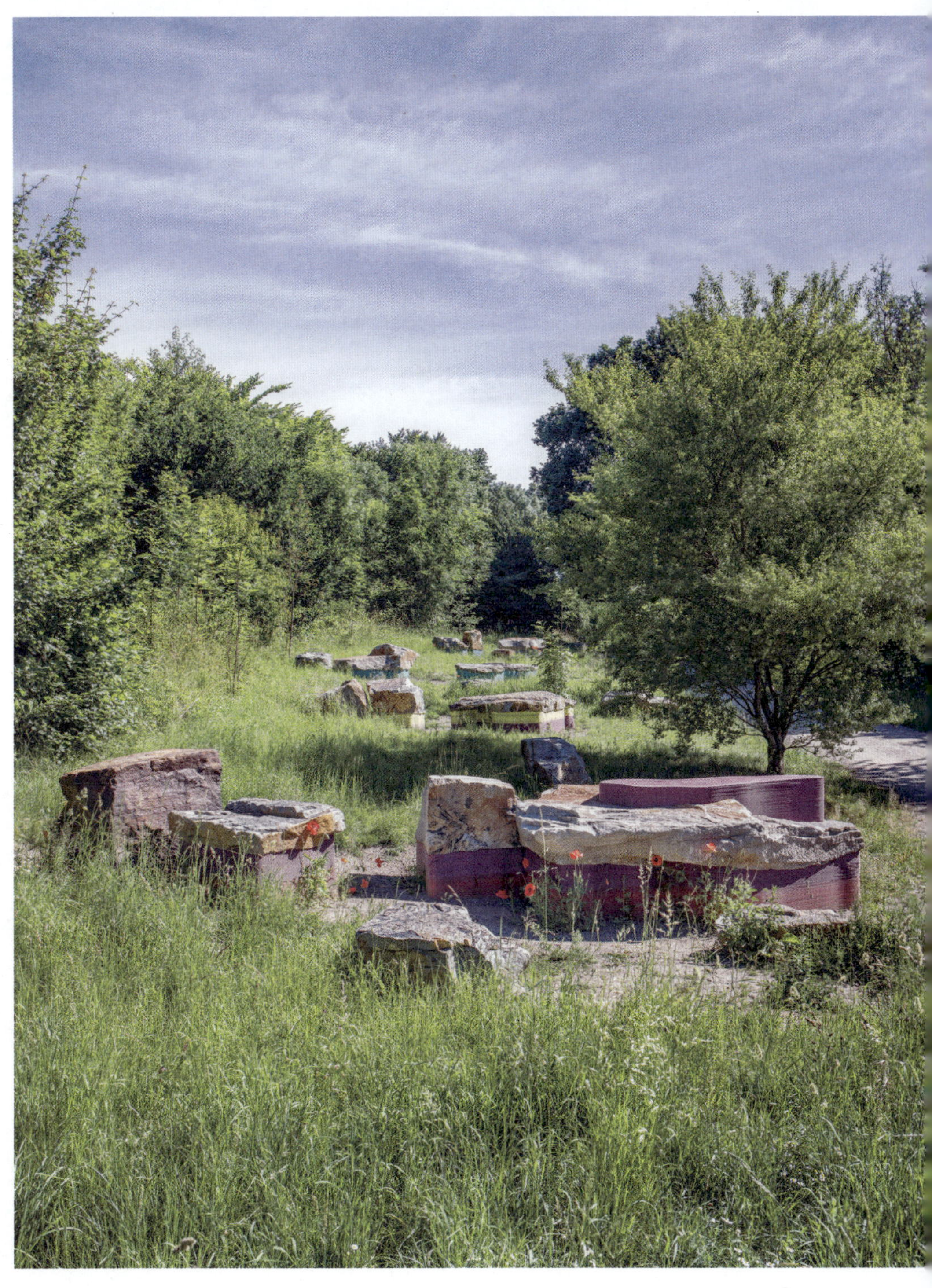

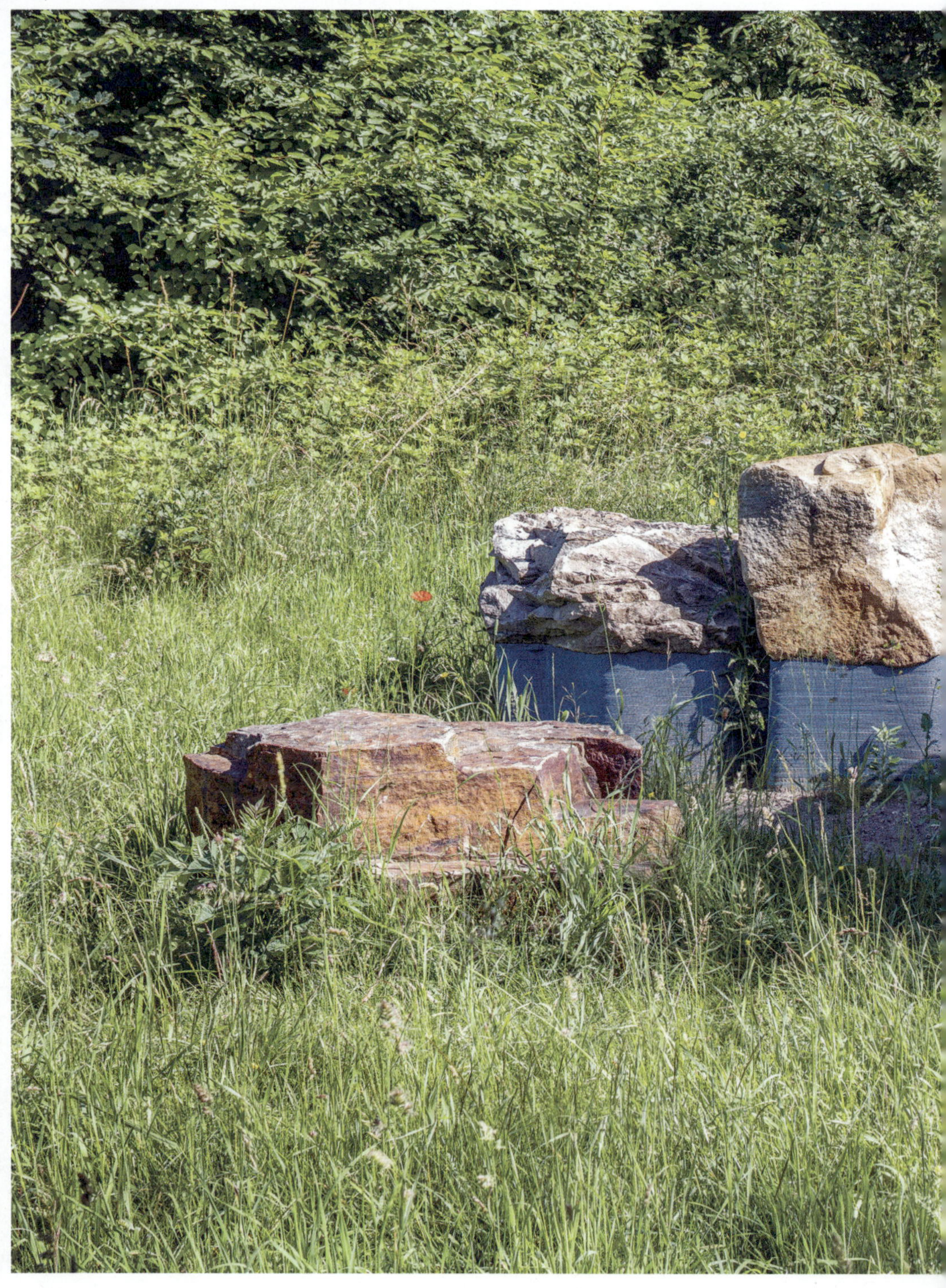

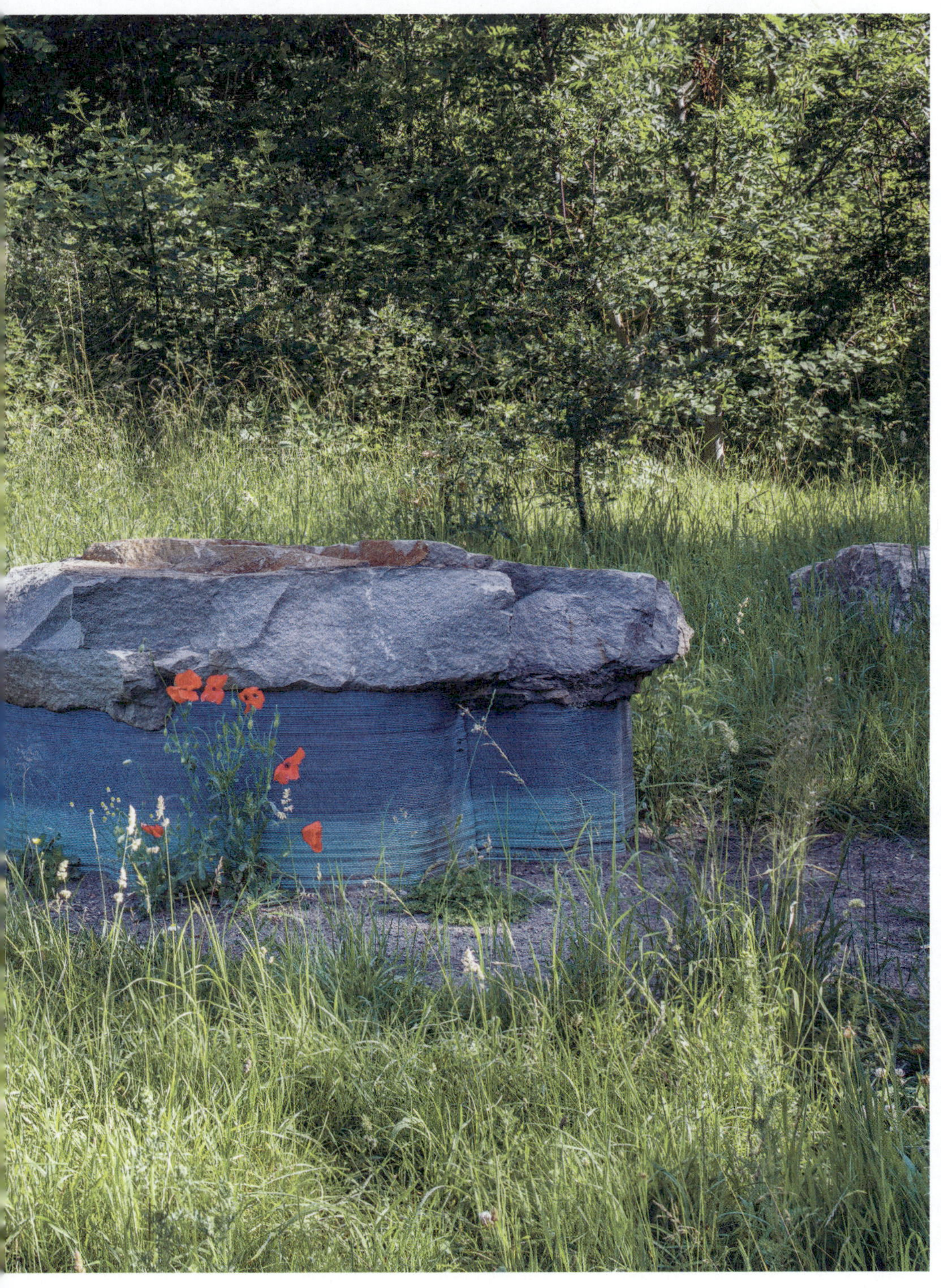

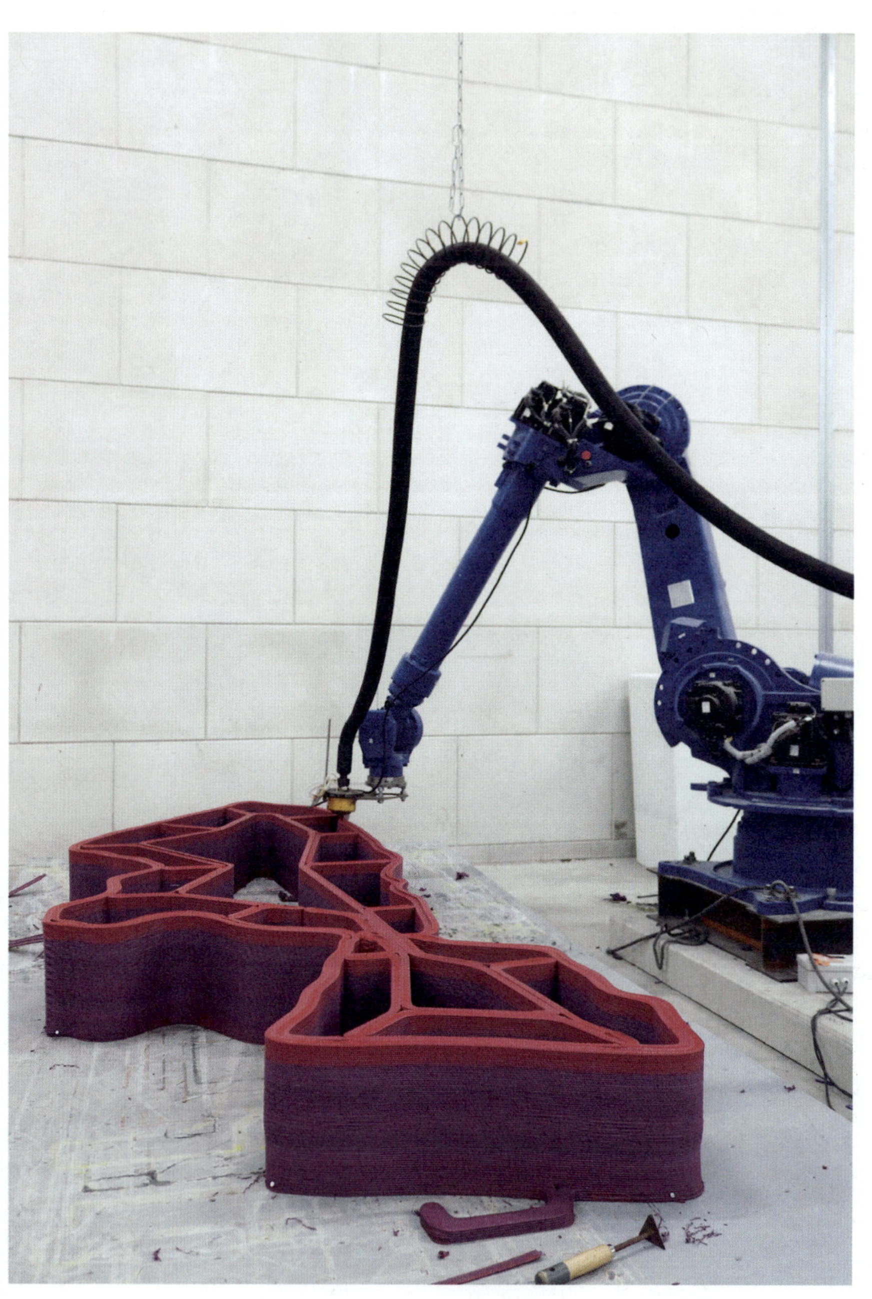

David Jablonowski's hybrid sculpture is located directly next to the Emscher-Weg cycle path in Dortmund. In it, the artist, who grew up in Bochum, explores the history and future not only of this particular place, but of the entire Ruhr area as well. At the same time, he has created a contemporary monument that resembles a natural landmark and can be regarded as referring to the ecological improvements that have been made to the Emscher river system. In this multipart installation, the artist combines sandstone and plastic. 3D printed elements made of recycled plastic and broken sandstone from the Ruhr region are stacked on top of each other like sediments. The resulting amorphous, artificial formations protrude out of the ground in a seemingly random fashion.

The sandstone comes from the nearby town of Sprockhövel. It was formed about 320 million years ago and is one of the most resistant types of sandstone in Germany. Unlike this raw material that has been used by humans for millennia, the use of recycled plastic elements produced by 3D printing pro-vides a glimpse into a digital, green vision of the future. 3D printing, or additive manufacturing technology, is in principle based on data for computer-aided physical translation. Through 3D printing, Jablonowski implicitly refers to invisible infrastructures that are created by the digital data traffic of public communica-tion. He also juxtaposes waste, which is a material that needs the help of digital technology to become a resource, with geological materials that are quarried in a traditional way. This innovation through the combination of new technologies, nature and artistic interventions also reflects the project of a generation of restoring the Emscher river.

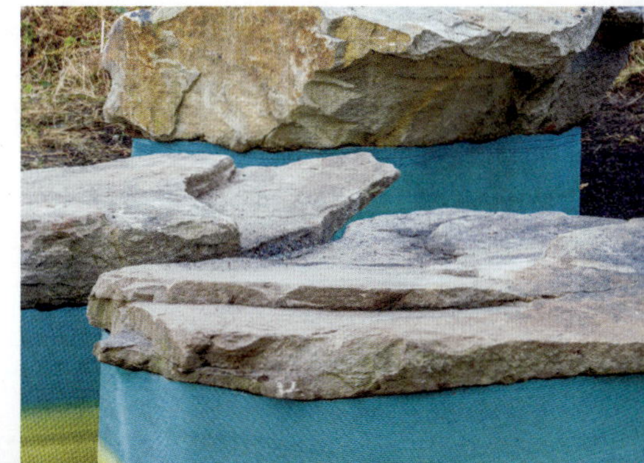

SAND-STONE-PLASTIC

Noor Mertens
on *Public Hybrid*
by David Jablonowski

In late autumn 2021, following a year-long planning phase, David Jablonowski's work *Public Hybrid* was unveiled in the Schüren district of Dortmund. Jablonowski's childhood coincided with large-scale, continuous transformation processes in the Ruhr region where he grew up: when the economically challenged mining and steel industries were being further dismantled, the artist's parents took him along to workers' protests in Bochum and his father gained his PhD with a dissertation on the decline of the mining industry; Jablonowski himself was attending school with the children of migrant workers, witnessing how former industrial sites such as the Zeche Zollverein [Coal Mine Tariff Union], the Hüttenwerk Meiderich [Meiderich Steelworks] which is now the Landschaftspark Duisburg-Nord [Landscape Park Duisburg-Nord] were being effectively transformed into leisure sites and tourist attractions.

David Jablonowski's artistic practice can be described as a sculptural archaeology of technological developments; it explores the aesthetic form of such changes and questions their social and communicative impact. Hybridity is a recurring theme in his works; Jablonowski deliberately uses this term to emphasise the diversity of technical devices, the wide-ranging opportunities they create and their external forms. His artworks demonstrate how he regards hybridity as an essential element of history and the material environment, and how it provides the impetus for his complex installations.

This specific focus in Jablonowski's practice, along with his inside knowledge of the major — and often painful — upheavals in the Ruhr district, make him the ideal artist to examine and appreciate the contradictory nature and complexity of the Emscherkunstweg [Emscher Art Trail], and to develop a new work for a post-industrial natural setting.

Jablonowski's multipart installation *Public Hybrid* combines two contrasting materials: sandstone from the Ruhr region and recycled plastic. The stone elements were extracted from a quarry in the nearby town of Sprockhövel according to the artist's instructions. Both the quarry in Sprockhövel and the site in Schüren where the sculptural group is now installed are «Urorte» [primordial sites] that have been left behind by the excavation of raw materials. Mines were operated in this area as early as the sixteenth and seventeenth centuries, in places where coal seams were located close to the surface of the earth. The source and history of the Ruhr sandstone — a particularly hard type of sandstone — are important to Jablonowski. A total of twenty-seven stones were broken to obtain the particular size and density he wanted. These stones were individually scanned to create animations of the objects, and these were then used to produce their plastic counterparts. The plastic components were matched very precisely to the simulations of the stones they were going to support. Jablonowski describes this process as a kind of science fiction, as it was the first time he had worked with 3D printing on such a large scale. In addition, the raw material — existing plastic objects that were melted down specifically for this purpose — has a utopian quality. The recycling process not only highlights the extent of mankind's exploitation of the earth and its resources; it also emphasises the fact that producing new objects from waste products is the only real alternative. Compared to other works by the artist that visualise data processing devices (such as laptops) or infrastructures (such as the internet) in the work itself, the process of creating this piece shows how digital media and information technologies influence Jablonowski's aesthetic and his use of materials and data.

Once the plastic components had been 3D printed, the stones and the supporting elements were taken to the chosen location in Schüren and the process of measuring and fitting them together precisely got underway; the different parts were thus combined to create hybrid objects.

The different colours of the plastic elements correspond to their spatial arrangement. Warm, industrial colours are placed at the front, while cooler tones are set further back; this creates a landscape effect as they progress from warm to bright to cool. The use of recycled plastic to produce this artwork is based on the «cradle-to-cradle» approach: in principle, the pure material could be reused (the exact composition of the material is listed on the objects via QR code), although art's inherent claim to eternity naturally contradicts this.

The *Public Hybrid* installation was carefully designed and staged by the artist. Visitors and passers-by are free to touch the artwork and, with reaching a maximum height of one metre, it is neither too monumental, nor does it overpower the surrounding landscape. The walking and cycling trail runs directly past the installation. Narrow paths run between the stones and from one to the other; these have been trodden by visitors since the work was first unveiled, indicating that people are using the objects — most likely to sit, rest or play on — in precisely the way Jablonowski intended with his non-monumental piece.

Public Hybrid in Dortmund is not the first public sculpture Jablonowski has created; nor is it his first work with this title. In his ongoing series of works, the title *Public Hybrid* refers not only to the ambiguity pertaining to the use of materials but also to the ambiguity and transformation in terms of function. In 2019, he realised an installation of erratic boulders and 3D printed prototypes of furniture items for a public square next to the Centraal Museum in Utrecht. The assemblage served as a temporary vision of the future for the furniture industry, created in a city that is home to the long-established furniture manufacturing company UMS Utrechtsche Machinale Stoelen Meubelfabriek [Utrecht Chair and Furniture Factory] and to a museum with a renowned collection of art and design. Jablonowski stacked the 3D-printed pieces to create an unusable structure, combining them in a loose arrangement with old rocks that were found in the area around Utrecht.

From a curatorial point of view, Jablonowski's work for the Emscherkunstweg refers to the history and future of the Emscher region, without being an uncritical reflection or approval of either. Up to now, the industrial history of the region has been characterised by a desire for innovation and technological progress. While the future may be uncertain, it will definitely be shaped by the need to deal with the environment in a less exploitative manner than before. Jablonowski's work plays with different temporal references and technologies: the centuries-old mining industry; the quarry in Sprockhövel that has been in use for an equally long time; new methods that allow existing objects to be precisely scanned; recycled materials; and the use of 3D printing techniques

to produce an artwork that is then
embedded in the landscape like a
modern megalith. What consequences
do technological developments and progressive thinking have for ecological and
sociological transformations? For the
people responsible for such innovations,
the consequences are largely unfore-
seen; often they are not confronted with
the effects of their actions, which can
be catastrophic or at least unexpected.
Technologies are continuously evolving,
as Jablonowski's work illustrates, and
it is not always possible to predict future
repercussions, which may in turn
generate sociological needs that did not
previously exist. This complex hybridity
and interdependence between technology, humankind and the world around
us is precisely what Jablonowski is
exploring and articulating in his works. ←

SPIRITS OF THE EMSCHER VALLEY
Studio Orta

2016

MATERIAL
Vogelfrau [Birdwoman]
Aluminium
150 × 232 × 100 cm

Totem mit Elster [Totem with Magpie]
Aluminium
442 × 148 × 90 cm

ADDRESS
Emscher-Weg
near Faßstraße
44263 Dortmund

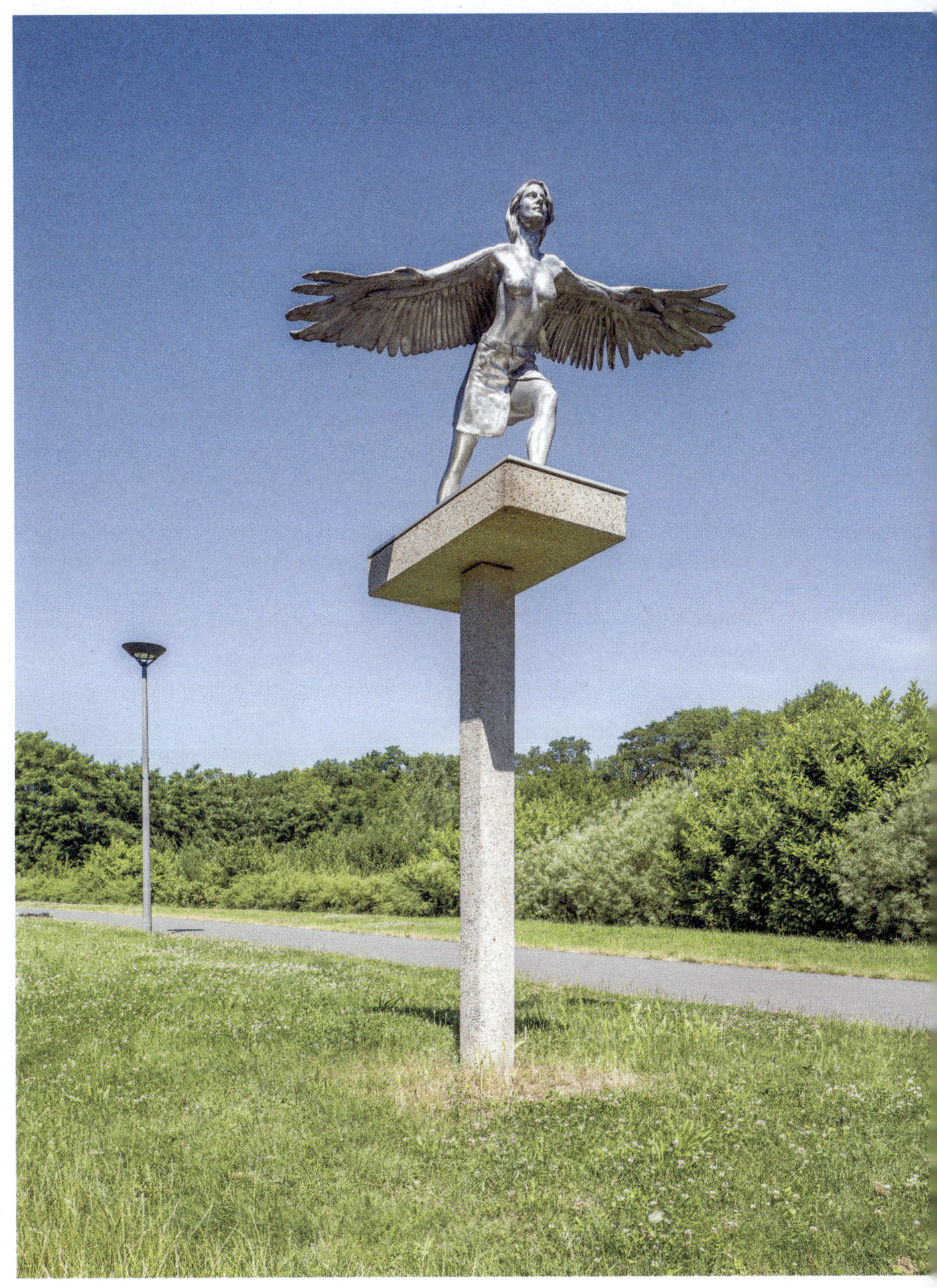

Originally, Spirits of the Emscher Valley was intended for the 2016 *Emscherkunst* exhibition as a kind of parkour linking three sculptures. The *Spirits* consisted of the two works *Vogelfrau* [Bird Woman] and *Totem mit Elster* [Totem with Magpie] that were installed during the exhibition on the southern shore of the Phoenix Lake in Dortmund's Hörde district, then later shifted to the Emscher-Weg bike path on the other side of the lake. A third sculpture, *Beobachter (Oraculum)* [Viewer (Oraculum)], was originally installed on the grounds of the Hansa coking plant in the Huckarde district of Dortmund but is now no longer preserved.

The works came about in a participatory process with people who have a personal relationship to the Huckarde and Hörde districts near Dortmund. In this way, the artists Lucy and Jorge Orta wanted to give expression to the spirit of the new Emscher Valley. The aluminium sculptures were developed from tales and collective memories recounted by the participants, and from their philosophical reflections. Many of the participants had actively witnessed the era of the steel industry in the Phoenix-West and Phoenix-Ost foundries that were gradually shut down prior to 2001, thereby marking the end of Dortmund's heavy industry. The Phoenix-Ost plant was dismantled and exported to China. In its place, in 2011 the grounds of the former steelworks were transformed into the Phoenix Lake as a local recreational area and are now a premium residential district. In allusion to the name of the former steel foundry and the new lake, the *Vogelfrau* represents a chimera between a woman and a bird, a reference to the legendary phoenix of Greek mythology. The *Vogelfrau* arises like a «phoenix from the ashes» and looks vigorously towards the future. The *Totem mit Elster* is composed of three figures of children carrying each other on their shoulders, with a magpie perched on the outstretched arm of the uppermost figure. The youth at the bottom bearing the other two is standing on a lump of coal, jutting out of which is a diamond. As the most precious manifestation of carbon, the gem alludes to the region's formidable economic past. With its use of naturalistic formal language, the artists' collective is playing on historical and mostly heroised depictions of coal miners. On the one hand, *Spirits of the Emscher Valley* pays tribute to the people who laboured in the steel and coal industry; on the other hand, the youth of the figures therein depicted deliberately shifts the focus onto a new generation.

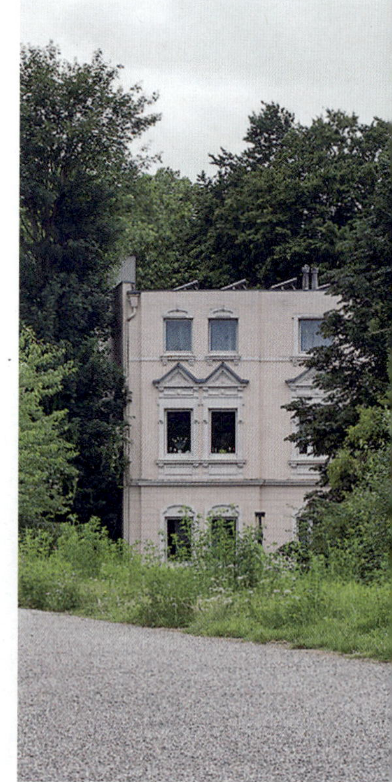

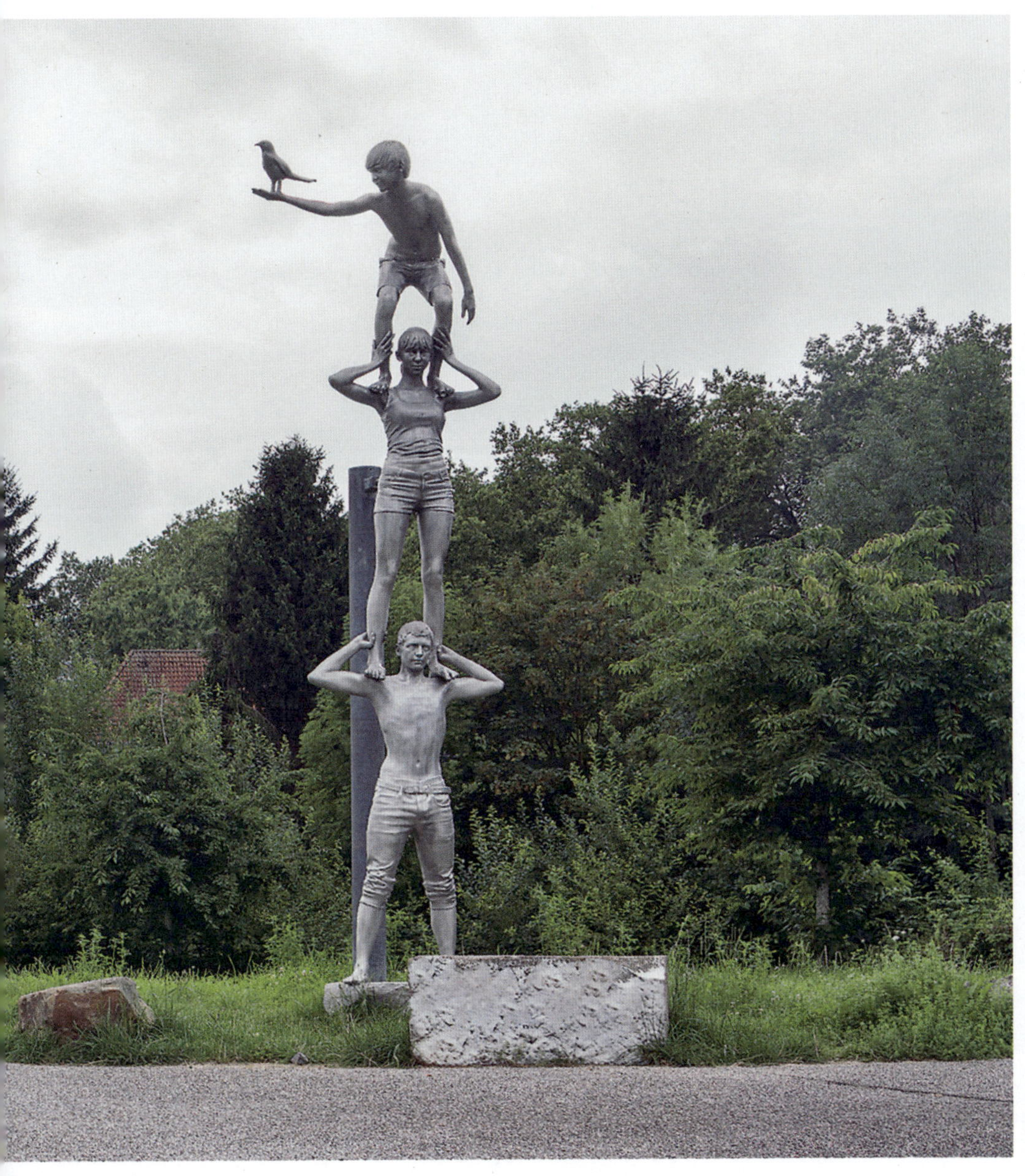

VOGEL
Samuel Treindl

2016

MATERIAL
Neon letters, acryl glass
330 × 72 × 15 cm

ADDRESS
Rheinische Straße 131
44147 Dortmund

108

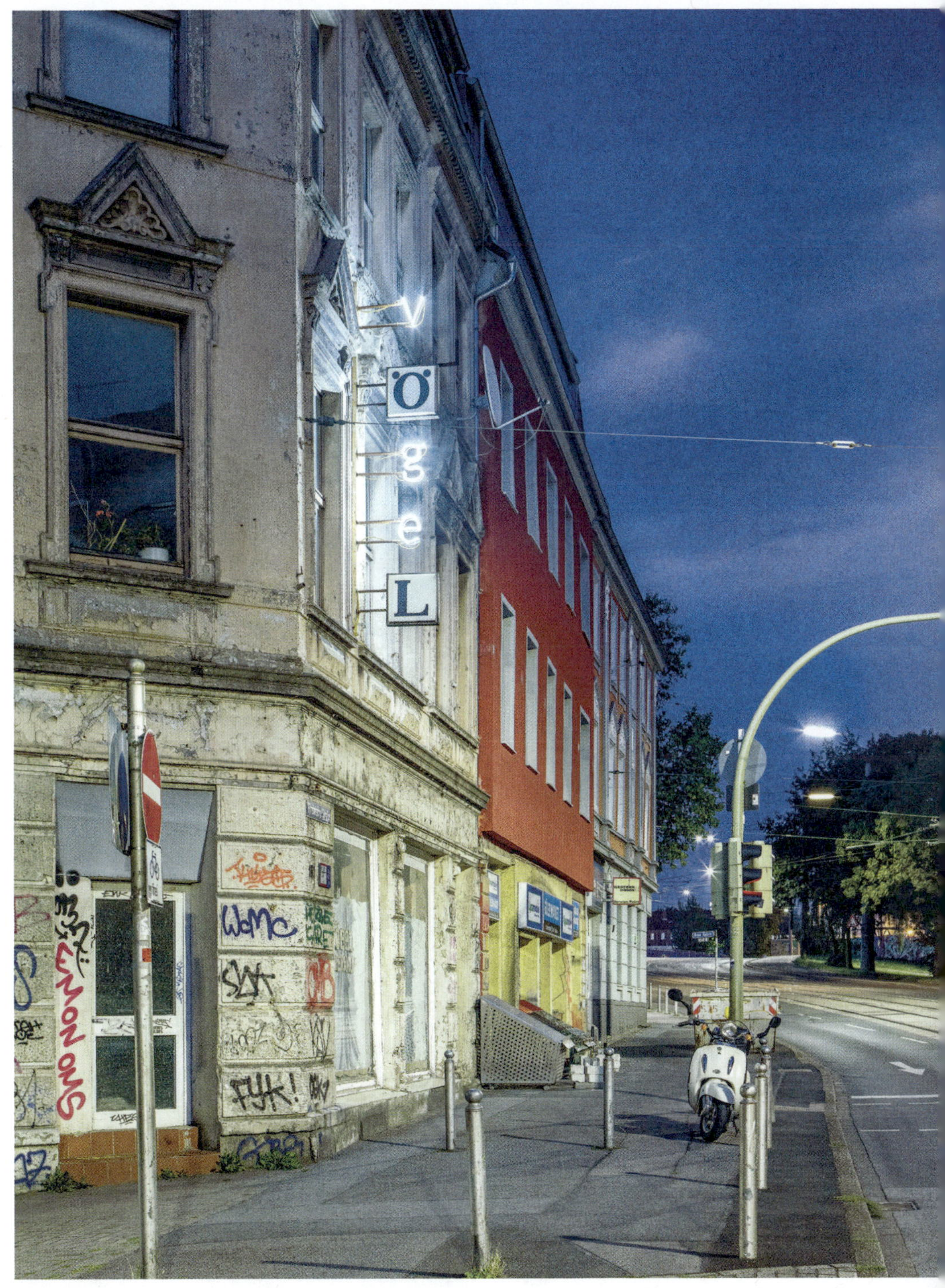

V
Ö
g
e
L

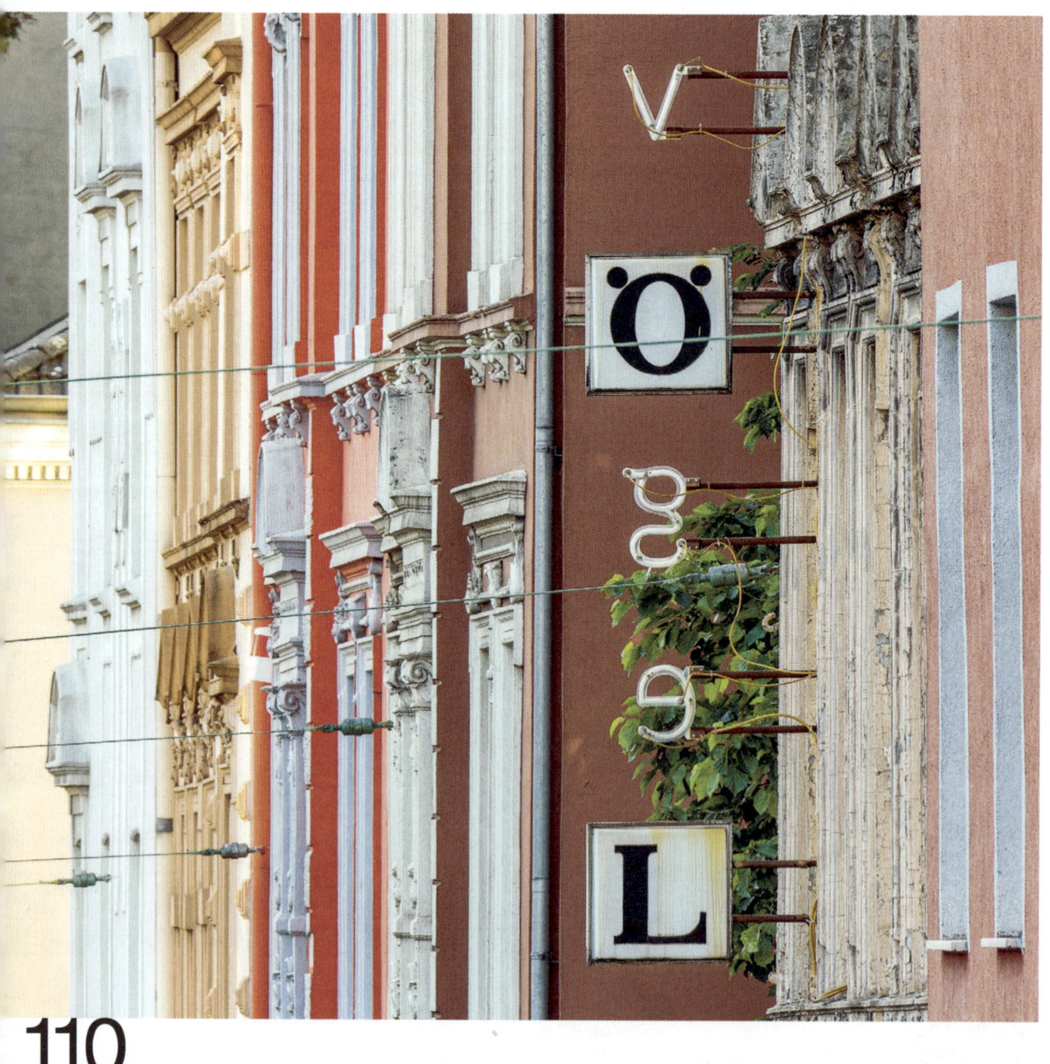

The Kunstakademie Münster was invited to develop a contribution for each of the three editions of *Emscherkunst* [Emscher Art]. In an internal competition in 2016 fifteen projects in total were selected by the academy and realised under the title *Stadt Raum Bewegung* [City Space Movement] in the vicinity of Rheinische Straße in Dortmund. Among them were Samuel Treindl's *Produktionsskulptur* and his artistic intervention *Vögel* [Birds].

The collaborative project *Produktionsskulptur* (together with David Rauer) consisted of a kind of open studio with a production line situated in Westpark. In several workshops local residents were invited to create objects of their own that could modify urban space. Treindl's own works in or for public space often consist of process-led and participatory elements through which he calls into question production processes and perceptual habits, concepts of art and design, and overall aesthetic and social categories.

The point of departure for *Vögel* was a disused shop at Rheinische Straße 131, where a now only partially intact neon sign on the dilapidated façade was a reminder of better times. The only remaining letters of the former shop name «MÖBEL» [furniture] were »Ö« and «L». Although these in themselves still spellt the word «ÖL» [oil], their spacing was an invitation to find others to fill the gaps. In a play on meaning and purpose, the artist hand-crafted the neon letters «v», «g» and «e», thus transforming the former advertising message into the word «Vögel». In doing so, he didn't simulate the original typography but gave the letters a fresh design to make them stand out clearly. The shop sign now no longer calls for customers and trade but offers an irritation: What message does it seek to convey? The humorous and poetic gesture of supplementing letters can sharpen our attention to advertising in urban surroundings, but it also guides our gaze upwards to the sky and perhaps lends wings to our imagination.

ZUR KLEINEN WEILE
raumlabor

2016

MATERIAL
Prefabricated reinforced concrete,
shotcrete construction, steel skeleton
with railings on concrete foundation
approx. 920 × 540 × 550 cm

ADDRESS
Emscher-Weg
Huckarder Straße 260
44147 Dortmund

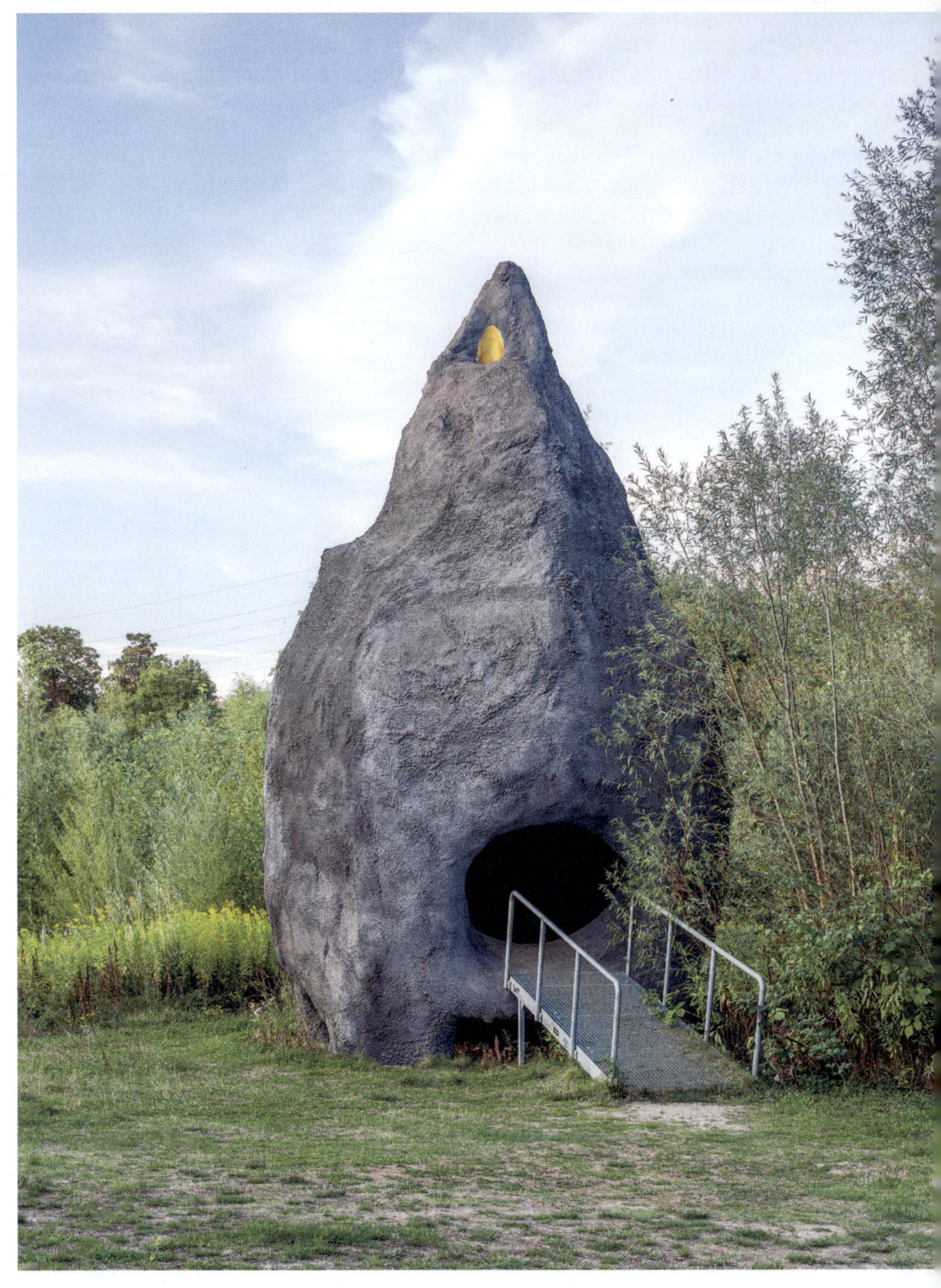

113

Situated between the renaturated Emscher river in Dortmund-Huckarde and the Emscher cycle trail is the work *Zur kleinen Weile* [For a Short Spell] by the Berlin collective raumlabor. It was created for the third edition of the *Emscherkunst* exhibition in 2016, which showed temporary art in the eastern part of the Ruhr region, stretching from the source of the Emscher river to Herne. This sculpture by raumlabor is one of five artistic perspectives from the 2016 exhibition that were preserved for the Emscherkunstweg [Emscher Art Trail].

Cycling alongside the Emscher from Dortmund's Huckarde district towards Castrop-Rauxel, in the distance one suddenly spots a monumental grey rock looming out of the rampant vegetation. Something golden flashes at the peak of the sculpture that is set against the backdrop of a flyover. Getting closer, one catches sight of an opening in the belly of this amorphous edifice which tapers to a point. Hovering slightly above the ground, the concrete sculpture can be entered via a ramp. The object's misshapen exterior with its irregular surface of shot concrete stands in sharp contrast to the perfectly globe-shaped space that opens up on the inside and is fully painted gold. Small apertures below and a larger round opening at the top create an unusual acoustic setting in combination within the smooth, spherical interior. Visitors are encouraged to try out this sound experience by using their own voices and then pausing «for a short spell».

With their work, raumlabor has created a space for contemplation, a tranquil haven in a countryside where nature constantly battles with urban sprawl and traffic noise. In this spot beside the ecologically converted Emscher, the river is now barely visible, since nature has managed to reclaim its refuge.

The work was executed by Andrea Hofmann and Markus Bader from raumlabor, in collaboration with Claire Mothais, Federica Teti, Louise Nguyen and Maria Garcia Perez.

KUNSTPAUSE
atelier le balto

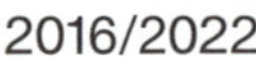

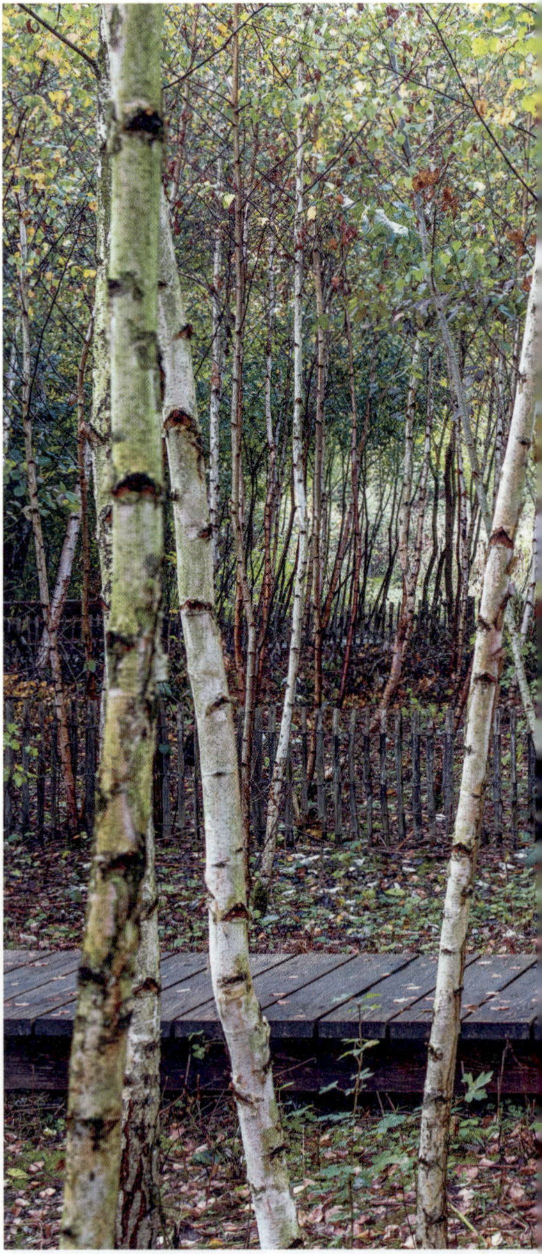

2016/2022

MATERIAL
Area with palisade (stakewall) fencing,
wooden terracing and steps
Dimensions area: approx. 10,000 m²

ADDRESS
Emscher-Weg
Huckarder Straße 197
44369 Dortmund

116

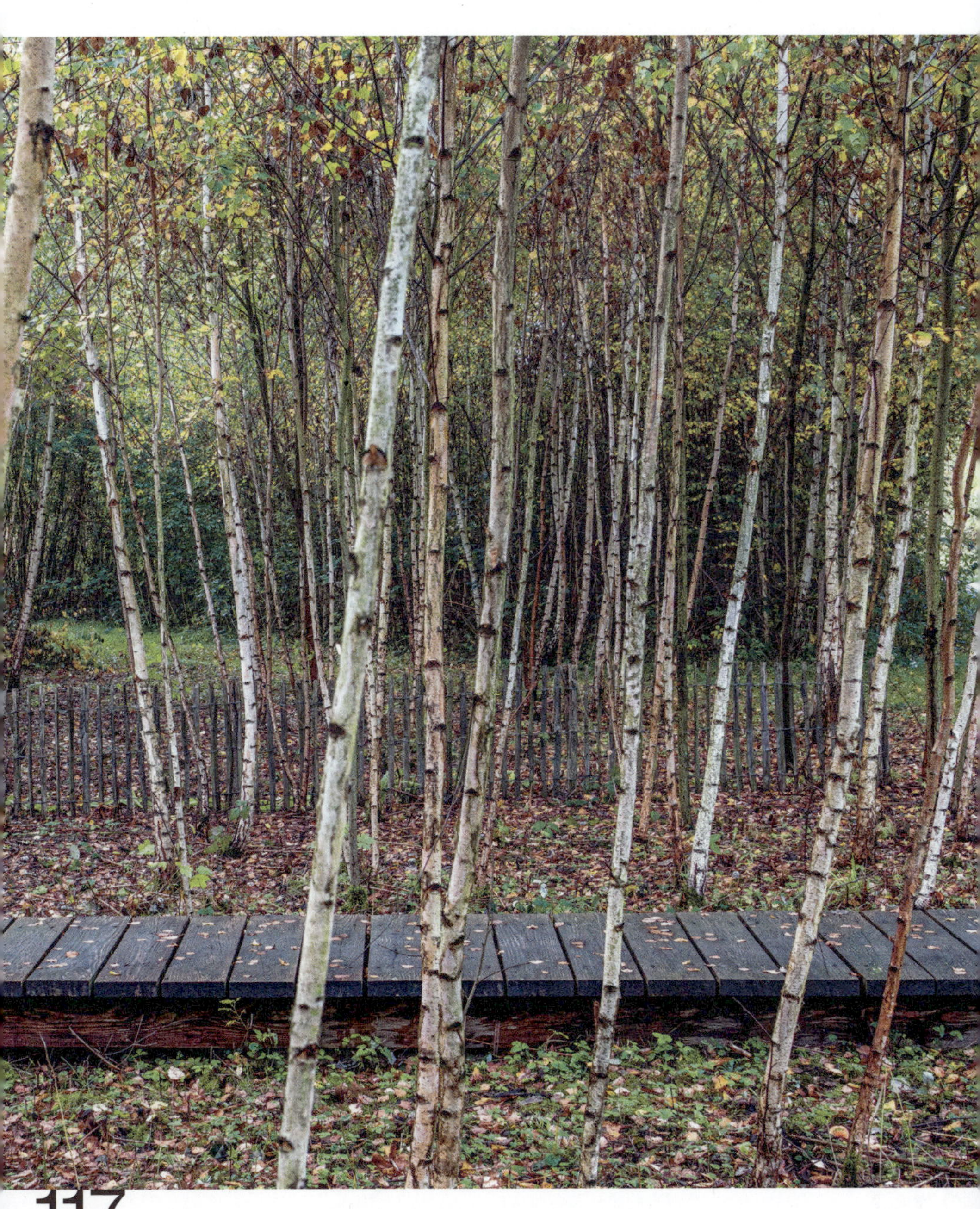

For *Emscherkunst* exhibition in 2016 the Berlin landscape architecture office atelier le balto transformed a large, overgrown hazelnut grove close to a motorway slip road in Dortmund into a place for repose on the banks of the Emscher river entitled *Kunstpause* [Art Break]. The landscape design preserved the site's original character, whereby atelier le balto incorporated sculptural accents by making targeted removals and additions of the site's vegetation. In addition, the area in and around the hazelnut grove was structured with wooden walkways, decks and paling fences.

The artists discovered this unusual location in Dortmund during an exploratory cycle tour they undertook along the Emscher. What first appealed to them was the hazelnut grove, which consisted of several large bushes, reminding them of a naturally grown spatial architecture. Furthermore, it struck them that the site — although ostensibly somewhat inhospitable — was much-frequented. It is situated between an industrial zone and Dortmund's harbour area, while at the same time quite close to the city centre.

atelier le balto describes the site itself as a kind of prototype of a «non-place», a term coined by the ethnologist Marc Augé. The debate surrounding this theme often provides the context for the group's artistic work. But here, the non-place is also a place of transit. Lodged beneath a six-lane road and the twin-track railway line, it is also used by people out walking and cyclists as a place of refuge between the former Emscher wastewater canal and a further multi-lane traffic artery.

In a simple yet striking gesture, the collective has infused the previously undefined space with a new dimension: the quality of lingering. The wooden structures with walkways and terraces encourage passers-by to linger and stay, making it a place that can be experienced. Allow yourself to be led and you will arrive in centre of the grove and discover a change in perspective as well as a different acoustic ambient. Suddenly, all noise of traffic and trains is muted. A rising, tribune-like structure close to the Emscher river offers a tentative glimpse over the already renatured waterway.

Between 2016 and 2021, the vegetation has changed considerably and the place itself has also been given new attributions. For example, a skate park with the sculpture The Stage by the artist Roberto Cuellar is now located in the immediate vicinity of the art break. These changes prompted atelier le balto to carry out a major design overhaul in 2022, opening up new points of reference to the surroundings.

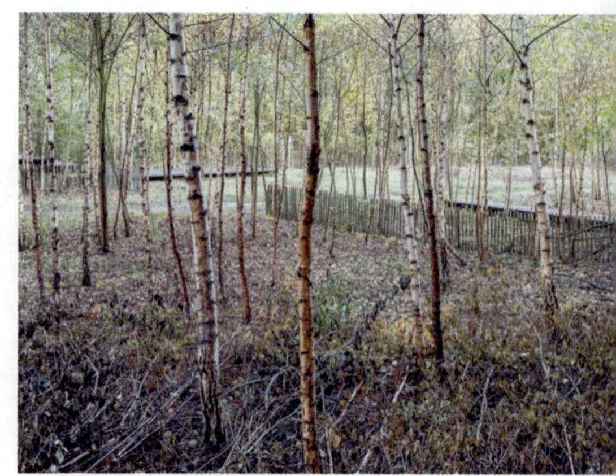

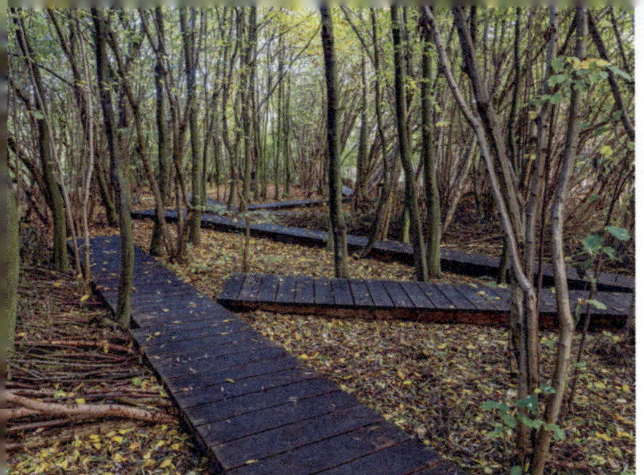

Birches are pioneer plants; since 2016 they have been establishing themselves next to the hazelnut grove.

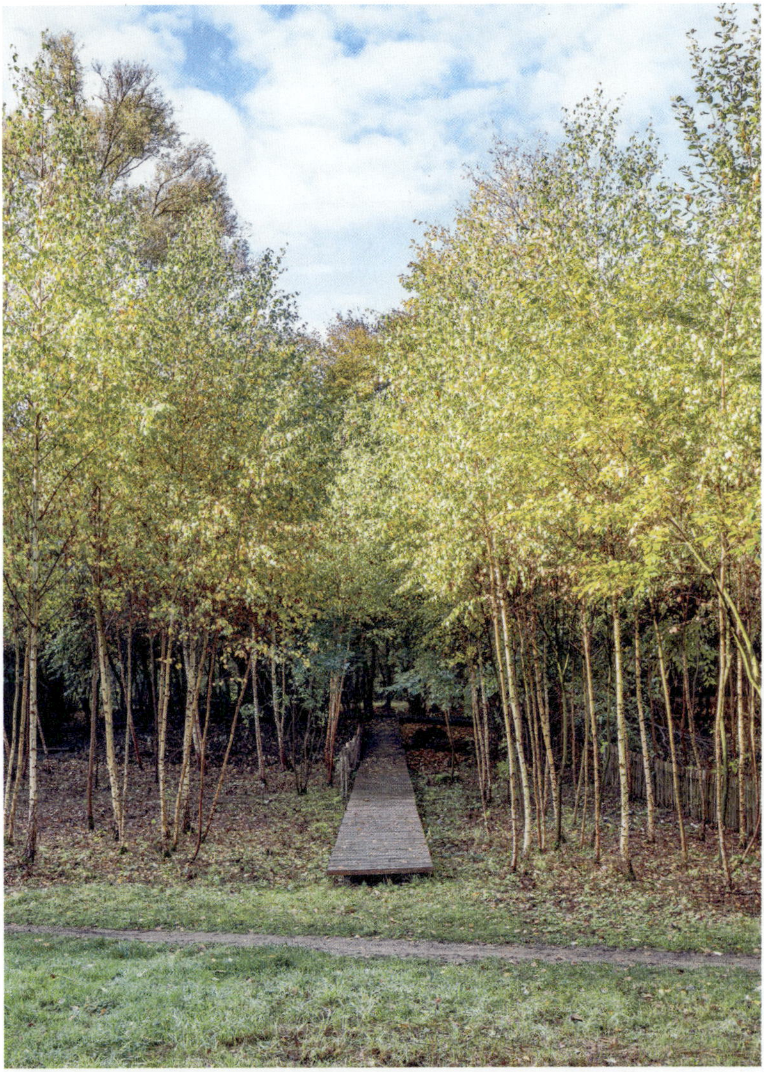

DASPARKHOTEL_
INSIDE-OUTSITE_
Andreas Strauss

2022

MATERIAL
Earth mound, corrugated steel,
wooden benches, wicker in steel fence
converted concrete tubes for
overnight stays, bedding and linen,
wall painting
2,40 × 2,40 × 3,21 m

ADDRESS
Hof Emscher-Auen
Rittershofer Straße 170
44577 Castrop-Rauxel

Overnight stays
from May to October,
bookable at
dasparkhotel.net

120

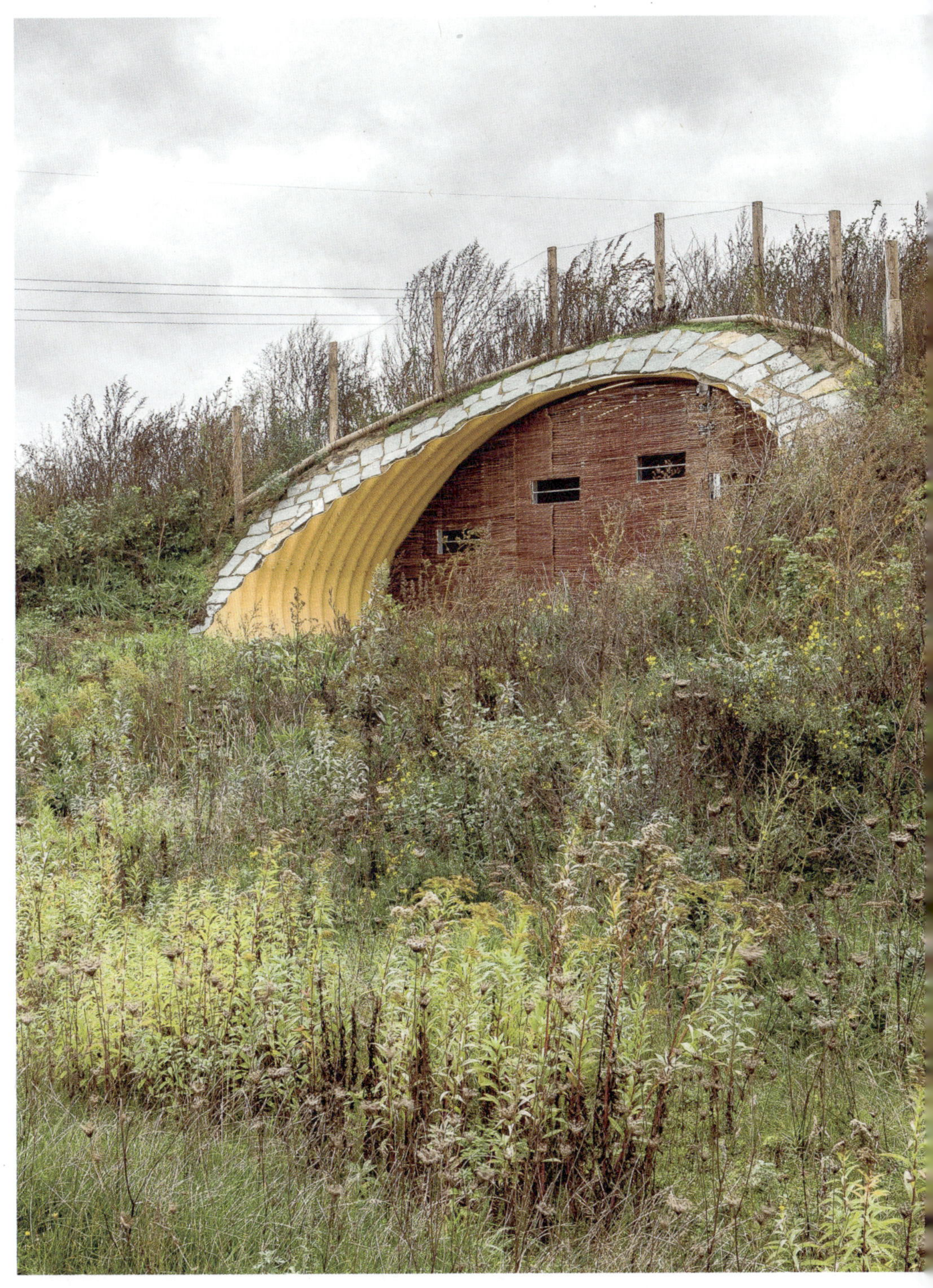

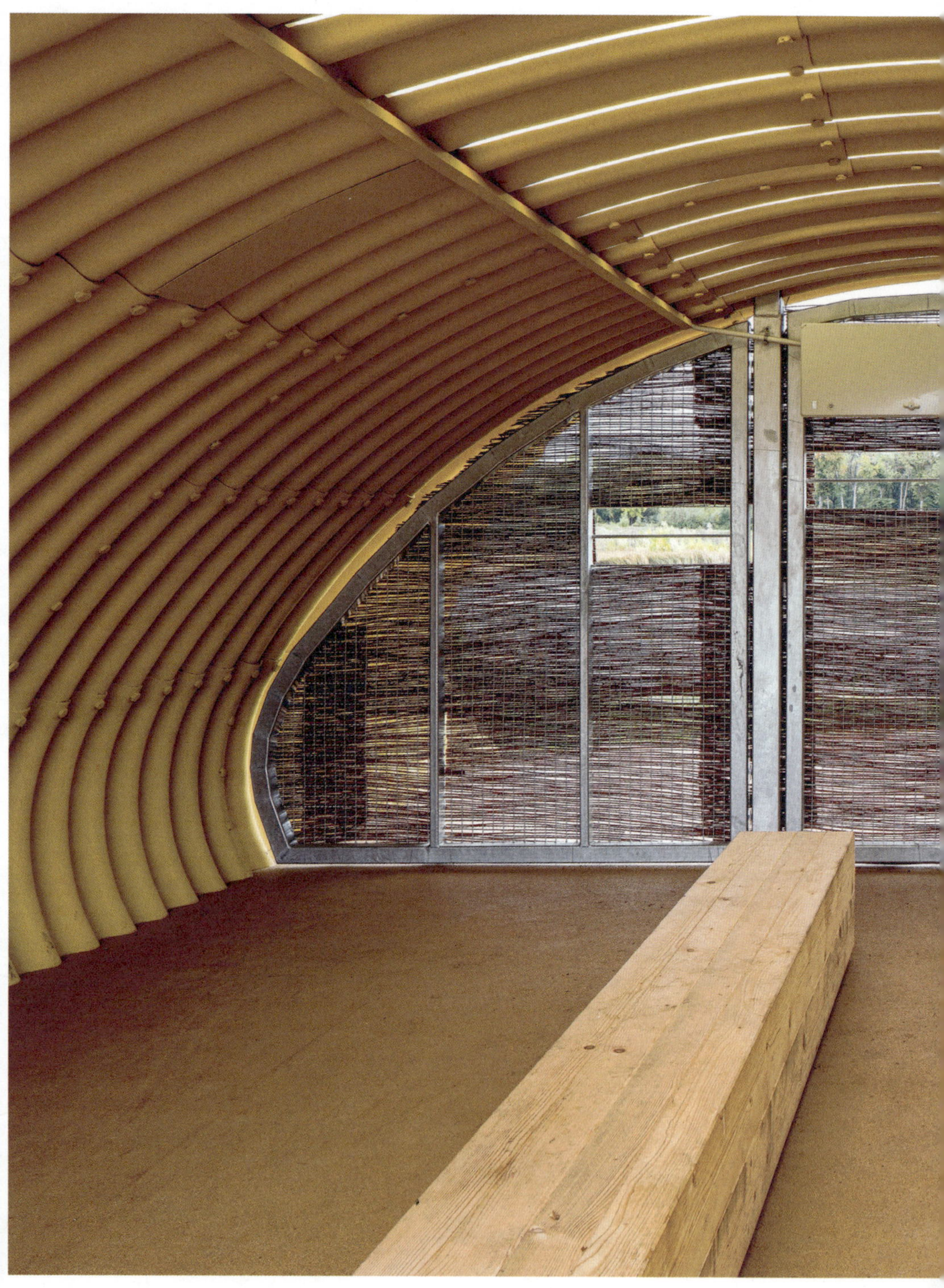

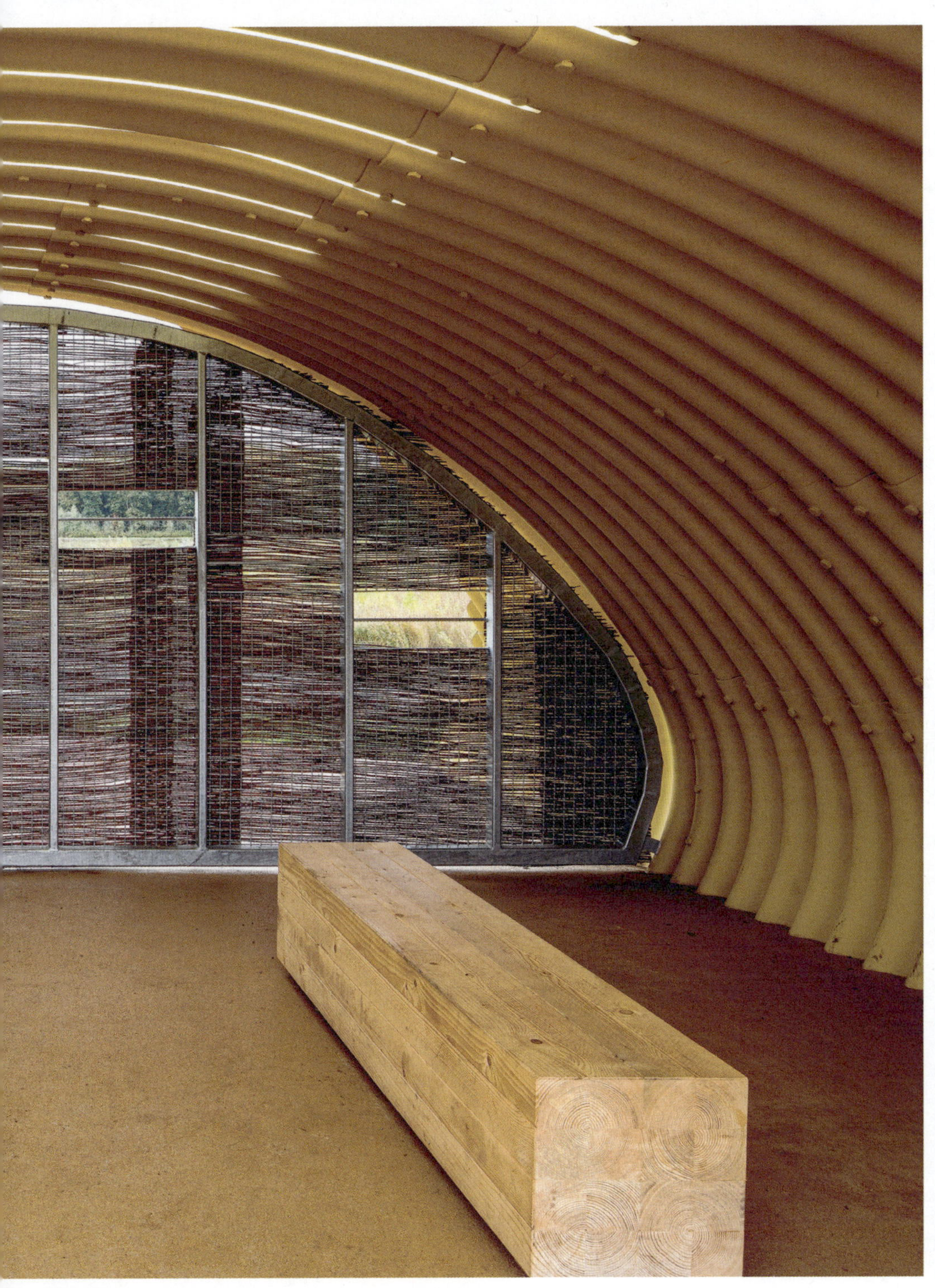

From the very first beginning it was the idea of the artist Andreas Strauss to create a network of these unusual accommodation options. The first *dasparkhotel* was built in Austria in 2005. In May 2022, *dasparkhotel_inside-outsite* was opened at Hof Emscher-Auen [Emscher-Auen Farm] in Castrop-Rauxel as part of the artistic revision and expansion of the Emscherkunstweg [Emscher Art Trail]. It is the second location of *dasparkhotel* on the Emscher. There has been a branch in Bottrop's BernePark since 2010.

At the Hof Emscher-Auen, three sleeping tubes made from industrially manufactured sewer tubes now offer the opportunity to spend the night. Andreas Strauss also developed the *inside-outsite* pavilion especially for the location, which invites you to observe nature and especially birds.

In order to be able to observe flora and fauna, Andreas Strauss designed the shelter, which, like the park hotel, consists of industrially prefabricated parts. In this case he used corrugated steel, which is commonly used in hydraulic engineering. Created in an artificial mound of earth, it invites visitors to the park and amateur and professional ornithologists as well as overnight guests to the sleeping tubes to linger. It represents a protective space against the weather, which is artistically integrated into the landscape and equally provides insight, perspective and outlook.

With the overnight accommodations at Hof Emscher-Auen in Castrop-Rauxel and in the BernePark in Bottrop, the Emscherkunstweg can be experienced on its almost one hundred kilometres of cycle paths in the form of a tour lasting several days. The concrete sleeping cabins can be opened and closed individually using an electronic code-locking system. They offer space for one to two people and are opened in the warm season between May and October.

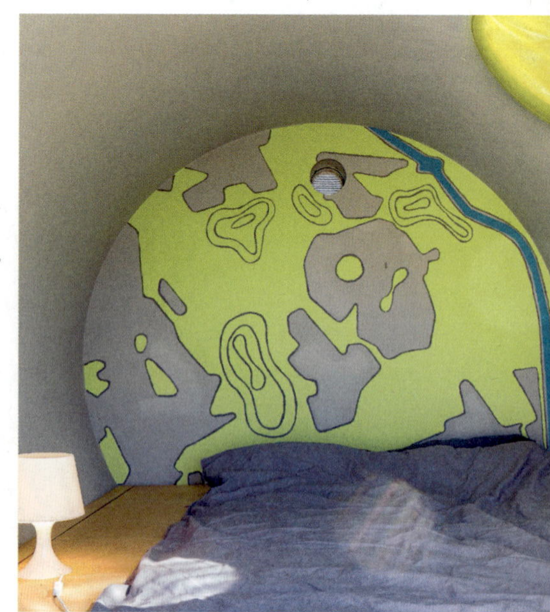

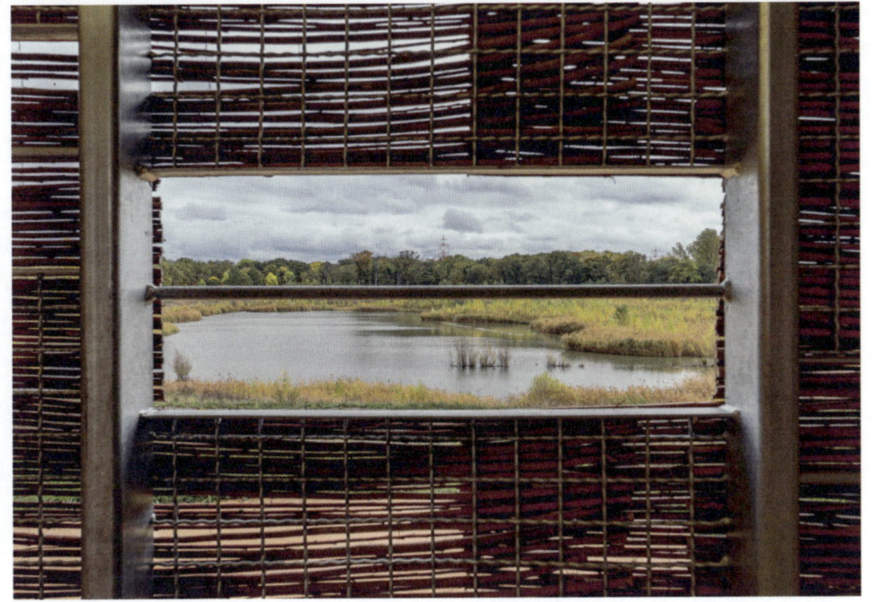

Andreas Strauss has worked at the
Emscher Auen Farm with inmates
from the neighbouring Castrop-Rauxel
correctional facility.

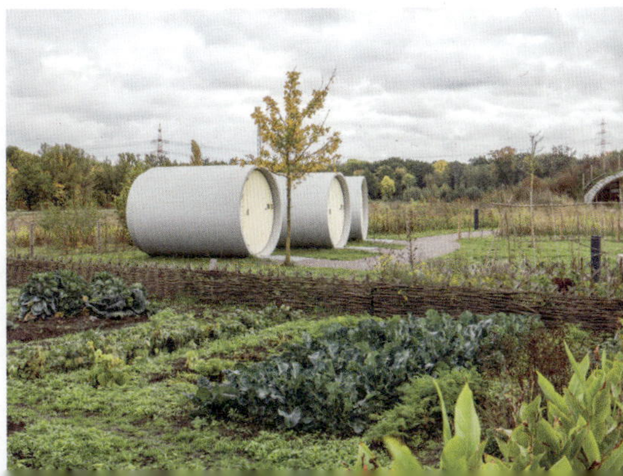

BLACK CIRCLE
SQUARE
Massimo Bartolini

2016

MATERIAL
Reinforced concrete
construction, swimming pool
with black surface coating
Dimensions installation:
10.5 × 10.5 m,
total depth 4.20 m
Dimensions swimming pool:
Ø 7.83 m
Height railings: 1.25 m

ADDRESS
Hof Emscher-Auen
Rittershofer Straße 170
44577 Castrop-Rauxel

126

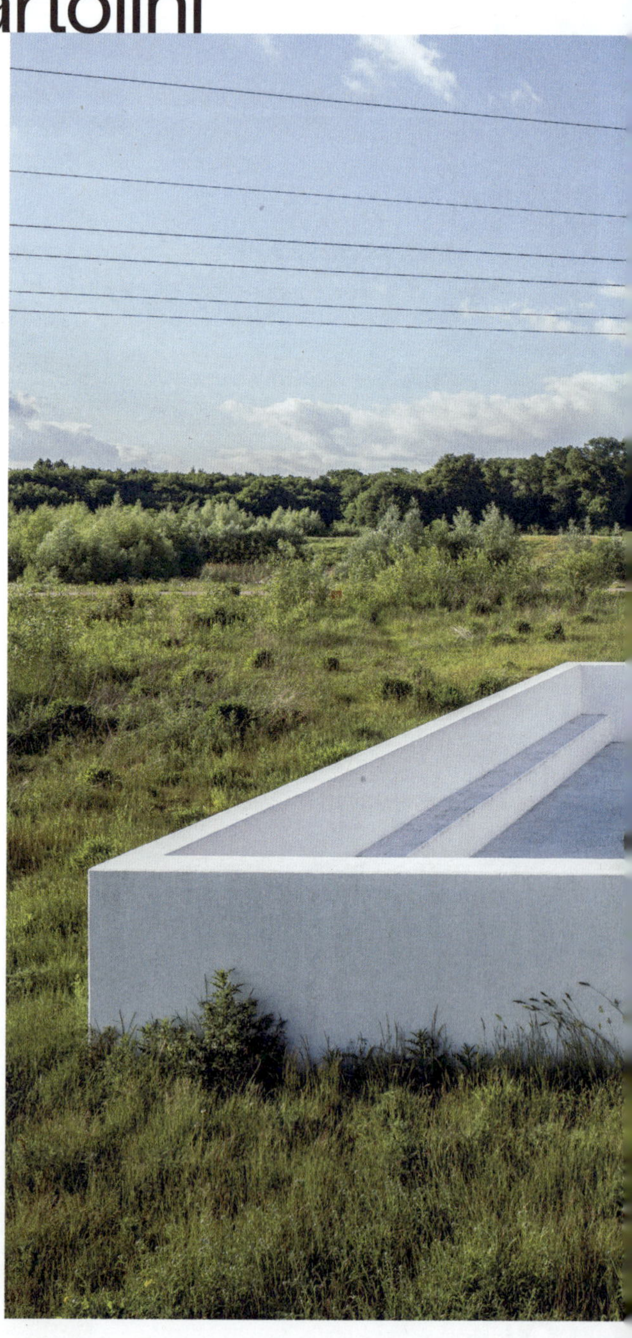

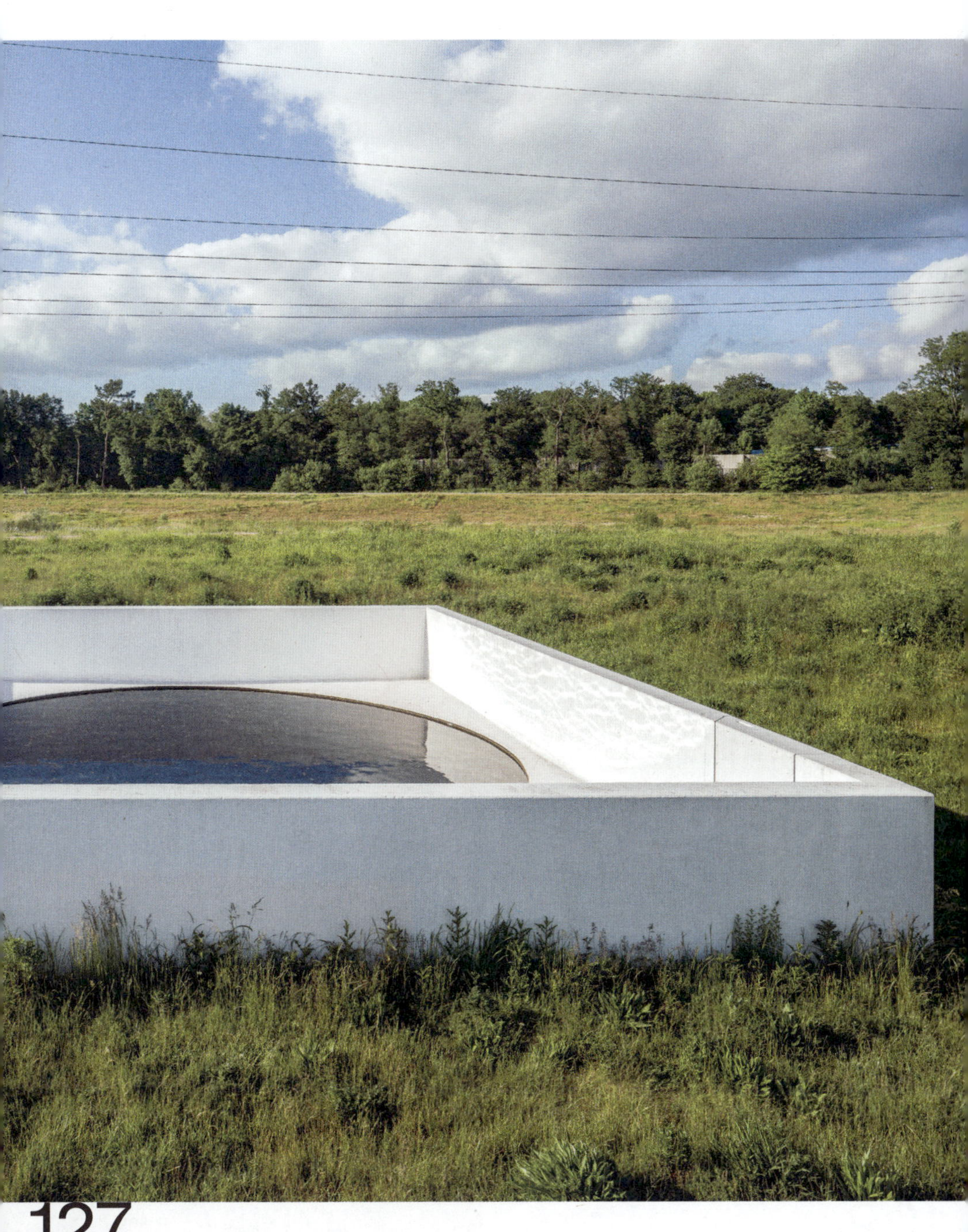

Located at Hof Emscher-Auen [Emscher-Auen Farm] in the Mengede district of Dortmund is the work *Black Circle Square* that was developed by Massimo Bartolini for the 2016 *Emscherkunst* exhibition. Looming out of the middle of the sweeping landscape around the flood retention basin is a gleaming white square surface measuring 10.5 × 10.5 metres along the perimeter and framed inside a small white wall. Inserted into the white concrete square is a circular opening of almost eight metres in diameter that holds a sheet of water. The four-metre-deep water basin beneath the surface is coated in black, so that, viewed from above, one perceives a black circle inside a white square. In formal terms, the work makes a direct reference to Kazimir Malevich's 1915 painting *Black Square*, which became an icon of modernist art. With this work Malevich marked the change from figurative to radically non-representational painting, for which he is considered the pioneer of Suprematism.

Bartolini transformed the painting of the Russian avant-gardist into the third dimension, as it were: the point of departure for *Black Circle Square* was Malevich's painting *Black Circle,* also from 1915, which Bartolini reproduced in tenfold enlargement as a spatial object. The Italian Concept artist also supplemented the inert basin with a performative component: for the duration of the exhibition a former coal miner regularly cleaned the black pool with a mop in a kind of spiritual ritual. A saxophonist and a synchronised swimmer were further protagonists in performances that animated the artwork's presence. At the same time, the minimalist artwork serves permanently as a fire pool for the neighbouring farm complex of Hof Emscher-Auen.

In this way Bartolini proposed a link between Malevich's art, whose absolute reduction of artistic means marked the «zero point of painting», and the situation in the Ruhr region, which since the mid-twentieth century has faced the task of reinventing its own future. Concretely, Bartolini saw the decision to renaturate the Emscher as a central impulse regarding the possibilities for shaping an alternative future.

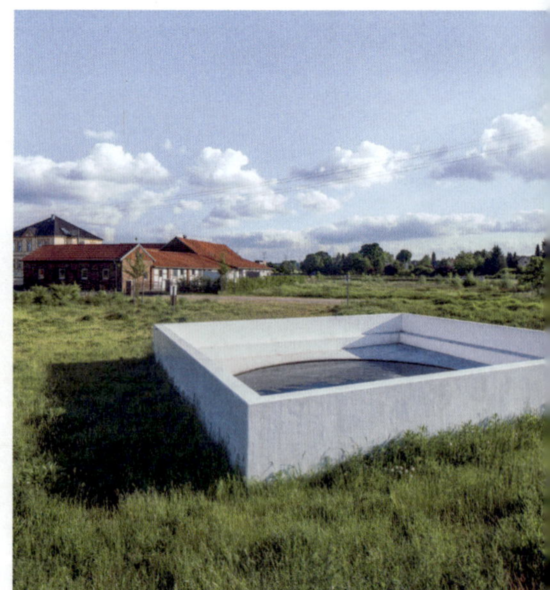

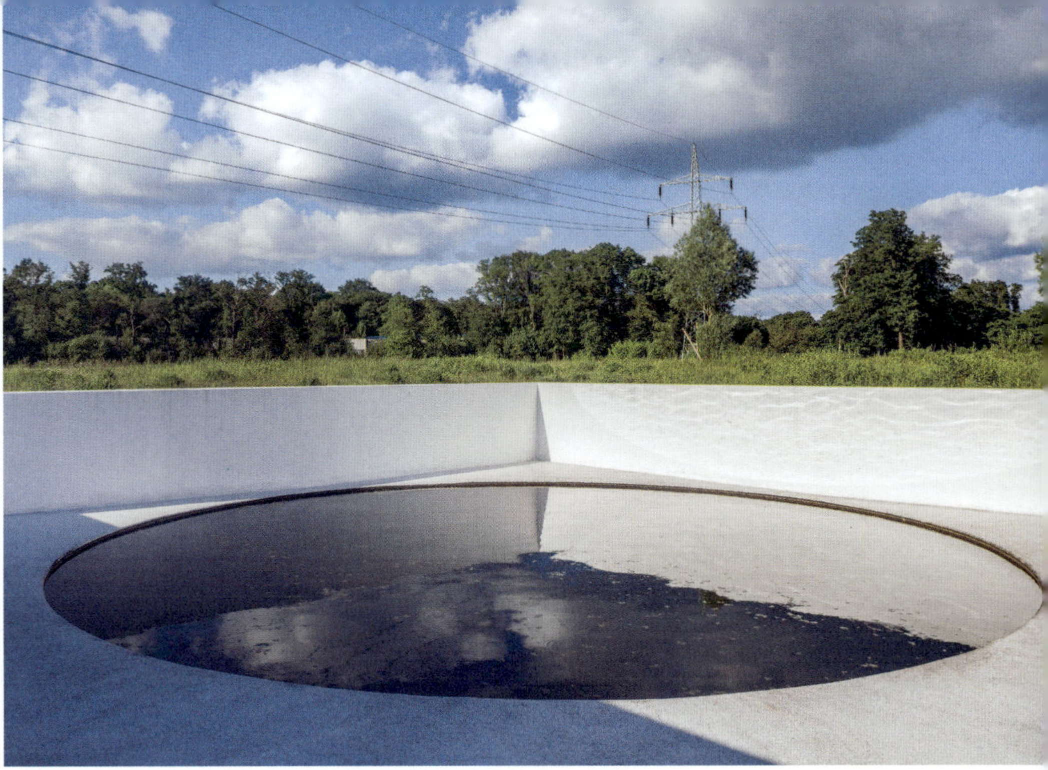

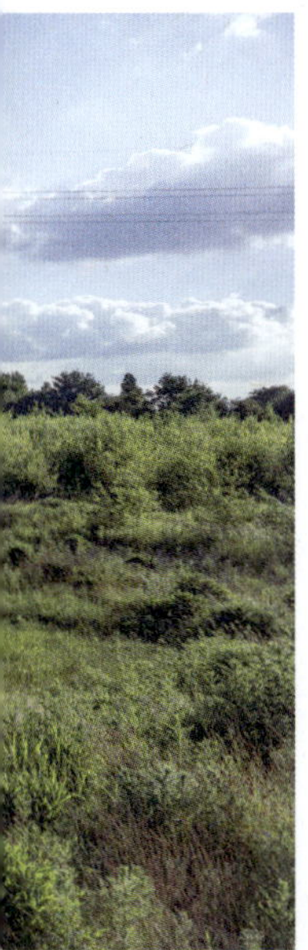

←

Black Circle Square also serves as a fire pond and holds over 200,000 litres of water.

WALKWAY AND TOWER
Tadashi Kawamata

2010/2019

MATERIAL
Web and observation tower
Concrete construction, larch wood
Height tower: approx. 12 m
Length web: approx. 120 m

ADDRESS
Emscher-Weg
near Emschertalweg 62
45665 Recklinghausen

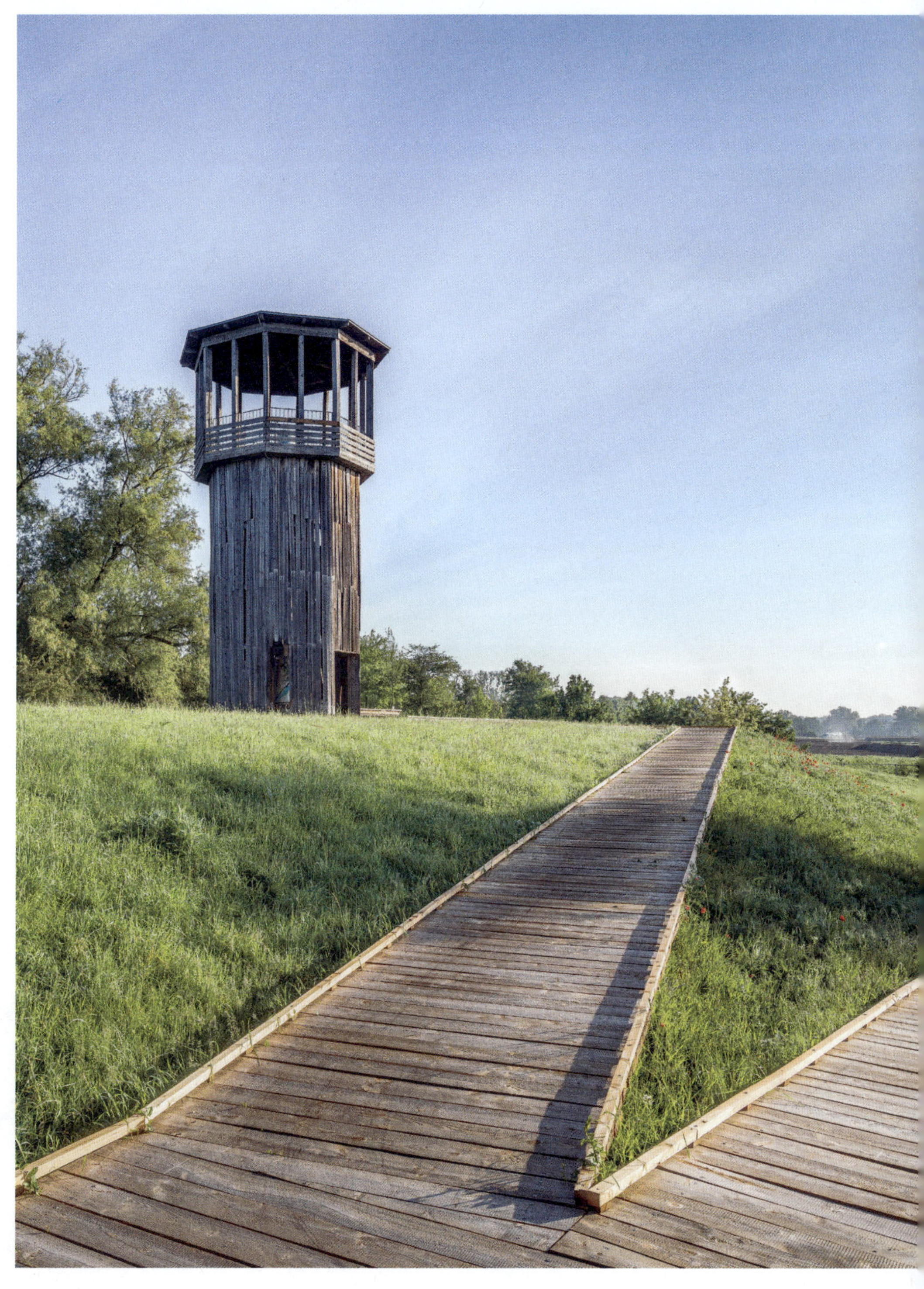

Today, the tower stands in the
middle of the Emscherland Park.

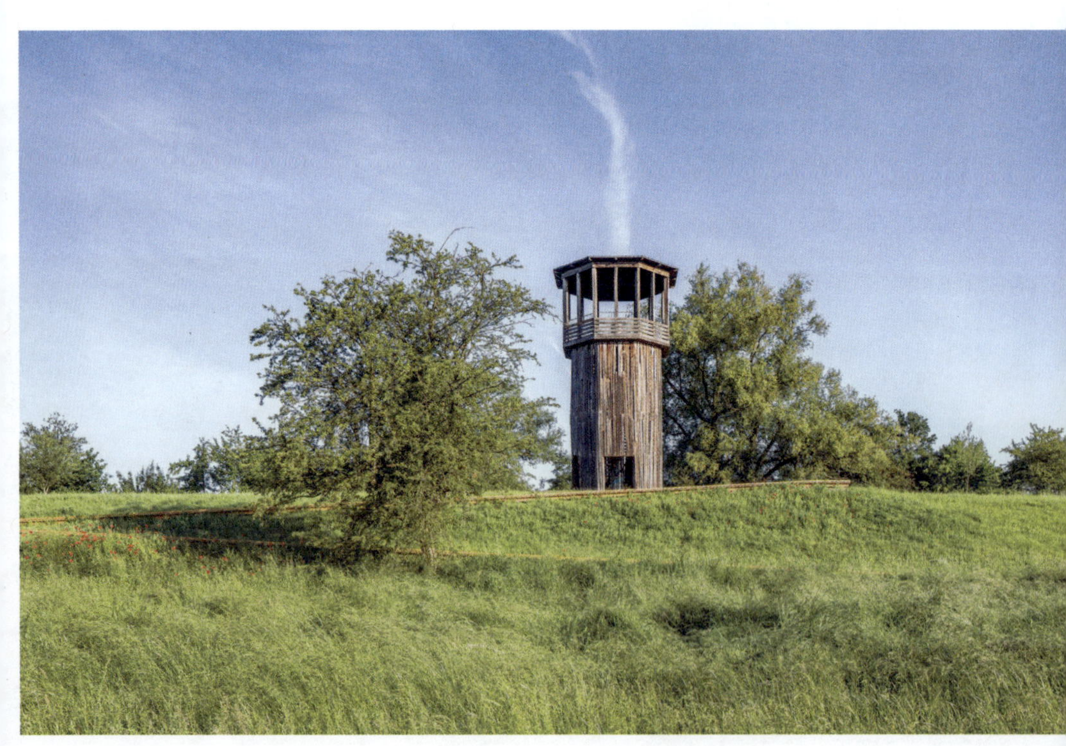

For his work *Walkway and Tower,* Tadashi Kawamata chose a location close to the waterway junction of the Emscher river and the Rhine-Herne Canal on the city margins between Recklinghausen and Castrop-Rauxel. It is situated at the eastern tip of the so-called Emscher Island, a thirty-four-kilometre strip of land running between the river and the canal. Following extensive renaturation measures, in 2010 it was converted into a local recreational area and became the venue for the first edition of *Emscherkunst* [Emscher Art]. Today, as then, the surroundings are marked by the conversion of the Emscher river.

In his 2010 work Kawamata contrasted the horizontal sweep of the landscape with a vertical landmark in the form of a wooden observation tower. *Walkway and Tower* is a blend of architecture and sculpture, although the edifice's function is hard to define. The twelve-metre-high tower stands on raised ground beside the Emscher trail and can be accessed via a zigzagging wooden walkway. Having reached the top, visitors encounter not so much a spectacular panorama as a view over a calm and sparsely populated region. With the *Walkway and Tower* the artist prompts viewers to engage in active perception of the surroundings from several perspectives, but also to meditatively turn their gaze to their inner selves — a reminiscence of Japanese garden and landscape design.

Kawamata deliberately chose wood to build his construction. For, similar to the surroundings on view from the tower, the wood it is built from is also in a permanent state of transformation through weathering, passing seasons and, not least of all, human intervention. Likewise, the provisional character of the edifice stands allegorically for the constantly changing landscape. With *Walkway and Tower* Tadashi Kawamata has created a place of contemplation which at the same time urges critical reflection on human interaction with nature as manifested in particular in such post-industrial regions as the Ruhr.

As part of restoration measures in 2019, the course of the wooden walkway was extended and slightly redesigned by the artist.

REEMRENREH
(KAUM GESANG)
Bogomir Ecker

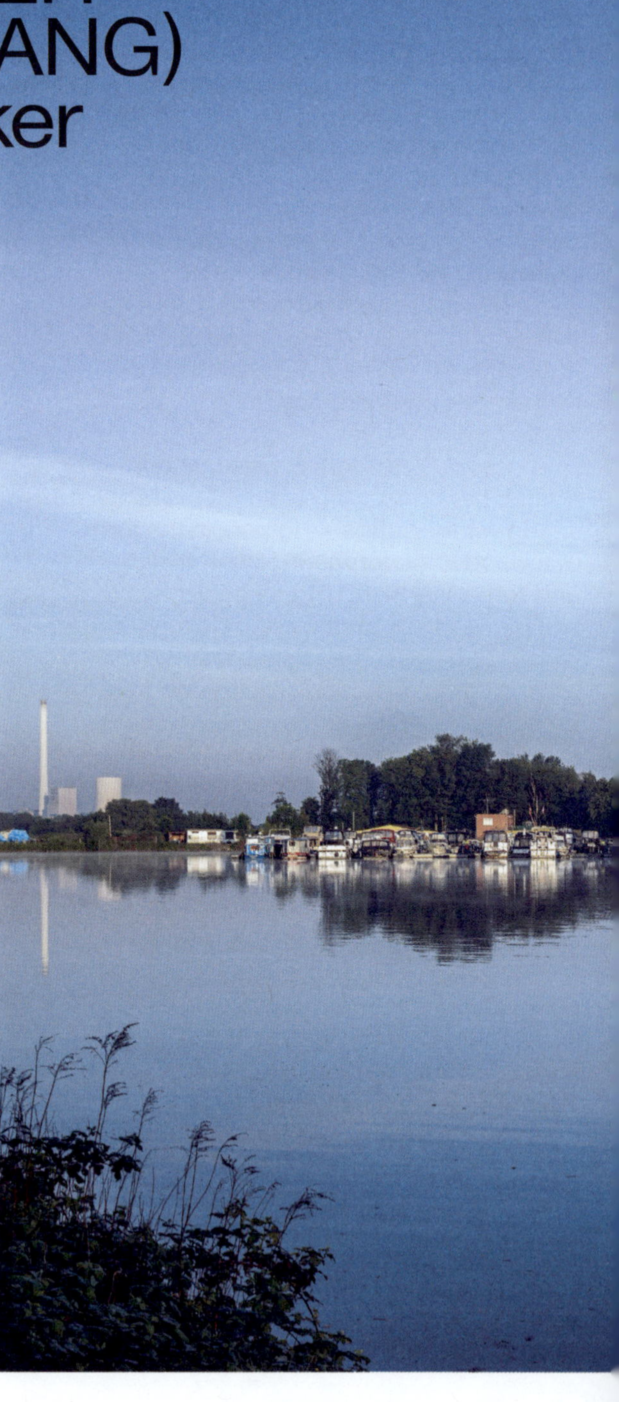

2010

MATERIAL
street lamp
Aluminium sheet,
aluminium cast,
steel, varnish
23 × 2.3 × 2.1 m, 7.6 × 1.7 × 1.2 m
Height street lamp: 16 m

ADDRESS
Herner Meer
near Gneisenaustraße 204
44628 Herne

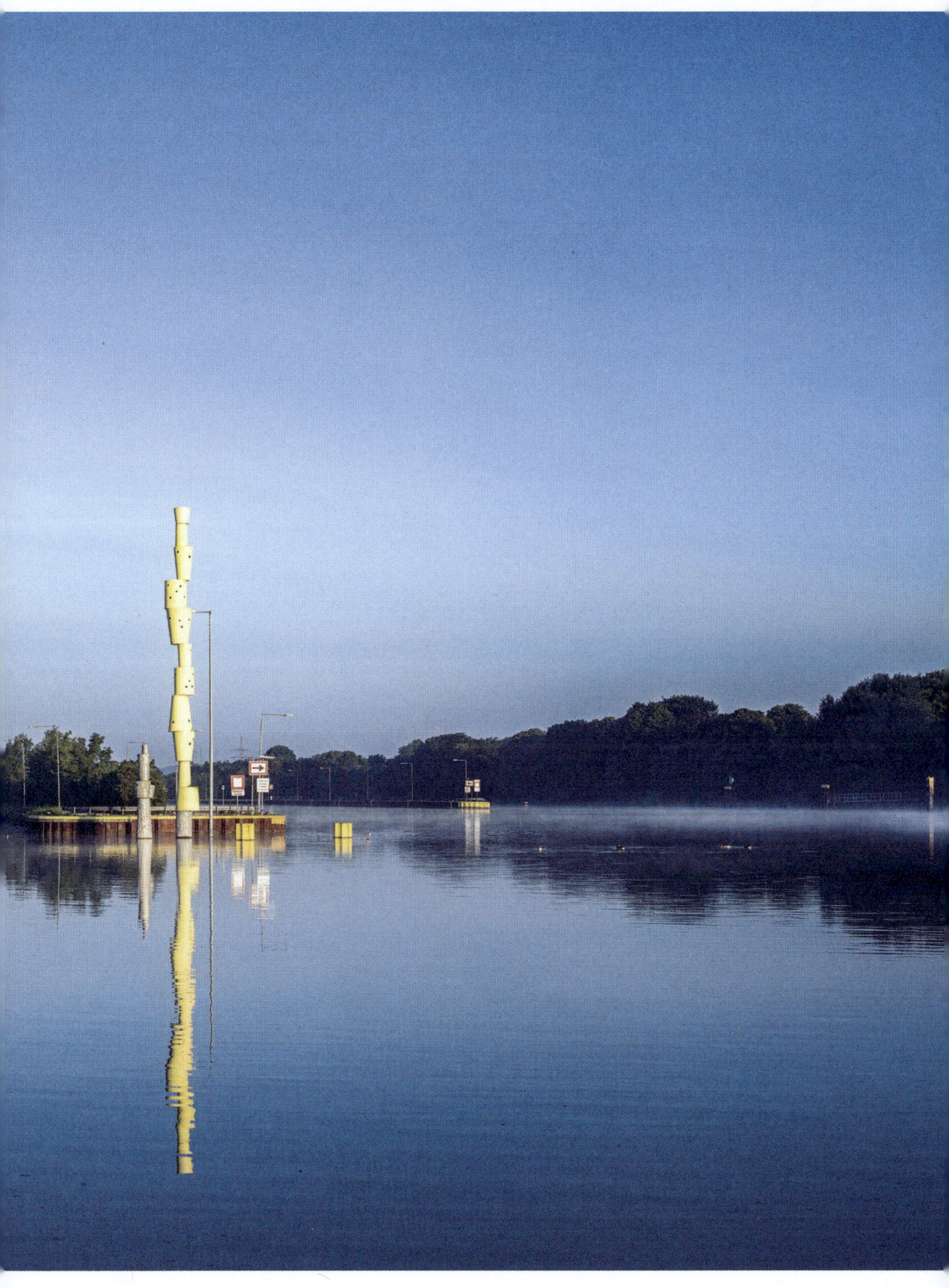

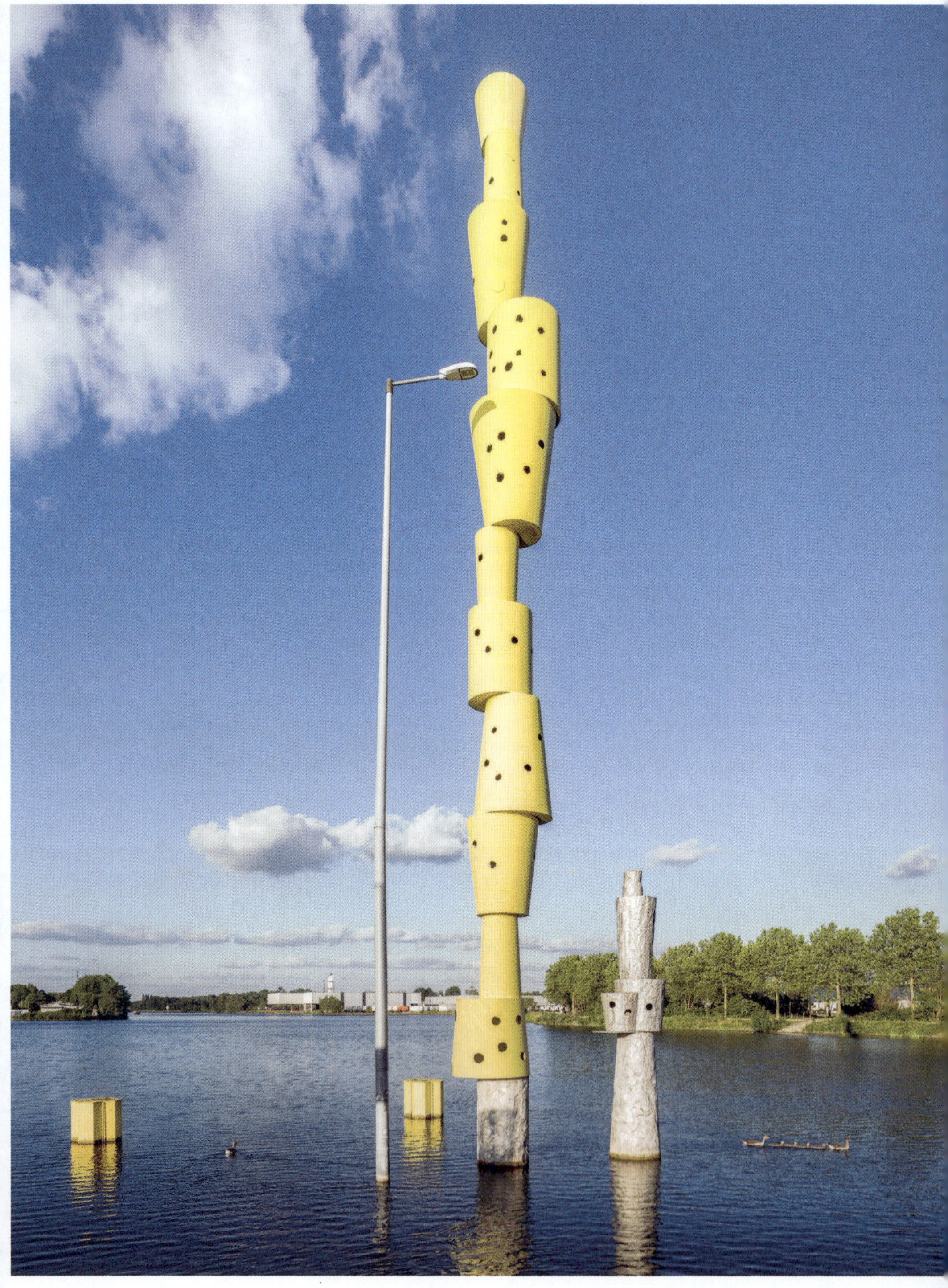

136

Being a flat, languid river, the Emscher was never suitable for industrial inland shipping, even though in the process of being straightened it was debated whether it should be converted for this purpose. Instead, in the early twentieth century the Rhine-Herne Canal was constructed, which today is still one of the busiest freight transport routes in the Ruhr region and in part courses through the Emscher's old riverbed. Beginning in Castrop-Rauxel, the canal widens increasingly towards the Herne-Ost Lock where it joins the so-called Herner Meer [Herne Sea]. Here, positioned at the end of a jetty, is a work of art by Bogomir Ecker. The artist conceived the three-part ensemble with the seemingly cryptic title *reemrenreh (kaum Gesang)* [reemrenreh (Barely Singing)] for the 2010 *Emscherkunst* [Emscher Art] exhibition and placed it directly in the lake.

Cylindrical and cone-shaped yellow forms are stacked to form an approximately twenty-three-metre-high construction. With its bright yellow surfaces and impressive height, the work's perforated hollow bodies are also dubbed locally the «cheese straw». Whistling through the holes, the wind produces sounds but «barely any singing», as the title suggests. But read backwards, the title reveals the work's location: Herner Meer. Jutting out of the water alongside the yellow edifice that is visible from afar is another sculpture, a kind of «little sister» in grey. At night the group of figures is lit up by a — seemingly — ordinary street lamp. In reality, standing sixteen metres high, it towers above its roadside colleagues, which generally reach heights of just three to six metres. Yet in this spot the lamp truly looks too small in relation to the yellow sculpture.

As early as 2009, Bogomir Ecker created a formally similar, monumental sculpture for public space in Brussels. His work *Aliud* (meaning «something other» in Latin) in the Duisburg inner harbour also bears formal resemblance to *reemrenreh (kaum Gesang),* but is suspended mid-air from a steel girder between two buildings. Likewise, with its seemingly makeshift composition, *reemrenreh (kaum Gesang)* also appears to defy gravity. These abstract figures that somehow look like gadgets and have strange titles are typical of Bogomir Ecker's sculptural work. Here too, the sculpture retains a disconcerting quality, even if, when viewed from a distance, it marks the jetty as a threshold between the yacht harbour and the lock.

GLÜCKAUF: BERGARBEITERPROTESTE IM RUHRGEBIET
Silke Wagner

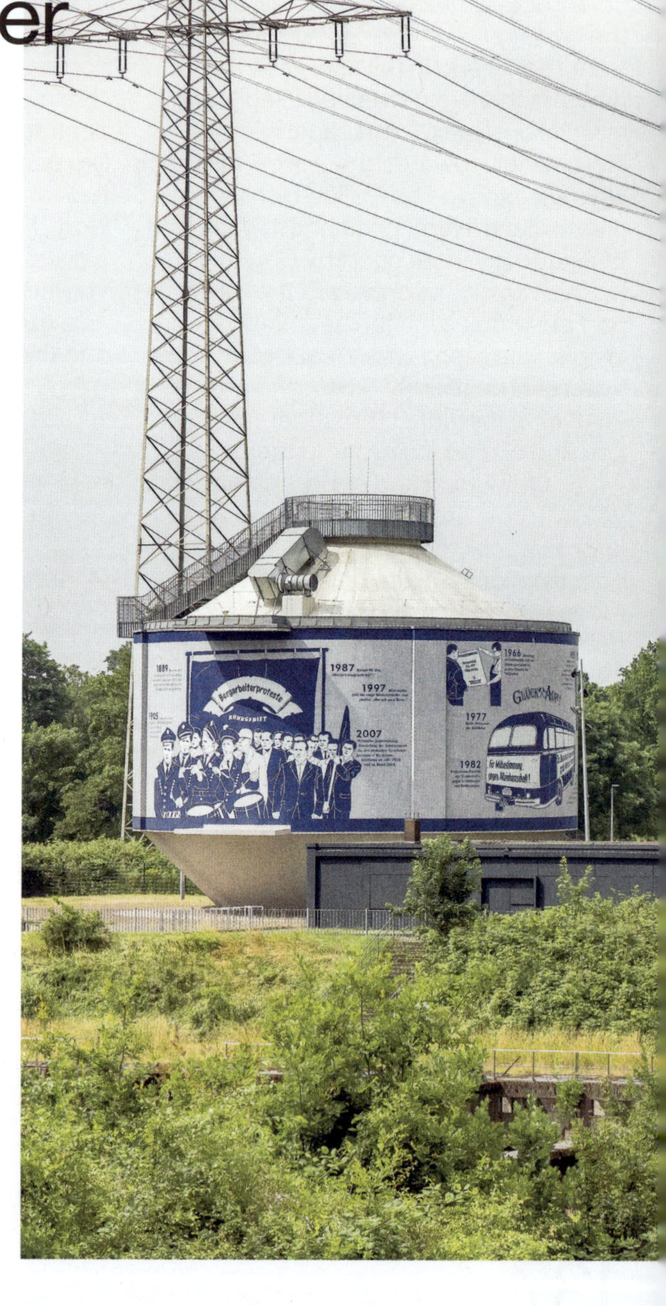

2010/2021

MATERIAL
Digestion tower of the former
treatment plant Herne,
outer shell with wall mosaic
Dimensions wall mosaic:
66.6 × 9.3 m
Glass mosaic stones:
10 × 10 mm each

ADDRESS
Former Kläranlage Herne
Vockenhof 1
44629 Herne

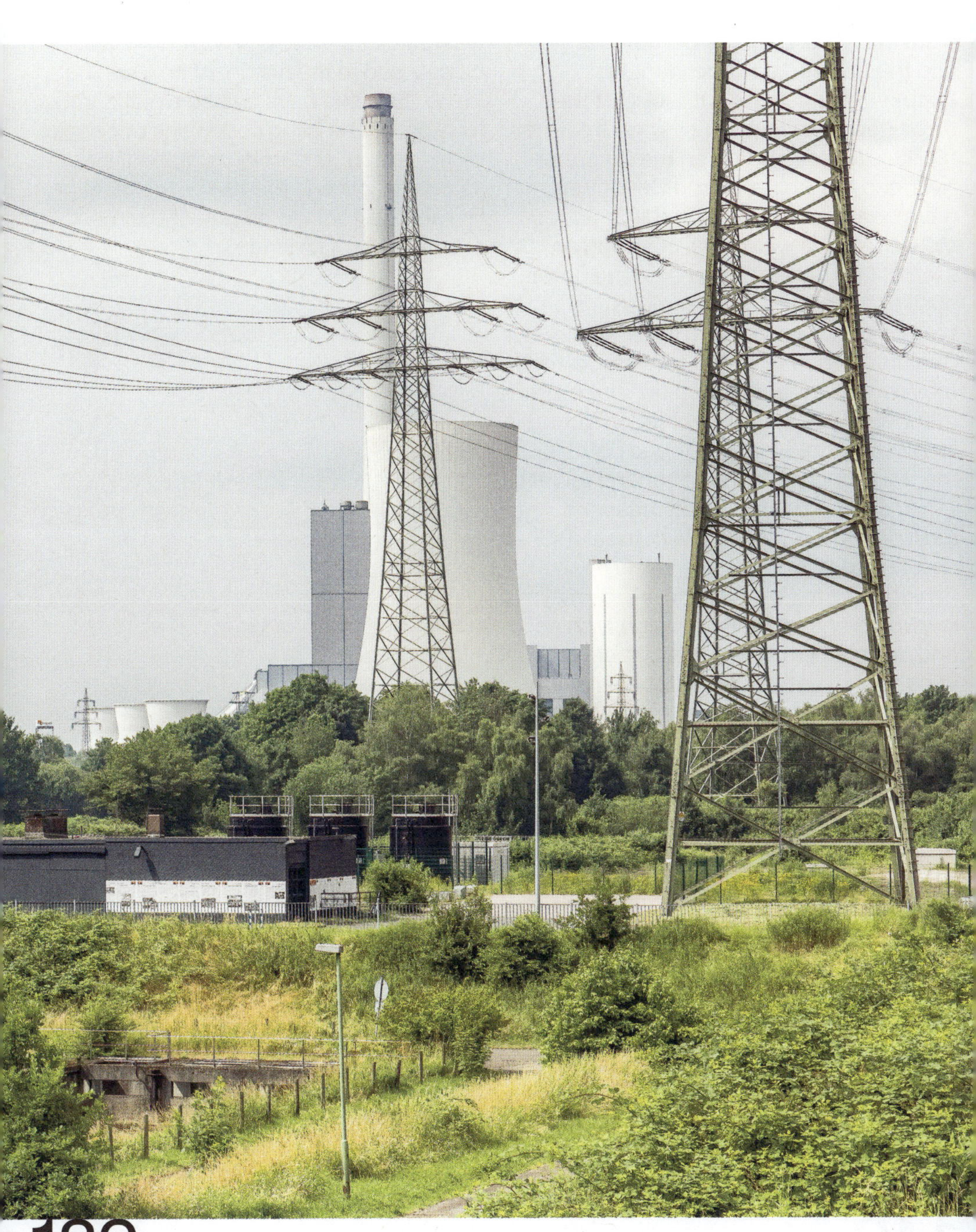

As the site for her contribution *Glückauf. Bergarbeiterproteste im Ruhrgebiet* [Good Luck. Miners' Protests in the Ruhr Region] to the 2010 *Emscherkunst* [Emscher Art] exhibition artist Silke Wagner chose the former sewage plant in Herne. Besides BernePark and the disused sewage plant in Läppkes-Mühlenbach, it is one of the three decommissioned sewage treatment facilities located between the Emscher river and the Rhine-Herne Canal that have been preserved as publicly accessible sites. In a wall mural covering an area of 600 square metres on the outer shell of the gutted, former digestion tank of the sewage plant, the artist depicts scenes from the miners' protest movement in the Ruhr region. The mural's monochrome blue-and-white colouring is inspired by the tiling in pithead baths and the traditional patterns of miners' towels.

Starting with the first mass strike in 1889 and ending with the 2007 decision to stop subsidies to the coal mining industry, the wall mosaic displays keywords and images based on archive and newspaper photographs to depict important events in the history of mining protests. As part of her research Wagner closely collaborated with the historical archive of the «Haus der Geschichte des Ruhrgebiets» at Ruhr-University Bochum. In 2010, this cooperation gave rise to a «Protestzeitung» [protest newspaper] to accompany the wall mural, documenting the history of miners' protests in greater detail. Inspired by the miners' protests and strikes, solidarity campaigns and politicising developments spread throughout Germany. In the course of the twentieth century these contributed crucially to society's advancing democratisation. With this work Wagner has erected a kind of monument to the politically committed miners and their labour, seeking to preserve their memory beyond the closure of Germany's last colliery in 2018.

In addition, the location of the disused sewage treatment plant in Herne brings into focus the achievements of wastewater technology, which are also closely tied to the history of coal mining in the Ruhr and have helped significantly to improve the living conditions of people in this region. Accordingly, at the time of its construction in the 1920s, the plant in Herne was considered one of the most progressive of its kind.

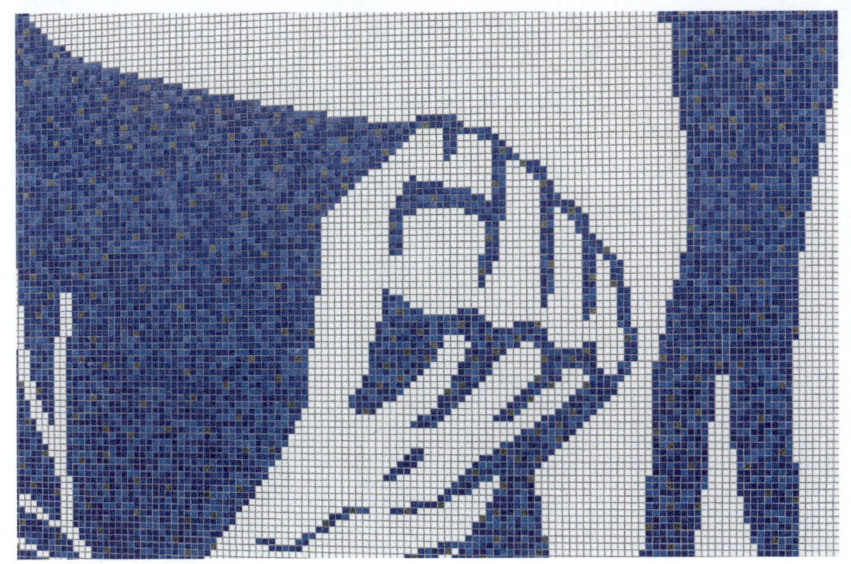

→

Around 5.8 million stones
are built into the mosaic.

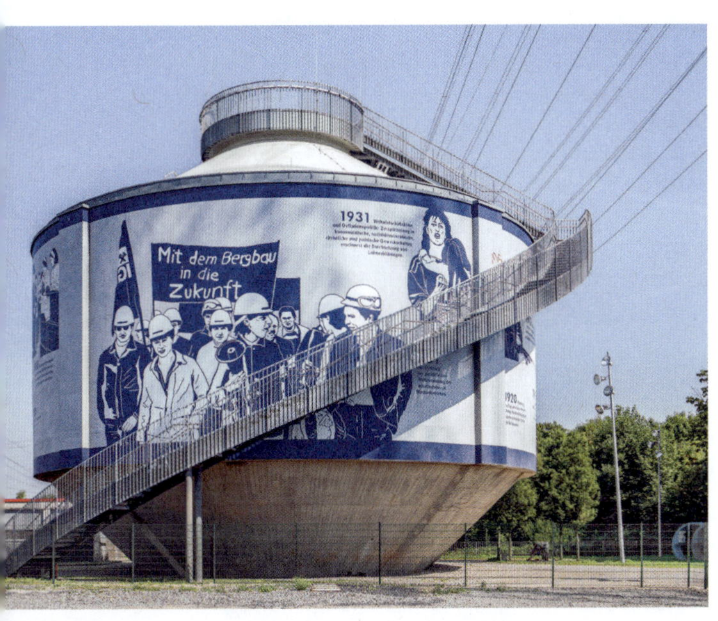

KØNIGSGRUBE
Markus Jeschaunig

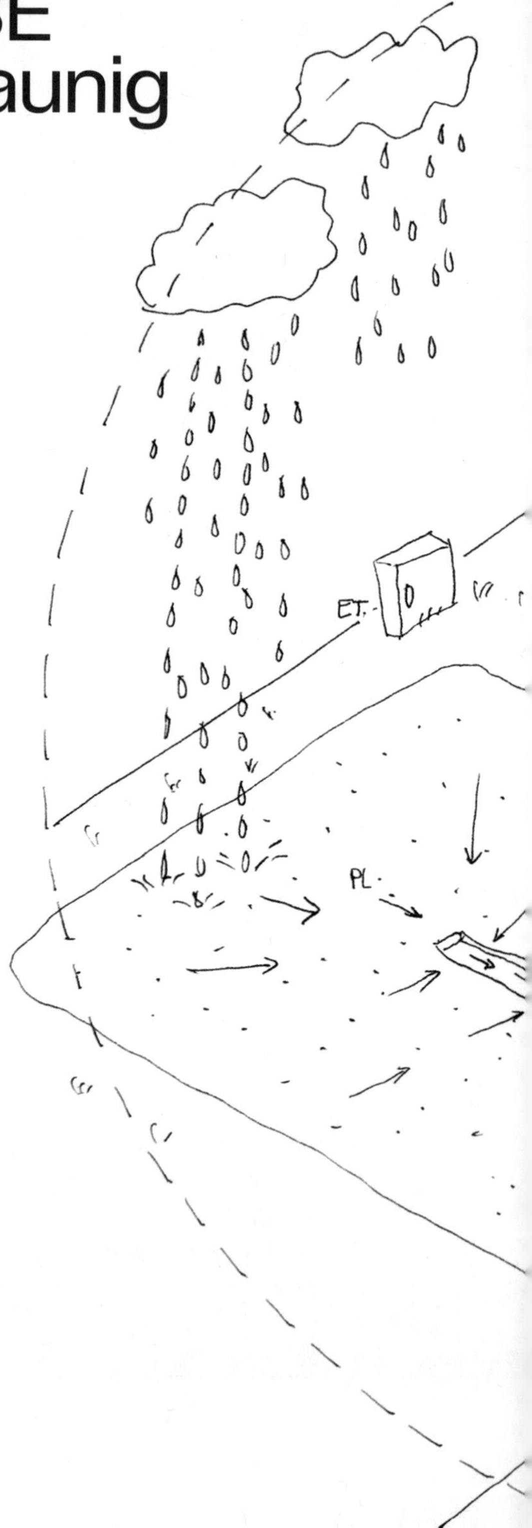

2024

MATERIAL
Concrete structure
(fragment of the former pumping station)
Steel pipe duplicates, fence elements,
iron grating, concrete stairs
(from original parts)
Water cistern, storage substrates,
water pump, PV pergola, storage gravel,
control switchboard, water gutters
Quarry forest vegetation
(sedge, fern, mint, black alder, etc.)
Sound installation, drip installation,
synthetic resin casting

Dimensions quarry forest: 13.10 × 11.70 m
Dimensions of total area: 24.90 × 21.60 m
Depth of back-filled former
pump room: 12.50 m

ADDRESS
Hofstraße 24
44651 Herne

142

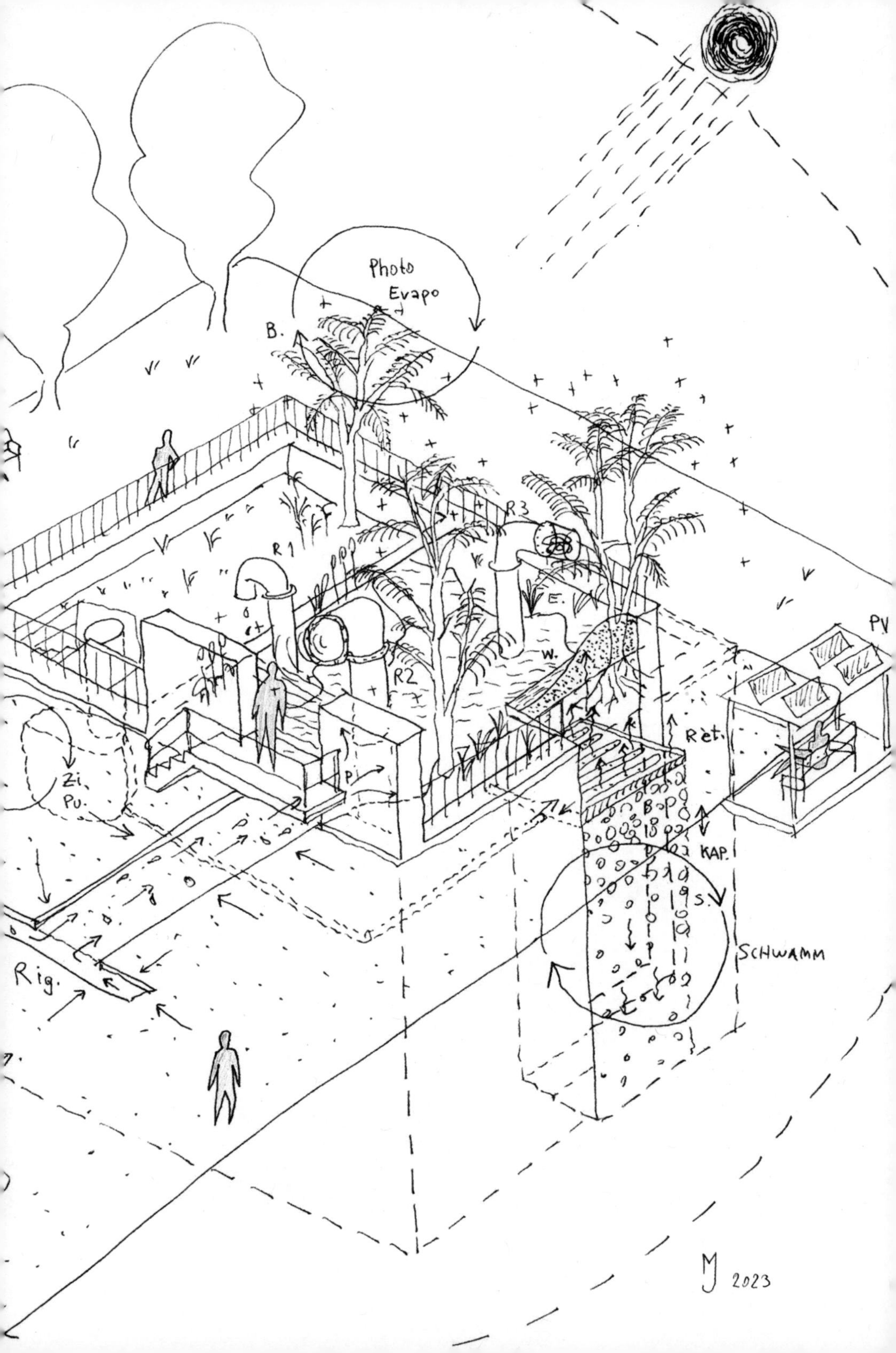

Photo
Evapo
B.
R1
R2
R3
E.
W.
P.
PV
Ret.
KAP.
B.P.
S.
SCHWAMM
Zi.
Pu.
Rig.
MJ 2023

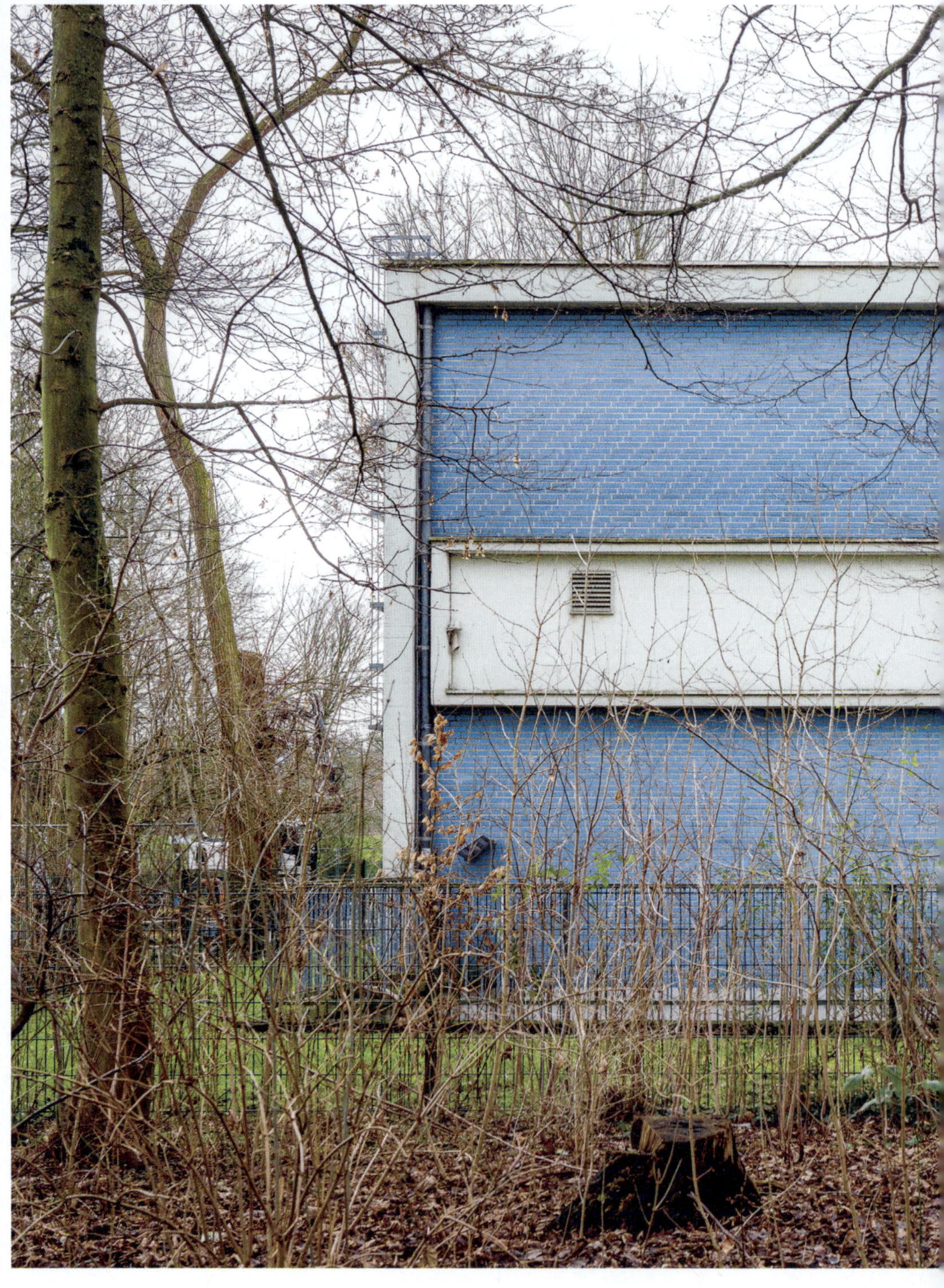

144

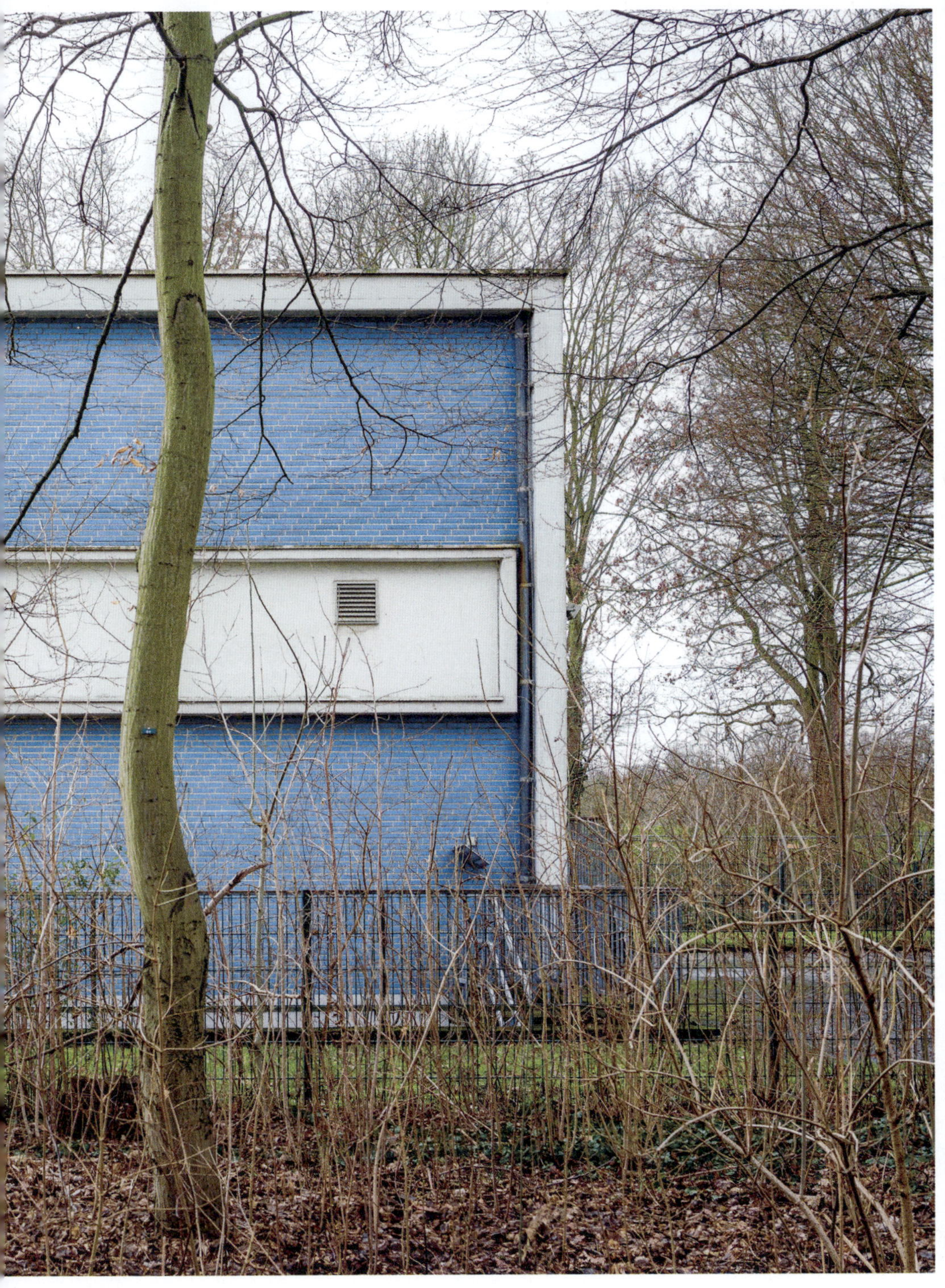

A former pumping station of a disused coal mine is now an installation; the name it retains has an auspicious ring to it: *Königsgrube* — the King's Mine. The past and the present shape Markus Jeschaunig's work in which he has transformed fragments of the dismantled building into a hybrid landscape.

From 1860 to 1967, coal mining at the Königsgrube pit in Herne-Röhlinghausen was extremely productive; but once the black gold had been fully removed the ground that remained was depleted and riddled with holes. The subsidences amounts to up to ten metres. The pumping station's purpose was to channel the wastewater from neighbouring municipalities into the Hüller Bach stream, and from there into the Emscher. The closure of the coal mine made underground wastewater disposal possible and the pumping station was shut down. Jeschaunig used the partially filled-in foundations to build an installation that sculpturally integrates various elements of the building: a part of one staircase has been preserved; three pipes tower up to create a solar-driven fountain from which water drops and sounds emerge. Where the over twelve-metre-deep clarifying basin once stood that prevented rainwater from seeping away, a marsh forest has evolved, a biotope of six nursery-grown black alders that thrive in damp ground and bring to mind the pre-industrial wetlands that once bordered the Emscher. Rainwater is collected in a cistern on the paved forecourt and, together with the photovoltaic pergola, enables completely self-sufficient operation. As an artistically reshaped ruin, Jeschaunig's work alludes both to the outstanding technology and to the enormous ecological devastation brought on by coal mining, while at the same time showing a way for new life and «climate-positive» places to emerge in the city.

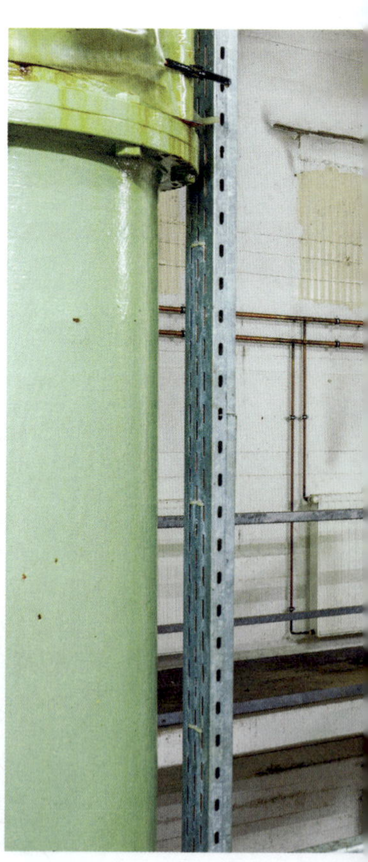

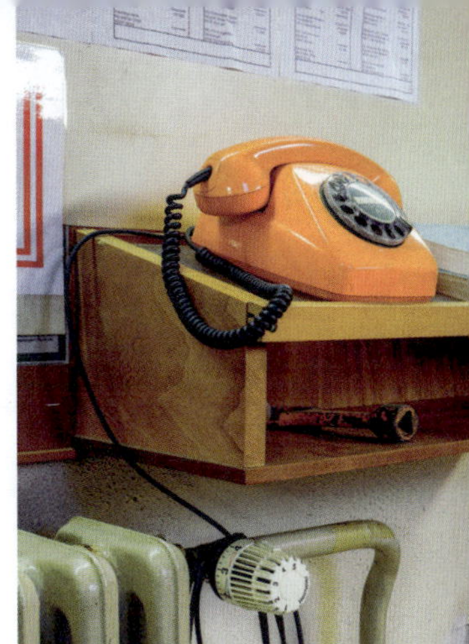

→

The installation was still being set up
as this book was going to press.

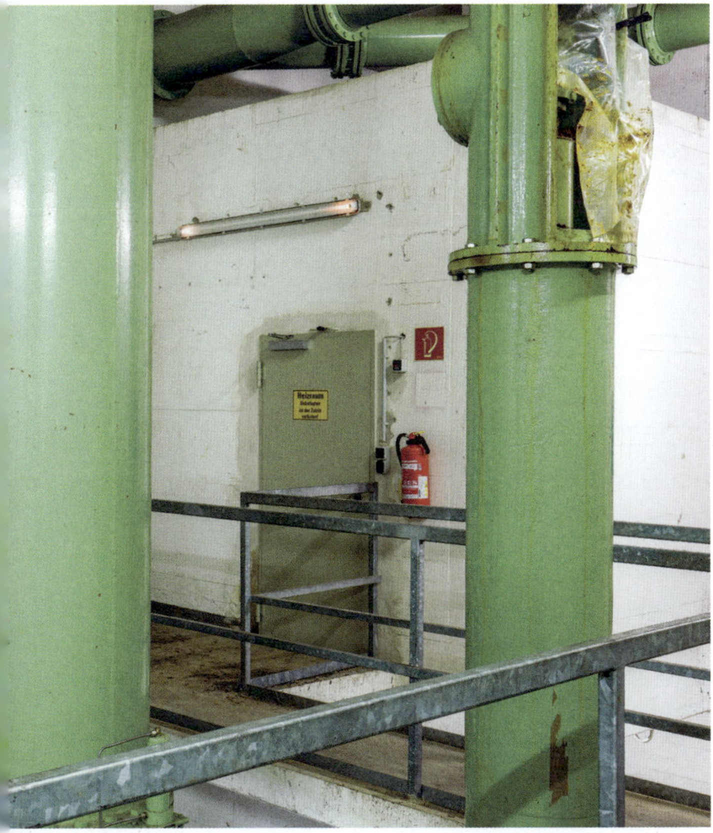

147

ETERNAL TASK

Brigitte Felderer on
Königsgrube by
Markus Jeschaunig

The artist Markus Jeschaunig causes the pump station Röhlinghausen to disappear in order to preserve the memory of it.

On a Sunday afternoon in February 2023, the team of Urbane Künste Ruhr [Urban Arts Ruhr] invited the public to a presentation and public discussion into the Volkshaus Röhlingshausen. Markus Jeschaunig presented his art project for the pump station Herne-Königsgrube [King's pit] to an attentive audience. A group of people familiar with the area gave insights into forthcoming plans and into the building's history, and told stories about it. Until its closing, the station pumped wastewater from the municipal areas of Bochum, Herne and Gelsenkirchen into the nearby Hüller Bach [Hüller brook], from where it finally flowed into the Emscher river. During the times of coal mining, an underground disposal was not yet possible. Drain pipes could not have withstood the massive soil movements, because the area sank over the years at times by as much as ten metres. The Hüller Bach, which in its concrete shells also provided protection from flooding, reached the houses as an open sewage canal, and on hot days it stank to high heaven. The polluted brooks and rivers were as much part of nature in the Ruhr region as the coal dust and the fumes that came from the coal mines and their plants. Wastewater canals, coal mining plants and residential areas all merged. For example, in 1928, a bridge had to be constructed in Röhling-hausen to enable neighbours to cross the machinery of the coal mine with less risk, which since the beginning of mining seventy years before had got danger-ously close to residential areas. This «asthma bridge» — it owed its nickname to the coal gas that those crossing the bridge had to breathe in — had become a landmark of the place until it was pulled down in 1976; the coal mine Königsgrube had been closed down in 1967. The mine Königsgrube started operations in 1860, and in 1863, with a workforce of 427, 408,742 Prussian tonnes of black coal were mined, which corresponds roughly to 81,750 metric tonnes. Profits were as great as they were merciless; only a little more than twenty years later, the workforce had nearly tripled to 1,195, and a tremendous 376,336 tonnes of black coal were mined. In 1930, 488,087 tonnes of black coal were mined by 1,564 pitmen. In 1960, there were still 1,199 people employed by the coal mine, who mined 541,028 tonnes of black coal.

While the plant of the coal mine was finally demolished in 1974, the Volkshaus Röhlinghausen, established in 1921, has remained a vibrant place in this part of Herne. The building's structure has changed, but for one hundred years, celebrations have been taking place there which are still informed by a sense of belonging to Röhlinghausen, and not least also by its significance for the history of the workers' movement.

On that afternoon in February, Jeschaunig presented his designs; many had come and then walked to the pump station to get an idea of the immediate future of its redesign.

Jeschaunig will leave stairs as well parts of the building's foundations reaching deep into the ground. The pipes that are up to five metres high will inter-mingle with the new plantings that are suitable for forming a new carr or marsh-land forest, a «hybrid place», as the artist puts it, of technological history and the presence of a new nature. The remain-ing fragments of the technical plant are reminiscent of a time when people as well as the landscape were subjected to an excessive increase in mining, and visions of the future were oriented on profit. The artist plans an «architecture of absence»[01] as a ruin that will also remind people, how briefly such industrial plants are needed and used, and what long-term liabilities they leave behind. When Jeschaunig sets up a carr, he steps back as an artist and designer. His concept aims at setting the visible and the hidden up in such a way that a new nature, a planned wilderness emerges. Such carrs or marshland meadows also grow without any intervention in industrial wasteland and meadows when an area sinks or the groundwater line rises or sinks significantly. They are a natural expression of a resilience that reacts to extreme circumstances and in the end creates new conditions.

Jeschaunig plans a process of disappearance that gives rise to a blossoming notion of eternity, beyond the expiration date of industrial exploitation. The point is not to eradicate the past, or to forget, but rather draw attention to a visible absence. Jeschaunig's artistic approach recognises the symbolic power of the few remaining coal mine plants for the people of Röhlinghausen, for the Ruhr region, for the pride of looking back on such hard times that forged connections between people and that led to solidarity and social cohesion.

In his projects, the artist frequently explores the possibilities of realisable utopias. He is not content with the vision, the idea — he wants to actually realise them. For example, he used the exhaust air of a bakery in Graz to create the climate required for a banana plant. He was inspired by architectural utopias such as *Oase No. 7* by the group Haus-Rucker-Co from 1972, which designed temporary housing with low-cost materials, subversively and in a visionary way disregarding existing built structures. The banana plant in Jeschauning's *Oase No. 8* flourished in a transparent plastic bubble that had been installed between two houses in the densely built city. This biosphere created an energy cycle and at the same time a visible urban intervention that moved an equation, or rather the conflict between city and nature, in favour of nature. The plant lay claim to an empty urban space which had previously not even been perceived as such.

By now using elements of the building to remind us of the pump station, and reconstructing the former plant into a ruin, Markus Jeschaunig transforms a formerly inaccessible site of industrial infrastructure into a space of public and communal use. Nature becomes a protagonist, and the artist uses artistic strategies and the generally accepted rules of technology and science to create a vision of a future landscape where new uses can be experienced. Urbane Künste Ruhr supports the political demand for communally used spaces and advocates that a «new wet place», as Jeschaunig calls it, can emerge which also leads to new responsibilities. The pump station is not placed under heritage protection, but rather subjected to the protection of nature. This artistically shaped commemorative culture does not create any sentimental nostalgia, but rather a historical awareness that is oriented towards the future. Markus Jeschaunig does not let architecture and nature collide, or supersede one another; rather, he lets them get entangled, and he allows us to witness how nature takes, as it were, revenge on the functional building. The function is suspended, and the artist leaves open what his project

may trigger. Will the small delicate carr
that is now emerging perhaps even
become a model for other places in the
Ruhr region? For new wetlands? Keep
following the Emscherkunstweg, today
and tomorrow! ←

01 Kai Vöckler, *Die Architektur
der Abwesenheit: Über die
Kunst, eine Ruine zu bauen*
(Berlin, 2009).

MONUMENT FOR A FORGOTTEN FUTURE
Olaf Nicolai, Douglas Gordon & Mogwai

2010

MATERIAL
Artificial rock and
sound installation
Steel construction,
concrete, render,
sound system
Dimensions rock:
approx. 10 × 9 × 17 m

ADDRESS
Emscher-Weg
near An den Schleusen 1—29
45881 Gelsenkirchen

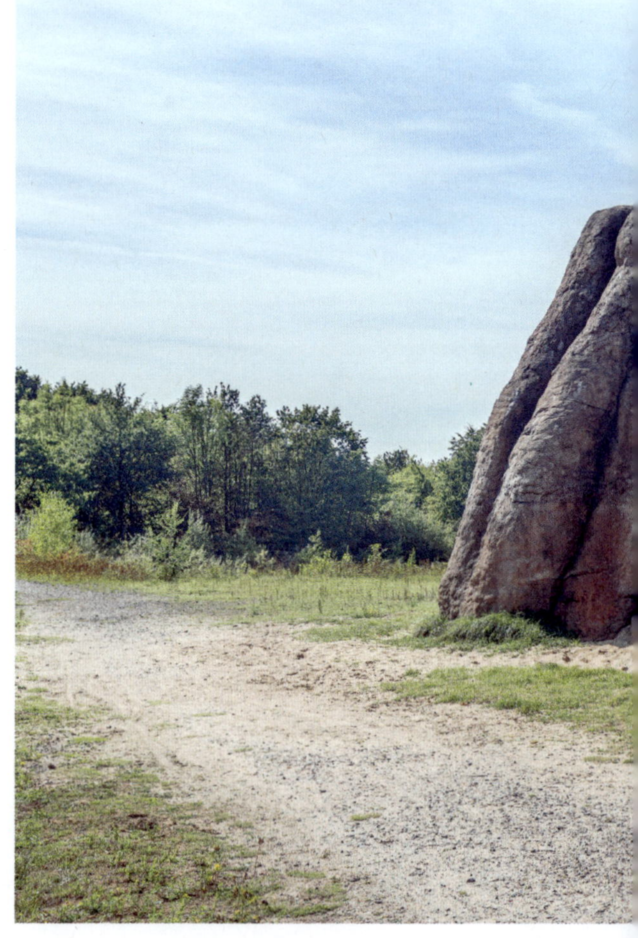

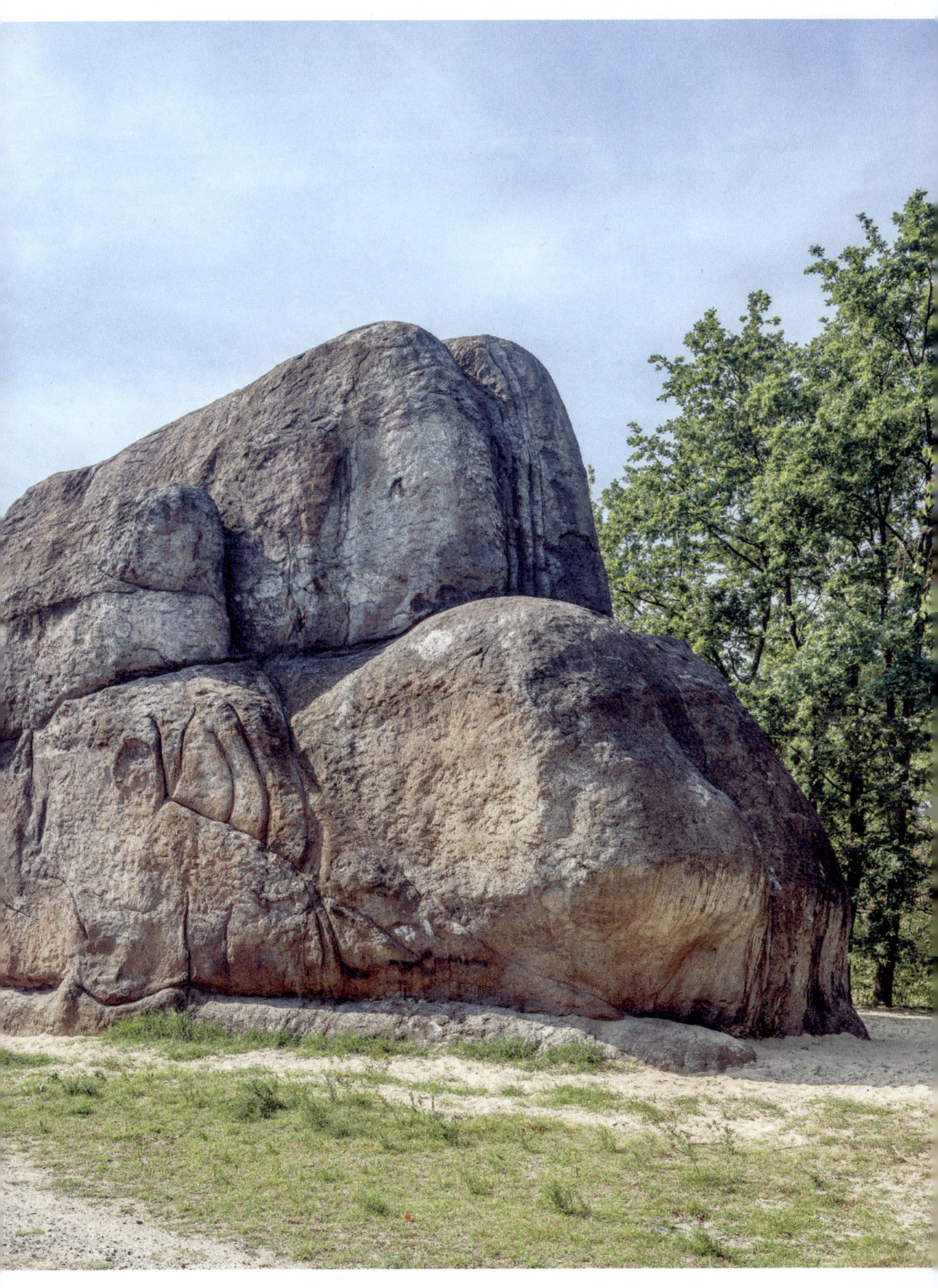

↓

As you approach the rock, the *Music for a Forgotten Future* can be heard more and more clearly.

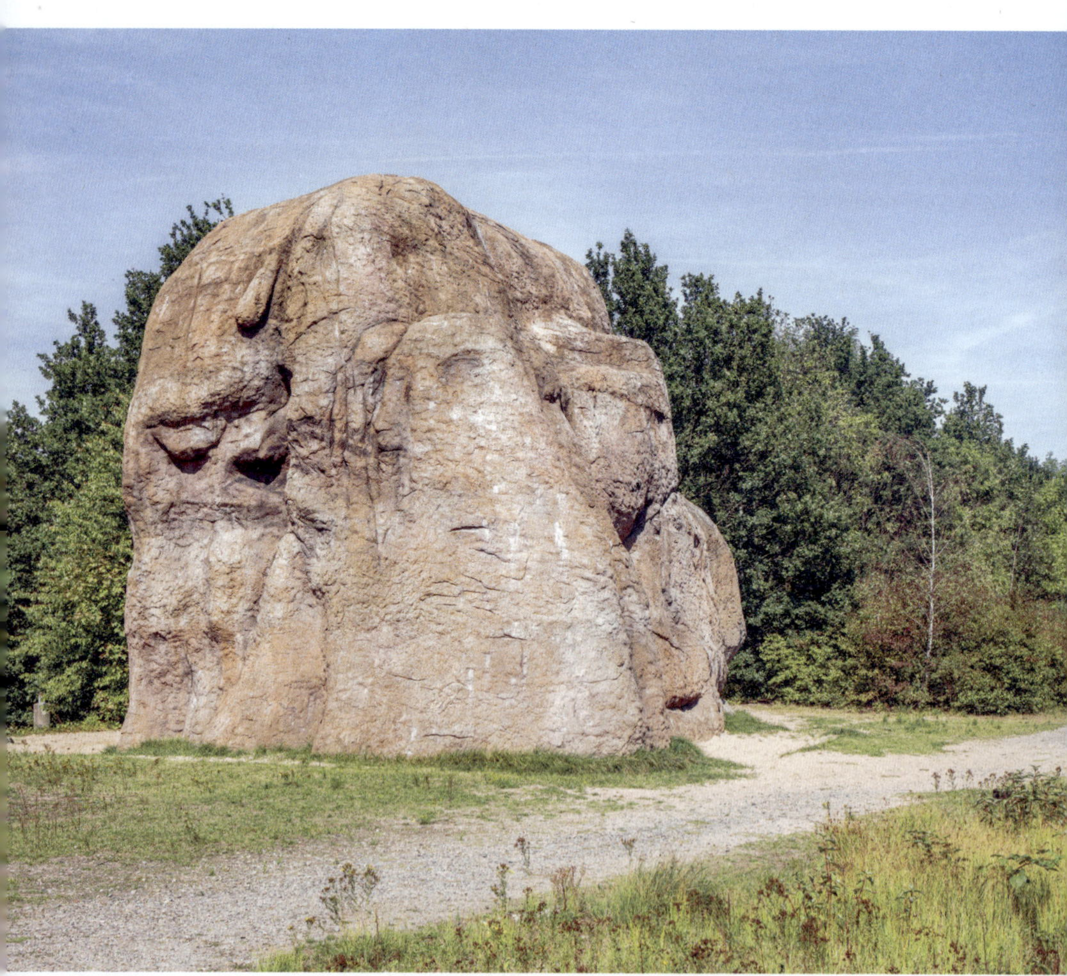

On the Emscher Island near the Gelsenkirchen Locks, just a short distance from the cycle path next to the Emscher, one unexpectedly encounters a huge rock formation. As one approaches, a quiet music becomes audible that seems to be emanating from inside the mountain. Embedded on sand, the mountain has a strange appearance, as if a glacial boulder had somehow found its way to this spot. In fact it is an artistic work by Olaf Nicolai and Douglas Gordon, created for the 2010 *Emscherkunst* exhibition.

Olaf Nicolai built a faithful reproduction of a rock formation in the Joshua Tree National Park near Los Angeles und installed it on the highest spot of the so-called Wild Island between the Emscher river and the Rhine-Herne Canal. The artificial mountain itself sits on top of an artificial mound, namely a waste tip made of the soil excavated during the construction of the nearby locks and the Rhine-Herne Canal. This aside, nature here has been left to its own devices. Visible in the background is the vast industrial scenery of the Ruhr Oel refineries.

This «unnatural natural phenomenon», as Nicolai describes the work, consists of a steel frame coated in shot concrete, which at first sight looks deceptively similar to a massive natural rock formation. But the mountain is hollow, and on the inside harbours a sound system which during the summer months plays a looped, twenty-three minute composition by the Scottish band Mogwai, *Music for a Forgotten Future (The Singing Mountain)* that was commissioned by Douglas Gordon.

Monument for a Forgotten Future can be taken as a symbol for the extensive conversion of the landscape in the Emscher valley and emphasises that even seemingly wild nature can in fact be human-made and thus subordinate to human interests. At the same time, this allusion to one of the most famous national parks in the US evokes a romantic image of untouched nature: the touristic fascination of Joshua Tree's desert landscape lies not only in its unique vegetation and characteristic rock formations, but also in its status as the epitome of the US «frontier landscape», whose romanticism and monumentality stand for the departure into the New World.

155

CARBON OBELISK
Rita McBride

2010/2022

MATERIAL
Carbon, synthetic resin
Height: 14 m

ADDRESS
Emscher-Weg
near Karnaper Straße 30
45329 Essen

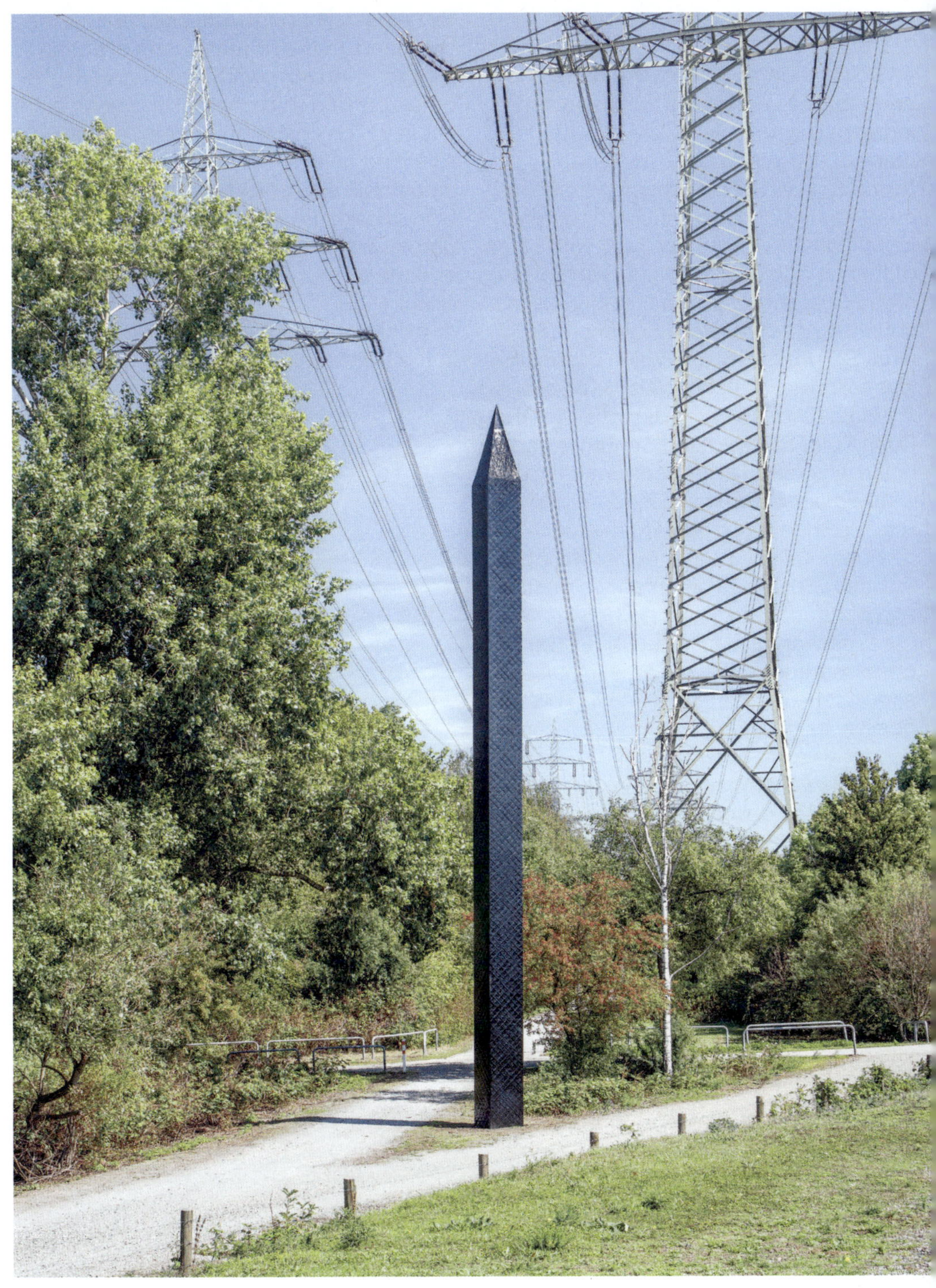

In the Ruhr region there are over 250 waste tips — up to 140 metres high, artificial mountains of mining waste, slag and rubble — witnesses to mining and industrial history. Since the late 1980s many of these tips have been transformed as part of the *Internationale Bauausstellung* [International Architecture Exhibition, IBA] *Emscher Park,* with some of them made over into sites for monumental installations. The first large-scale sculpture was Raimund Kummer's 1987 work *Schwelle* [Threshold] in Essen; this was followed in 1998 by Richard Serra's *Bramme für das Ruhrgebiet* [Slab for the Ruhr Area] on top of the Schurenbachhalde waste tip. In her contribution to the 2010 *Emscherkunst* exhibition, sculptor Rita McBride responded to the two monumental sculptures by her male colleagues with a less ostentatious gesture. At a nondescript crossroad between the Emscher river and the Rhine-Herne Canal in Altenessen, the artist installed a fourteen-metre-high, gleaming black obelisk. Its title, *Carbon Obelisk,* simply describes form and material.

However plain and familiar its form might be, the delicate pointed pillar with its hi-tech, lozenge-shape patterned shell of carbon fibre resembles an alien presence standing at the dusty fork in the path. In ancient Egypt, monolithic obelisks original represented a link to the world of gods; later, Roman conquerors removed them and installed them as trophies of victory in prominent places around their empire. In more modern times, obelisks have performed cartographic functions by marking distances. Even if the site and size of this sculpture seem less prominent than the landmarks on top of the waste tips, McBride's work nonetheless suggests diverse references to its location.

By using carbon the artist alludes, on the one hand, to the hi-tech material and to progress-driven civilisation, while, on the other, carbon also denotes the geological era in which coal was formed, thereby referring quite simply to the origins of industrialisation. Not least of all, as this work marks the junction of several cycle paths between the Rhine-Herne Canal and the former Emscher wastewater canal, McBride is also playing on the current period of cultural transformation in the Ruhr region.

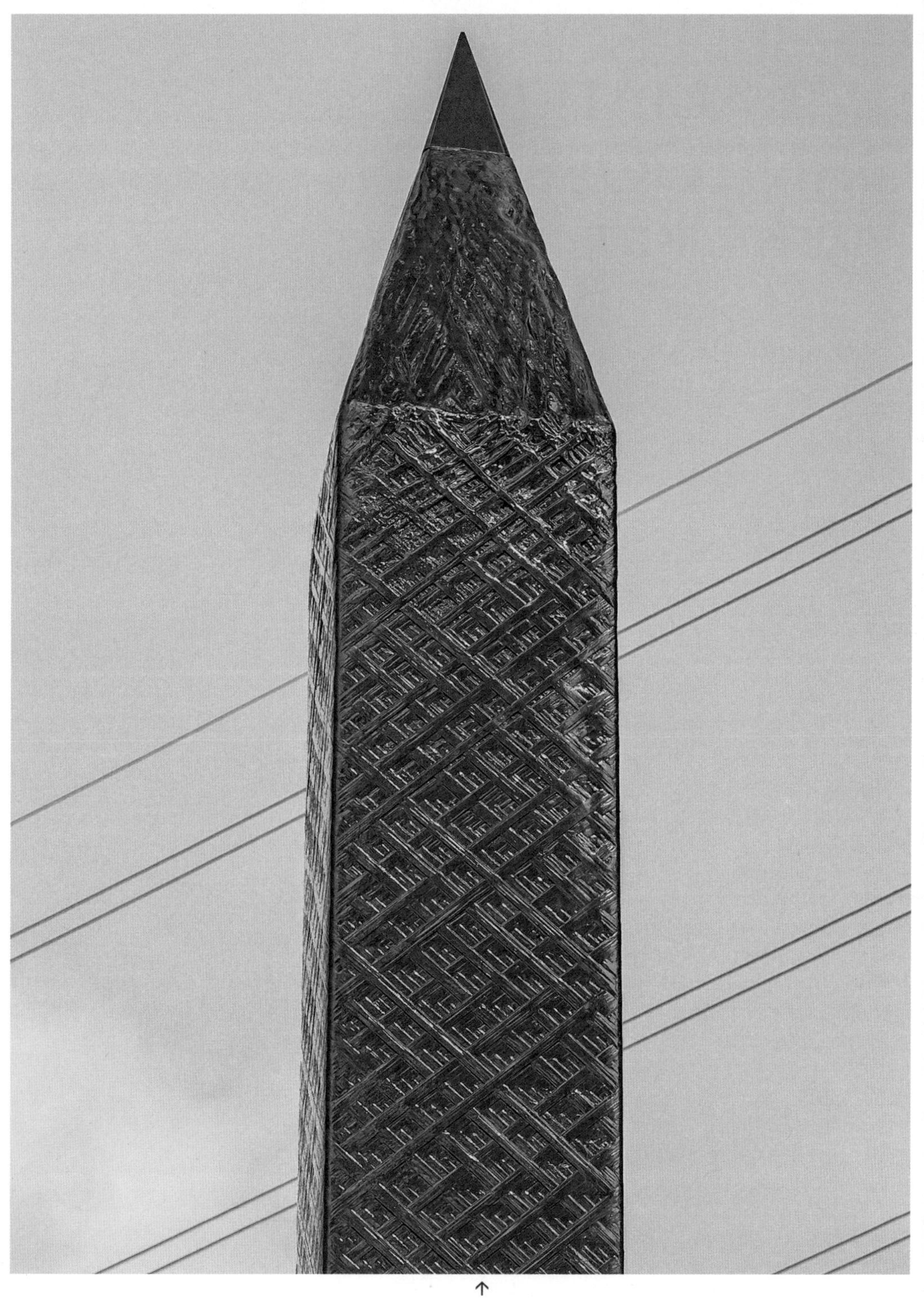

The shiny black surface of the obelisk is made of carbon. The composite material made of carbon fibres is extremely light and unbreakable.

GESELLSCHAFT DER AMATEUR-ORNITHOLOGEN
Mark Dion

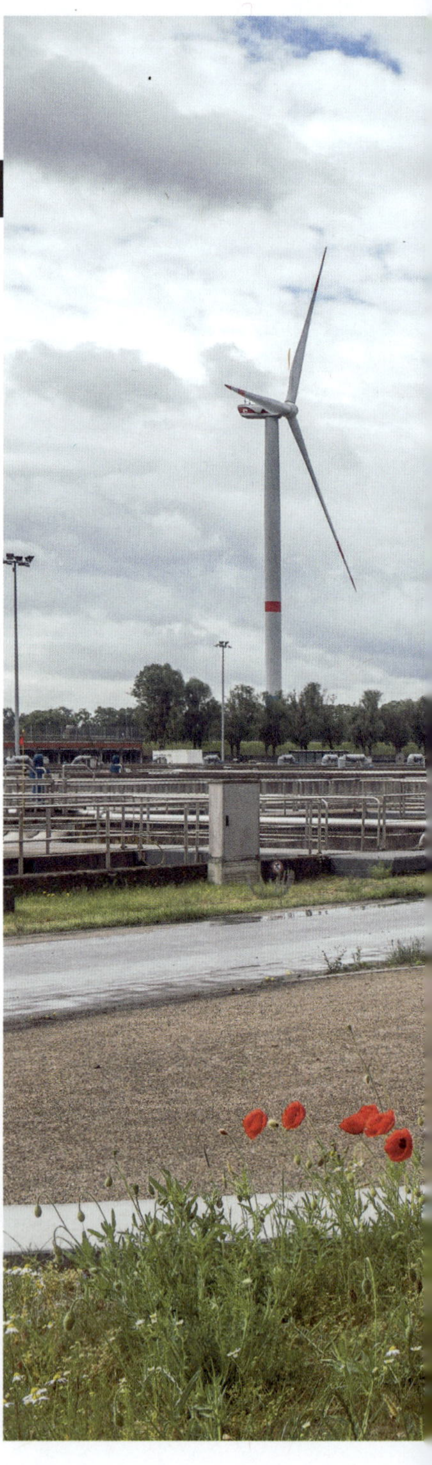

2010

MATERIAL
Former gas tank,
modified and arranged
Steel, acryl glass, used furniture
and carpets, ontological instruments,
articles from a flea market
Dimensions gas tank:
approx. 8.50 × 3.10 × 3.50 m

ADDRESS
Kläranlage Bottrop
In der Welheimer Mark 190
46238 Bottrop

The artwork can only
be visited on request.

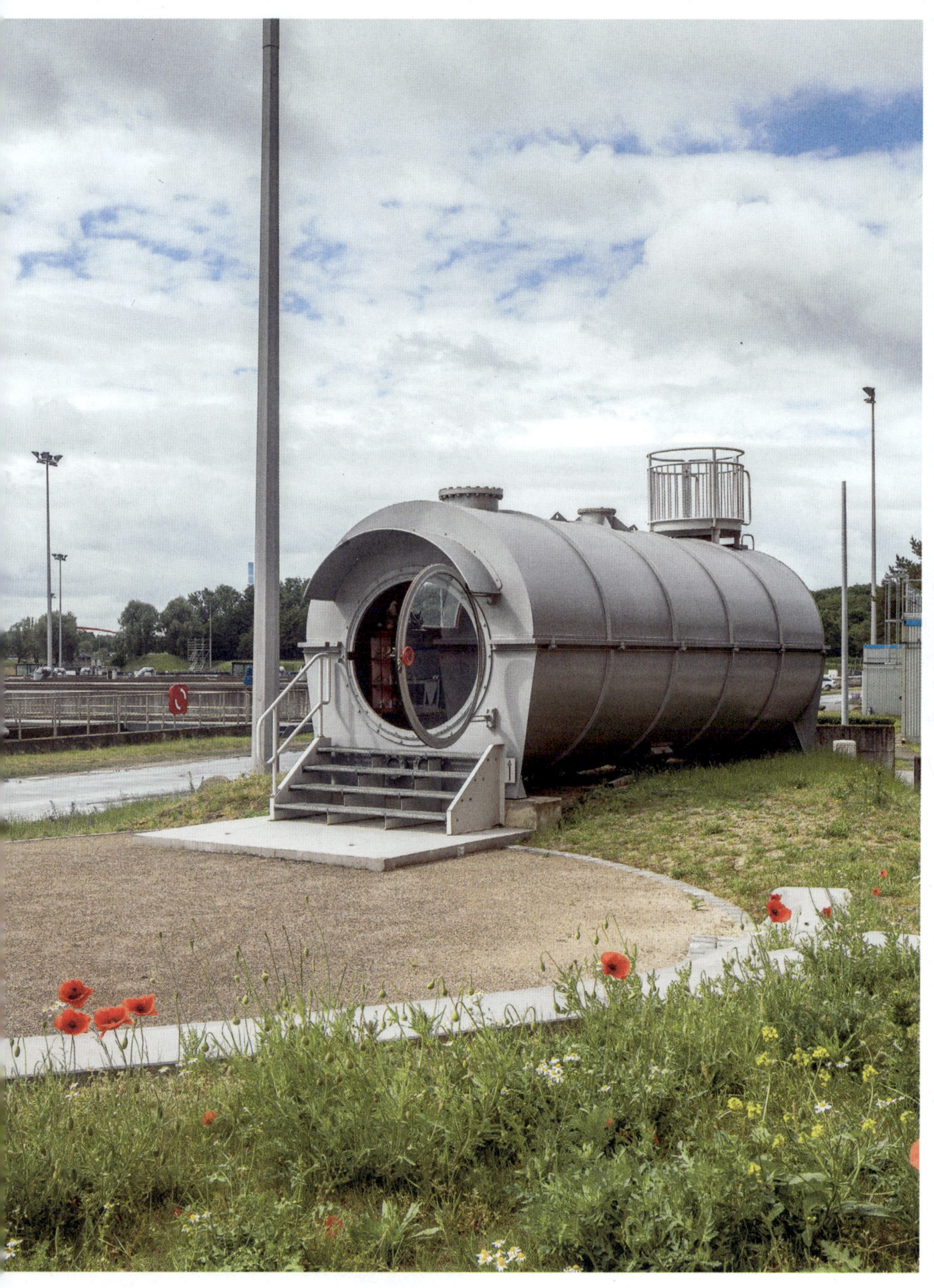

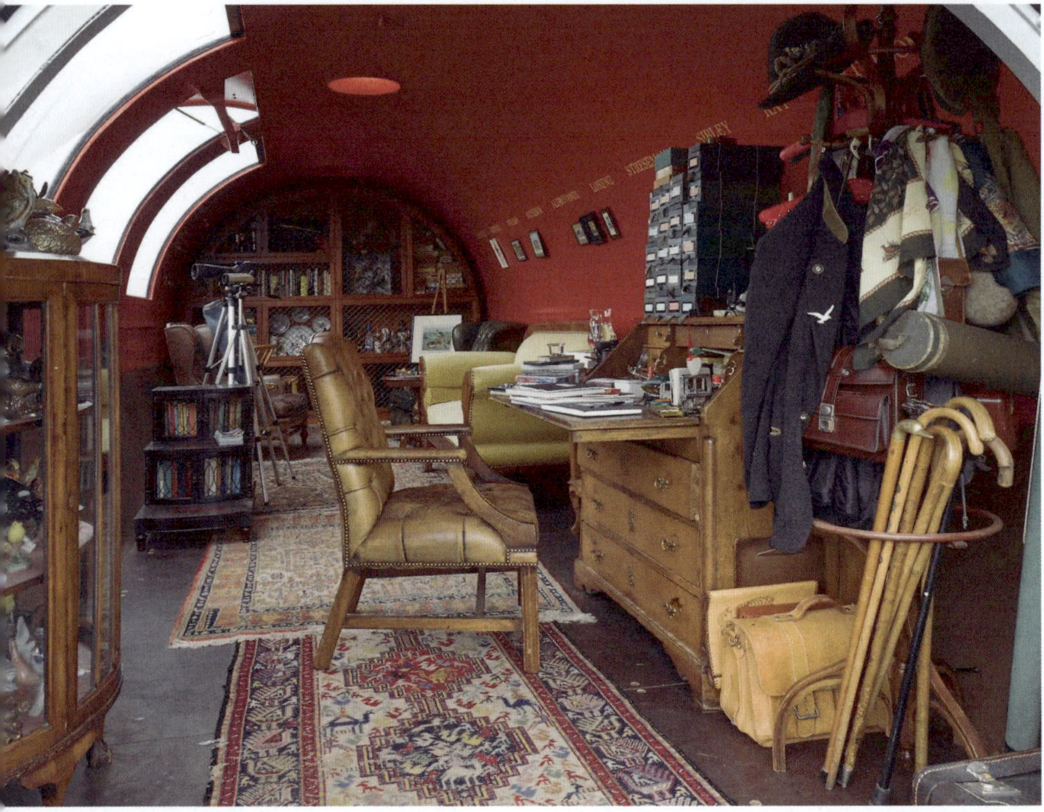

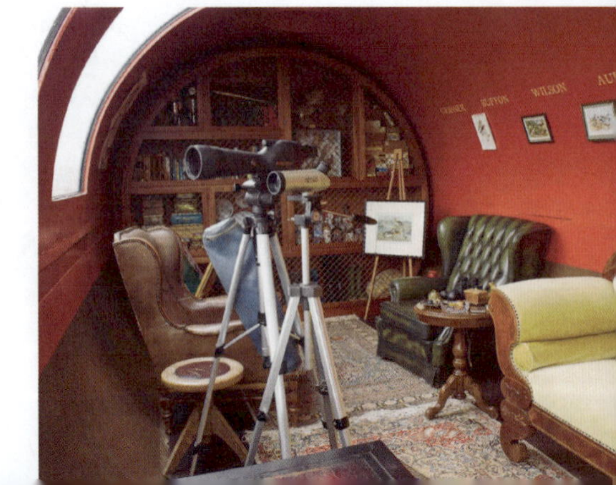

For his contribution to the 2010 *Emscher-kunst* exhibition Mark Dion had a disused gas tank converted into a kind of bird observatory. He came across the object at the former Herne sewage treatment plant, where the artist Silke Wagner also realised her work *Glückauf. Bergarbeiter-proteste im Ruhrgebiet* [Good Luck. Miners' Protests in the Ruhr Region].

Entitled *Society for Amateur Ornithologists,* Dion transformed the barrel-shaped vessel into a free-standing, walk-in edifice. To one side of the entrance with a roofed porch and stairs a large window opening was inserted into the side wall and two windows installed in the ceiling where previously supply pipes had been con-nected to the tank; in addition, a small observation platform was built onto the roof. In contrast to the tank's plain outward appearance, its interior has been fitted with sophisticated furnishings. Reminiscent of a clubhouse, it brings to mind images of nineteenth-century curiosity cabinets. The artist furnished the space with old carpets and antique furniture, supplementing it with numerous ornithological objects and books he had purchased from various flea markets around the region. Aligned telescopes, books opened up on the bureau and crystal bowls filled with sweets give the impression that a hobby ornithologist has just left the observatory. Visitors are encouraged to use all the objects in the observatory, thus themselves becoming this same «amateur ornithologist» and part of the artwork — like the birds that allow themselves to be observed from this spot and the process of observing itself.

Since its initial setup, Mark Dion's installation has changed location on several occasions. In 2010 the object was located by the so-called Herner Meer [Herne Sea], in direct proximity to the Herne yacht harbour. For the 2013 *Emscherkunst* exhibition it was shown on the lift bridge in Duisburg-Walsum. After the work was presented in 2016 at Hof Emscher-Auen [Emscher Auen Farm] near the flood retention basin in Dort-mund-Mengede, it has now been allotted a permanent site in the grounds of the large Bottrop sewage treatment plant. The former industrial object that serves as a camouflaged bird observatory has constantly adapted to changing locations in the post-industrial landscape of the Emscher region without losing any of its impact.

DASPARKHOTEL
Andreas Strauss

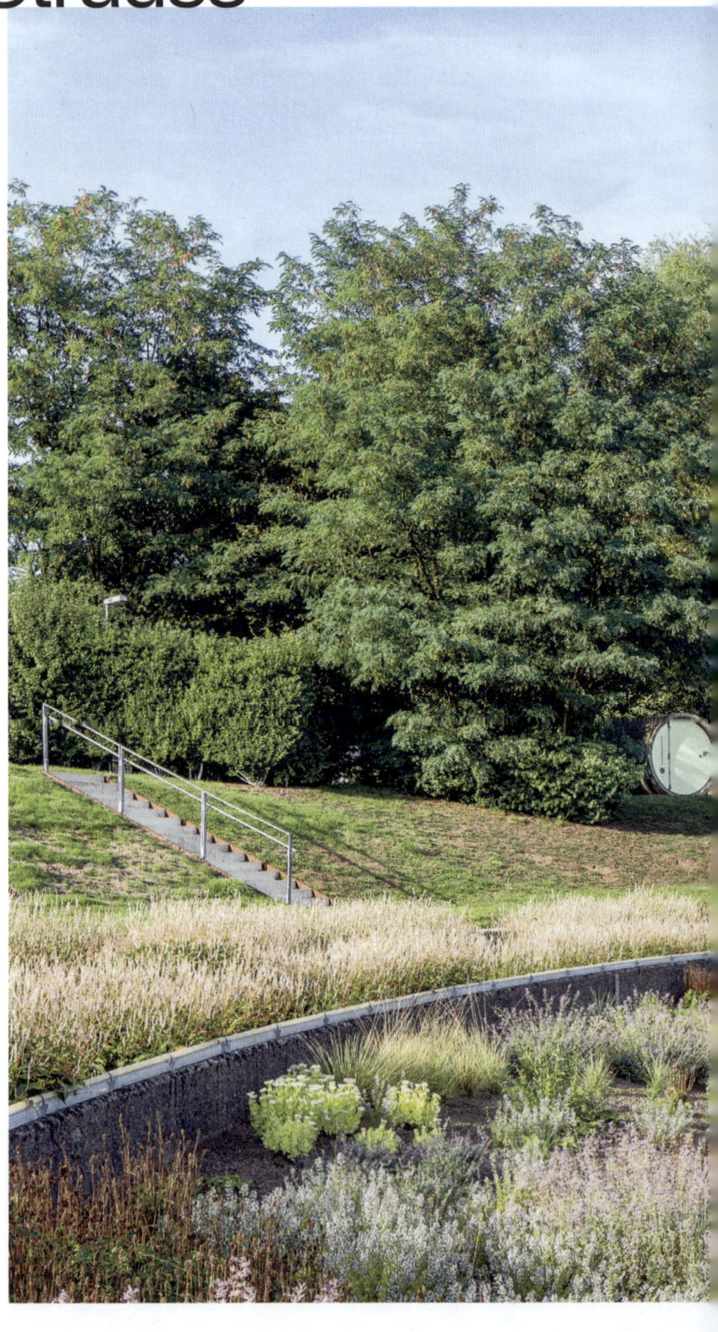

2010/2022

MATERIAL
Converted concrete tubes
for overnight stays,
bedding and linen,
wall painting
Dimensions:
2.40 × 2.40 × 3.21 m

ADDRESS
BernePark
Ebelstraße 25a
46242 Bottrop

Overnight stays
from May to October,
bookable at
dasparkhotel.net

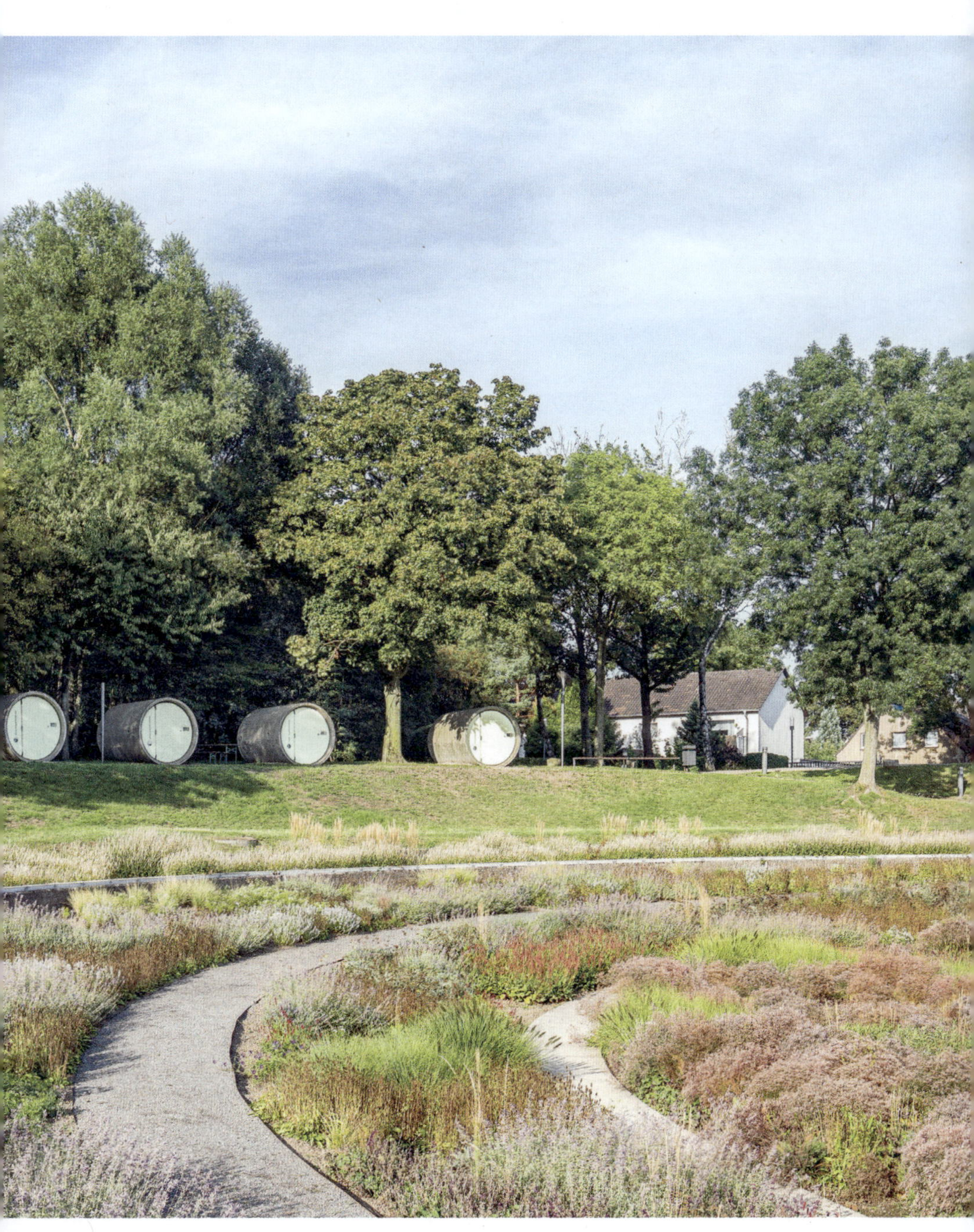

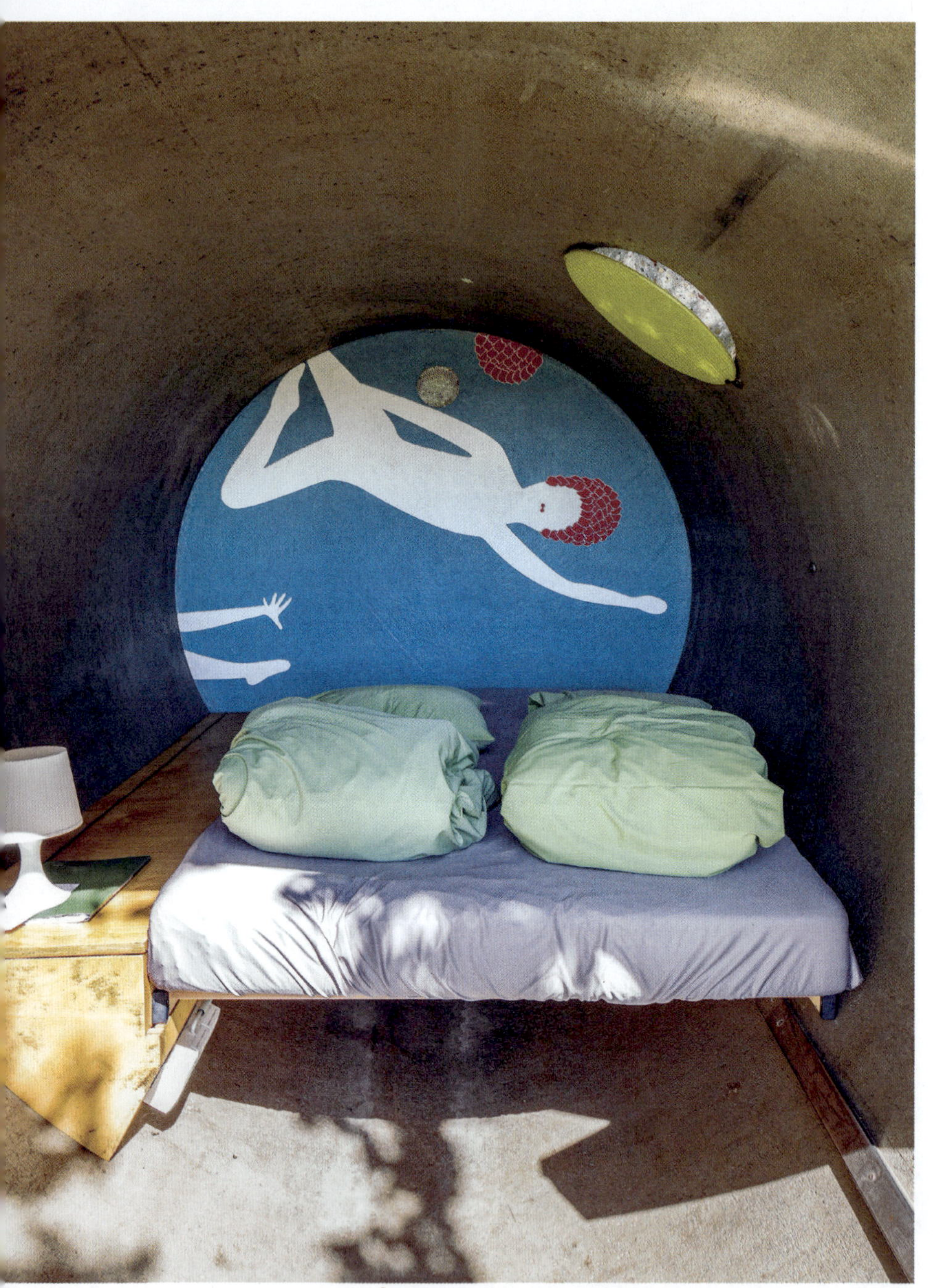

Can you imagine hotel rooms that are as simple and uncomplicated to use as a station luggage locker? Prompted by this idea, the artist Andreas Strauss developed his project *dasparkhotel.* For this, he converted commercially available sewage pipes into sleeping cabins that can be used individually by overnight guests at all hours, just by means of an electronic code-locked system of access. Each pipe is furnished for up to two people, including storage space and a bedside lamp, with a window for natural daylight.

dasparkhotel was first set up in Donaupark in Linz in 2004, then moved a year later to be permanently installed in Rodlgelände park in Ottensheim, Upper Austria. In the meantime, a specially developed sanitation pipe has been added. In 2010 a further site went into operation near the former sewage treatment plant in Bottrop-Ebel where altogether five «sleeping pipes» and one sanitation container were installed. On the rear wall inside each of the pipes the artist Sophie Grebe created an individual wall painting.

From the outset, the artist's idea was to create a network of these unconventional accommodation units based on a notion of common economic good. Situated on the banks of the Emscher, these refunctioned concrete pipes also allude to the larger purpose of the Emscher conversion: the river that was formerly subordinate to industrial purposes has now been invested with a new hospitability for people and nature.

The «hospitality devices», as Andreas Strauss calls the sleeping pipes, dissolve the boundaries between private and public space, and combine the individual experience of nature and the cultural realm with the comfort of an urban capsule hotel. In this respect, the work's title *dasparkhotel* can be read as an ironic comment on the lure of commercial, touristic pledges. Besides its easy, 24/7 access via online booking, the non-profit-oriented operating concept is an integral conceptual component of the project which aims to offer accommodation to everyone for just a small financial contribution.

Completed in October 2010, since spring 2011 *dasparkhotel* in BernePark has been offering overnight stays during the warm season of the year for all-comers — whether cyclotourists, hikers or fugitives from everyday life. In 2019 *dasparkhotel* was adopted as a permanent artwork of the Emscherkunstweg [Emscher Art Trail].

THEATER DER PFLANZEN
Piet Oudolf
GROSS.MAX

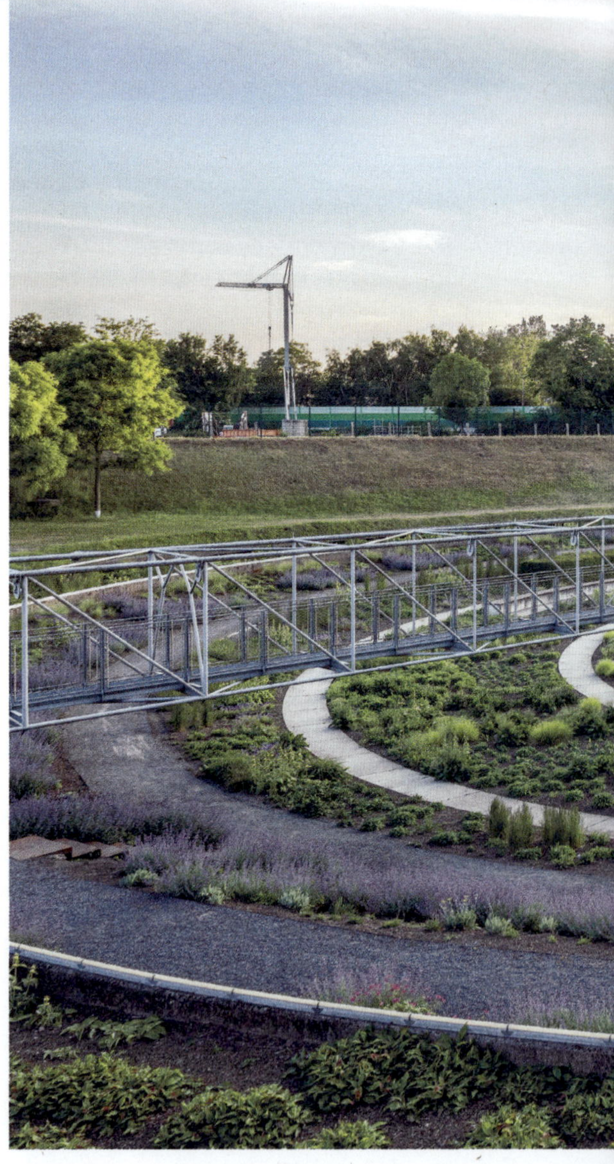

2010

MATERIAL
Landscape architectural
forming of both settling basins
Calibre of settling basins:
73 m each

ADDRESS
BernePark
Ebelstraße 25a
46242 Bottrop

168

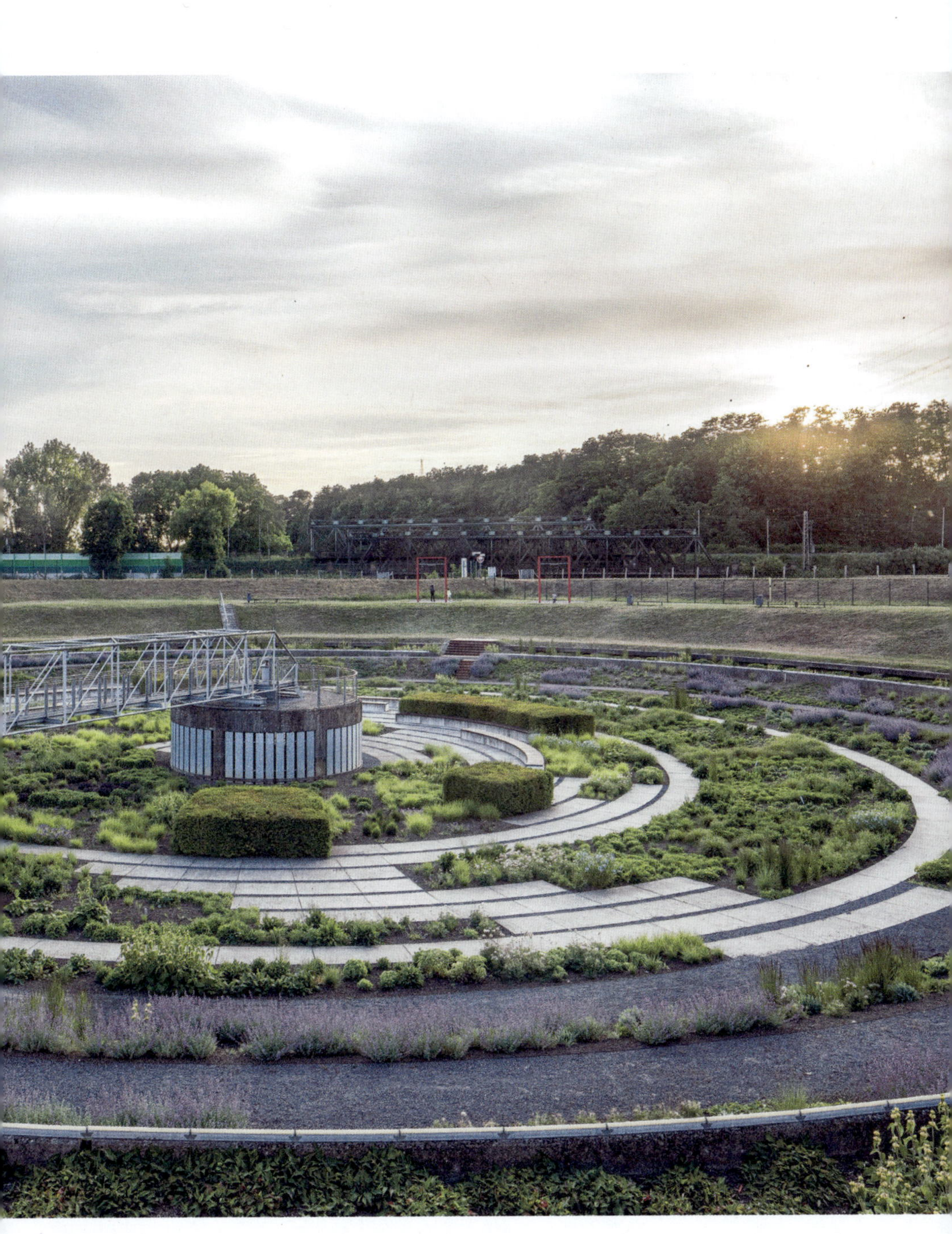

In the 1990s, in connection with the restoration the Emscher river to a close-to-natural condition and the construction of an enormous, subterranean wastewater canal, numerous relatively small sewage treatment plants were shut down. One of those which closed in 1997 was the plant in the Bottrop-Ebel district, where the Berne river flows into the Emscher. Rather than being demolished, it was chosen not only to be preserved as an industrial monument, but also to fulfil a new function as a park to meet the recreational needs of the local community. The landscape architecture office David | Terfrüchte + Partner proposed a masterplan which on the occasion of the 2010 *Emscherkunst* exhibition was supplemented with artistic interventions. The garden artist Piet Oudolf, collaborating with the landscape architects GROSS. MAX, created the work *Theater der Pflanzen* [Theatre of Plants]. The concept was based on a conversion of the two former round clarifying tanks. Whereas one tank remains filled with water, for the other Oudolf and GROSS.MAX designed a gyrating, descending, walk-through garden. To this end, the basin was filled with earth and arranged in a horticultural composition of shrubs and grasses. Paths and seating structure the garden into a kind of labyrinth. Oudolf's choice of plant varieties was guided primarily by aesthetic criteria, taking into consideration their changing conditions through the different seasons of the year. The beds are arranged in clusters, whereby various shrubs and grasses are repeated, but always with one particular plant dominating the ensemble and setting the tone. Through his work with perennial plants Oudolf is associated in gardening circles with the so-called New Perennial Movement, which champions the idea of

sustainable garden design. In BernePark this concept also reckons with a regular flow of local visitors keen to witness the ever-changing spectacle of nature in flux.

The *Theater der Pflanzen* [Theatre of Plants] consists of over 21,000 perennials and other plants.

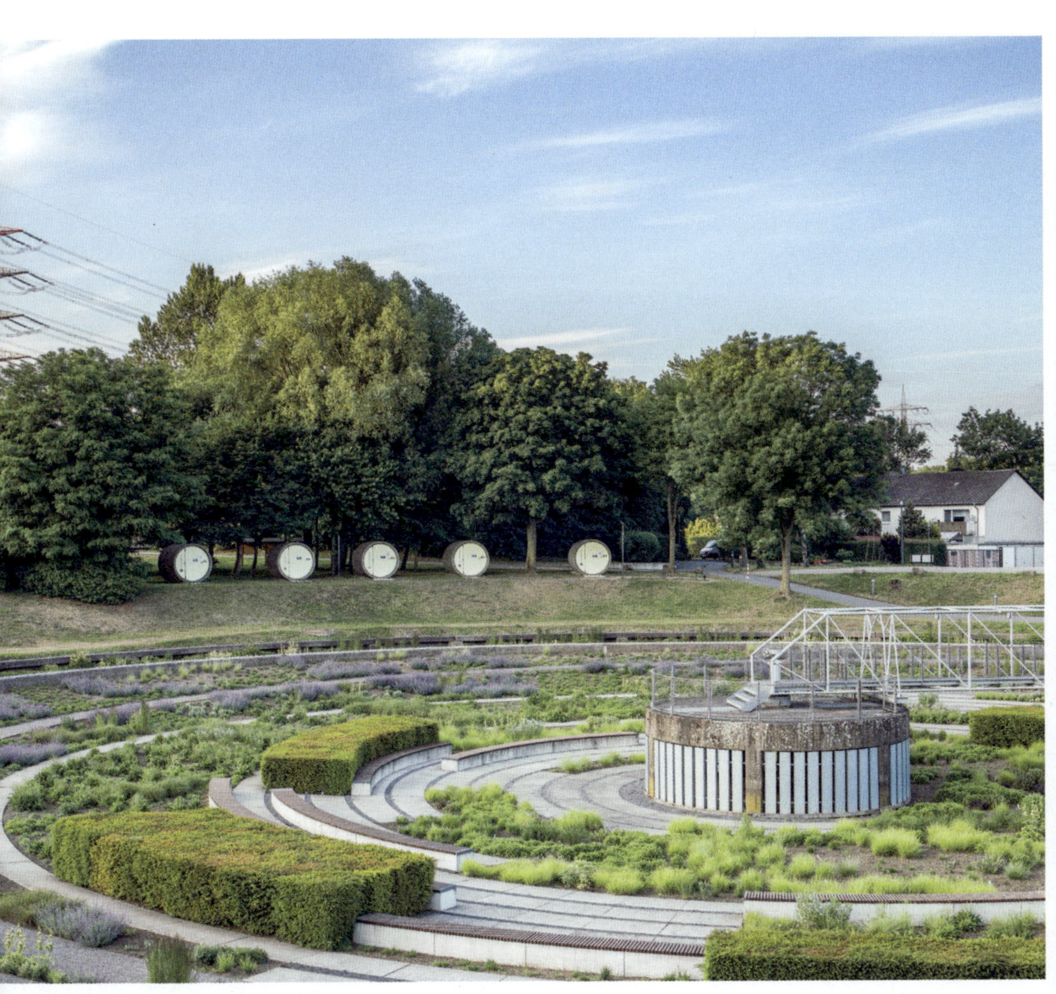

CATCH AS CATCH CAN
Mischa Kuball
Lawrence Weiner

2010/2021

MATERIAL
Rotating light installation
in both settling basins,
lettering on the roof of the
former operations building
Fluorescent LED tubes,
metal construction

ADDRESSE
BernePark
Ebelstraße 25a
46242 Bottrop

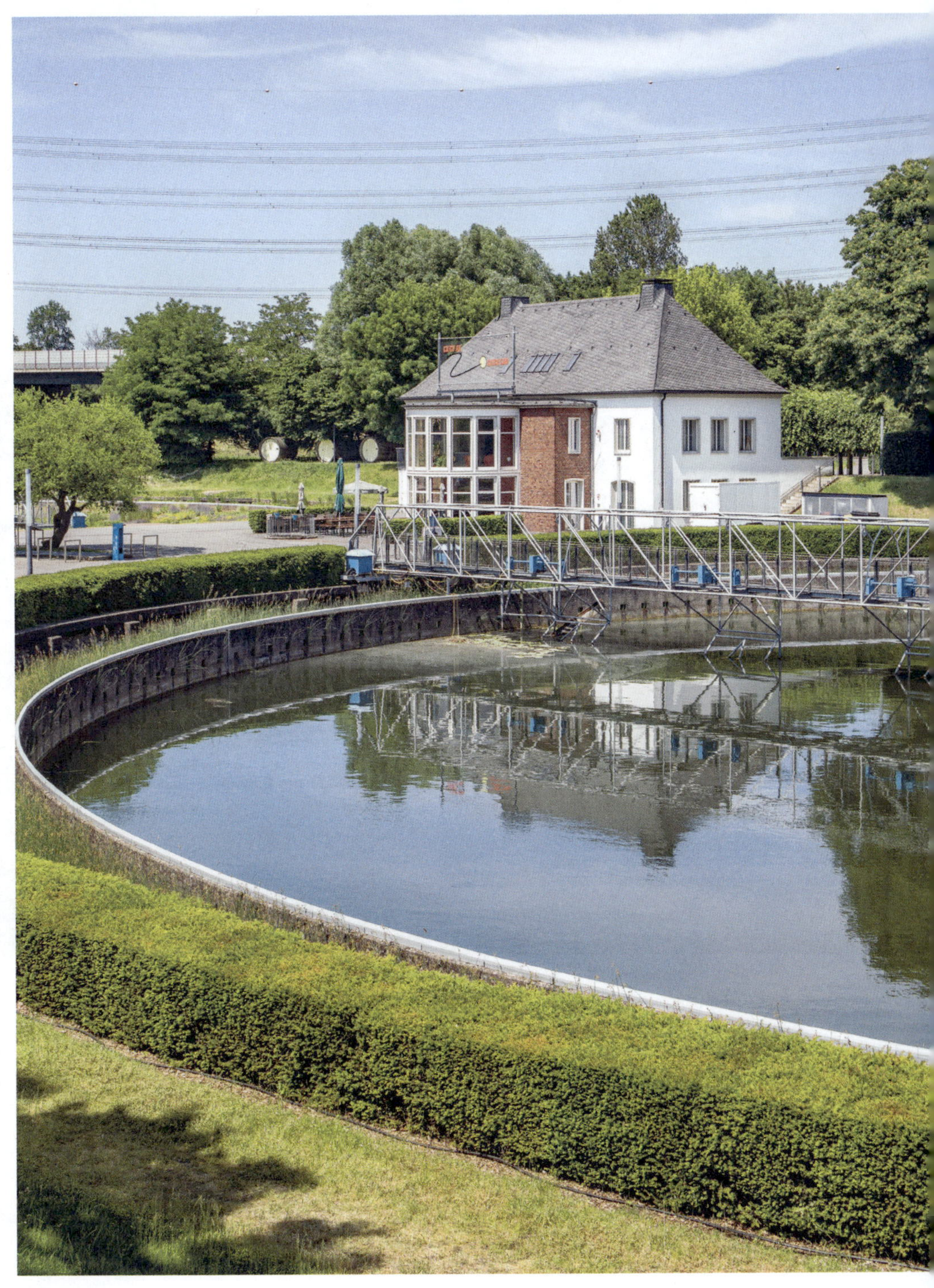

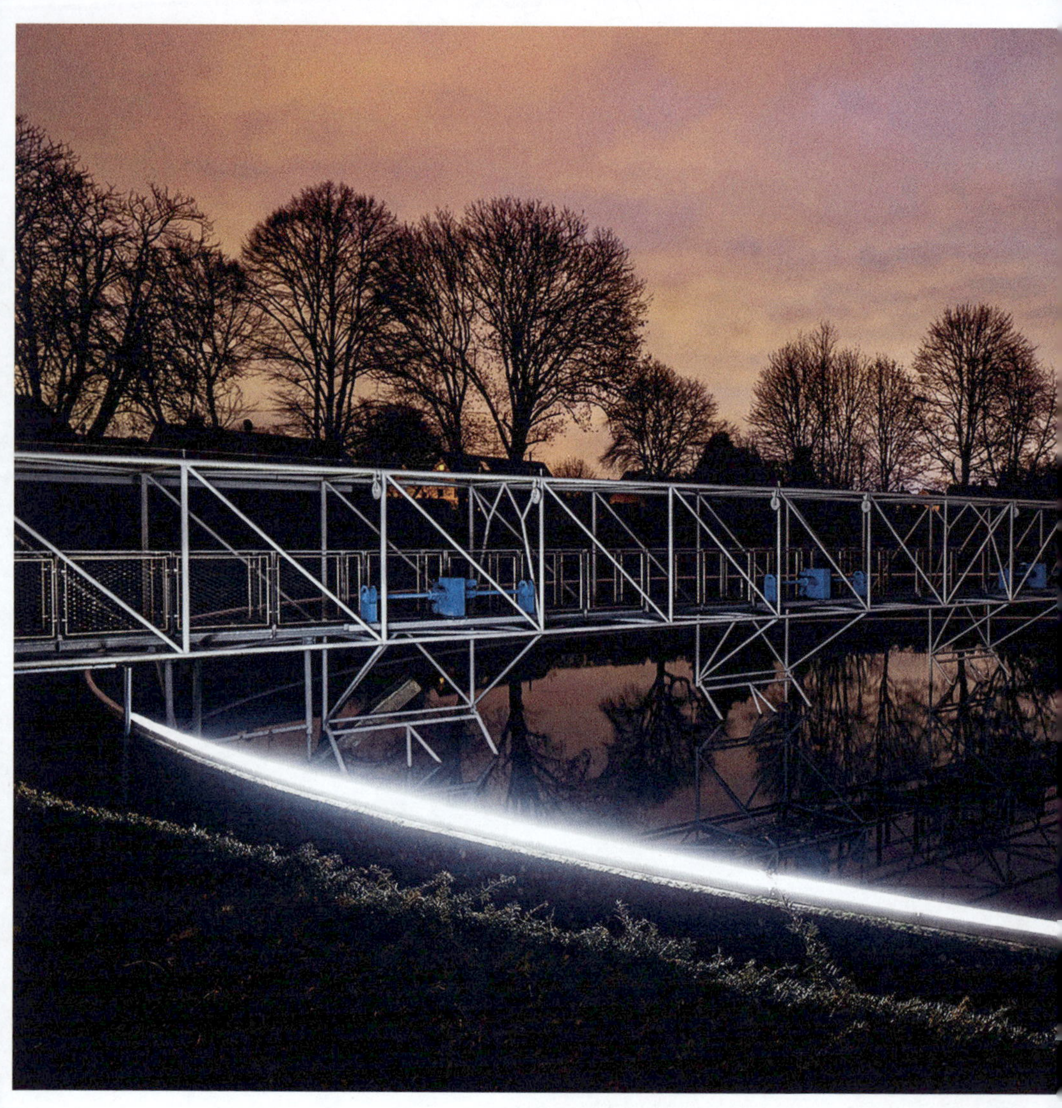

From nightfall, Mischa Kuball's light installation
in the two former septic tanks glows.

The two artists Mischa Kuball and Lawrence Weiner were invited to each contribute a work to the 2010 *Emscherkunst* exhibition. Their collaboration first developed during the preparations and planning for the former Bottrop-Ebel sewage treatment plant, which resulted in the joint work *CATCH AS CATCH CAN.*

The present-day BernePark instantly appealed to a number of artists back then. So with Piet Oudolf & GROSS.MAX, and Andreas Strauss, altogether five different artistic strategies are represented here. If the Ruhr region is associated predominantly with disused collieries and steelworks, sewage plants are surely some of the more unusual former industrial sites to have found new uses by becoming public parks and, at the same time, monuments. Up until the late 1990s, they were still an essential part of the above-ground Emscher waste-water system throughout the region which since the early twentieth century had regulated the flow and treatment of grey water from industrial works and private households, thereby also ensuring the containment of epidemics such as typhoid and cholera.

Under a shared title the two artists created independent works in their respectively typical media of light and text, which they turned into a dialogue with one another. At night Mischa Kuball's light installation illuminates the plant's two former clarifying basins with a strip of white light that constantly revolves around the edge of each basin. The dynamic movement of the circling light is echoed in Lawrence Weiner's flamboyant illuminated lettering of *CATCH AS CATCH CAN* mounted on a fine wire construction, which initially was installed on the roof of the plant's main building. Restoration work on the listed historical building required the object to be shifted, so since 2020 its new location has been on the flat roof of the semi-circular extension building. In an ironic commentary Weiner casts the entire premises of the former sewage treatment plant in the light of this proverbial motto, saying «make the best of what you have». In a manner typical of the artist, Weiner works with text and typography – in this case in the form of an old-fashioned advertising panel in the style of the 1950s and '60s, thereby referencing the period of the plant's construction. Nowadays, BernePark is extremely popular as a site for leisure and recreation.

ZAUBERLEHRLING
Inges Idee

2013/2019

MATERIAL
Steel with surface coating
Height: 35 m

ADDRESS
Gehölzgarten Ripshorst
Ripshorster Straße 306
46117 Oberhausen

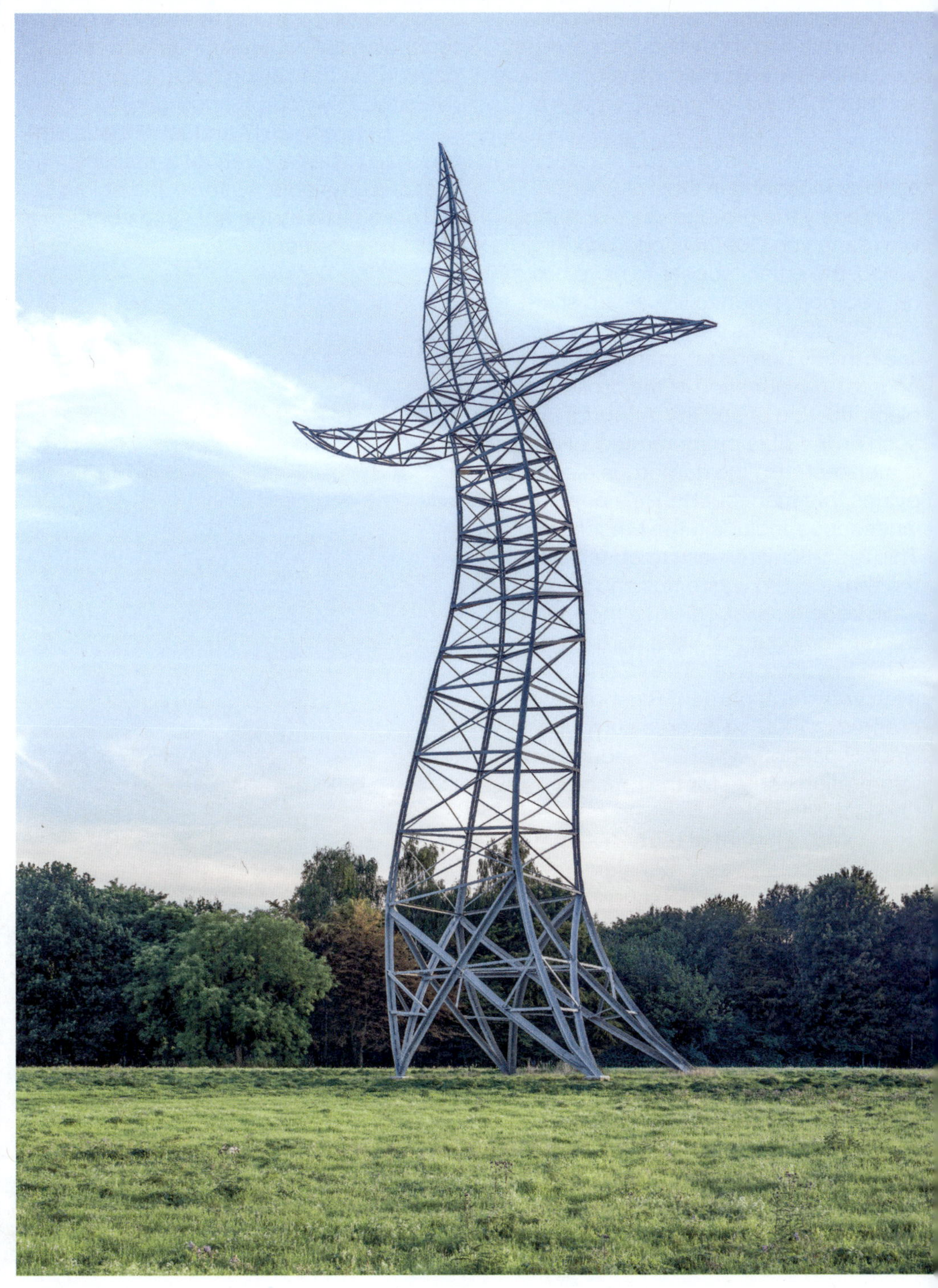

In connection with the 2013 *Emscher-kunst* exhibition the artists' group Inges Idee [Inge's Idea] created the enormous sculpture *Zauberlehrling* [Sorcerer's Apprentice], visible from a great distance and installed in the tree and shrub garden at Haus Ripshorst in Oberhausen. Inspired by the protagonist in Johann Wolfgang von Goethe's eponymous ballad, the artists appear to have brought an electricity pylon to life, which since its installation has been «dancing out of line». In this humorous manner the artists address the question of the proliferating electrification of society. Although as such an invisible phenomenon, electricity is manifested in the numerous electricity pylons that mark our densely populated landscapes, including the Emscher valley. This is particularly easy to observe from the renaturated waste tips and parks that have been developed since the 1980s on the former industrial sites north and south of the Emscher river. The «Gehölzgarten» [tree and shrub garden] Ripshorst was created in 1999 on an area surrounding Haus Ripshorst, which now houses an information centre for the Emscher Landschaftspark.

With a height of thirty-five metres, the steel sculpture's dimensions and form match those of a traction current pylon. Yet, to achieve the structure's flowing form each element had to be individually drafted and produced.

The dynamic of its apparent movement changes depending on the viewer's perspective. Its dancing, playful character is especially striking when seen from the West: from this point of view *Zauberlehrling* joins the company of a number of other, variously shaped electricity pylons, further emphasising its animated character. For all its playful irony, the allusion to Goethe's poem «Zauberlehrling» is intended as a warning to treat our use of technological achievements with critical caution. As the saying goes, «Spirits that I've cited // My commands ignore».

Between 2017 and 2019 the sculpture had to be renovated for stability reasons. The object's form and colour were adjusted by the artists to conform to static requirements.

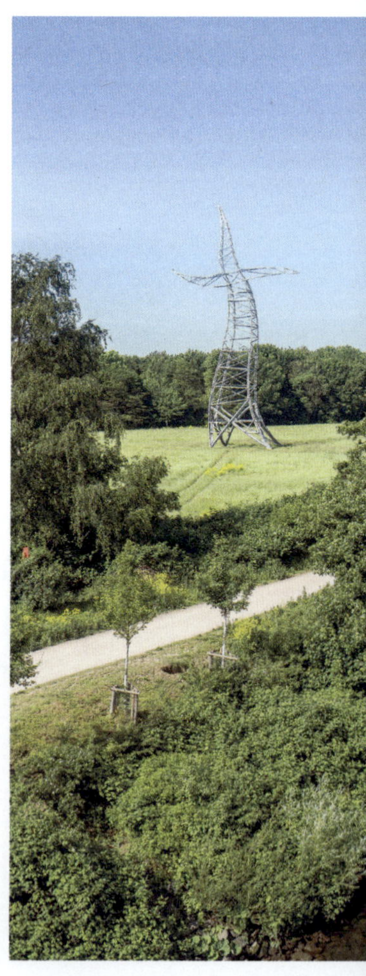

Zauberlehrling [Sorcerer's Apprentice]
is thirty-five metres high and consists
of a total of 24.4 tonnes of steel.

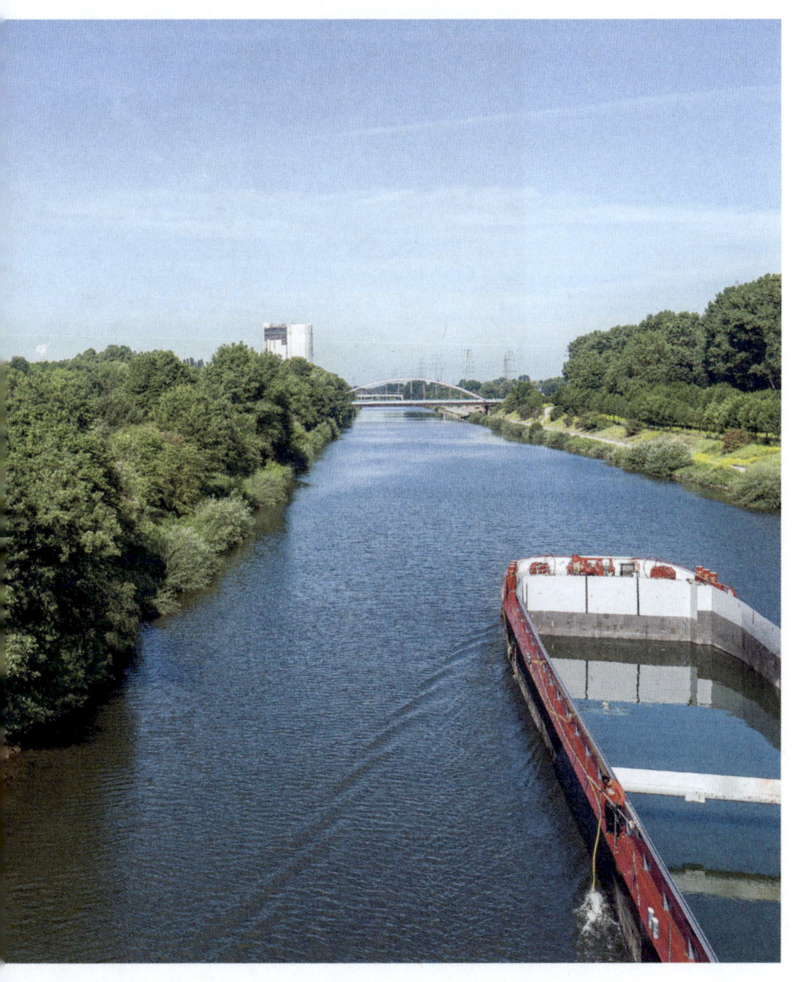

SLINKY SPRINGS
TO FAME
Tobias Rehberger

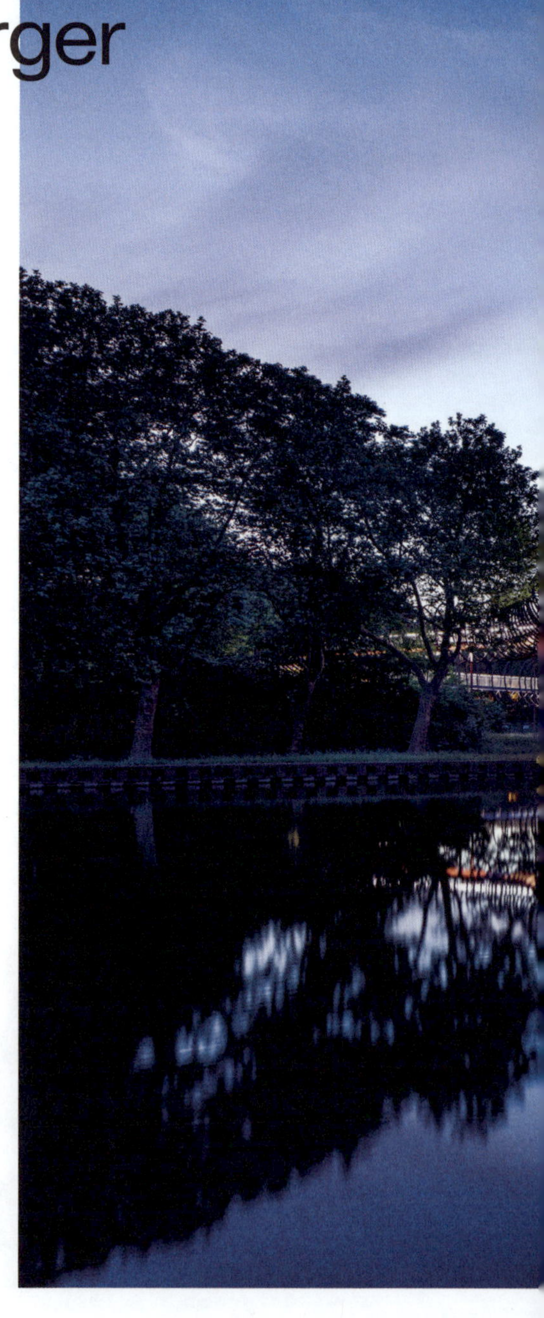

2010

MATERIAL
Stress ribbon bridge
Steel, tartan floor,
LED-lightning

Total length: 406 m
Amount helices: 496
Calibre helix: ca. 5 m
Width bridge: 2.67 m
Surface bridge: 1.085 m²
Height above water: 8.50 m — 10 m

ADDRESS
Emscher-Weg
near Konrad-Adenauer-Allee 46
46049 Oberhausen

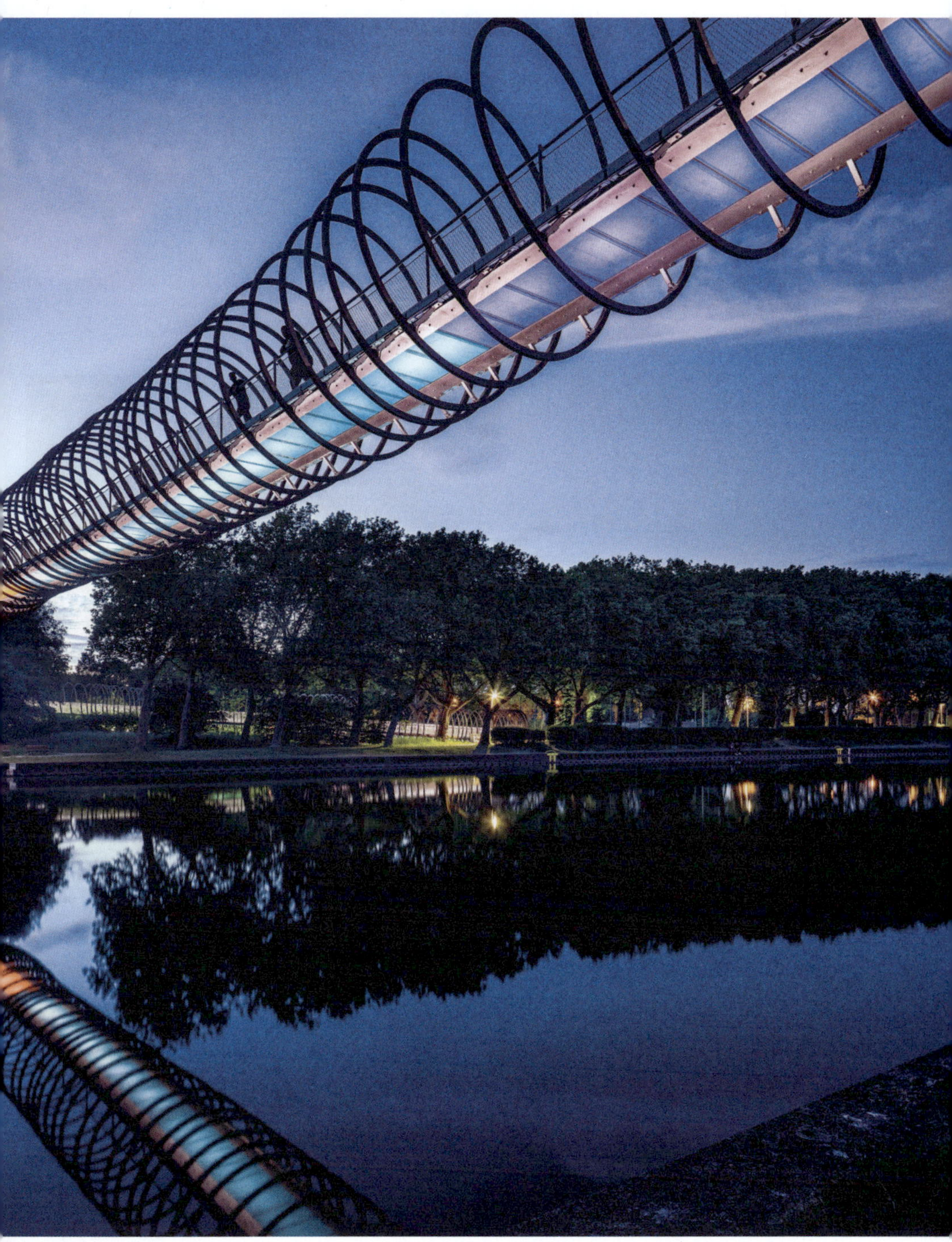

406 metres of LED luminaires
were installed in the handrail.
The 496 spirals contain further
luminaires in the lower centre.

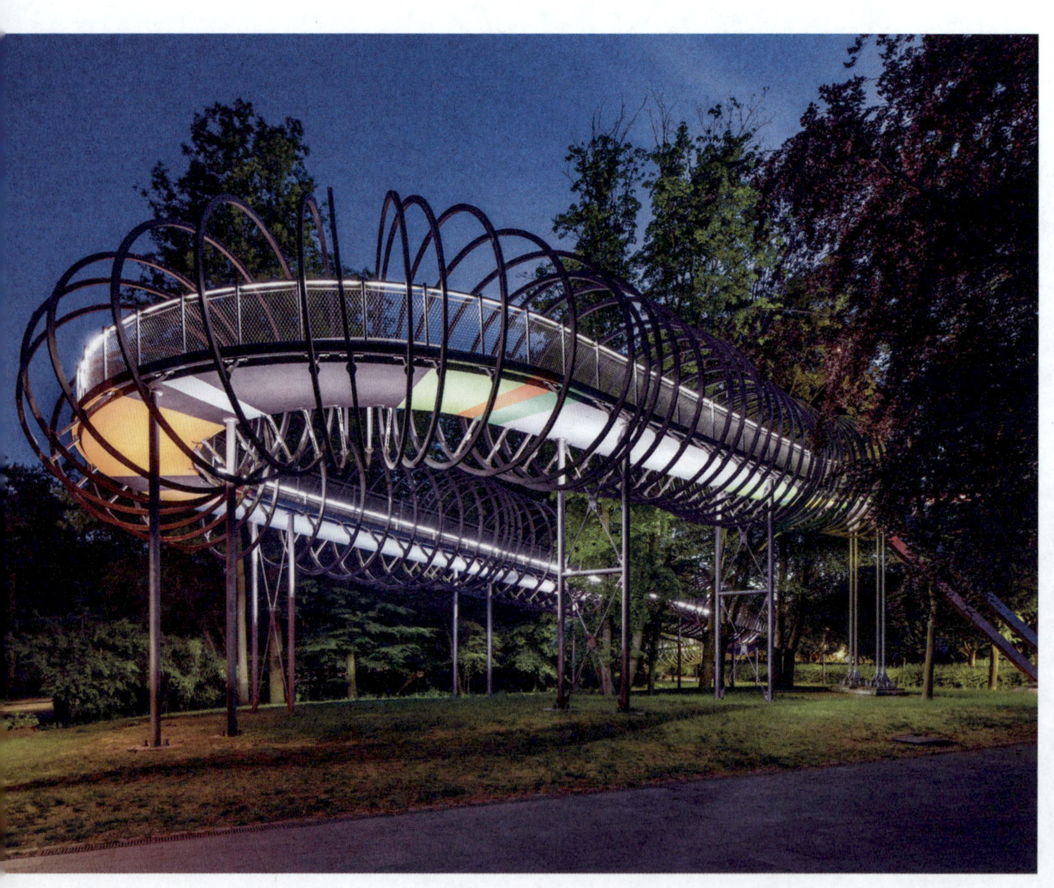

182

Forming 496 hoops, the spiralling bridge *Slinky Springs to Fame* coils nonchalantly across the Rhine-Herne Canal in Oberhausen. Tobias Rehberger designed the bridge as a contribution to the *Emscherkunst* exhibition during Essen's year as Capital of Culture in 2010, situating it in the place where a now disappeared bridge once connected the Emscher Island with the historic Kaisergarten park. Carried out by the Stuttgart-based engineering company Schlaich, Bergemann and Partners over a five-month construction period, the stress-ribbon bridge was opened in 2011. In engineering terms the bridge is a unique and highly complex construction: due to the container ship traffic on the Rhine-Herne Canal the main bridge had to be placed over the canal at the unusual height of ten metres. The fragile conditions around the bank on one side and the nature of the ground on the Kaisergarten side, where there is an old river meadow of the Emscher, posed particular challenges for the planners. In addition, the artistic design envisaged the bridge resembling a rope loosely thrown over the water with a light, wild and irregular feel. In order to achieve the construction's desired litheness the walking surface itself was made into the supporting framework, allowing the coils to spiral freely around the structure and act as the salient visual feature of the bridge's design. At both ends the bridge sweeps round in a broad arc, so that the entire work can boast a total length of 406 metres. The walking surface consists of a soft tartan flooring which in irregular sequence alternates through sixteen different colour fields from yellow, orange, pink and red to blue and turquoise.

Named after and inspired by the popular child's toy «Slinky», whose dynamic coils can somersault down a set of stairs, the footbridge seeks to animate not just children to take a buoyant walk across the canal. Cyclists who have biked down the Emscher trail will be greeted on the other side by the historical Kaisergarten dating back to the nineteenth century with an animal enclosure and the Schloss Oberhausen that houses the Ludwig Gallery. The bridge is particularly worth visiting after sunset: with the night-time illumination of the handrail, together with 293 further LEDs installed beneath the coiling spirals, the structure comes ablaze with light, creating dramatically colourful reflections in the water.

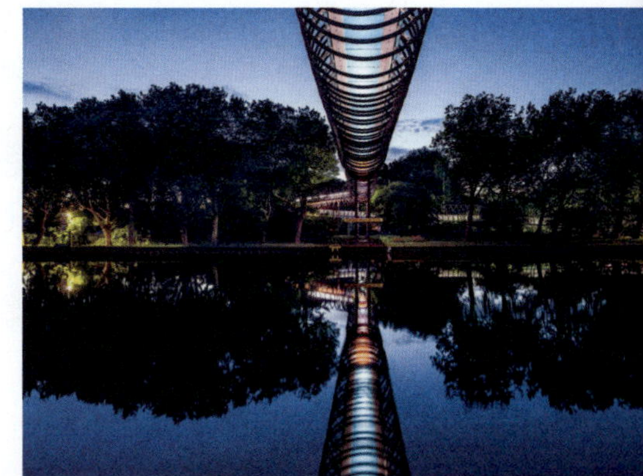

NEUSTADT
Julius von Bismarck
with Marta Dyachenko

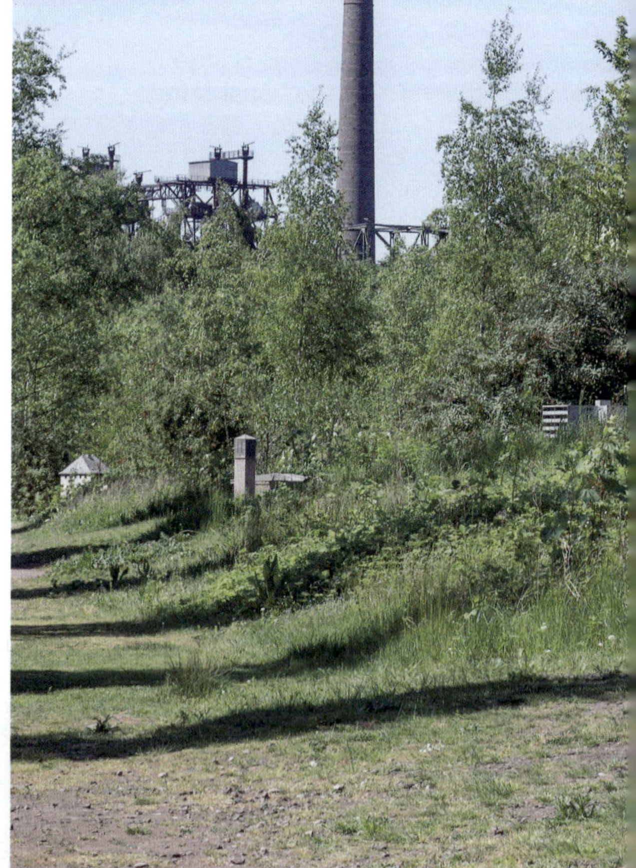

2021

MATERIAL
Installation in several parts,
consisting of 22 sculptures
of buildings
Concrete, steel, stainless
steel, acrylic glass

ADDRESS
Landschaftspark Duisburg-Nord
Emscherstraße 71
47137 Duisburg

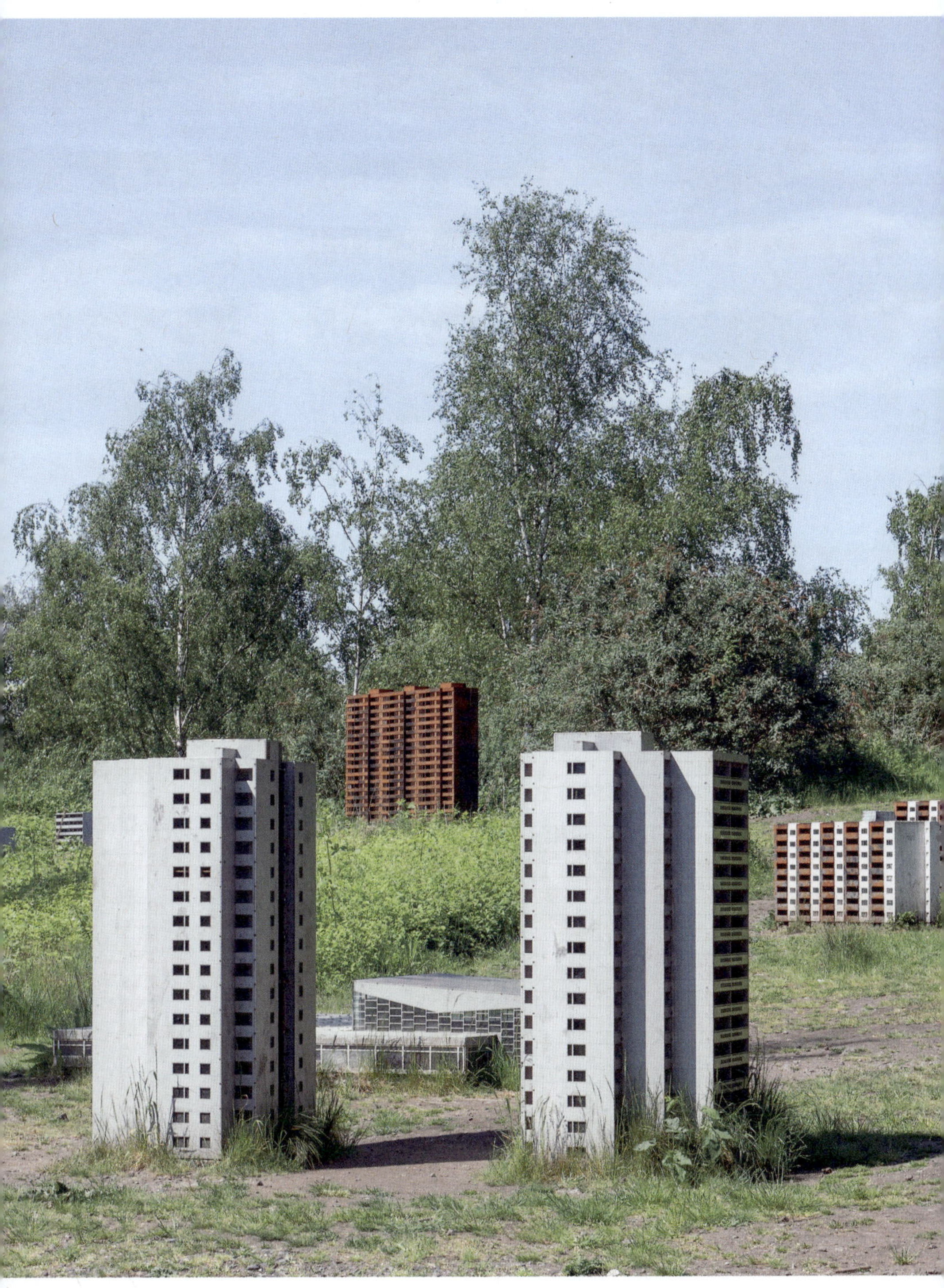

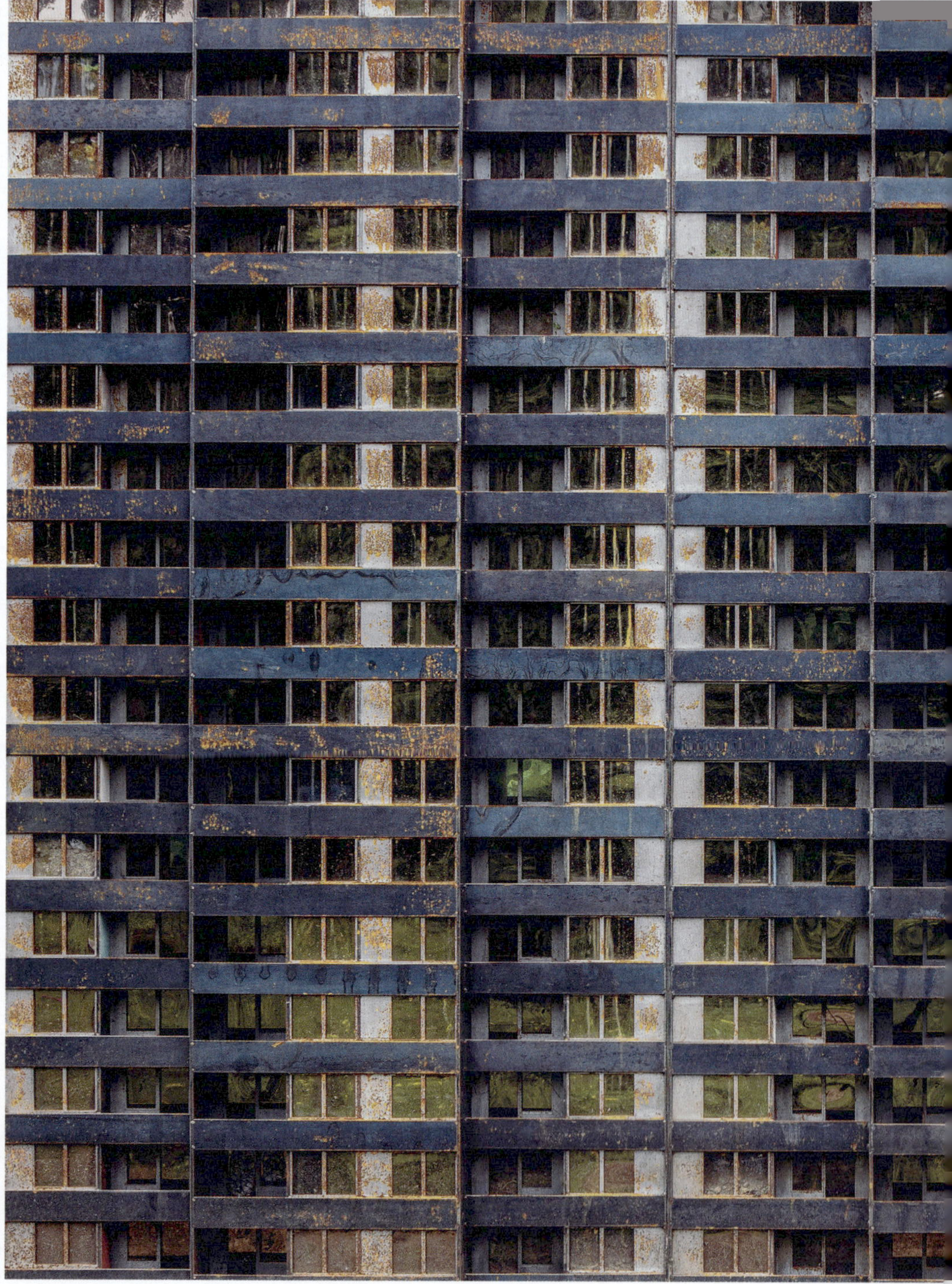

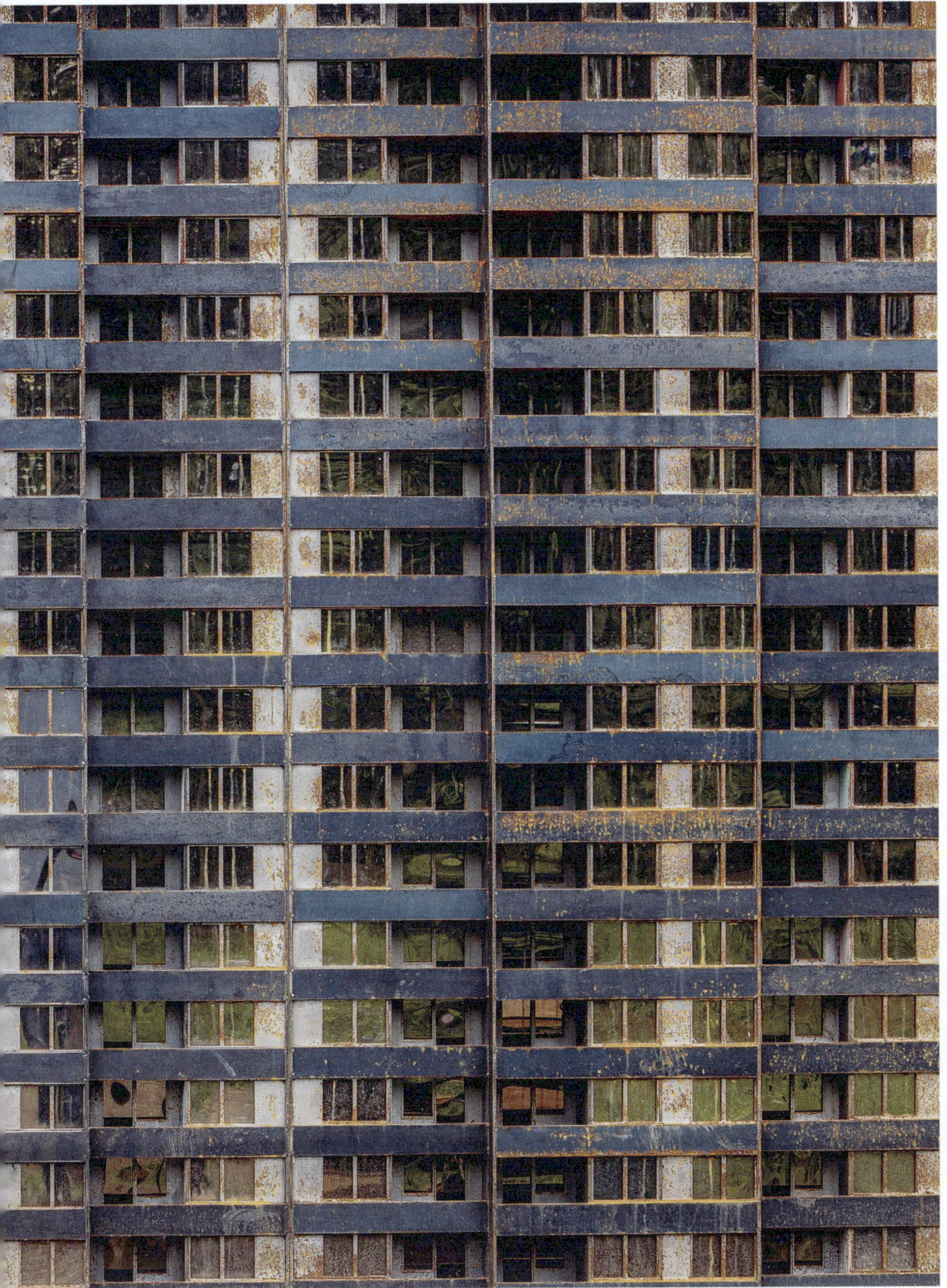

Julius von Bismarck is one of the first artists to have been invited to develop a new work for the Emscherkunstweg [Emscher Art Trail], which was inaugurated in 2019. Together with the artist and architect Marta Dyachenko he conceived the installation *Neustadt* [New Town], which is located on a grassy area in Landscape Park Duisburg-Nord, between the Alter Emscher river, the cycle track «Grüner Pfad» [Green trail] and the A 42 motorway.

Altogether twenty-three sculptures make up a fictive town that has been assembled from 1:25-scale models of various real buildings in the Ruhr region which have been demolished since 2000. The choice of types and functions of building was not based on any rigorous system but followed aesthetic and sculptural criteria and the wish to show a cross-section of local urban architecture.

In addition to a block of flats from Essen dating back to the Gründerzeit period, there is, for instance, a residential complex from a former model estate in Marl built in 1965, while further residential units in a prefab plattenbau style speak of social history in the 1970s. The Paulskirche church in Duisburg or St. Joseph's Church in the Kupferdreh district of Essen, built in 1904 in neo-Gothic style and torn down in 2015, are both examples of the social change that has also taken place within religious congregations. The sculptures of the Volkshochschule [adult education centre] in Essen with its unusual tiered architecture and washed concrete reliefs on the façade, or of the indoor swimming pool in Marl — once celebrated examples of post-war architectural modernity — raise questions as to the relationship between preservation and demolition.

The sculptural installation has been consciously integrated into what appears to be fallow land, yet which in fact was landscaped as part of the *Internationale Bauausstellung (IBA) Emscher Park* [International Building Exhibition Emscher Park] in the 1990s, and thus — in addition to the dramatic shifts in scale — reflects the relationship between nature and culture. *Neustadt* evokes numerous associations and memories, but also prompts us to explore questions about urban planning as well as the environment, which likewise are mirrored on a broader scale in the structural change of the Ruhr region and the Emscher river conversion.

→

As part of the artistic concept, the building sculptures were transported by barge from Berlin to Duisburg.

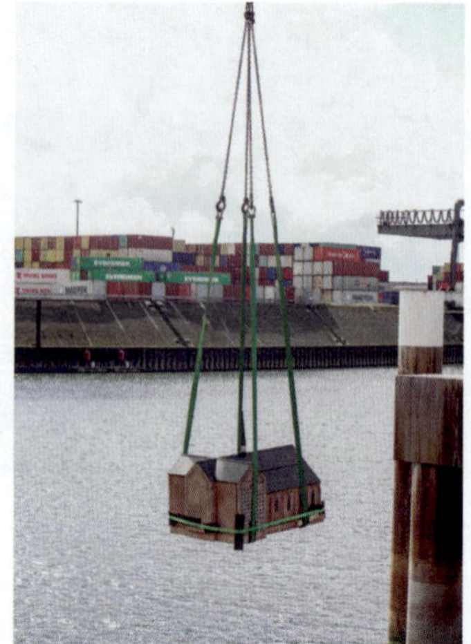

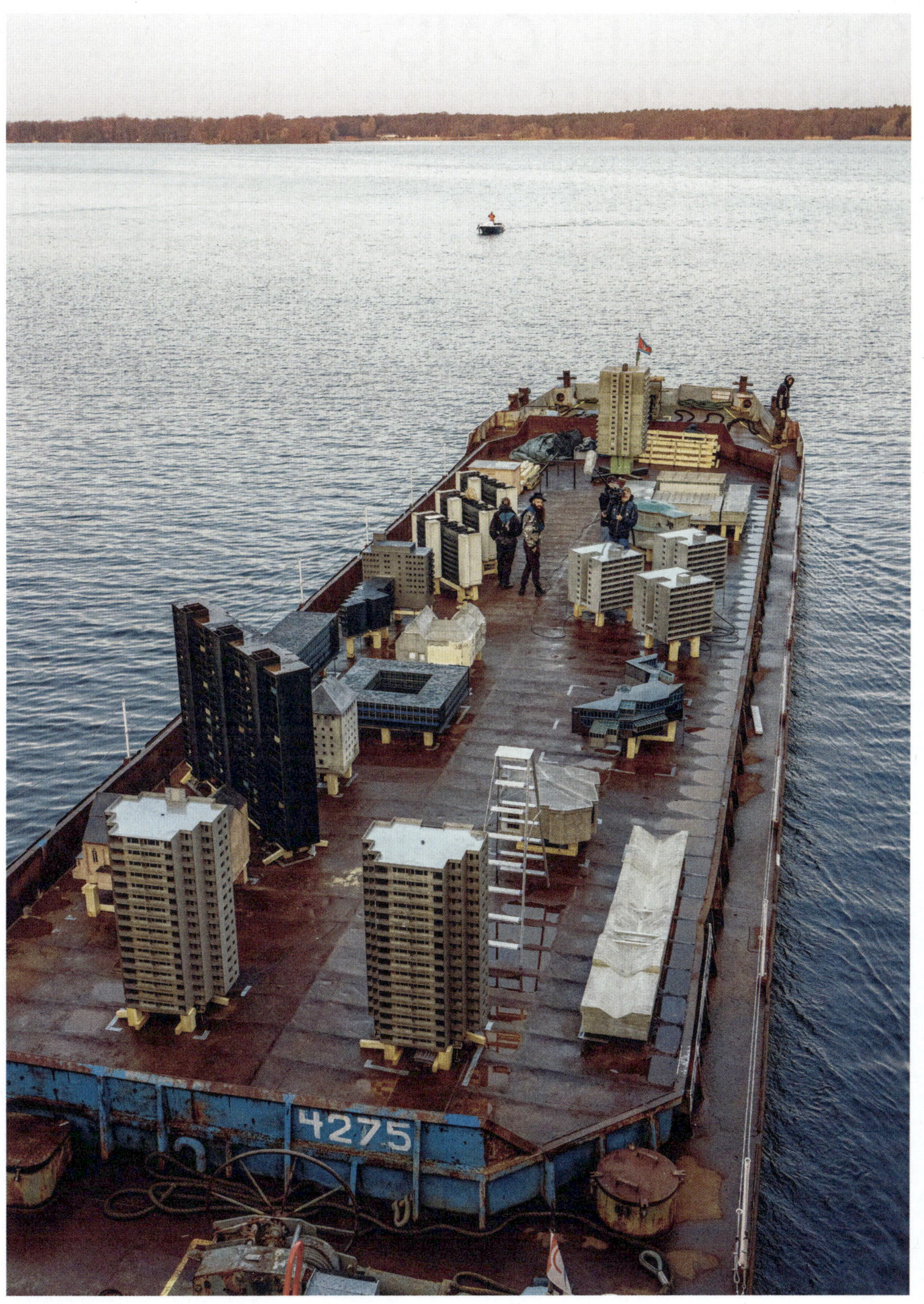

OF SKELETONS AND RUINS

Georg Imdahl
on *Neustadt* from
Julius von Bismarck
with Marta Dyachenko

The new town was built by the old Emscher river, alongside the motorway A 42. Visible in the distance is the silhouette of the Meiderich Steelworks, protected as a historic monument, which was converted into the Landschaftspark Duisburg-Nord [Duisburg-Nord Landscape Park] in the 1990s in the course of the *Internationale Bauausstellung (IBA) Emscher Park* [International Building Exhibition Emscher Park]. This, seemingly, is where the Ruhr region is its truest self, but the surrounding landscape was in fact created within the framework of that same *IBA,* the product of long-term planning. Since 2021, as part of the permanent sculpture trail Emscherkunstweg [Emscher Art Trail], one hill has seen the construction of residential buildings, school buildings, a supermarket, plus churches, swimming pools and administrative buildings. *Neustadt* [New Town] can be reached via two paths and in future is due to become greener — so green, in fact, that it will be completely overrun and even overgrown by vegetation. This is completely intentional: *Neustadt* was designed as a ghost town and will always remain one, as is the aim of the artistic project conceived by Julius von Bismarck and Marta Dyachenko.

As is instantly evident, their «new town» lacks any charm popular architecture might have; residential blocks and towers stoically occupy the impassable terrain, triggering desire for a shift in scale (1:25) as well as all manner of eschatological associations — but also memories of architectures that were doomed at some point in the last decades to disappear from everyday life in the Ruhr region. At the same time, *Neustadt* refrains from the usual clichéd coal industry folklore, easy enough to evoke with mine shafts, chimneys and pit-head frames; this sobriety is not mitigated by the nearby Gustav Knepper power station, which in 2019 was decommissioned and compacted into a crude block. Instead of the Hugo mine and the Victoria colliery, *Neustadt* is an assembly of scattered landmarks from the urban swathes of the mining region that in recent years have fallen victim to «re-building» — the German officialese for demolition. Such as the indoor swimming pool in Marl with its impressive glass roof, demolished in 2016, which was built in 1964 from a design by Heinz Burbaum, Günther Marschall and Hans Joachim Thielcke; or the St. Stephanus church in Essen's Holsterhausen district, a sophisticated ensemble with an imposing rotunda built in the 1930s by Emil Jung — an altogether regrettable loss. The choice of edifices for *Neustadt* was determined by aesthetic and sculptural criteria, based on a concept seeking to represent a cross-section of local urban development in the Ruhr region.

The wrecking ball also gives food for thought in regard to what, locally, were surely rated as the most hated apartment blocks, such as the «White Giant» in Kamp-Lintfort, Marl's «Goliath» and the city residential tower in Bergkamen: with its floors suspended from the core, the high-rise building seemed to ascend from a plinth (similar to Marl town hall by Johannes Hendrik van den Broek and Jacob Bakema, which is currently being restored). In the manner of their assembly here, these sculptures serve as a plea for the conservation of architecture and for greater imagination in all stages of planning, development and adaptive reuse.

In *Neustadt,* the Berlin artists have wisely refrained from any kind of cuteness. This is no vehicle for nostalgia. Rather, the project seeks to negotiate in the here and now the formal and aesthetic options of contemporary sculpture and to question their specific relationship towards the presence. Equally, as the buildings' appearance shows, this is also about the time factor. The edifices are weathering, are nestled among tufts of grass, are rusting, their façades raw, forbidding and rotting. You are no beauty, as Bochum's local pop hero Herbert Grönemeyer might sing to this town; you love yourself, by God, without make-up. But this is the only way it can function as an environment. The houses rise up as brittle, minimalist sculptures made of concrete, glass and steel, are simultaneously shells and ruins; colour occurs only sparingly. This creates distance and affords us the possibility to appreciate buildings, which we would normally encounter from a frog's-eye perspective, as whole objects at a single glance.

In art-historical terms, *Neustadt* can be ascribed to the tradition of the Düsseldorf «model builders» of the 1980s around Thomas Schütte and Ludger Gerdes. Later, the sculptors Rita McBride or Ina Weber also created architectural sculptures for exhibitions, and as early as in the 1960s, an adventure park called Minidomm was opened in the region, a tourist attraction in Ratingen's Breitscheid district containing iconic architecture in miniature format, which included Neuschwanstein Castle, the Leaning Tower of Pisa, the Brussels Atomium and Dortmund's Westfalenhalle. *Neustadt,* on the other hand, assembles signature buildings from everyday life in the Ruhr region and seeks to awaken critical and historical awareness. In it, layers of time overlap, while urbanity and periphery merge. Memory is sparked where one least expects it: on a walk along the promenade.

Neustadt does not indulge in just another celebration of concrete Brutalism. As an abstraction of architecture and the city the project seeks to establish spaces for thought along a broad front. On being invited to participate by Britta Peters, artistic director of Urbane Künste Ruhr [Urban Arts Ruhr], Julius von Bismarck was animated by the razing of Berlin's Palast der Republik [Palace of the Republic], as he explains in conversation, but such treatment of less prominent buildings is equally questionable, and not only in the Ruhr region. Indeed, what does it say about attitudes to architecture and urban development when a vast building is erected, torn down, replaced by something less promising and then, some twenty or thirty years' hence, approved for demolition again? It is these kinds of fundamental questions that *Neustadt* seeks to provoke, without allowing itself to be fobbed off with the conventional excuse that it costs less to build something new than to refurbish — which, below the line, is often not the case.

The two artists point to the «grey energy» that every building consumes from the first instant ground is broken, and to the «38 percent of global carbon dioxide emissions» accounted for by the construction industry. By leaving yesterday's undesirable architecture to its own devices, letting it weather and decay until it is clearly just ugly and needs to be knocked down — does this need be a never-ending cycle? This connection was also highlighted by their performative boat trip on a flat barge that transported the house sculptures from the artists' studio in Berlin down the canal network to Duisburg. On their way west they passed industrial zones on either side, sailing past great heaps of rubble and sand which in their raw state

represent the same materials later to
be used for new construction and, later
still, result from demolition. Aside from
its economic and ecological parameters,
this artistic project in particular quizzes
the scope of ideas for architecture. Why
is there so little aspiration in this country
to create buildings as interesting as the
«White Giant» and «Goliath»? This same
question is being asked by experts such
as Tim Rieniets from the Hannover-based
Institute of Design and Urban Design,
who contributed to the discursive events
supporting *Neustadt.* Rieniets proposes a
«culture of conversion», an «architecture
of change» and cites successful projects
such as the award-winning redevelopment
of the Cité du Grand Parc in Bordeaux
(which also involved the architects
Lacaton & Vassal), the Kleiburg high-rise
block in the Bijlmermeer satellite town in
Amsterdam and the Cosmopolitan in the
former commercial harbour of Brussels.
So why is there so much support for
new construction in this country? One
reason, says Rieniets, lies perhaps in the
capital-intensive construction sector we
have developed here.
        Against this background, Duis-
burg's *Neustadt* serves as a memorial,
but one where people can meet, hang out
and chill. The project will develop in its
own time. This too is an inspiring aspect
of *Neustadt* as art in public space: it is
evolving here as a process and unfurling
its own historicity. ←

193

PLAY_LAND
Apolonija Šušteršič

2013

MATERIAL
Transfigured area, youth centre
with skateboarding track
and playground

ADDRESS
Jugend- und Kulturzentrum
emscherdamm
Flugstraße 1
46147 Oberhausen

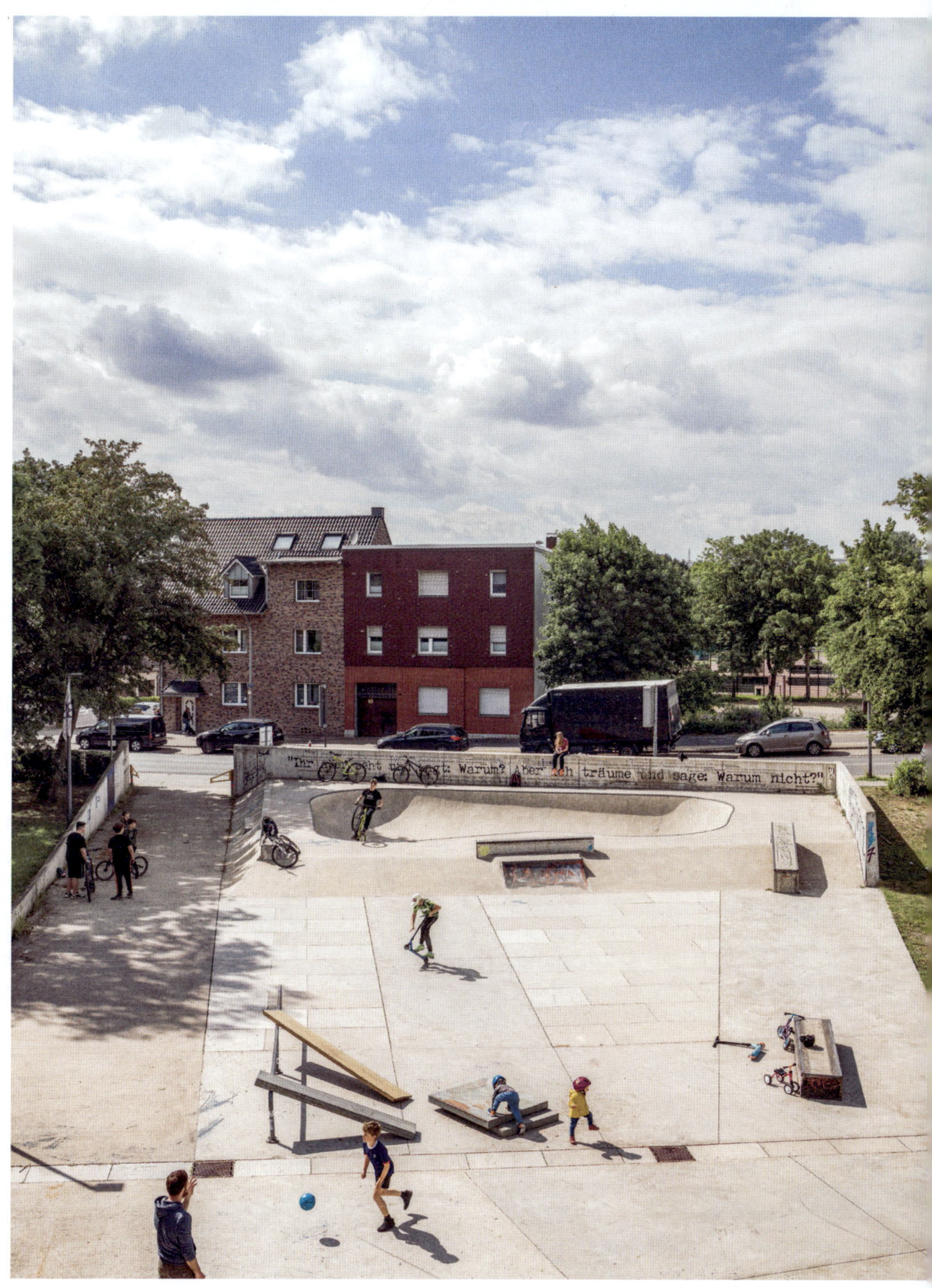

195

The construction of the new underground Emscher wastewater canal in 2013 required relocating the youth club emscherdamm and its playground from their previous location in the Holten district of Oberhausen to a new home on the nearby site of a former recreation ground and the adjacent skate spot. After two project proposals by other architects had already been turned down, artist and architect Apolonija Šušteršič was asked to develop a design for the new facility as part of the 2013 *Emscherkunst* exhibition.

The new locale was intended above all to meet the needs of young users and local residents. In a multi-stage process that started in 2011, parallel to the design for a new building Šušteršič also conceived a participatory pro-gramme. In a series of workshops and discussions children and young people from the neighbourhood, together with their parents, were incorporated into the planning, especially regarding the outdoor site. The penultimate stage of the conversion was a building camp involving children and young people during the period of the *Emscherkunst* exhibition. All the ideas that had been previously contributed and discussed were given expression with various artistic and handicraft techniques.

The result meets the diverse requirements for use and at the same time forms a single entity: the entire facility is screened from the residential area by a green hill-like earth mound. Housed within this hillock is a youth centre with a cafeteria section, recrea-tional areas and a bike repair workshop. The clearly structured façade made up of concrete slabs snakes out towards the road and leads to a 600-square-metre skateboard park. Abutting the rear of the building is a recreation ground that echoes the nearby Emscher wastewater canal in the form of sections of canal pipe that can be played in and around, and are decorated with colourful stencilled graffiti.

The entire project *PLAY_LAND* was completed by late 2013 in collaboration with various specialists and companies.

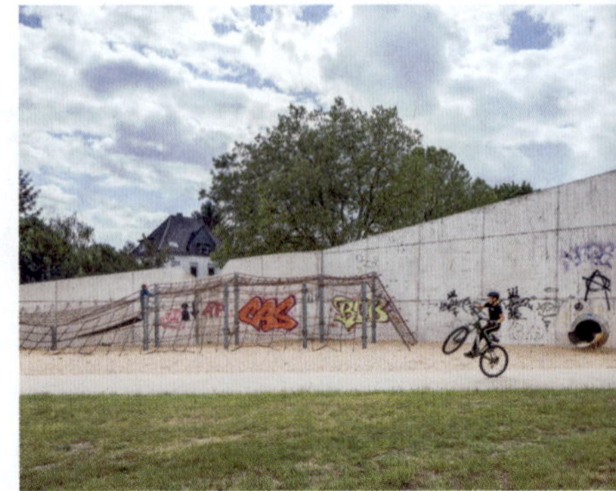

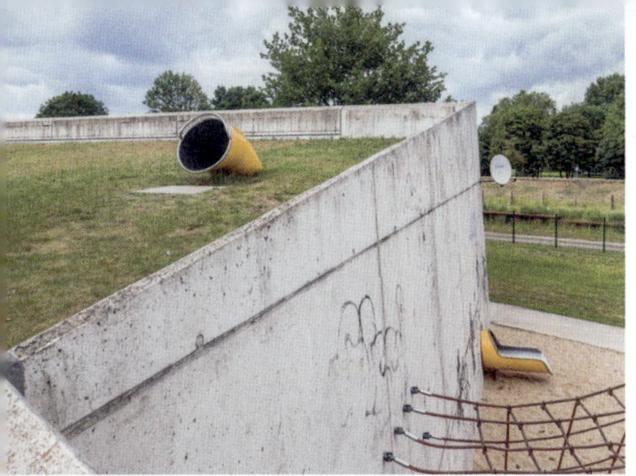

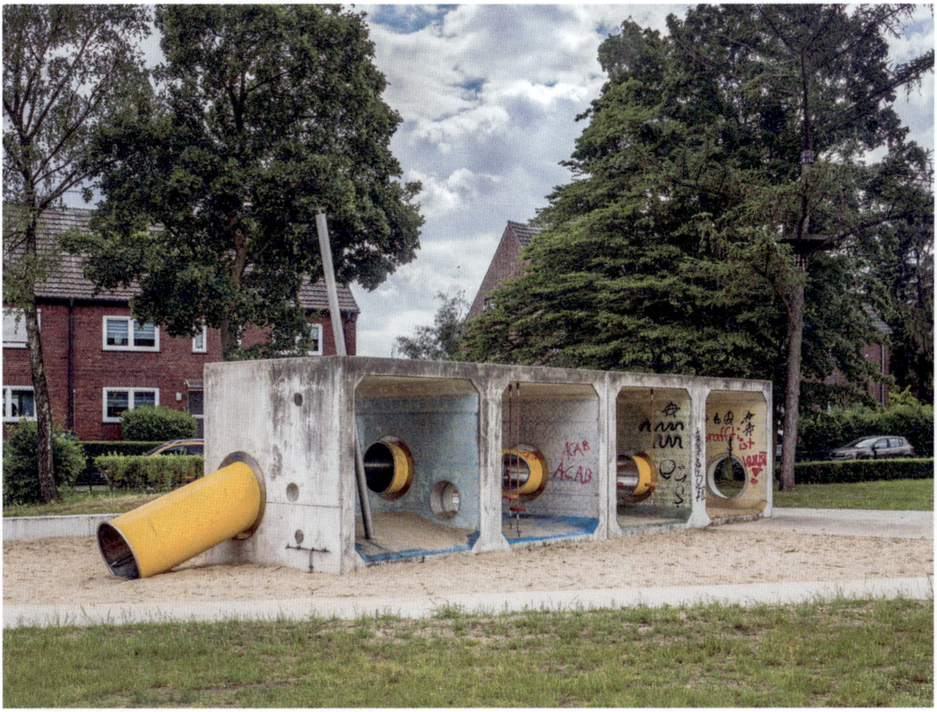

EMSCHER FOLLY
Nicole Wermers

2022

MATERIAL
Concrete foundation,
stainless steel tube,
modified bicycles

ADDRESS
Kläranlage Duisburg-Alte Emscher
Alsumer Straße 215
47166 Duisburg

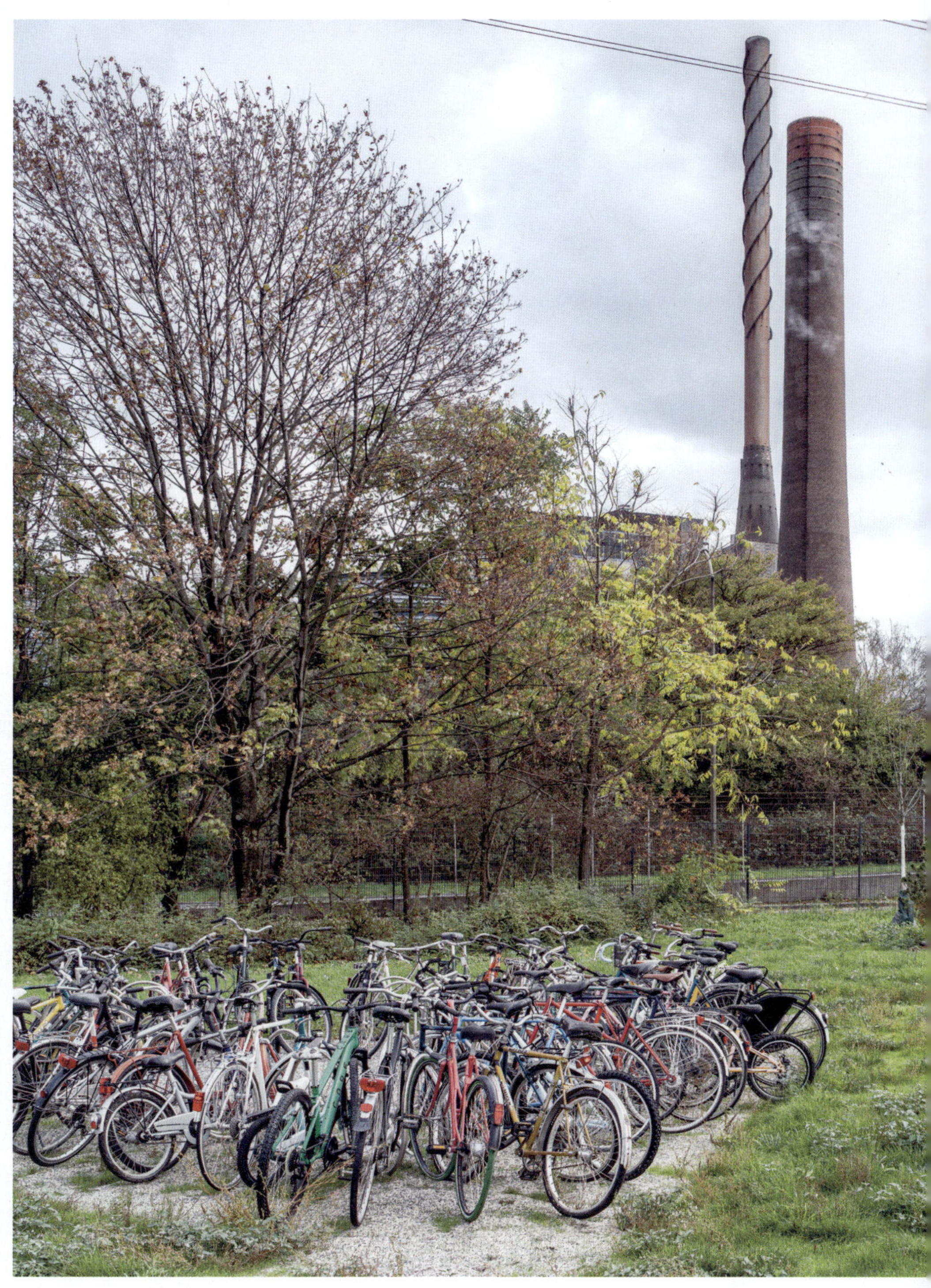

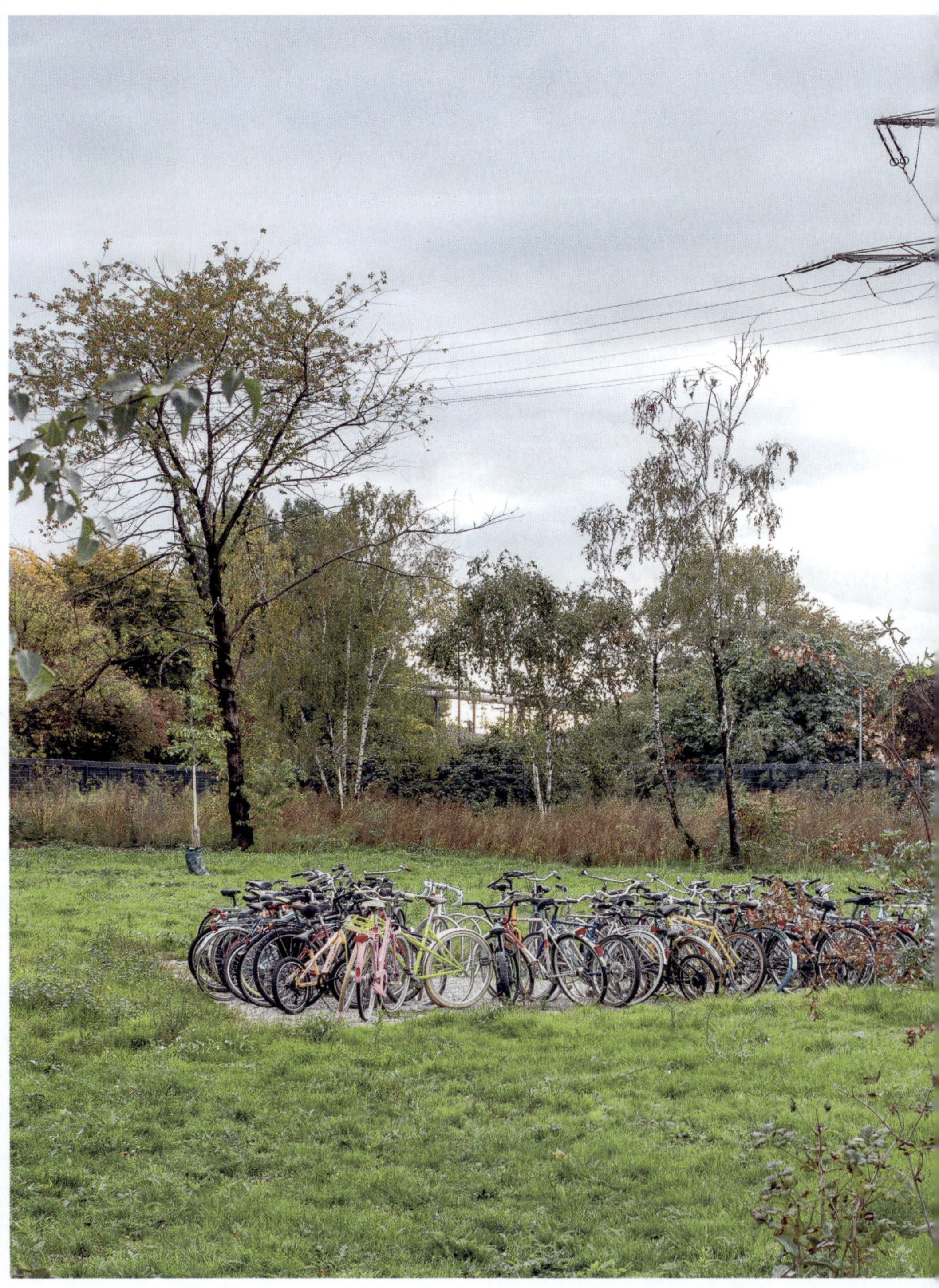

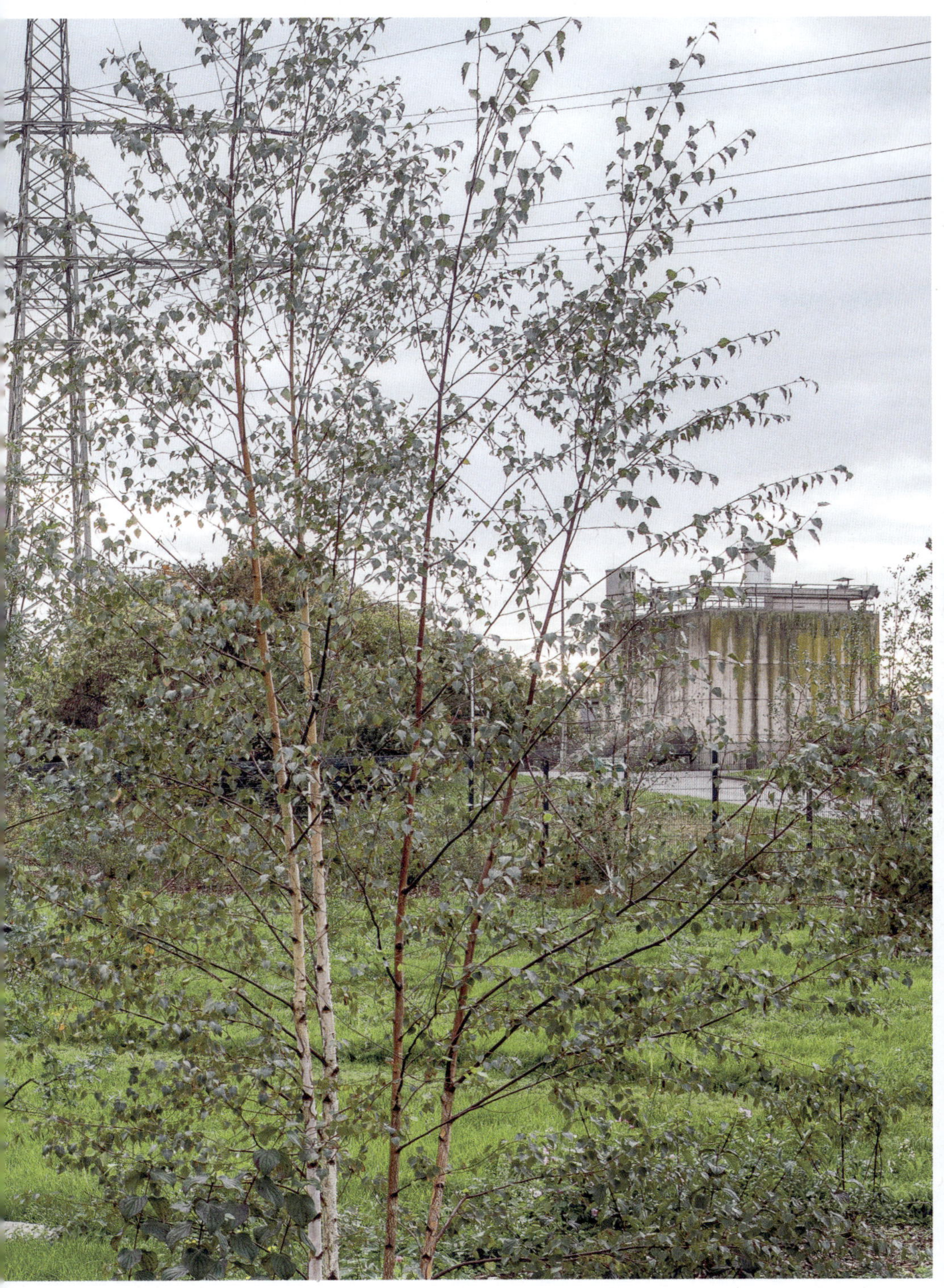

↓

From the cycle path on the Rhine dyke,
one overlooks the sewage treatment plant
with the Bruckhausen ironworks in the
background.

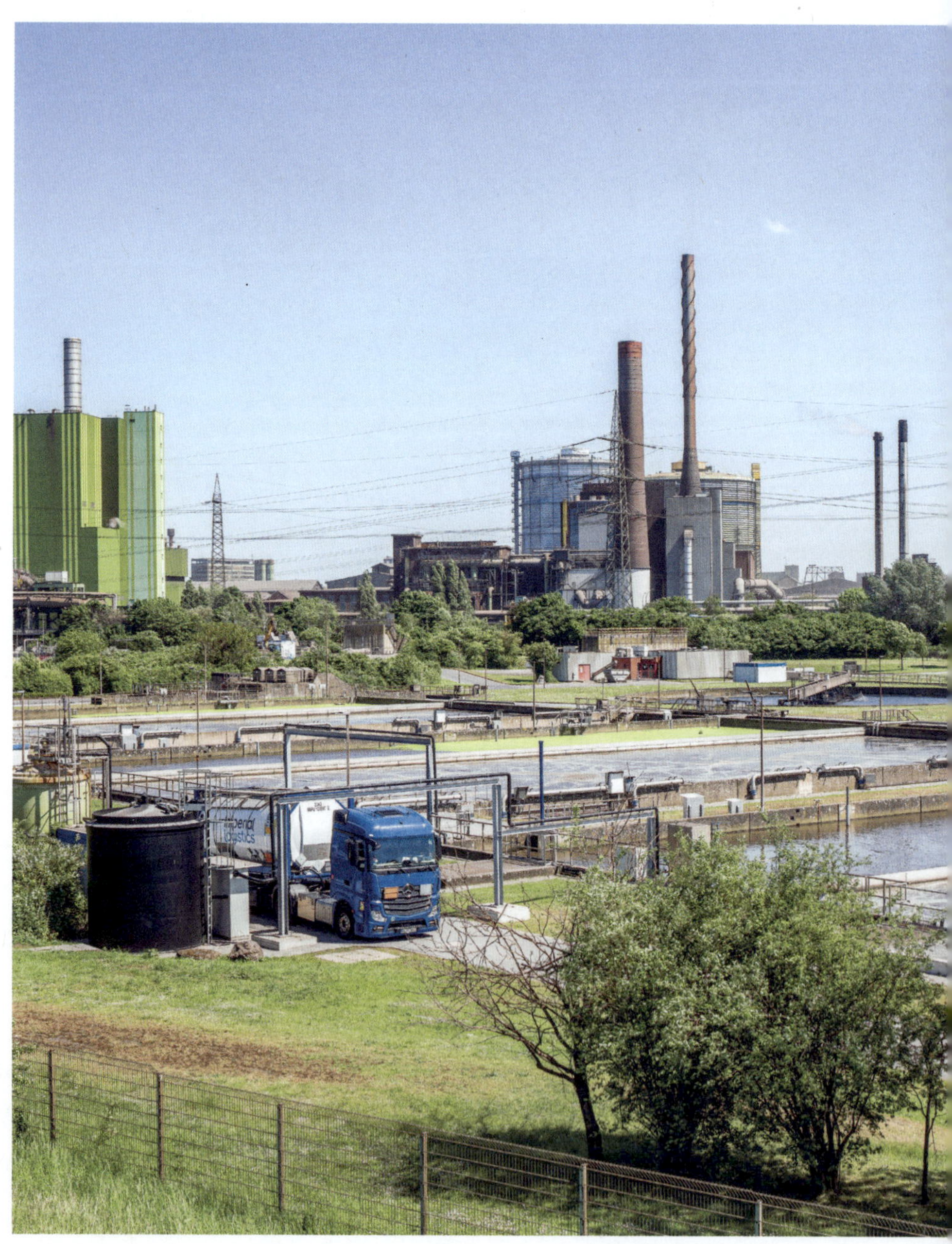

202

The sculpture *Emscher Folly* is located in an open space between the Duisburg Alte Emscher wastewater treatment plant, the Bruckhausen steelworks by the Alter Emscher river and the Alsumer Berg slag heap. Nearby is where the Emscher originally flowed into the Rhine.

Here, artist Nicole Wermers has welded dozens of bicycles onto a steel structure to create a triangular sculptural form. Her installation transfers an image familiar from urban contexts to an inhospitable locale defined by industrial production — a scenario also referenced in the work's title, *Folly.* Folly is the name given to a type of decorative architecture in eighteenth-century European garden and landscape design. Follies are ornamental, often eccentric edifices that suggest a function, but are in general without purpose. At the same time, Wermers's sculpture refers to the artificiality of a landscape that has been extensively shaped by human activity such as the Emscher region. Stripped of their intended purpose, the design of the bikes is all the more striking. Their being permanently welded to the steel tube base creates an aesthetic of sudden standstill and dramatic compaction.

In much of her work the London-based artist explores moments and zones of transition in public space. The focus of her sculptural and photographic works lies particularly on architectural threshold situations, but also on their materiality, such as different kinds of floor surfacing. Equally significant are gestures and sculptural codes that we have learned to intuitively understand and whose requirements we generally fulfil. For Wermers, the moment of locking a bicycle to a public bicycle stand is one such moment: bike racks are symbols of our present-day mobile imperative, while at the same time prescribing a structuring order. The *Emscher Folly* conserves this polarity, thereby taking it to absurd lengths.

ORNAMENTAL CONSTRUCTION AT THE SEWAGE PLANT

Vanessa Joan Müller
on *Emscher Folly*
by Nicole Wermers

Folly is the name given to an eccentric ornamental building in eighteenth-century European, and especially British garden and landscape architecture, that is distinguished by its unusual idea or extravagant design. Such buildings seek to stand out and almost provocatively display their lack of functional use. Likewise, their aesthetic correspondence to their surroundings is challengingly ambivalent, in contrast to decorative architecture which blends in harmoniously with its environment. In gardens — hence far from the more functionally defined sphere of urban life — follies experiment with calculated breaches of the rules of social and architectural norms, celebrating capricious abandon by freely playing with historical forms.[01] With formal designs shifting between sculptural and architectural appearance, follies should then be read primarily as symbolic installations whose significance derives primarily from the deviation from or meaningful displacement of prevailing typologies.

Nicole Wermers's *Emscher Folly,* with its deliberate and visible dislocation of form and function, its disparate incorporation within an industrially defined site and its artful play with proportions and material, quotes key aspects of garden stage-setting subsumed under the term «folly». The work consists of a sculptural ensemble reminiscent of a bicycle stand, but ostentatiously dysfunctional: over fifty bicycles have been welded to a metal structure that at first sight resembles what would seem to be a familiar object in an urban context, but that has been installed in the wrong place. Yet the way the numerous bicycles have been lined up along the bike rack, whose evenly wave-shaped design is vaguely reminiscent of classic tubular furniture, is anything but careful. This welded storage apparatus, which hardly tallies with the notion of short-term parking, clearly contradicts the concept of a bicycle parking facility in public space. However, it is precisely this deviation, subversion and disruption that animate reflection on the nature of such street furniture and the actions usually associated with it. Bicycle stands are there to park bikes and to chain them up as theft-proof as possible. As a symbol of contemporary mobility, the bicycle rack stands for structure and order. Situated in this place where there is no call for people to gather in numbers, nor any real need to secure a bicycle against theft, the welding together of bikes turns the essentially temporary moment of locking up into a state of permanence. Here, the mobility integral to cycling is not simply postponed, but enduringly suspended. Even the invitation to become active emanating from a regular bicycle stand comes to nothing. What the viewer encounters instead is an image of petrified compression, more a barricade than an ordering element. Furthermore, most of the bikes are pointing inwards, directed at a stage-like, yet inaccessible space lodged between them. The emptiness and inapproachability of this interior space defined within the triangular shape of the sculpture conclusively establishes the surreal extravagance of these out-of-place bicycles.

Wermers's works often make reference to architectural elements and everyday objects typical of city landscapes — functional but decoratively softened designs that appear as accessories to the urban. The emotional impact generated by the detailed design of public space and the functional design of the objects within it also strikes a chord in these works. Her sculptures in particular address everyday design that consciously or unconsciously shapes, regulates or regiments our interaction with urban space. As utilitarian things with a clear purpose, they control our movements and behaviour in the public sphere and the way these transition into more private domains: doormats, ashtrays in outdoor spaces, awnings, baby changing tables in restaurant toilets—or indeed bicycle racks.

An alienation effect arises on being transferred into the institutional context of art, where things are deprived of their function, but also with shifting proportions and forms, materials and intentions. Wermers explores and highlights decorative aspects by stripping the objects of their utility value, exposing the genealogies of design and by focussing on the sculptural dimensions within the mundane. Hers is an elaborate play on syntax, semantics and materiality. Paradoxically, however, in her emphasis on form, the gestures that were originally linked to the object and its attendant affects are brought clearly to the fore. Our everyday performative ritual with the object might have been suspended, causing the design invested in its programmatic functionality to evaporate into pure ornament, yet the appellative character of wanting-to-be-used still remains. In this manner, things whose design in everyday life often persist below the threshold of active perception are transformed by Nicole Wermers into markedly aesthetic objects that have forfeited their assigned context. Their functional forms, however, return as «disengaged mannerisms»[02] that address us directly as subjects.

The sculpture *Emscher Folly* transfers an image familiar to us from urban surroundings to a site that serves as a visibly contrasting backdrop. Wermers's artificial assembly of bicycles mounted into the modernistically styled frame clearly stands out on the grounds of the Duisburg Alte Emscher wastewater treatment plant, situated between the Bruckhausen iron- and steelworks and the Alsumer Berg slag heap.

But the term «artificial» — as highlighted by the reference to the historical typology of the folly — also applies to the industrially exploited Emscher region, which today has been largely redesigned as a near-natural landscape which is increasingly used for leisure and local recreation. As a landscape it could be considered the post-industrial equivalent of the designed nature of the eighteenth century, hence an ideal location for a folly as a pertinently positioned *point de vue.* Through it — and this too is one of the folly's historical characteristics — viewers are not only invited to reflect on the meaning of architecture and design, as well as their suitable form, but they are also virtually compelled by the sculpture's unorthodox form to include themselves in the equation.[03] ←

01 See Matthias Noell, «Follies, Enten und andere Verrückt- heiten — Anmerkungen zu einer Typologie der exzentrischen Dinge», in *Fiasco — ma non troppo: vom Designfehler zum Fehler- design,* ed. Matthias Goetz and Maike Fraas (Basel, 2014), pp. 315—29.
02 See Kerstin Stakemeier, «Keine Distanz», in *Nicole Wermers: Women Between Buildings*, exh. cat. Kunstverein in Hamburg (Hamburg, 2018), p. 32.
03 Noell, «Follies» (see note 1), p. 317.

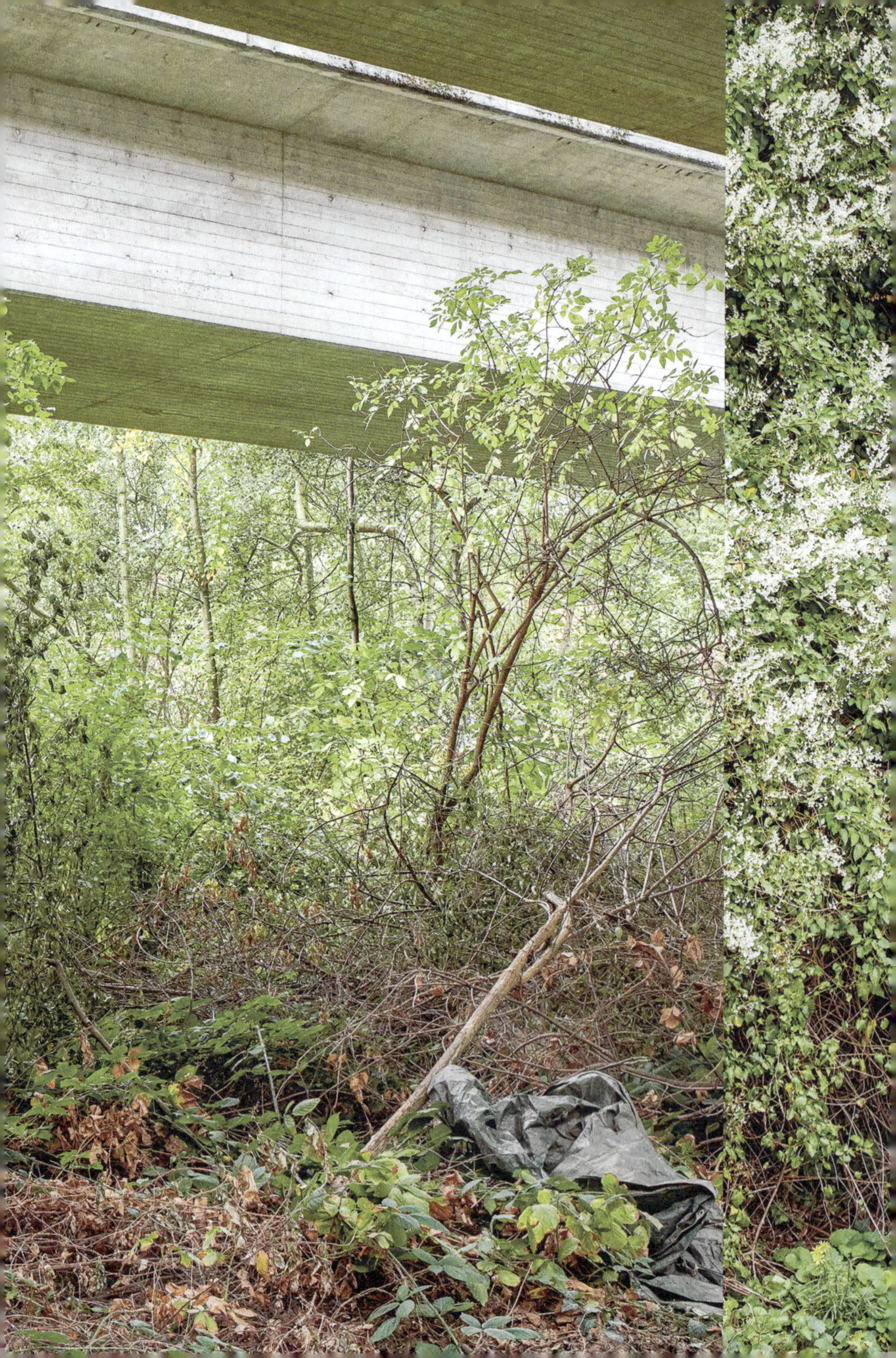

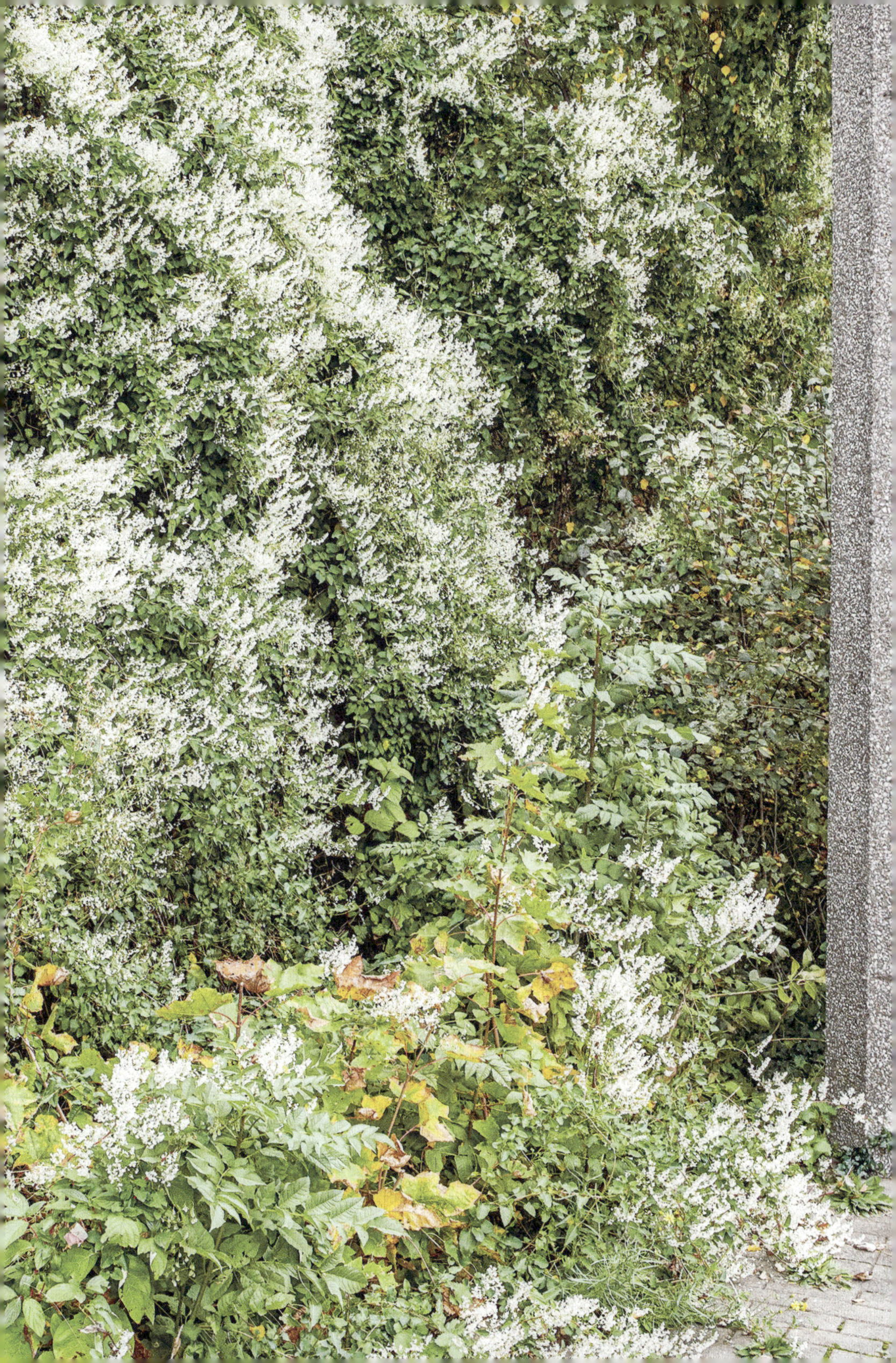

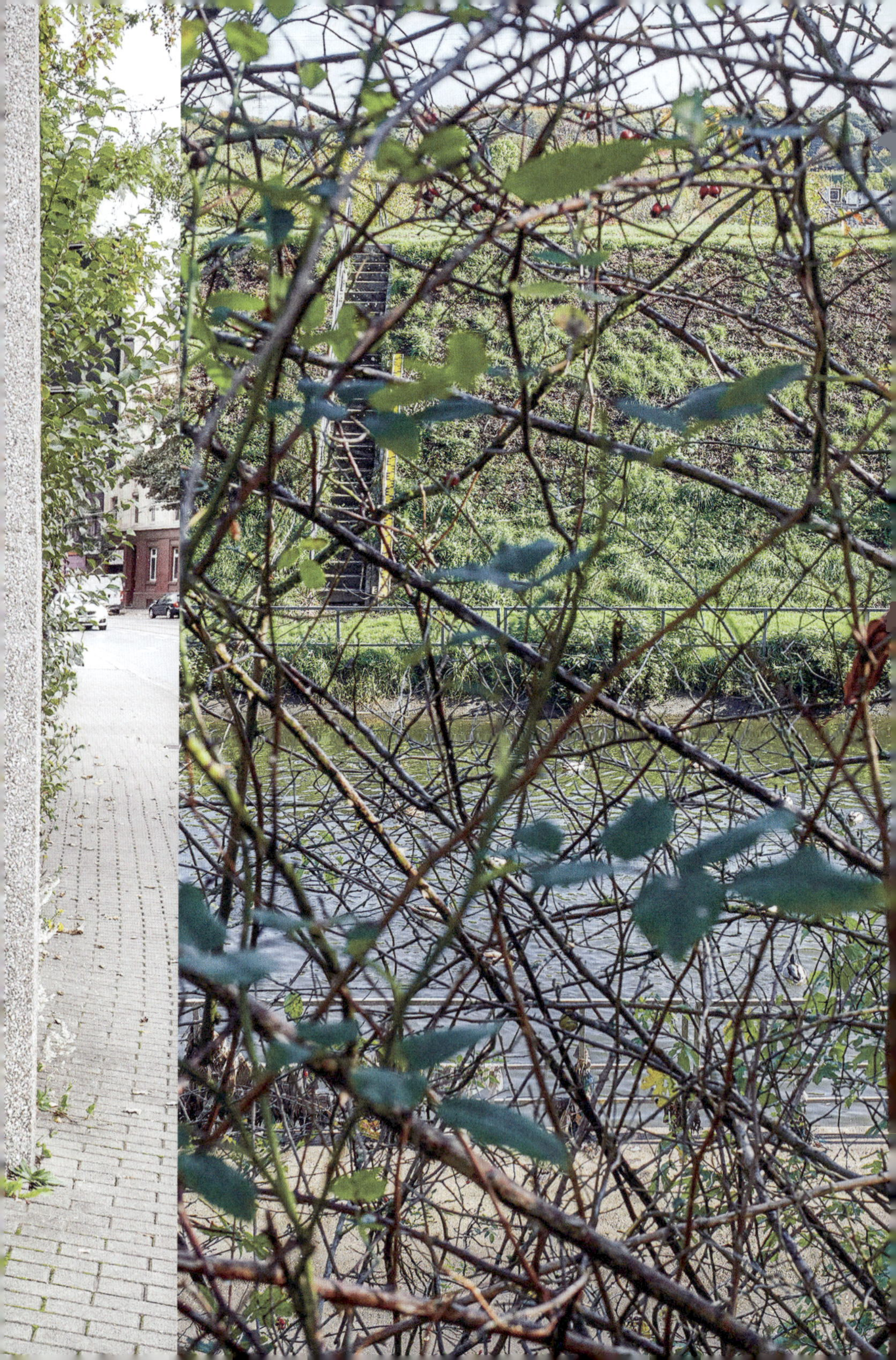

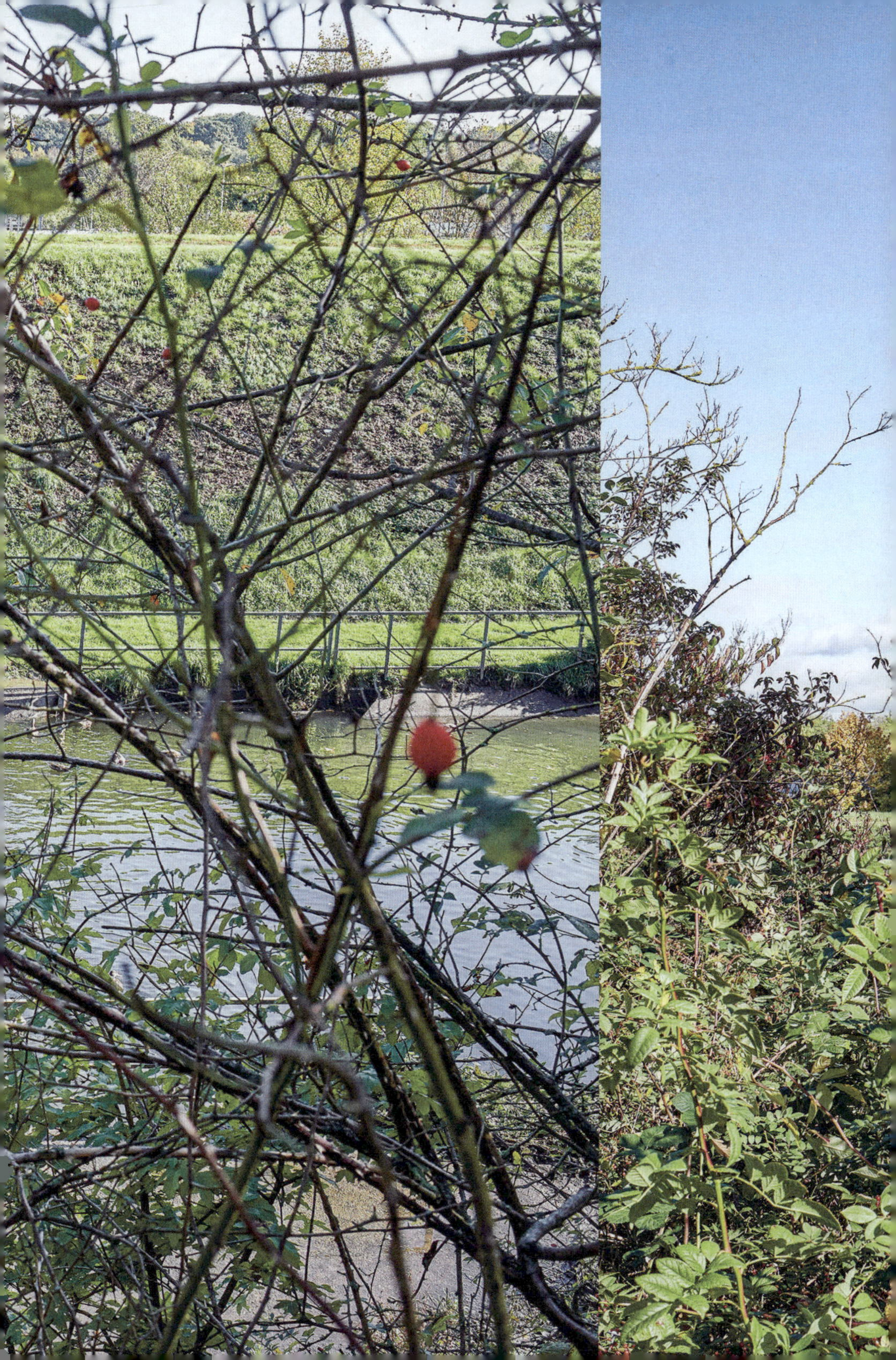

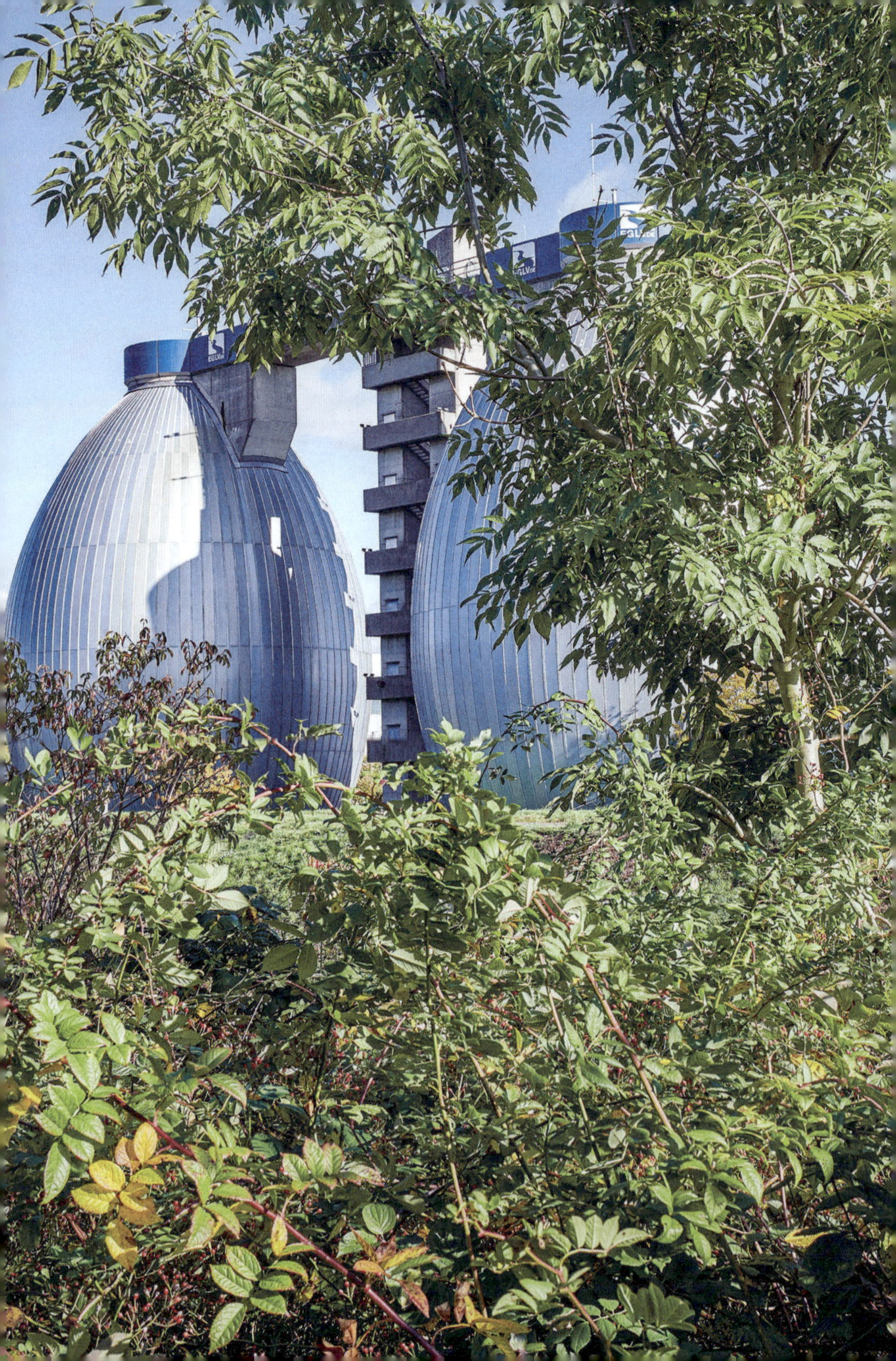

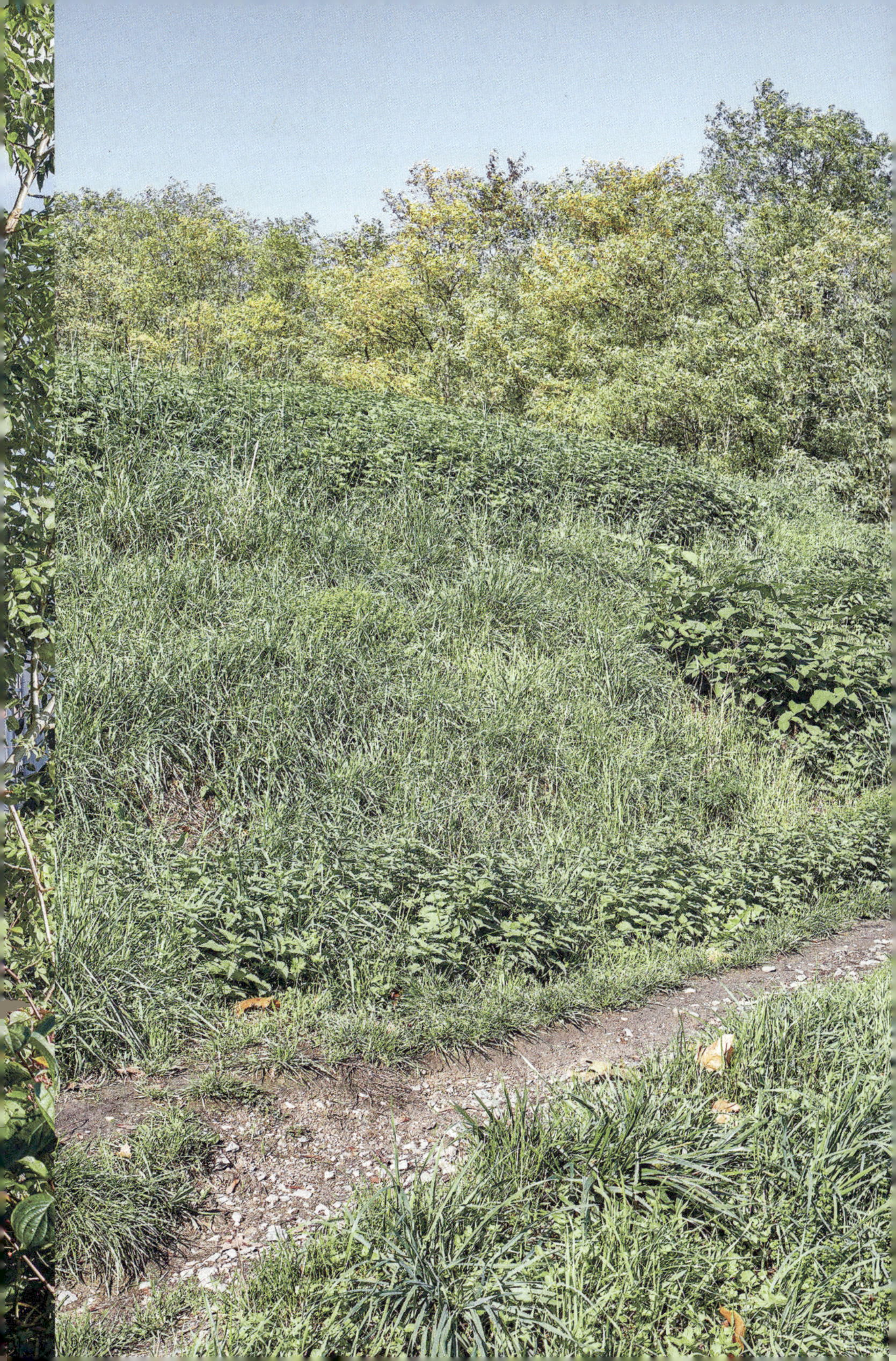

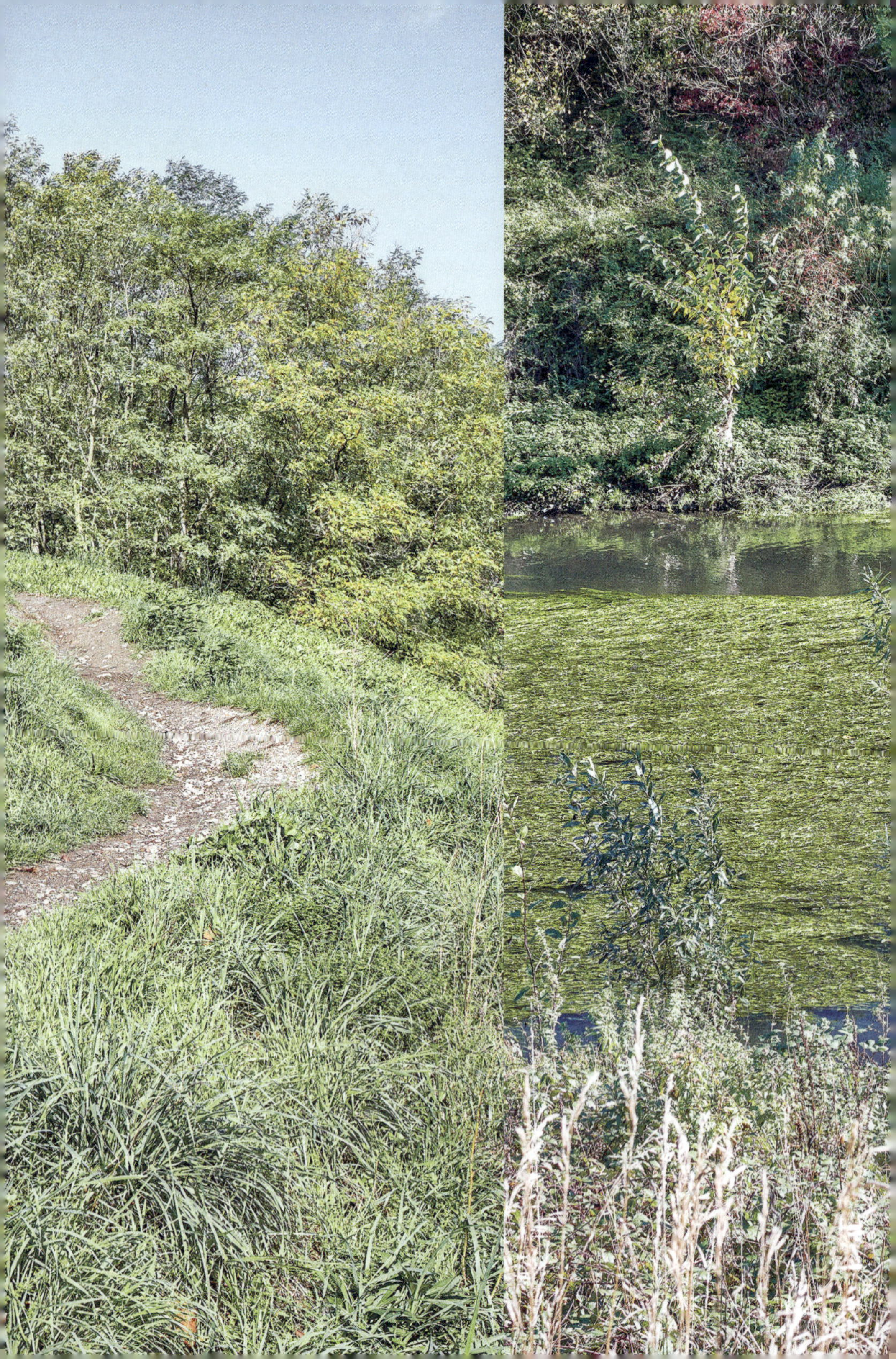

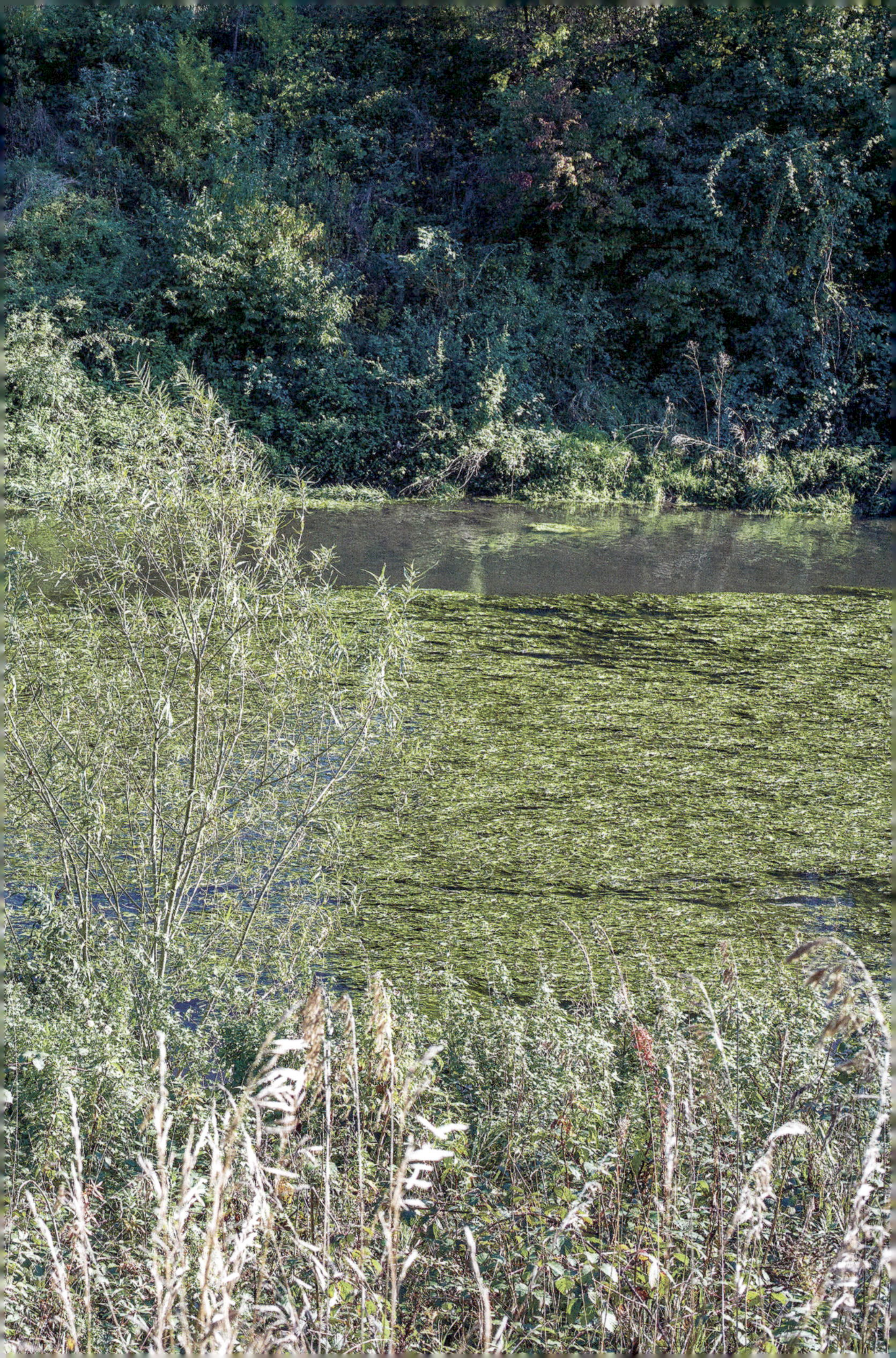

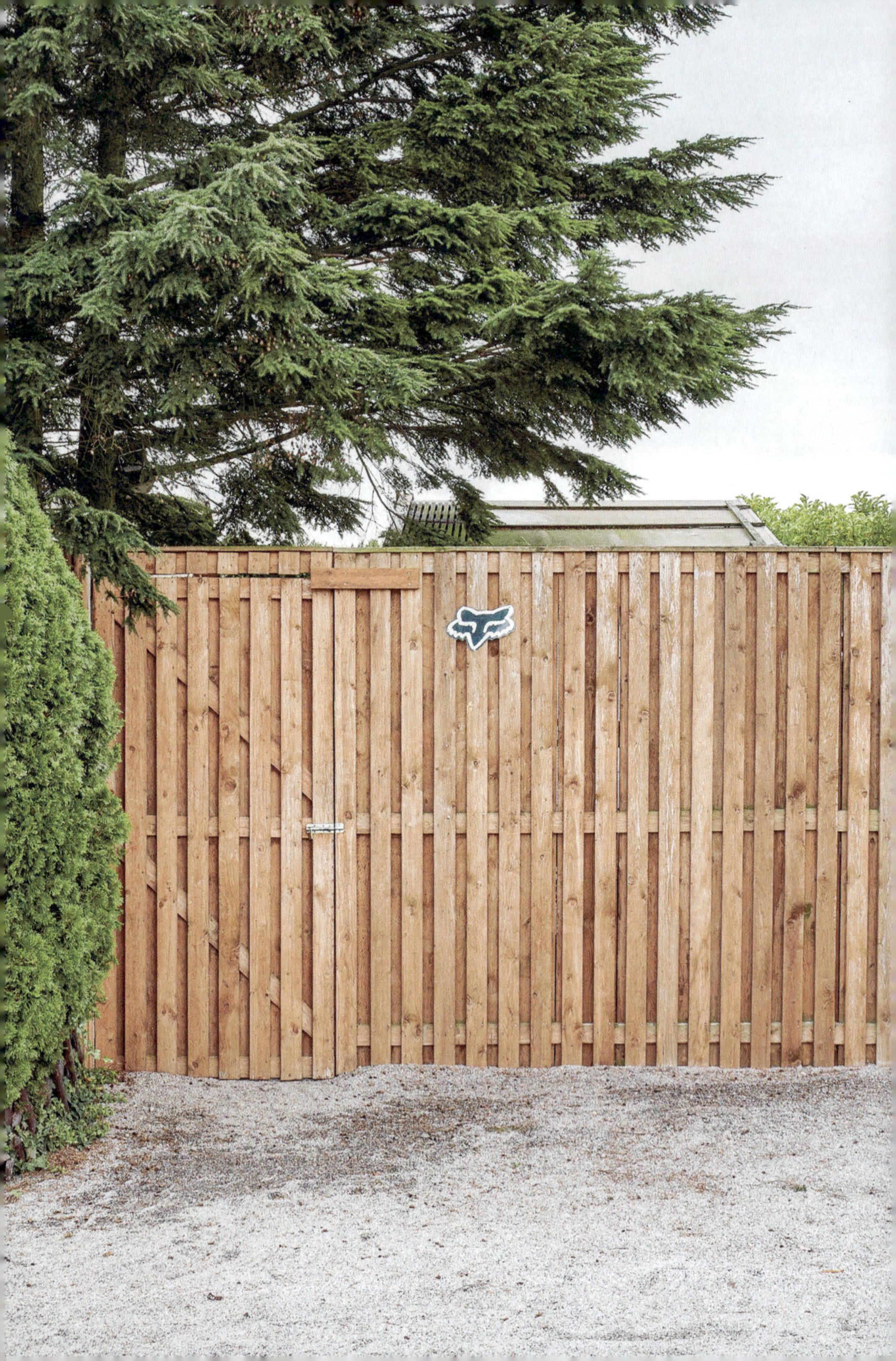

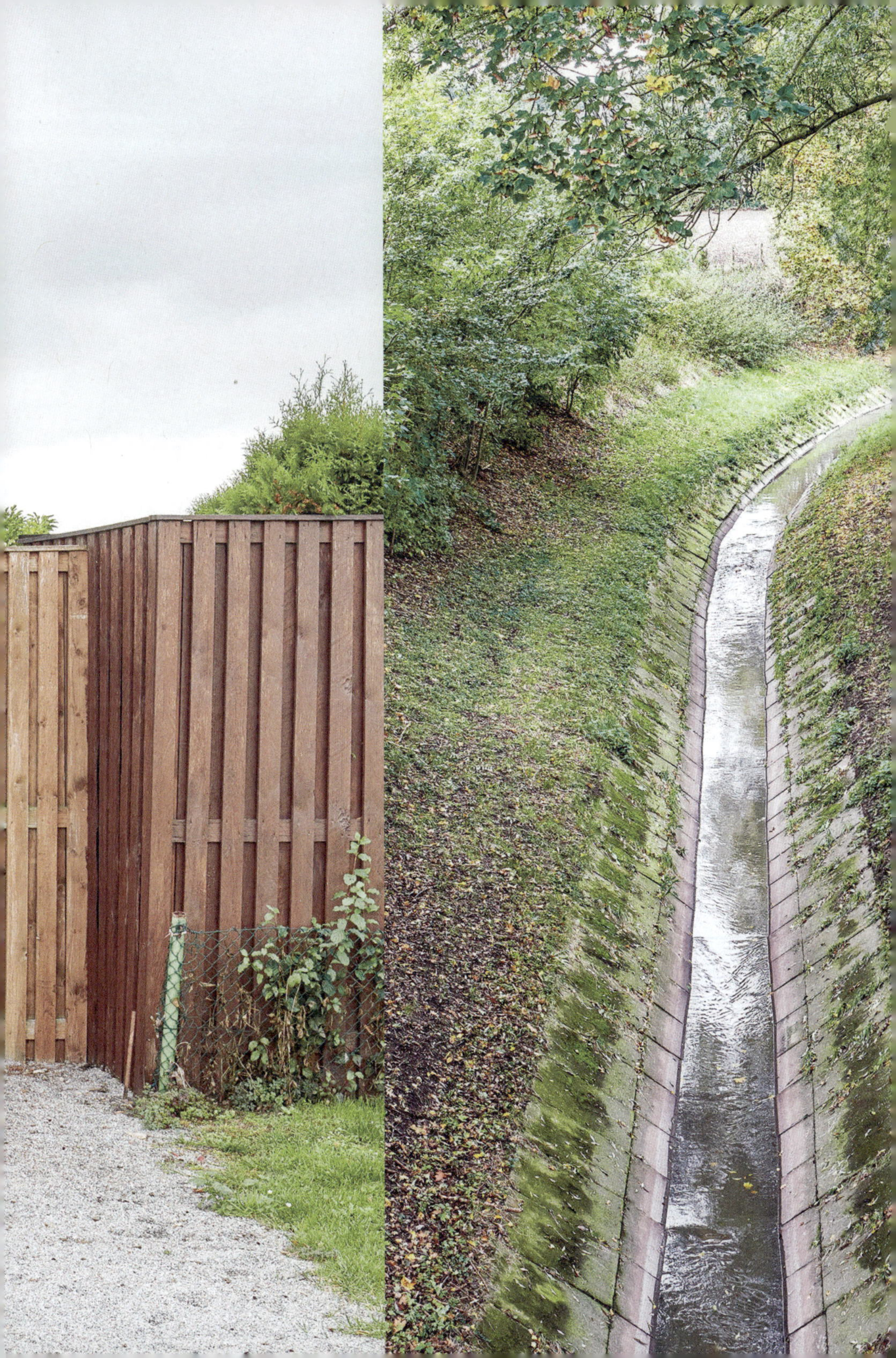

HUBS: THE EMSCHER KUNSTWEG AS A NEW LAYER OF INDUSTRIAL CULTURE

Jana Golombek

«I wanted to show that the entire Ruhr region can be fully transformed, because we are transforming it anyway. The entire river needs to evaporate, the entire river needs to turn into clouds.»[01]

Artist Reiner Maria Matysik's programmatic statement about his temporary artwork *Fluss wird Wolke* [River Becomes Cloud] from the 2013 *Emscherkunst* exhibition refers to the role that is frequently conceived for art during processes of transformation. It should turn everything on its head, provide new inspiration and pave the way to the future. In the process, it often begins as a tool and an element of planning processes and only then develops a life of its own. But what does this life of its own look like, what happens after the initial «unsettling» it triggers?

UPHEAVALS

At the time, the Emscher turned into clouds: the transformative artwork was located at the mouth of the river, where it flows into the Rhine near Dinslaken. Ten years later, the Emscher has not evaporated, but it has disappeared from the location of the artwork at the time. Its mouth has moved 500 metres to the north and no longer consists of a functional drop structure, but is a natural river delta that was flooded in November 2022 in a ceremonial act. Just two months earlier, the official conclusion of the Emscher restoration was celebrated. After thirty years of restoration, the Emscher is now free of sewage and its structural transformation has been completed, transforming what was once «the sewer of the Ruhr Region» into the «blue miracle».

But what remains to be completed is the river's investment with value on a narrative level and its new positioning within a region in transformation. *Emscherkunst* [Emscher Art] is a decisive element not only in the narrative reconstruction of the river, but also in preserving its history. It has accompanied the transformation of the Emscher system since 2010, initially as a temporary exhibition format for the year of Ruhr Region as European Capital of Culture, then expanded to a triennial in 2013 and 2016. As of 2019, it was transformwed into a permanent public art collection for the region, the Emscherkunstweg [Emscher Art Trail]. *Emscherkunst* itself underwent a dual transformation over the past years: along the shores of the Emscher, it no longer interprets and comments on the transformation of the river, but on the river's new function. As part of the Ruhr Region Memorial Landscape, consisting not only of monuments, artworks and buildings, but also immaterial memorial sites,[02] it has a greater impact on the sites of the respective artworks and the region around it. *Emscherkunst* is establishing a new network: the Emscherkunstweg with the Emscher as its backbone. It is time to define this location with an eye towards mythical origins, artistic reference points from prior historical layers[03] and current points of departure.

(NEW) MYTHS

The decline of bituminous coal mining made possible and required the second phase of the restoration of the Emscher; the pilot project of this second phase of restoration was the renaturation of Dellwiger Stream. In 1981, not far from Zeche Zollern [Zollern Colliery], a symbol of the transition from industry to industrial culture, a test run began for the restoration of the Emscher system. But a few years passed until *Internationale Bauausstellung (IBA) Emscher Park*

[International Building Exhibition Emscher Park] provided the decisive impulse to actually begin with the restoration and for an orchestrated public presentation intended to generate an emotional attachment to the plan among local residents. In the process of the narrative (re)construction of the Emscher, the planners profited from their experience and preliminary work for the IBA, which drove the transformation of the region's image in the eyes of the outside world and helped to generate a sense of local identity. It was able to develop «industrial culture» and «industrial nature» as central elements of a Ruhr regional identity, using the historical culture[04] of the region strategically and as a basis for further development.

The point of departure consisted of analyses from a circle of experts that first identified a «lack of legend formation» as a weak point that needed to be rectified, developing a «Masterplan for Visits to the Area» in 1997.[05] The Emscher, too, needed its own history in order to develop new myths. Thus, the Emschergenossenschaft [Emscher Cooperative] pursued the river's «rediscovery» and folklorification from early on. With the 1993 book *Die Emscher: Geschichte und Geschichten einer Flusslandschaft* [The Emscher: History and Stories about a River Landscape], Herbert Kurowski provided a historical overview with help of the Emschergenossenschaft[06] that «still today has great impact in terms of the politics of memory».[07] The volume *Emschervertellekes: Eine Region und ihr Fluss* [Emscher Narratives: A Region and its River],[08] the product of a joint call for contributions issued by the WAZ (Westfälische Allgemeine Zeitung) and Emschergenossenschaft, further helped to anchor the project in the regional historical culture. It collected personal memories, myths and songs as well as additional elements to contribute to the «establishment of a new myth of the Ruhr region».[09] And the book begins with an emotionally charged preface: «Whoever thinks the Ruhr region has lost its power, no longer capable of great things, should look at the Emscher that already is beginning to meander.»[10]

The dominant negative image of the Emscher as «basin of excrement» or «highway for faecal matter» provided a promising basis for a «phoenix from the ashes» narrative. On a material layer, the maintenance of the monuments of the industrial Emscher, such as the Emscher-Mündungsbauwerk [Emscher estuary structure], the sewage treatment plant at Bottrop-Ebel, today's BernePark, or several concrete shells from the old canals for the river, expanded the agenda in terms of memorial policy. Both the *Masterplan Emscher Landschaftspark* 2010,[11] as well as the *Masterplan Emscher-Zukunft*[12] took up these offers of identity and added to them: the new Emscher became the «spine» and Emscher Landschaftspark the «fitting spatial framework for the generation project of restoring the Emscher».[13] «Pride in our own history»[14] played an important role, together with art, which was to serve in part as a «transformer and source of commentary and inspiration».[15]

LAYERINGS

These demands made of art to provide a format for a gentle structural transformation were not new. The artistic approach had already proved useful as a tool that provided identity in the Ruhr region and was closely interwoven with the historical culture and the commitment of the residents of the region. The various layers of this engagement are still present today, from the works of Bernd and Hilla Becher, which document and aestheticise industrial culture, to the work of B1, a regional group of artists who took hold of the interpretive authority with pioneering ideas for landmarks, to the stockpile art of the *IBA,* with works by regional and international artists. Several artistic projects of the European Capital of Culture RUHR 2010 picked up directly from these prior works, such as *B1/A40 – Die Schönheit der großen Straße* and *EmscherPARK-autobahn.*[16] *Emscherkunst* used «the fixed foundation of a historically grown tradition»,[17] but provided entirely new approaches. During its move from the centre of Emscher Island to the mouth of the Escher in the west and finally to the source in the east, *Emscherkunst* took the residents of the Ruhr region along with it, inviting them to rediscover their region anew and not to stand still in the midst of transformation. Without the requirement of having to provide «aids for orientation and guides in an industrial landscape in transformation»,[18] as had been stipulated for the stockpile artworks of the *IBA, Emscherkunst* was able to act with more agility, be more complex and grow more organically into the memorial landscape.

HUBS
Especially since it has become permanent, the Emscherkunstweg has had the chance not only to take its orientation from prior historical layers in this memorial landscape, but to link them to one another, make them visible and contextualise them anew. Taking one work of the Emscherkunstweg as an example can illustrate how all works along the art path can serve as hubs.

Already with its name and its materiality, *Carbon Obelisk* opens various layers of interpretation: carbon in terms of a geological era and a link to the pre-industrial period, at the same time in a sense the foundation for the Ruhr region's very existence, carbon as a material for the future and carbon as chemical foundation for life on earth. As a form, the obelisk stands in the tradition of prior uses, that is, as a marking, a survey point or as a monument. The latter offers a point of departure for a symbol for the region in terms of memorial politics: monuments for the victims of mining accidents in the form of an obelisk, the first monuments with direct local reference, but without their own imagery. As a marking, it recalls a location with altered function, the transformation of the region, and also stands for a special point in time: the year of the European Capital of Culture 2010. As a spatial point of reference, it can be used to survey the region anew. But by setting itself in relation to other physical memorial sites in its direct environment that themselves represent various layers of time, these are opened anew and made once again visible: Nordsternpark, Schurenbachhalde or Zeche Carl.

But memorial sites that are no longer visible or scarcely visible can also be discovered anew by linking them to the obelisks, such as Zeche Emil-Emscher [Emil-Emscher Colliery], where four mineworkers died in a mining accident in 1969. All that remains of this location are several inconspicuous flame arresters and a mining pulley. The latter in turn is part of an early layer of regional memorial culture, the aestheticisation of everyday objects. As of the 1970s, many municipal governments, associations or initiatives installed «technical equipment that has been autonomised to art objects», usually from the realm of mining, to reaffirm a regional identity. The stockpile art works from a later period that recall historical structures, open new perspectives on a region caught in a process of transformation, and still require convincing, like Richard Serra's *Bramme für das Ruhrgebiet* [Slab for the Ruhr Area], are more visible and have an impact beyond the local area. This work in turn communicates with *Carbon Obelisk* in the valley, the surveys the Ruhr region anew from below, more reticently, rather a futuristic promise than a blatant assertion.

The potential of the artworks of the Emscherkunstweg as new hubs lies in looking more precisely and the many new perspectives offered on the Ruhr region as a memorial landscape, beyond identity marketing and folkorisation. They can allow for greater complexity and at the same time a playful lightness, because they take up existing narratives of industrial culture and transformation and profit from a temporal distance to the structural transformation. By engaging with an ever more complex and intricate environment, the special qualities of the region serve as a point of departure for more expansive debates. By becoming permanent, *Emscherkunst* itself has become part of industrial culture and creates offers to use the stories of the region for the future. An inclusion of aspects of historical and industrial culture from the surroundings of the artworks in education and outreach offers a great deal of potential here. While the Emscherkunstweg is a «sculptural path of its own kind, only understood by those who know the history of the area and the river»,[20] conversely the multi-layered aspect of the regional history and the river is better understood in our current time if we look at the works of the Emscherkunstweg.

223

01 «EMSCHERKUNST.2013: Fluss wird Wolke — Reiner Maria Matysik», YouTube video, 7:05 min., uploaded by «EMSCHERKUNST», 13 August 2013 → youtube.com/watch?v=K7mncxpJspA (accessed 23 March 2023).

02 For an extensive and multi-faceted survey and detailed exploration of sites of memory and the memorial landscape of the Ruhr region, see the volume: Stefan Berger et al., eds., *Zeit-Räume Ruhr: Erinnerungsorte des Ruhrgebiets* (Essen, 2019).

03 See on this Jana Golombek, «Mehr als Folklore? Das Ruhrgebiet in Schichten», *Transurban Magazin: Ruhrgebiet,* 1 February 2021.

04 On the concept of historical culture *(Geschichtskultur)* see Jörn Rüsen, «Was ist Geschichtskultur? Überlegungen zu einer neuen Art, über Geschichte nachzudenken», in *Historische Faszination: Geschichtskultur heute,* ed. Klaus Füßmann, Theo Grütter and Jörn Rüsen (Cologne, 1994), pp. 3—26.

05 Ministerium für Wirtschaft und Mittelstand, Technologie und Verkehr, *Masterplan für Reisen ins Revier: Bericht der Kommission* (Düsseldorf/Gelsenkirchen, 1997).

06 Hubert Kurowski, *Die Emscher: Geschichte und Geschichten einer Flusslandschaft* (Essen, 1993), p. 7.

07 Reiner Burger, «Von der Köttelbecke zur neuen Flusslandschaft: Erinnerungsort Emscher», in Berger et al., eds., *Zeit-Räume Ruhr* (see note 2), p. 135.

08 Gerd Niewerth and Jochen Stemplewski, eds., *Emschervertellekes: Eine Region und ihr Fluss* (Essen, 2004)

09 Burger, «Von der Köttelbecke» (see note 7), p. 138.

10 Niewerth and Stemplewski, eds., *Emschervertellekes* (see note 8), p. 9.

11 Projekt Ruhr GmbH, *Masterplan Emscher Landschaftspark 2010* (Essen, 2005).

12 Emschergenossenschaft, ed., *Masterplan Emscher-Zukunft* (Essen, 2006).

13 Projekt Ruhr GmbH, ed., *Masterplan* (see note 11), p. 92.

14 Emschergenossenschaft, ed., *Masterplan Emscher-Zukunft* (see note 12), p. A28.

15 Emschergenossenschaft, ed., *Masterplan Emscher-Zukunft* (see note 12), p. F7.

16 Uwe Rüth, «Industrial Land Art: 50 Jahre künstlerische Gestaltung des Ruhrlandes», in Burkhard Leismann and Uwe Rüth, *Industrial Land Art im Ruhrland* (Essen, 2009), p. 11.

17 Rüth, «Industrial Land Art» (see note 16), p. 11.

18 IBA Emscher Park, ed., *Katalog der Projekte* (Gelsenkirchen, 1999), p. 358.

19 Jürgen Zänker, *Öffentliche Denkmäler und Kunstobjekte in Dortmund: Eine Bestandsaufnahme* (Dortmund, 1984), p. 119.

20 Stefanie Städel: *Am Fluss der Ideen* → kulturwest.de/inhalt/am-fluss-der-ideen/ (accessed 2 March 2023).

VULNERABILITY IS THE THING; THE THING IS VULNERABILITY

Jes Fernie

When the curators of the Emscherkunst-weg [Emscher Art Trail] art-commissioning programme began discussions with artist Nicole Wermers about making a new work of art for this post-industrial landscape, conversations about potential damage went on for months, if not years. Will the work invite vandalism? Will that vandalism be more or less likely if we install the work here or there? How can we mitigate this? What type of materials should we use? The list of questions was endless and easily transferable to any number of other public art commissioning contexts. This road of enquiry inevitably leads to a point where we must address whether what we are making is art or just really well-constructed, embattled objects in space.

None of these discussions foresaw the fact that, when *Emscher Folly* by Wermers was finally installed in 2022, it was the birds that wreaked havoc on the work, not the kids. Our feathered friends took apparent joy in pecking the bicycle seats, on the hunt for chunks of foam to construct their nests, defying expectations about who, or what, gets to destroy art. Their interaction necessitated the swift replacement of parts of the sculpture with more durable, less bird-enticing options.

What I'd like to discuss here, in this text, is the important role that destruction plays in art-commissioning programmes, and how the vulnerability of a work of art is, in my view, intrinsic to its success. The ability of a work to forge a visceral relationship to its public (by which I mean human and non-human) is what gives it its traction. An artwork installed in the public realm is never a static entity — it is a hot-wire to the ever-changing political, social and environmental contexts in which it is located, and acts as a catalyst for all sorts of engagement and activity, sometimes disturbing or hurtful, at other times joyful or tender.

A charged example of this ever-shifting, often productive terrain is Robert Smithson's *Partially Buried Woodshed,* which was made in the grounds of Kent State University in January 1970. The artist dumped twenty truckloads of soil onto the central beam of an empty shed until the structure began to crack. His aim was for the shed to «go back to the land» and begin a process of «slow destruction». The conceptual thrust of the work radically changed when members of the National Guard shot at, and killed, four unarmed students protesting at the United States' involvement in the Vietnam War. This shocking, deeply traumatic event was commemorated on *Partially Buried Woodshed* with the words «MAY 4 KENT 70» painted on the central beam, presumably by a student — forever linking the work of art and the «breaking point» of the shed to the cultural shift that many consider the Kent State shootings to represent in American history. Much to the irritation of the university authorities, the work has assumed a different relation to its audience, shifting from a conversation around entropy to one that critiques the prevalence of American imperialism, and proselytises the importance of protest and civil defiance.

For public artworks that are destroyed by violent and disturbing aggressors, there too may, be scope for things reborn. When the queer bodies of Nicole Eisenman's temporary public fountain in Münster were defaced with a swastika and other offensive imagery in September 2017, the day before Germany elected a far-right party to the Bundestag for the first time since World War II, the outrage and upset was palpable. The commissioner *(Skulptur*

Projekte Münster) and the artist were thrown into a press frenzy that stirred up scepticism around contemporary art and its ability to forge a meaningful relation to its public. A group of local women worked with Eisenman to devise an ambitious plan to make a new — permanent — iteration of the work. This grassroots activity has resulted in the creation of an ongoing dialogue with the people of Münster about their city the role of art in society, and the importance of constructing inclusive spaces for all citizens. In this case, as in many others, destruction became a kind of gathering action in which a space is opened up for the creation of a work that forges a more expansive, powerful relation to the world.

Artworks that have remained untouched for years can become lightning rods for the expression of public emotion at a particular moment in history. The rationale of a work may be unpalatable in a different era (as we have witnessed with the recent widespread dismantling of racist, colonial and patriarchal monuments installed in cities across the world throughout the nineteenth and twentieth centuries), or societal conditions can create a situation in which a work is just used in a different way. Tadashi Kawamata's *Walkway and Tower* (2010) remained on site in Emscher largely untouched until the COVID-19 pandemic hit in 2020 and the desire to meet friends, flee the house and forge relationships became urgent, particularly among the young. This twelve-metre-high wooden observation point with accompanying walkway was explicitly designed by the artist to reflect the passing of time and trace marks of human interaction, which it had done movingly for ten years. However, during lockdown, the sculpture became a hangout for young people to meet illicitly, and inevitably, evidence of their presence was left in the form of discarded bottles, litter and tagging. Things came to head when a fire broke out, presumably the result of an ill-fated BBQ, and the work was temporarily closed. Exasperating, no doubt, for other visitors, as well as the sculpture park commissioners and the maintenance team, but this is artwork as public service — a vital, live, usable entity that reflects and provides for any given moment in time.

This commitment to the acceptance of the fallout of destruction is, of course, problematic in all sorts of ways and is vehemently contested within the visual art infrastructure. Destruction, after all, is the «antithesis of the process of making» — it works against our understanding of what it means to create.[01] More prosaically, but no less powerfully, it is also a threat to the machinery of the market which dictates that the value of an artwork is dependent on its status as a static, unchanging, sellable thing.

Beyond these powerful obstacles, there is the emotional impact of destruction. Many artists and commissioners describe a deep sense of failure and shame at seeing their work interacted with in such a way, on a public stage. The scepticism aimed at contemporary art by hardcore traditionalists, often stirred up by the media, serves to fuel this anxiety. «The emperor has no clothes», they seem to say — «see how the artists in their ivory towers are unable to communicate with the masses!» It is only in laying bare this complex set of emotions and broader societal issues that we can begin to carve out a space where taking risks and allowing for the unknown becomes an intrinsic part of all commissioning processes. The Emscher region has a gnarled

and problematic history that is born of
extraction, pollution, and destruction. This
is reflected in the rough-and-ready post-
industrial aesthetic of the landscape, one
which refutes a bucolic idea of the past
and grapples with the responsibilities of
the future. I like the idea that this commitment to veracity and fearlessness continues to be expressed in the artworks
that are installed in the landscape —
artworks which recognise that risk,
vulnerability and potential failure are an
intrinsic part of what we call art. ←

01 Claire Doherty, «Life Will Not Be the
    Same…», in *Archive of Destruction
    Reader,* ed. Jes Fernie (London, 2022).

EPIC JOURNEYS
CLOSE TO HOME

Martine van Kampen

233

A strange thing happened to Land Art Flevoland during the pandemic. Whereas museums were forced to close, make tremendous efforts to adapt to social distancing and struggle with plummeting revenues, this situation was different for public art in the Netherlands. Yes, we had to reschedule and adjust our activities, but the artworks themselves were available for people to be visited any time they wanted. Social distancing was easy; the fresh air was there to blow away any airborne virus particles. People could pick any time slot; no pre-ordered tickets were necessary. There was no need for high-tech visitor management solutions. And like the inner-city parks, which regained their public function and filled with people looking for things to do and other human bodies to be around, the land artworks in Flevoland were able to welcome many visitors. Before long, the national media found us as well and were happy to report on cultural outings that were still possible. The top museum director in the Netherlands wrote a series of articles on public artworks in the most renowned newspaper.[01] Suddenly, we were a viable alternative in a changing world.

This illustrates all that is good about public art and everything about it that clashes with the market economy. These are not the coolest artworks in the cultural scene; you can't buy or sell them on the art market, and you can't even earn ticket revenues with them. Even though they are often made by the same formidable artists of international exhibitions and biennials, collectors and galleries are hardly interested. They don't add value to the works that are bought and sold in the way museum exhibitions do. These artworks are often conceived with some form of common good in mind, with some kind of humility towards their locations and with respect for the communities surrounding them. They patiently sit there, risking vandalism and extreme weather — always available, generously offering their stories and meanings to those who are willing to engage with them.

Some public artworks are most certainly cooler than others. Probably the coolest ones are those that manage to escape the label «public art work» altogether. I would say Nancy Holt's *Sun Tunnels* from 1976 and Robert Smithson's *Spiral Jetty* from 1970 are technically kinds of public artworks, but they fall more comfortably under the label «land art». When trying to understand why they are cooler than other works, I think two aspects come to the fore: they were not commissioned by a government and thus defy the idea that they were meant to enforce power or, perhaps worse, to educate, and they have managed to instill a feeling of longing in those who see pictures of them and hence want to visit these destinations. Artists have made such large sites and objects as these out of an urge to break free from the constraints of the art world. They were aligned with the general cultural spirit of protest and political awareness of their time. Not only does this make for a very good origin story, but their location in deserted, spacious landscapes, which require some effort to, travel to must also help. In Flevoland, the term «land art» has been adopted because of the shared artistic history and the way this was connected to the specific story of making land (reclaiming it from the sea) that was going on at that time. Nonetheless, we must accept that we are, or have become, part of the force field of public art and that, as an institution, we are probably not so cool.

Although Emscherkunstweg's [Emscher Art Trail's] artworks have an origin story that starts later — around 2010 — the history of this area is older than Flevoland's. I think «industrial heritage» is the cool factor here. This is where the Ruhr district's transformation, in which architecture and the arts have played a major role, has been an inspiring example to many post-industrial sites, cities and areas worldwide. Another important factor is that an infrastructure of art professionals was already in place between the commissioners and the artworks to ensure that artists were given as much freedom as possible within the restricted format of the public art commission. The initial aim of this infrastructure was mainly to realise good-quality artworks created by a mix of renowned and younger artists while also reflecting topics that, while current in the art world, are also specific to the region. Yet, after the area had been developed and the artworks realised, after the temporary programmes had ended, the audience went home and the art world and the media turned their attention to new things.

There has never really been a good vision or widespread debate about what it is exactly that we do with all the public artworks that have been realised by all the renowned and not so renowned artists. Do we keep them forever? Do we get rid of them at some point, and, if yes, on what grounds? The once-cool and new artworks that shook things up and changed our perspectives, that told us stories we didn't know and were eager to hear, are starting to gather moss and air pollution residue, and the world keeps changing slightly as they stand still. Slowly, these artworks enter the realm of heritage. Both Emscherkunstweg and Land Art Flevoland are dealing with this transition. As they become heritage, the focus inevitably shifts towards their value, both culturally and economically. If what I said earlier about the noble qualities of public art versus market greed was a bit of a caricature, this is where it bites me in the ass.

I would argue that, in order for public artworks to prosper the way they deserve, they need to be tied to some form of economic activity. For lack of a thriving, institutional regional art infrastructure that can provide this value to the artworks — something Flevoland and Emscherkunstweg share — tourism is the next best thing. Tourism is linked to all kinds of cultural heritage — from castles, to fortresses and monuments. By understanding the land art in Flevoland as a form of shared heritage, we can both provide the works with the necessary protection from decay while also working to reduce their invisibility. So we start by tying a ribbon around them, presenting them as a collection and telling their origin story. We pave the way for people to come and see them, making routes and placing signs with QR codes. We basically do what museums do: we organise guided tours and provide audio tours. We point out the best local restaurants and, even though you can't exit through the museum shop, we make sure you can buy a catalogue. At the same time, we work on strengthening the collection, while editing existing works and realising new ones and looking at what is missing and what new audiences would respond to. All of this is adding value. In a way, it's marketing. It's not noble, but it does do two more things that are important: it makes the artworks interesting to policy-makers and potential sponsors, and it offers a wide, local audience a familiar way to relate to them.

If visiting the *Sun Tunnels* and the *Spiral Jetty* in the American desert could be considered the pilgrimage of art-related travel — requiring personal sacrifice, while inspiring longing and rewarding you with a mythical experience — the day trips on offer by Emscherkunstweg and Land Art Flevoland try to provide a more user-friendly format. An artist once told me that he walked through Flevoland from artwork to artwork, sleeping at farm houses and experiencing the rational, agricultural landscape in a completely unintended and thought-provoking way. There are epic journeys to be made in unexpected places close to home. As the world changes and the climate, social inequality and pandemics bring new challenges into our lives as well as our heritage and our museums, it seems smart to invest more effort into having viable alternatives around — ones that don't require air travel or entrance tickets and are fit for social distancing, ones that provide many opportunities to build on, to experiment with and to amplify with temporary programmes like *Emscher-kunstweg: Vor Ort* [On Site] and *Land Art Live,* and ones that invite people to redis-cover the landscape around them.[02] ←

01   The series by former Rijks-museum director Wim Pijbes in the newspaper *NRC* was titled «outside gallery». See, for example, his article «Inter-nationale allure, gewoon op het kruispunt» [International air, right at the intersection] from 7 May 2020.

02   *Land Art Live* started in 2013 with a programme of artist interventions on the land art sites in Flevoland, culminating in the exhibition, *Once More, with Feeling* (2017) at KAF in Almere and the book *Land Art Live: The Flevoland Collection* (Rotterdam, 2020).

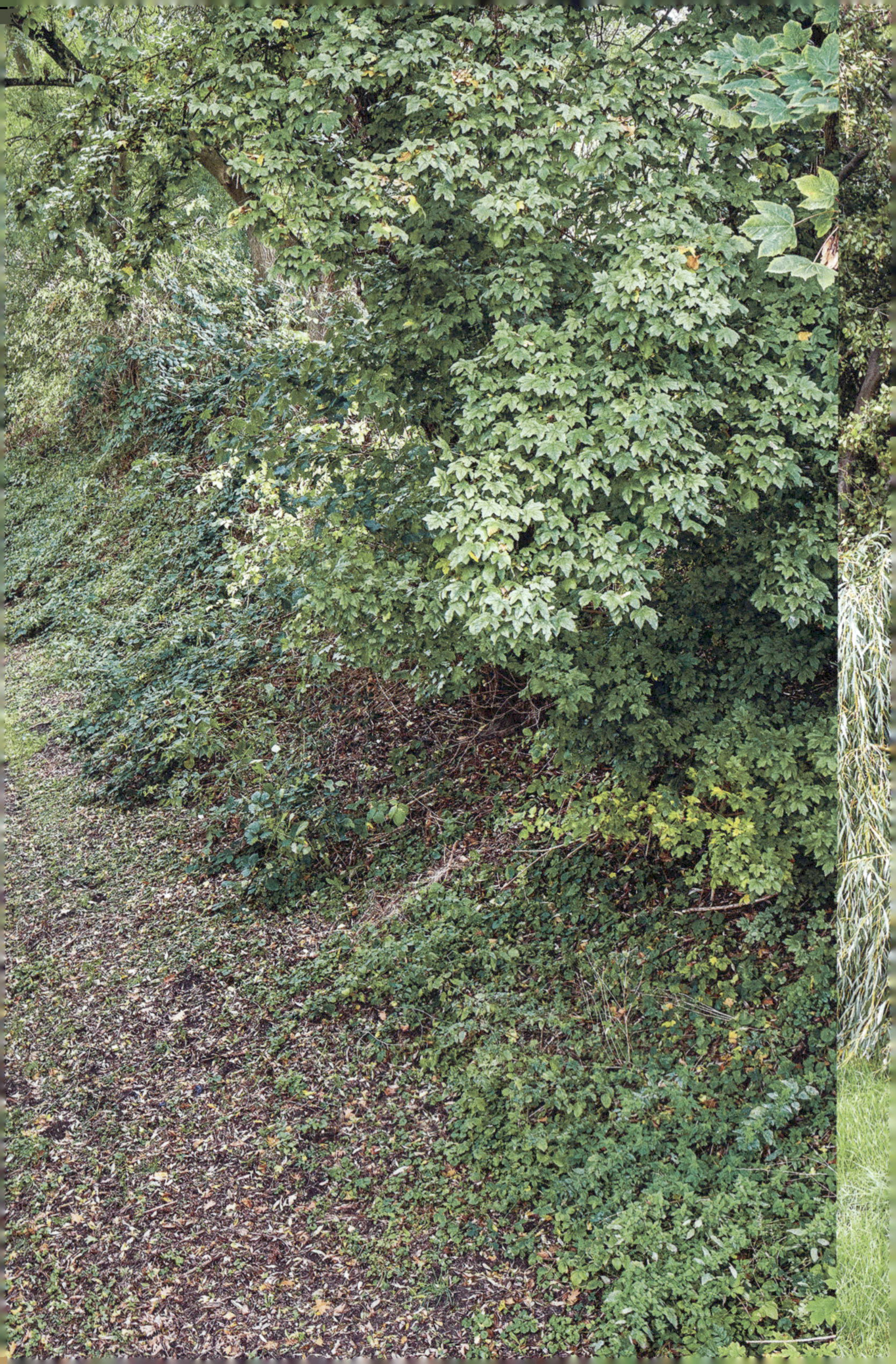

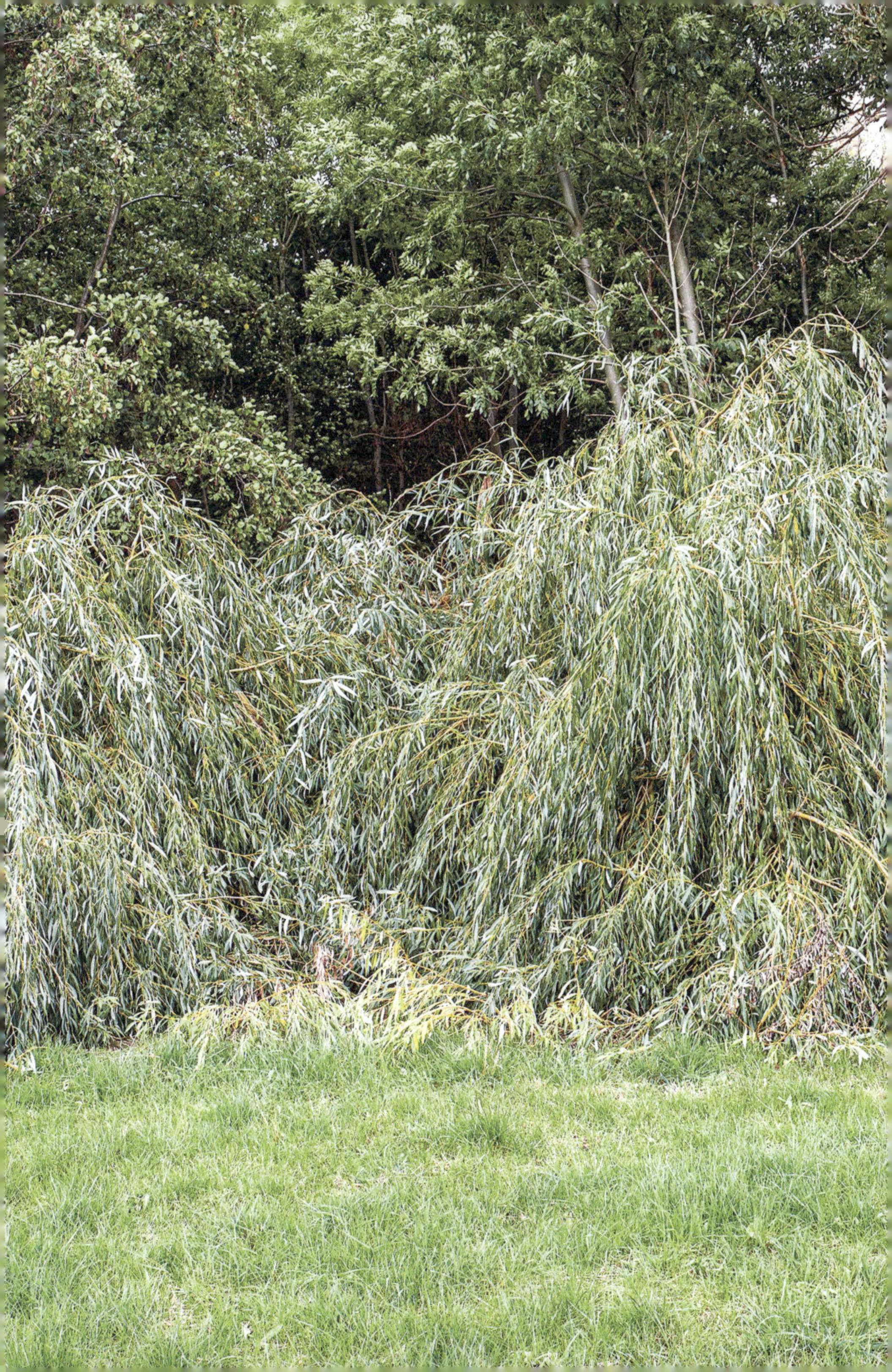

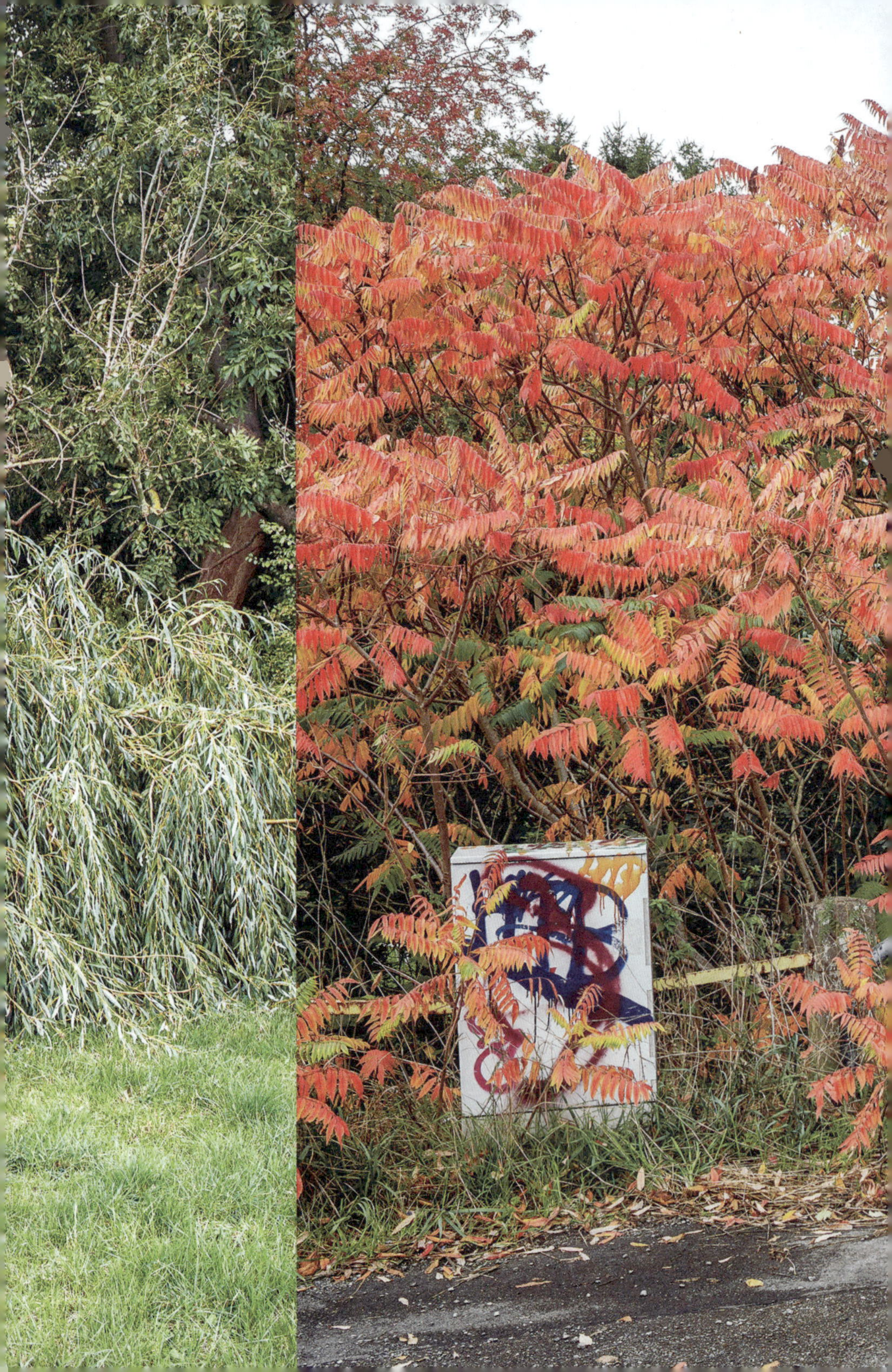

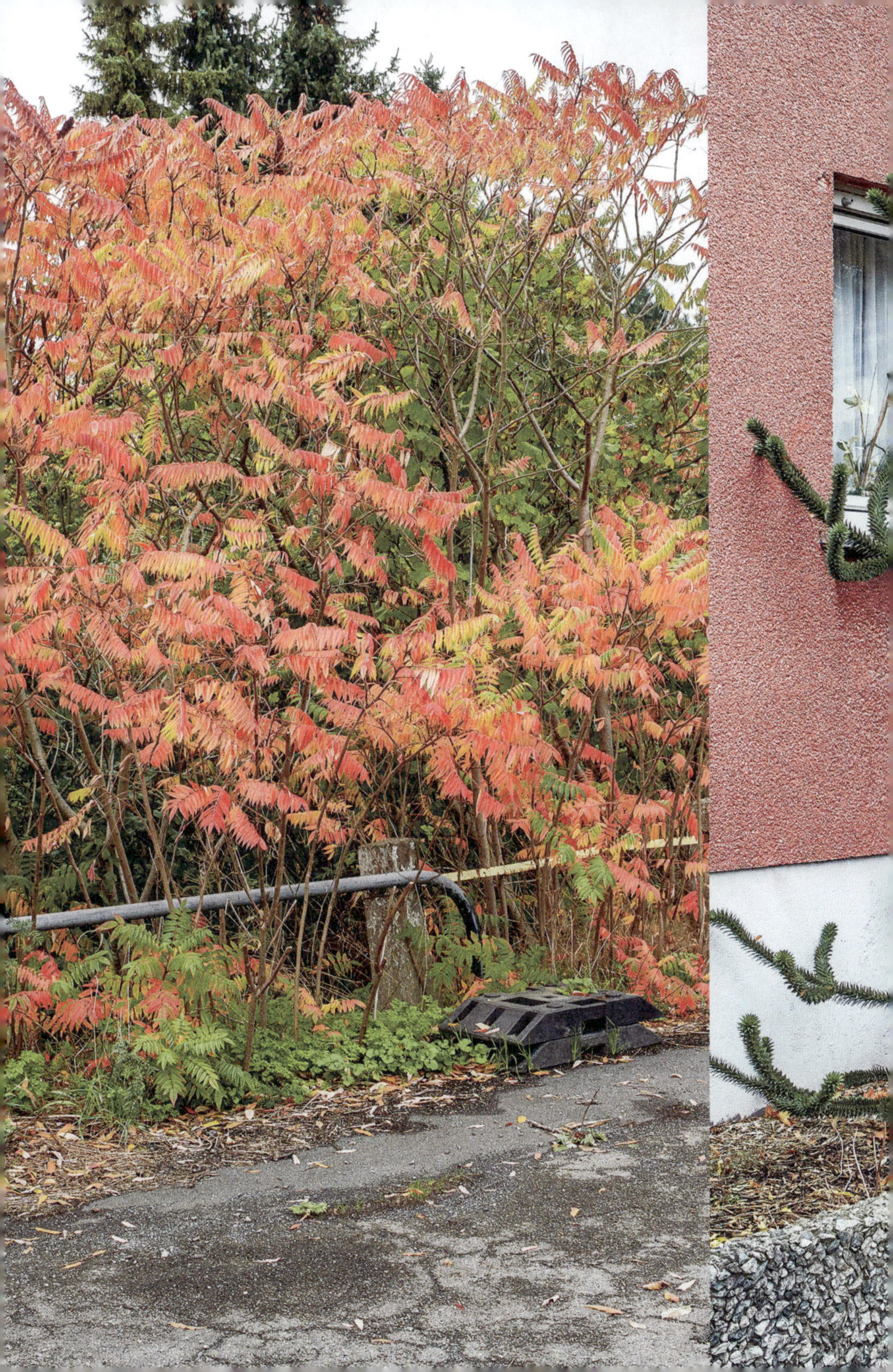

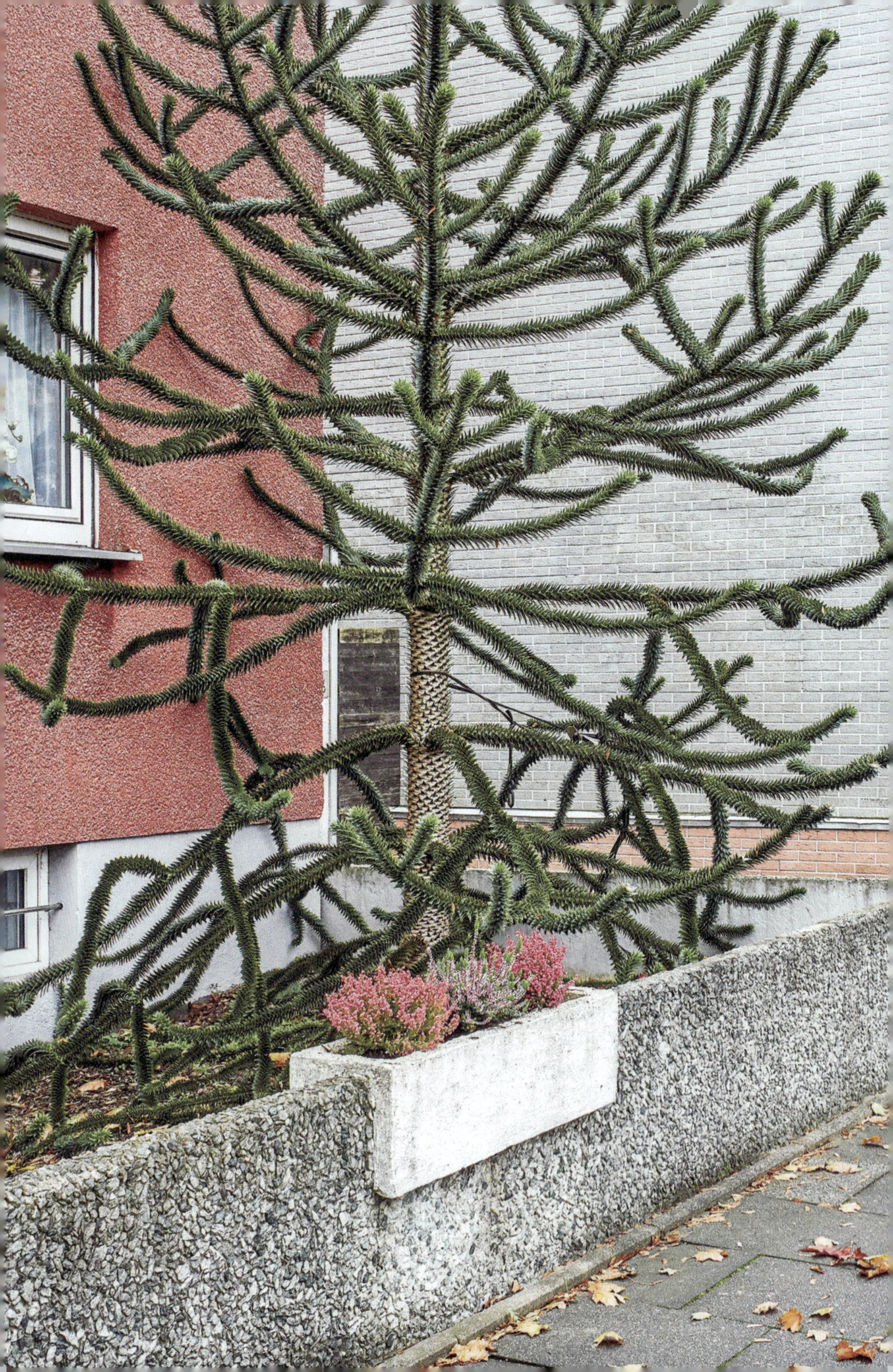

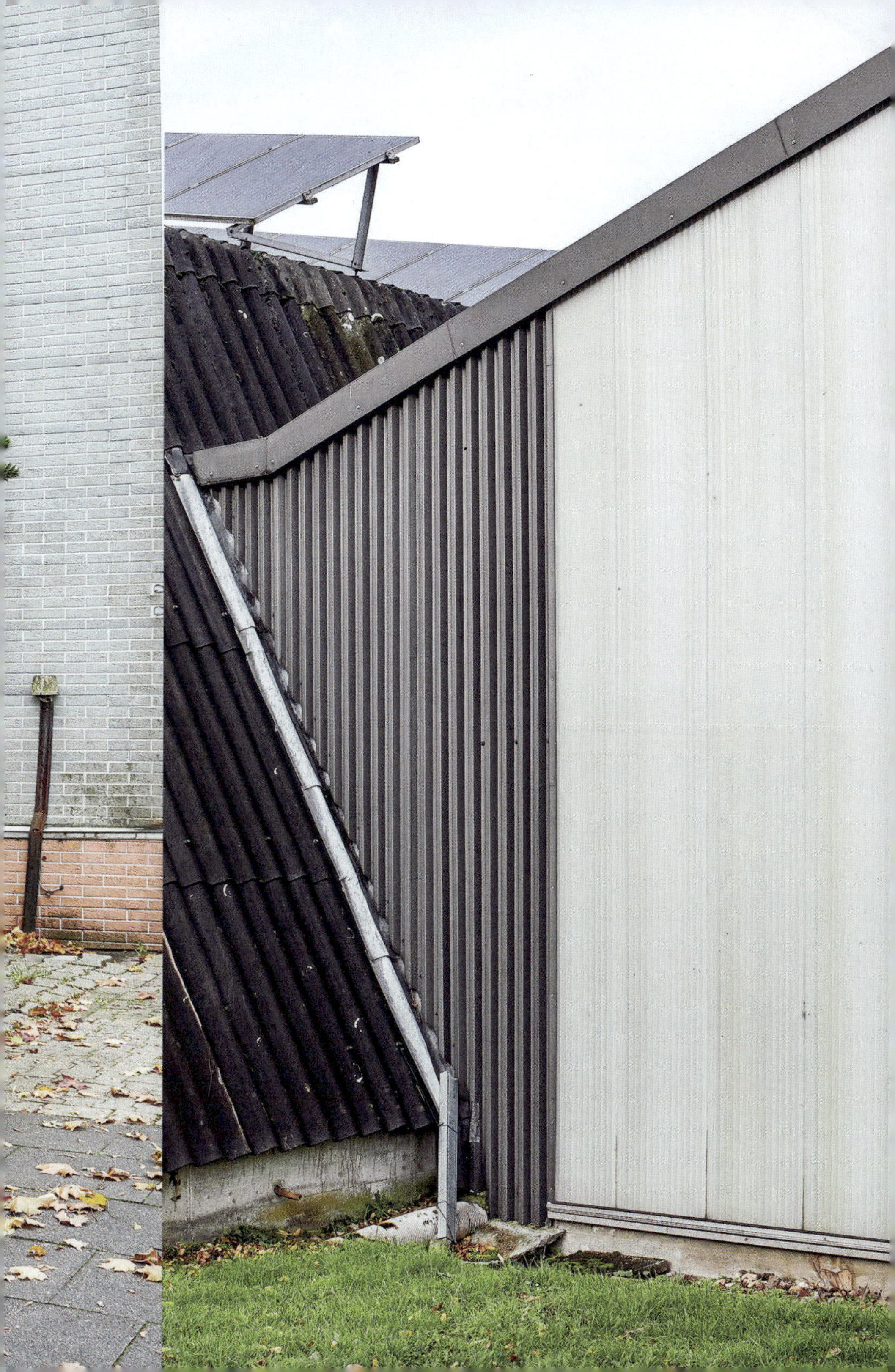

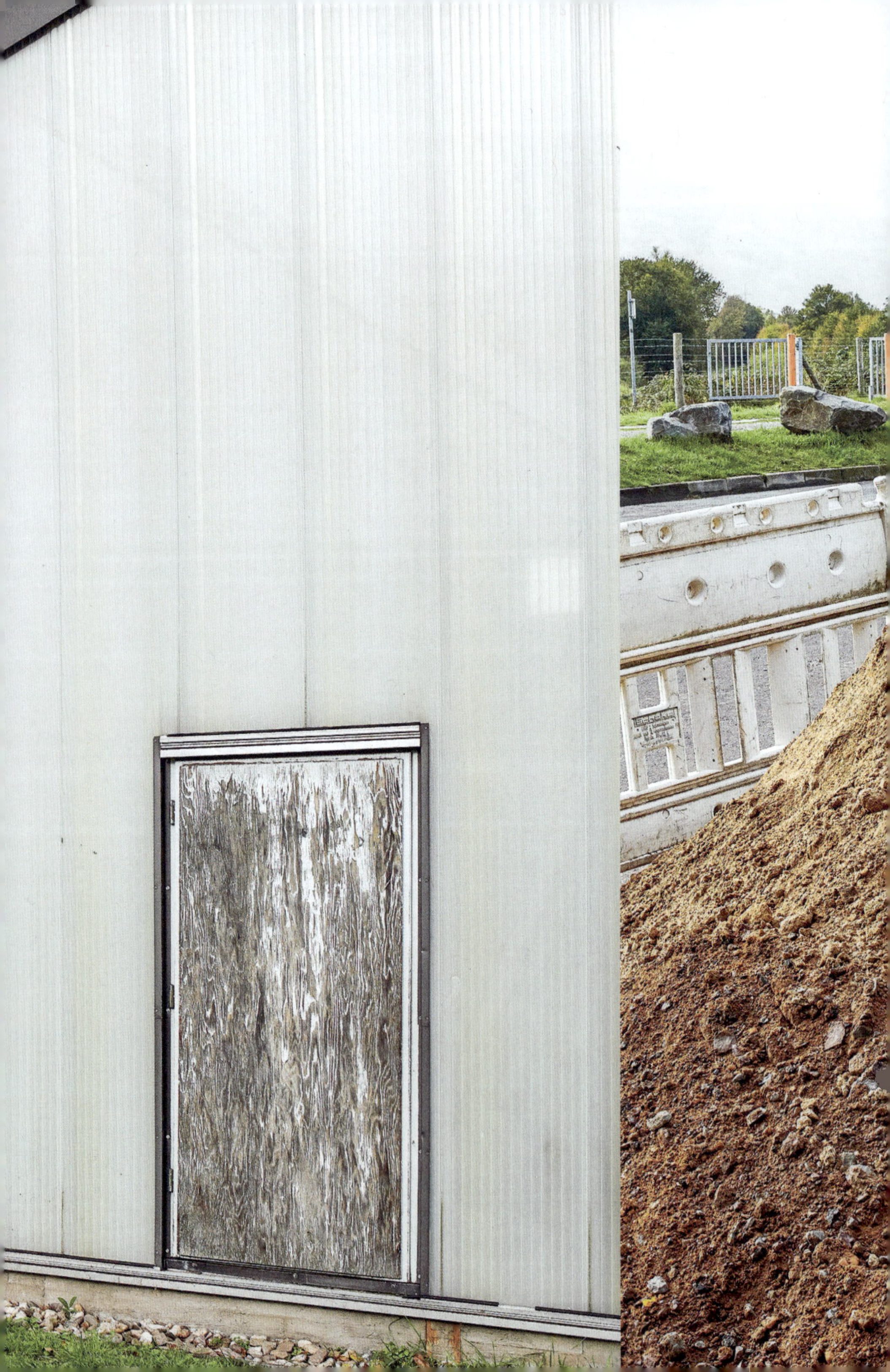

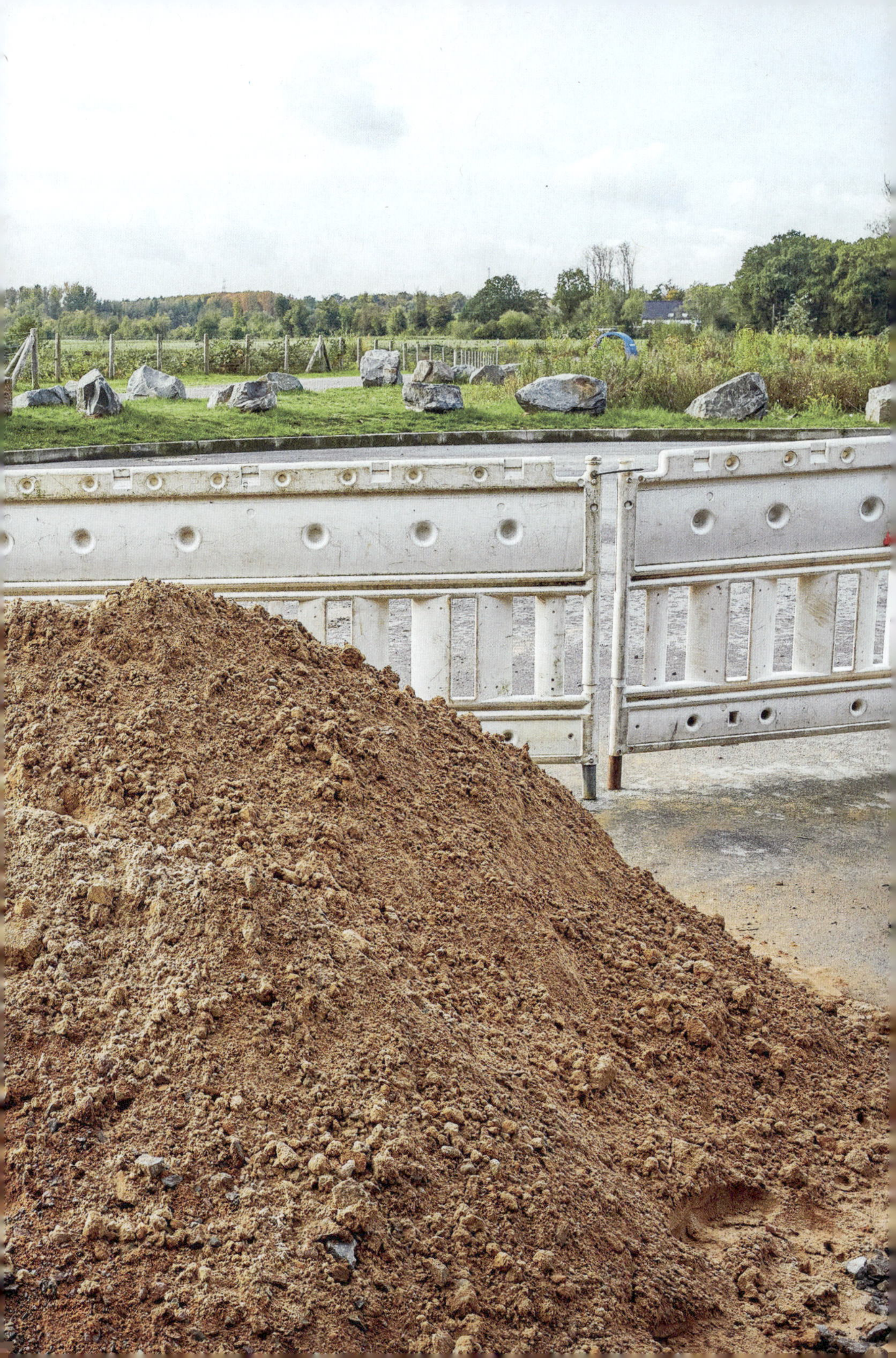

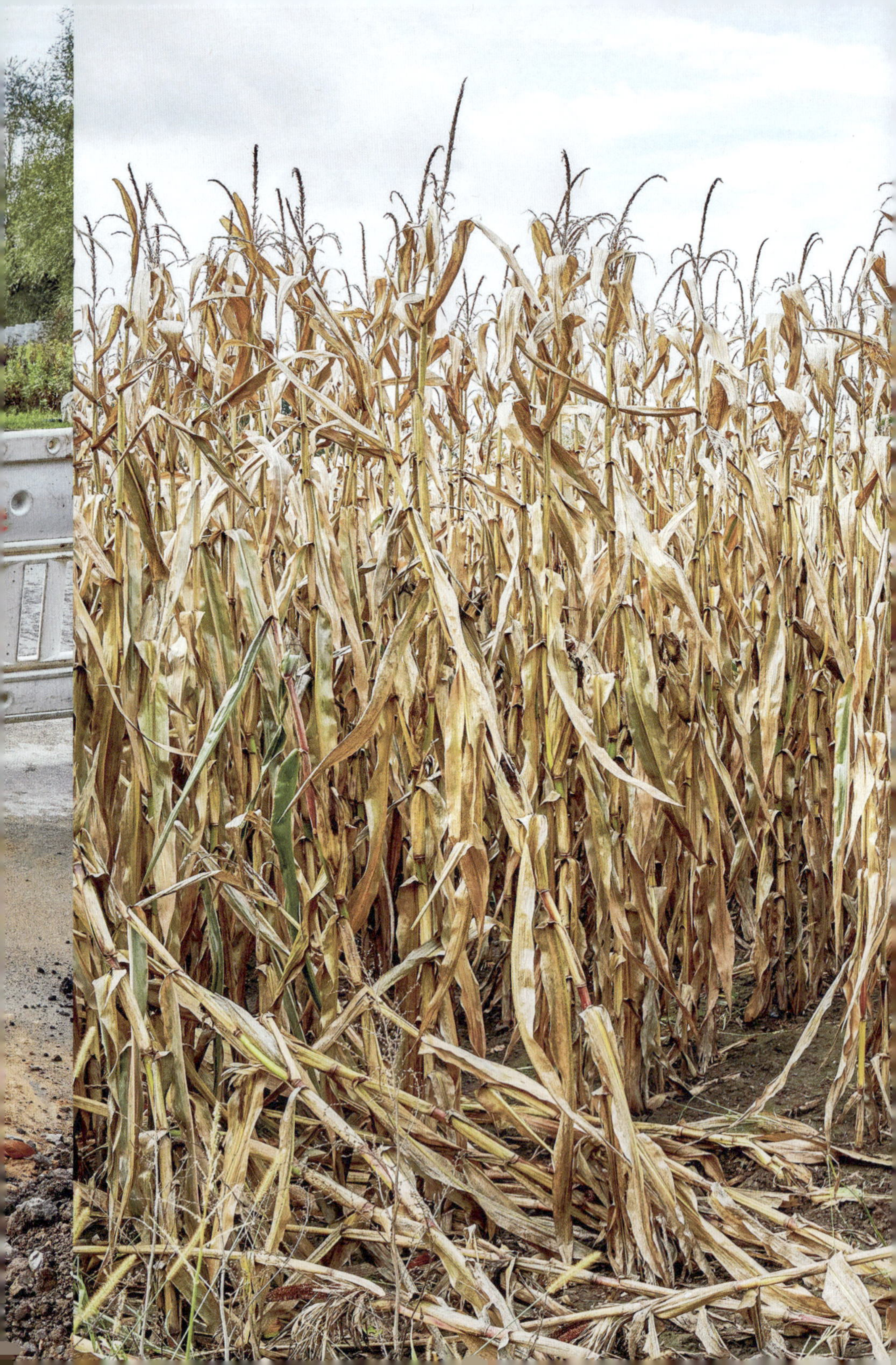

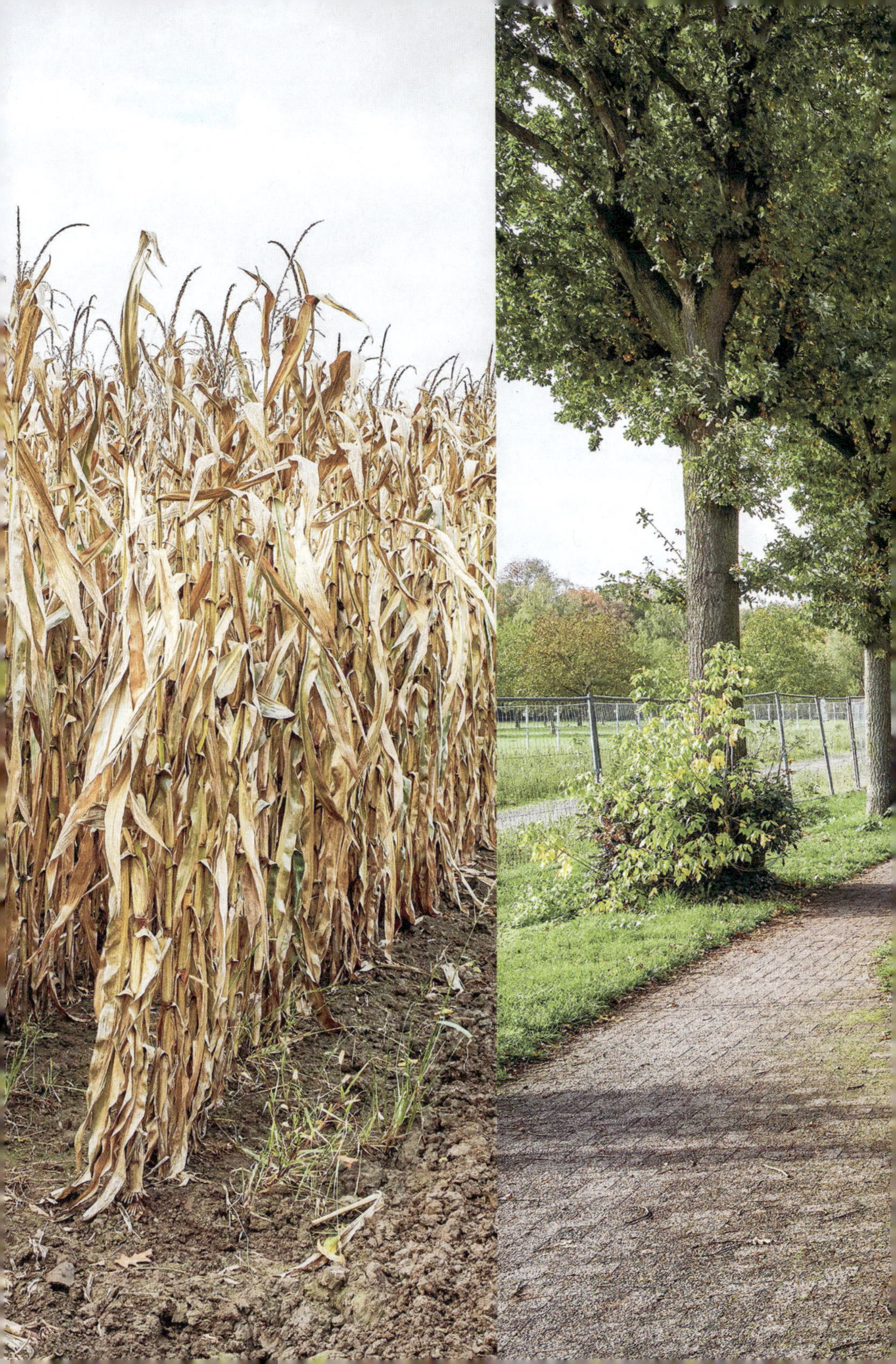

Thomas Voßmerbäumer
checks:

CARE AND MAINTENANCE ALONG THE EMSCHERKUNSTWEG

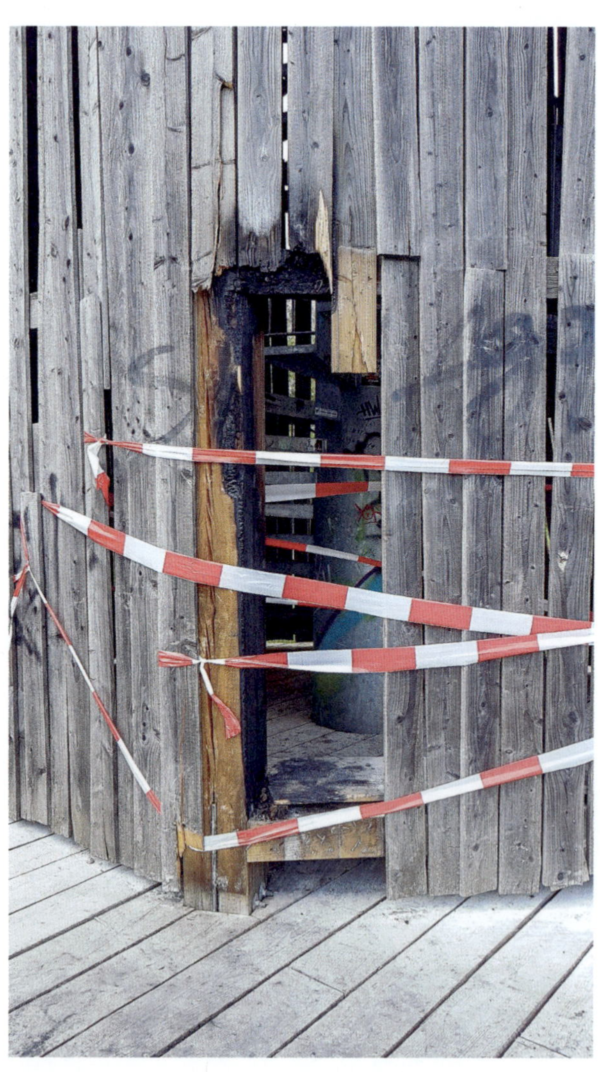

As a structural engineer, my job is to maintain the artworks along the Emscherkunstweg [Emscher Art Trail] on both an artistic and a technical level. It is very important to have more than a purely technical understanding of the pieces and to have some sense of what the artworks are and represent in themselves. My job starts by considering these outdoor artworks in public spaces as engineering structures. At the same time, I also try to bear in mind the artists' ideas of how each work should develop and evolve. Rosy red and deep grey have to be combined again and again, so to speak, for as long as an art work remains in situ. This is one of my key tasks in managing their maintenance.

From the very first discussion I have with the artists, I try to gain a sense of the art works: you have to have a feel for them. What does the artist really want to say and show here? Some things can actually be done too well — particularly when it comes to build quality or cleaning. One example that comes to mind is the concrete pipes of the new *dasparkhotel* in Castrop-Rauxel at the Hof Emscher-Auen [Emscher-Auen Farm], which the manufacturer unfortunately delivered in far better quality than we expected or wanted. The pipes were delivered not in their raw state but with a coating that would protect them from weathering. The manufacturer thought this would be a kind gesture. But the artist Andreas Strauss was very disappointed that in this state the pipes with their beautiful light grey coating would not be able to pick up an additional patina. He had imagined that they would gradually take on moss and turn green, which will not happen for years now due to the coating.

We also have other works in the collection such as the *Walkway and Tower* by Tadashi Kawamata, whose wooden construction is exposed to changes through weathering and the seasons. It is intended at first sight to appear provisional and temporary; however, the tower must always be absolutely fit for purpose and technically flawless. The structure is not supposed to look like it is complete and built to last for ever. Maintaining this balance — repeatedly looking to see what the technical requirements are and what has to be done to maintain the work — is what I try to achieve. For *Walkway and Tower,* I regularly have to test the state of the wooden structure and see if I can improve it while on the other hand always keeping the technical specifications in good order. For example, here we not only experienced damage due to vandalism; at one point the whole lightning protection system was stolen. Nobody had expected that to happen. Of course, security devices of that kind have to be replaced immediately. That is part of the long-term maintenance of an engineered structure.

In maintaining the works, we encounter three core problems: there is graffiti, the problem of litter in many outdoor public spaces and there is mechanical damage. One example of mechanical damage is surfaces being scratched, or, as we discovered on one occasion with Tadashi Kawamata's art work, the screws on a wooden terrace were all loosened three-quarters of the way. However, we have learned that damage in locations that we care for passionately and keep in good condition is markedly reduced. *Glückauf. Bergarbeiterproteste im Ruhrgebiet* [Good Luck. Miners' Protests in the Ruhr Region] by Silke Wagner in Herne is worth mentioning here. In this case,

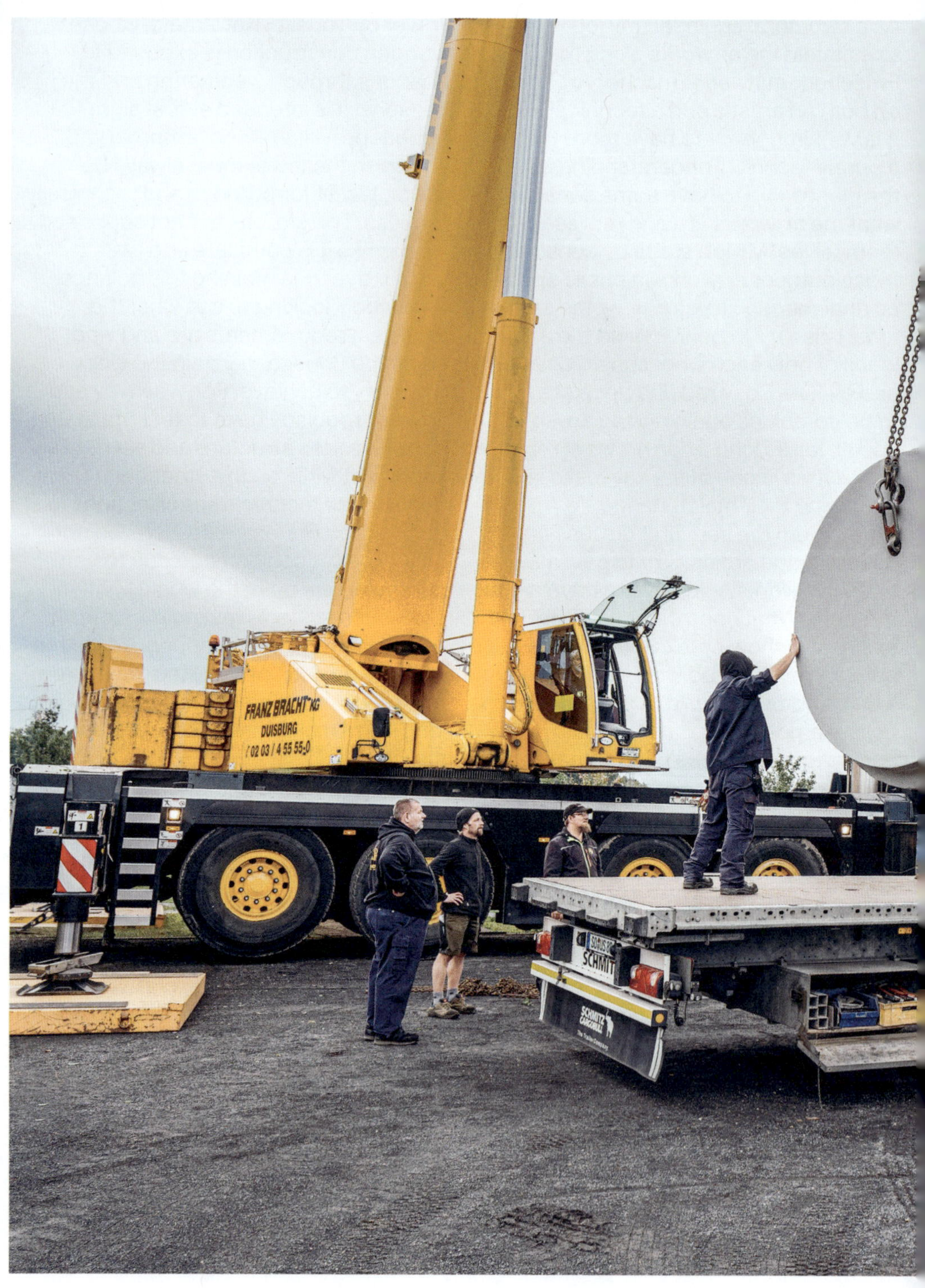

FRANZ BRACHT KG
DUISBURG
/ 02 03 / 4 55 55-0
SCHMITZ

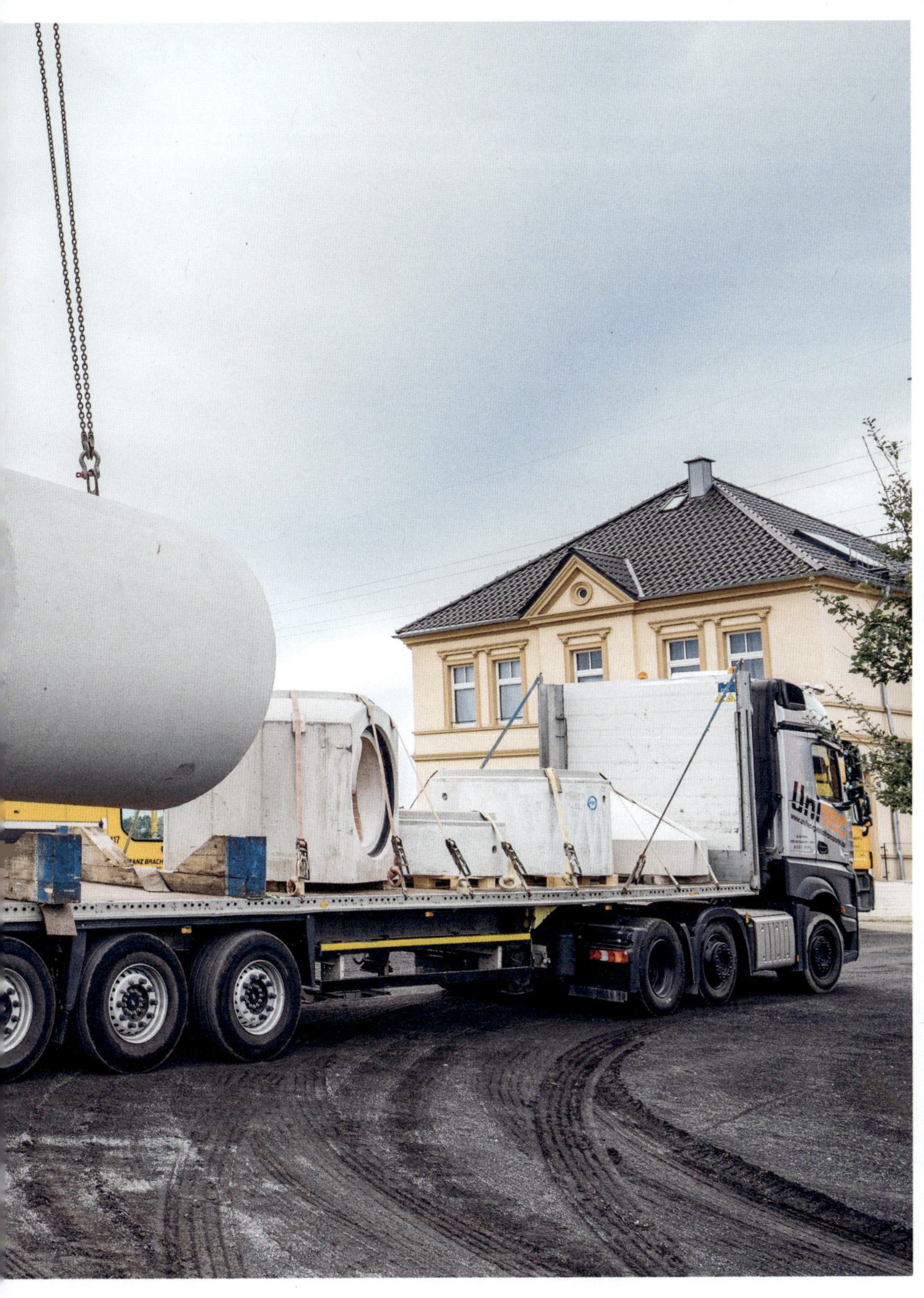

we painted the former administrative
building next to the artwork an anthracite
colour and always reacted immediately
whenever any graffiti appeared. Together
with the artist we also thought about
what else we could do and then put up
posters of the protest newspaper that
provides a more detailed chronicle of the
mineworkers' rebellions and originally
formed part of the artwork in 2010. Since
then, more or less nothing has happened.
Well-maintained sites clearly find greater
acceptance than those that are not cared
for. We also try to talk repeatedly with
the artists as part of the ongoing maintenance process in order to consider
jointly how we can and should deal with
damage. *Neustadt* [New Town] by Julius
von Bismarck and Marta Dyachenko is a
good example: with the replica buildings
that are intended to weather in natural
surroundings, the question arises of how
much graffiti the artists are willing to
tolerate. But we also check to see where
there is damage like dented panels and
have to continually reassess the safety of
the public passing through. What damages
are part and parcel of the metamorphosis
of the work and where are we legally
obliged to intervene? Where do we reach
the borderline where we are obliged to do
something?

All these aspects have to be
coordinated with each other because
the viewer should always be presented
with the impression that the work is in a
clean and orderly state, a well-kept, professional state, one with which the artists
are in agreement. So we repeatedly have
to strike a balance between the requirements we have from a technical or maintenance point of view and the objectives
that are important from an artistic point
of view. This means that regular contact
with the artists is essential. ←

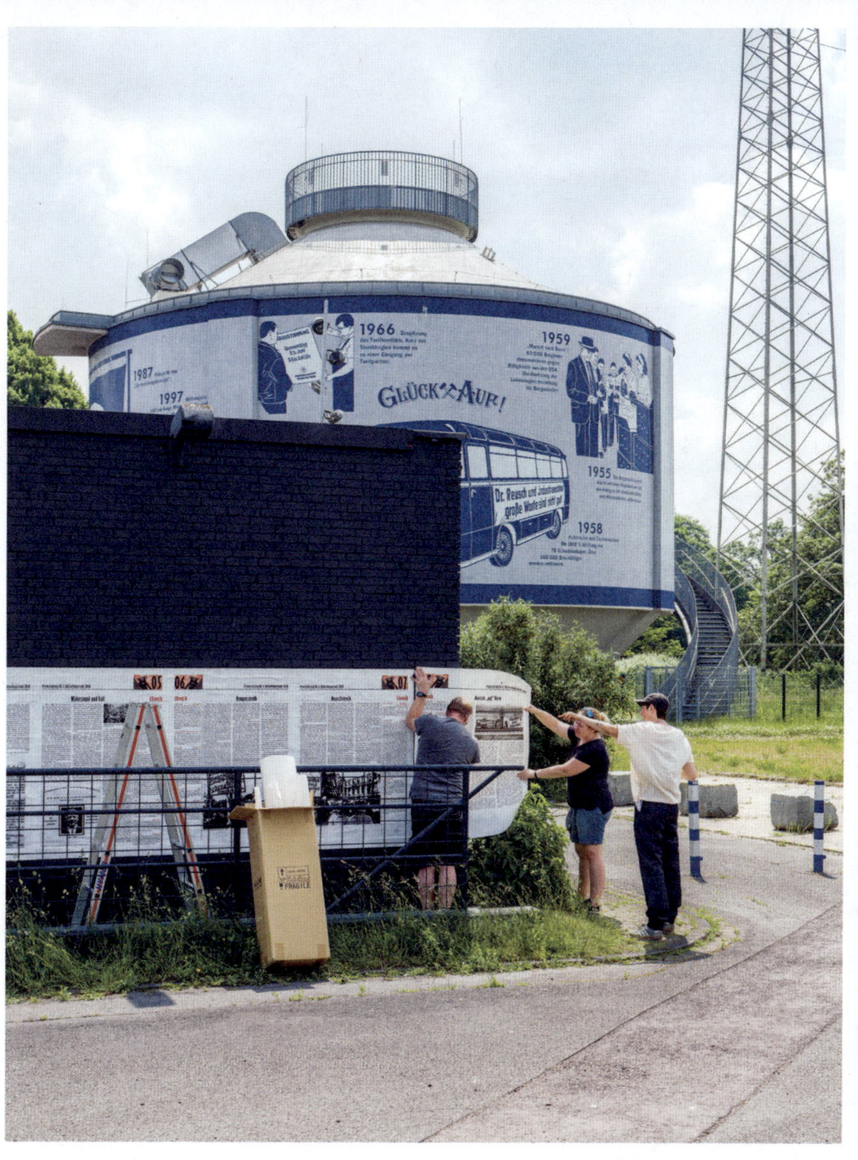

↑

Artistic revision together
with Silke Wagner

Glenda Mense
cycles:

BETWEEN ART AND INDUSTRIAL NATURE

257

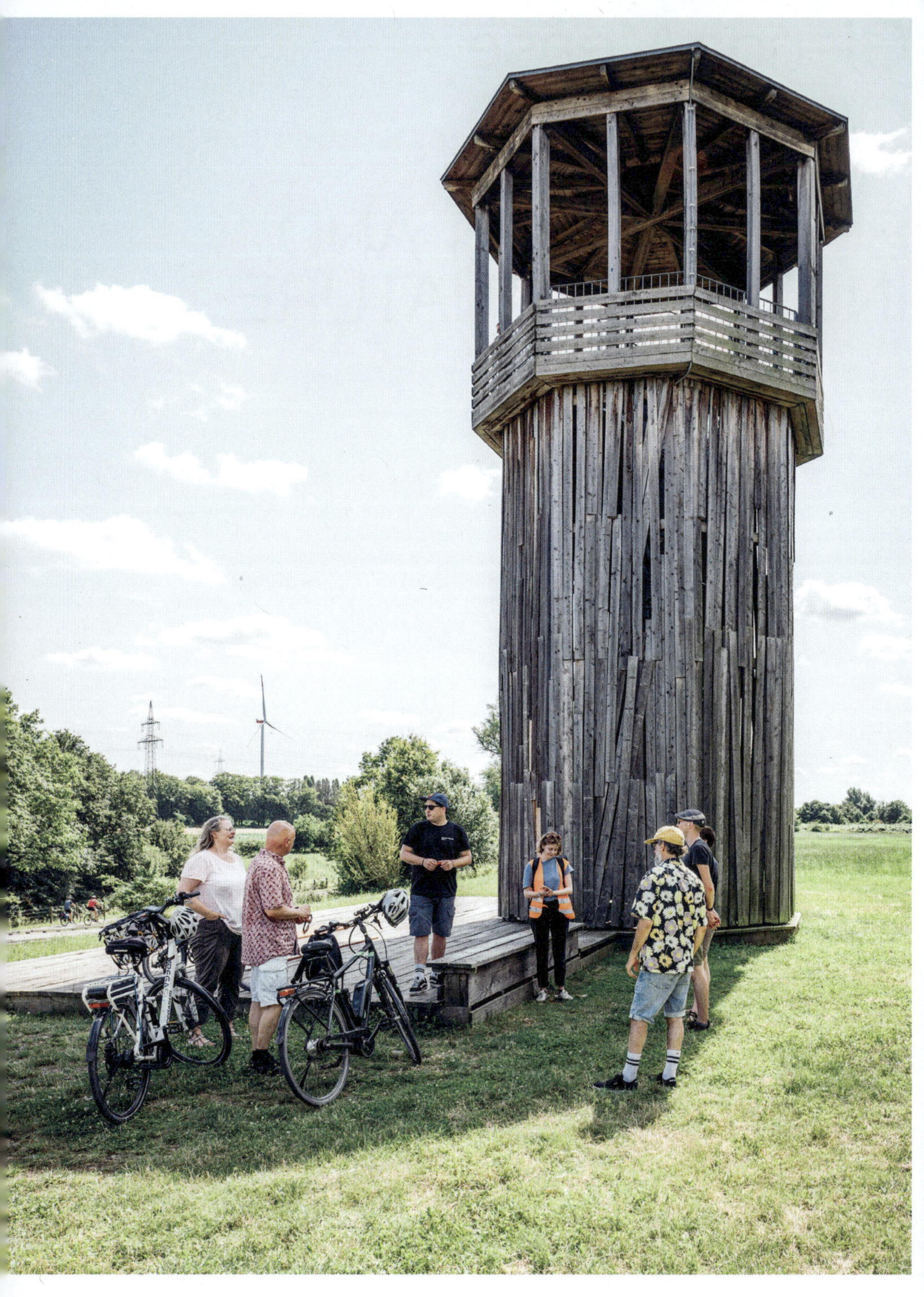

Our bikes are parked and our thigh muscles are aching. It's time to wash our sweat-stained T-shirts with the Emscherkunstweg [Emscher Art Trail] logo and put them back in a drawer.

Two thousand twenty-two was a special year. It was the first year after all the COVID-19 lockdowns, and we could finally take people on cycle tours to see the new artworks and exhibition sites. Two temporary formats were included in some of the tours for the first time: the *Beyond Emscher* exhibition at Zollverein and *Healing Complex,* an art project and community centre run by Urbane Künste Ruhr [Urban Arts Ruhr] in the former church of St. Bonifatius. Three new art projects had also been added: *Emscher Folly, Public Hybrid* and *dasparkhotel_ inside-outsite.* This of course meant that new routes had to be conceived and integrated into our tours.

Vera Bücker, Alicia Jütte, Harald Ophüls and I sat down together in November 2022 to share our experiences of the past season. First of all, we swapped notes on who had gone where, and when. Had we covered all the existing and new tours between us? Indeed we had.

As tour guides, we are the connecting link between the cycling tour, the artworks, the history of the Emscher region and the participants. Our different backgrounds and interests mean that we can offer varying perspectives on the routes travelled and the works viewed. Vera from Oberhausen and Harald from Herne, for example, are keen cyclists and know many of the routes inside out. Alicia from Essen rides a racing bike, whereas I, a dreamily distracted art historian from Dortmund, often rent a bike when I want to explore my surroundings.

When it comes to new building sites — of which there are many in this region — we all agree that we rely on our experience and intuition to find a way around them, and fortunately the participants don't get upset if a detour doesn't work out as expected. Many are able to see the funny side of such situations. According to Alicia, the best approach is to «say from the outset that we are going on a journey of discovery. After all, building projects are integral to the process of transforming the Emscher.»

The artworks enter into a symbiotic relationship with these constantly changing surroundings, combining to create a new image of the Emscher region. Districts that were once disparaged due to their proximity to the former «Köttelbecke» (a regional expression that translates roughly as «dung stream»!), along with the art that has been integrated into this environment, can be viewed from a different perspective.

Some visitors are surprised to learn that artists are also interested in exploring social structures. Take Apolonija Šušteršič, for example, who collaborated with local people to create her work *PLAY_LAND,* a new youth centre in the Holten district of Oberhausen. «This shows how the concept of art has evolved,» says Harald. «In the same way, the *Healing Complex* in Gelsenkirchen's Erle district is not immediately perceived to be an artwork or accepted as such. The idea has to grow. It takes time to find out whether projects like these will work.» This has already happened in Oberhausen: during a break on their cycle tour, one group got talking to a parent, who told them he had been bringing his kids to the new youth centre regularly since it was built because, as he said, «there's always something new happening here». This prompted a discussion within the group about the

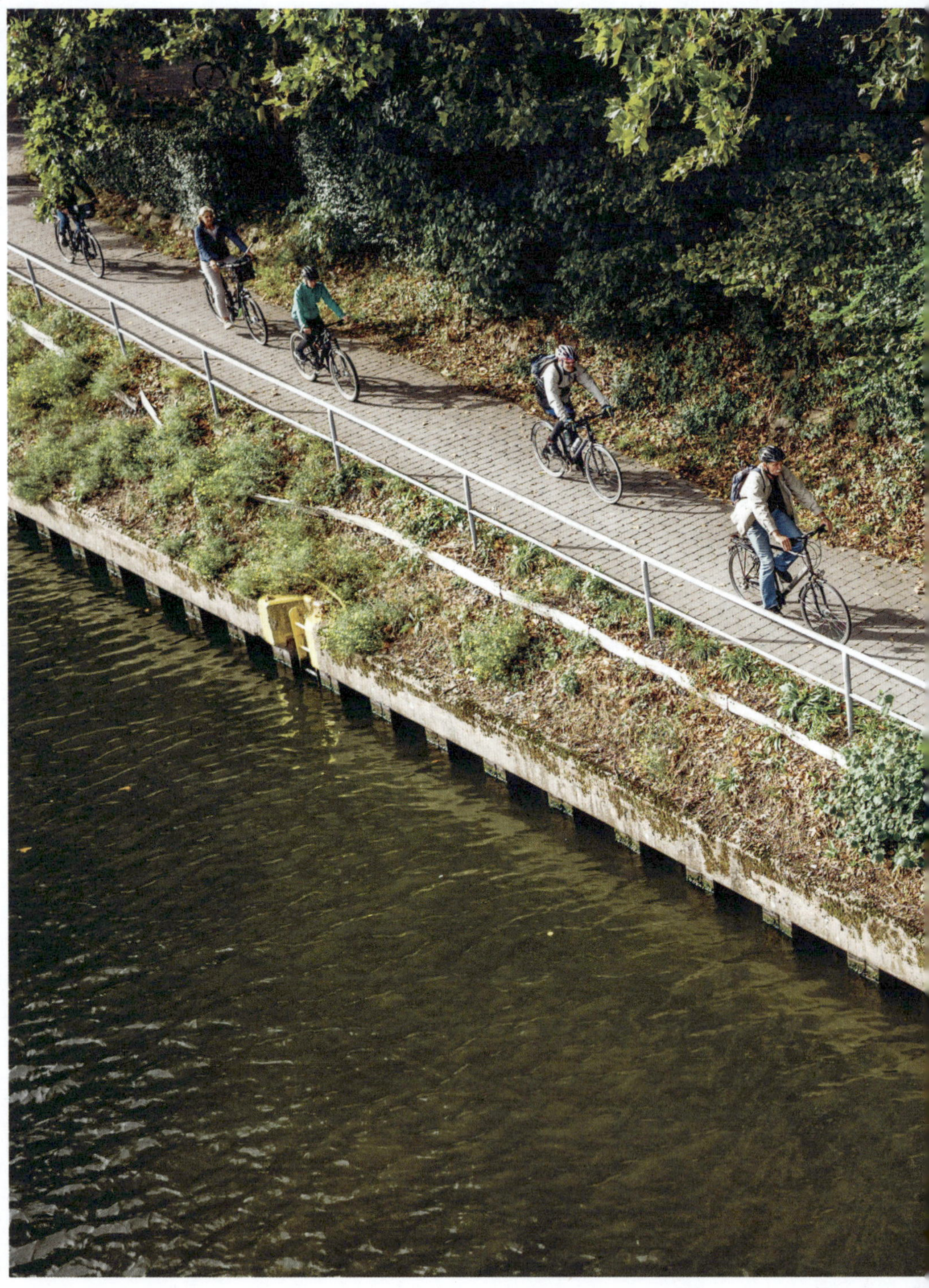

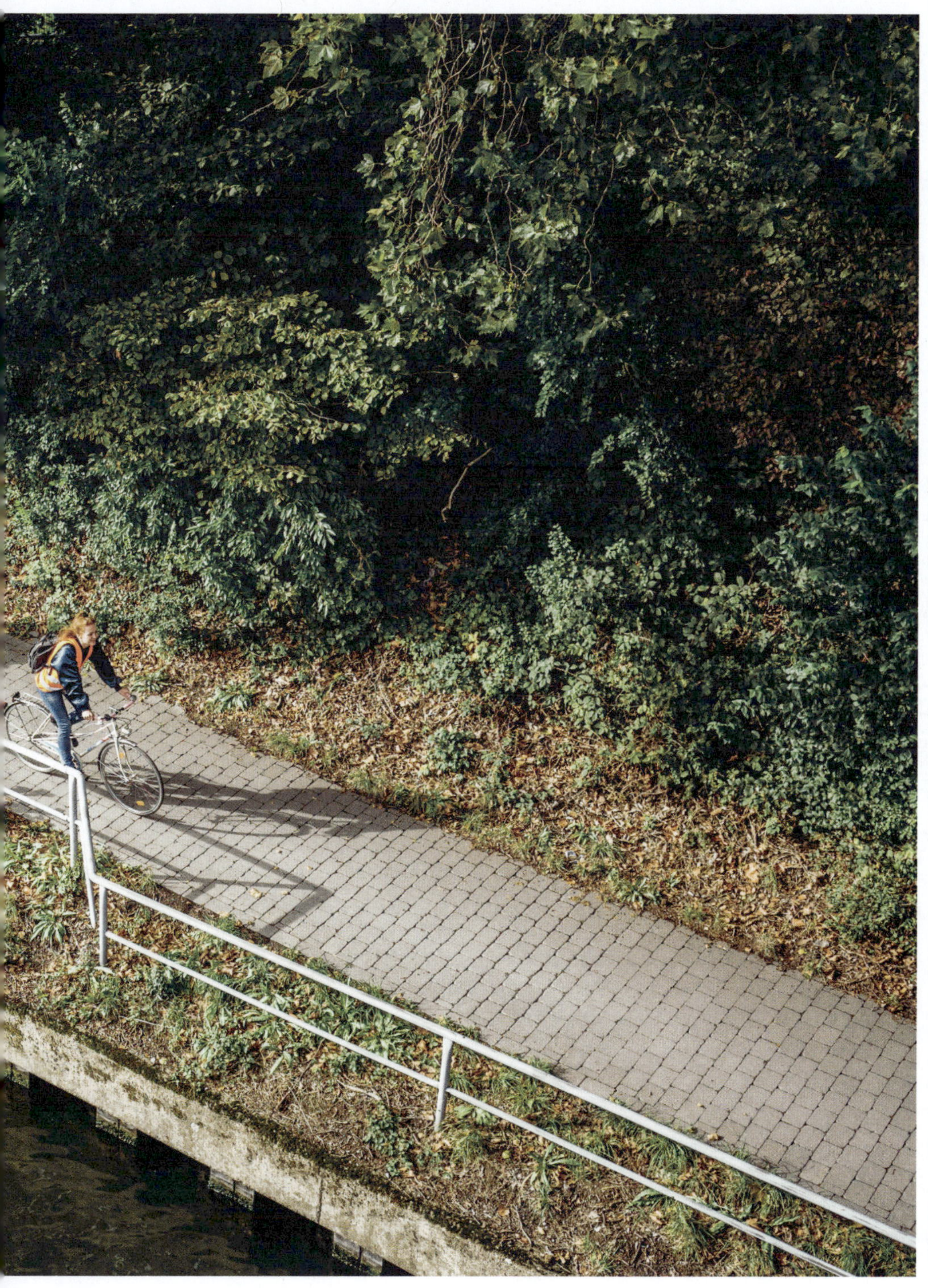

context sensitivity of art. How does it change our own view of art? A short time later, further up the Emscher river, the tour participants found themselves standing on the viewing platform of the new Oberhausen pumping station, silently contemplating the restructured terrain. You could almost say it was romantic.

The participants in the cycling tours come from diverse backgrounds. Some have prepared for their chosen tour and its particular conditions, while others have not. And those who thought they already knew the route had a very different memory of it, and were all the more surprised to see how much things have changed — usually for the better. «One couple from Cologne had been worried that it might be a bit boring — that we would spend the whole time cycling along a straight stretch of the river, and were relieved to find that wasn't the case,» Harald recalls. And one cyclist from Castrop seems to have taken part in just about every tour. «I remember him too,» Vera says. «This year, people came from further afield — Cologne, Münster, Düsseldorf, Bielefeld — as well as from the surrounding area. That was nice.» «One woman was planning to e-mail me afterwards,» Harald adds, «because we disagreed about specific elements of Rita McBride's work.»

Some of the participants cycle back along the route on their own; others continue to chat with us as we make the return journey by train. «You could see that people were continuing to share their impressions of the trip.» My personal aim is to give the participants a new viewing experience, one that varies from work to work. This will hopefully encourage them to reconsider aspects of the old (demolition), the mundane (a feeder bridge) and the new (3D printing), and stimulate some interesting discussions. The conversion of the Emscher involves continual transformation. To the east of Dortmund, the region presents itself as an idyllic landscape of hills and valleys, with the Emscher trickling through it as a little stream. Along the canal, by contrast, the river is broader and has a more striking presence. On the stretch of the river in Duisburg-Nord, its natural course — the Old Emscher — can barely be perceived. Only when it reaches the industrial quarter with the spectacular processing plants that characterise the city does the river gradually reappear, accompanied by a familiar cliché: its acrid smell. Nothing new about that.

«Many of the participants found the *Emscher Folly* very puzzling,» Harald recalls. «They felt that it didn't really fit in.» He is referring to Nicole Wermers' installation of bicycles, which seem rather incongruous in this location between the Bruckhausen steelmaking plant and the Duisburg-Alte Emscher wastewater treatment facilities. Bicycles in an off-land setting, I thought to myself — unusual but also ingenious. And typical of the Emscherkunstweg.

I have come to realise that every tour we do (with people we are unlikely ever to meet again) gives us, the art educators, the chance to enjoy a pleasant experience in our own backyard, as it were. But regardless of whether you are a tour guide or a visitor, everyone who takes part in this project should ideally gain a new perspective on the Emscher and its surroundings, or be able to add a new idea, an anecdote, or some inside knowledge to their overall image of this area. And we as the tour guides are closely involved in this process. Everyone ends the season with a new sense of the Ruhr region, and this was especially true in 2022.

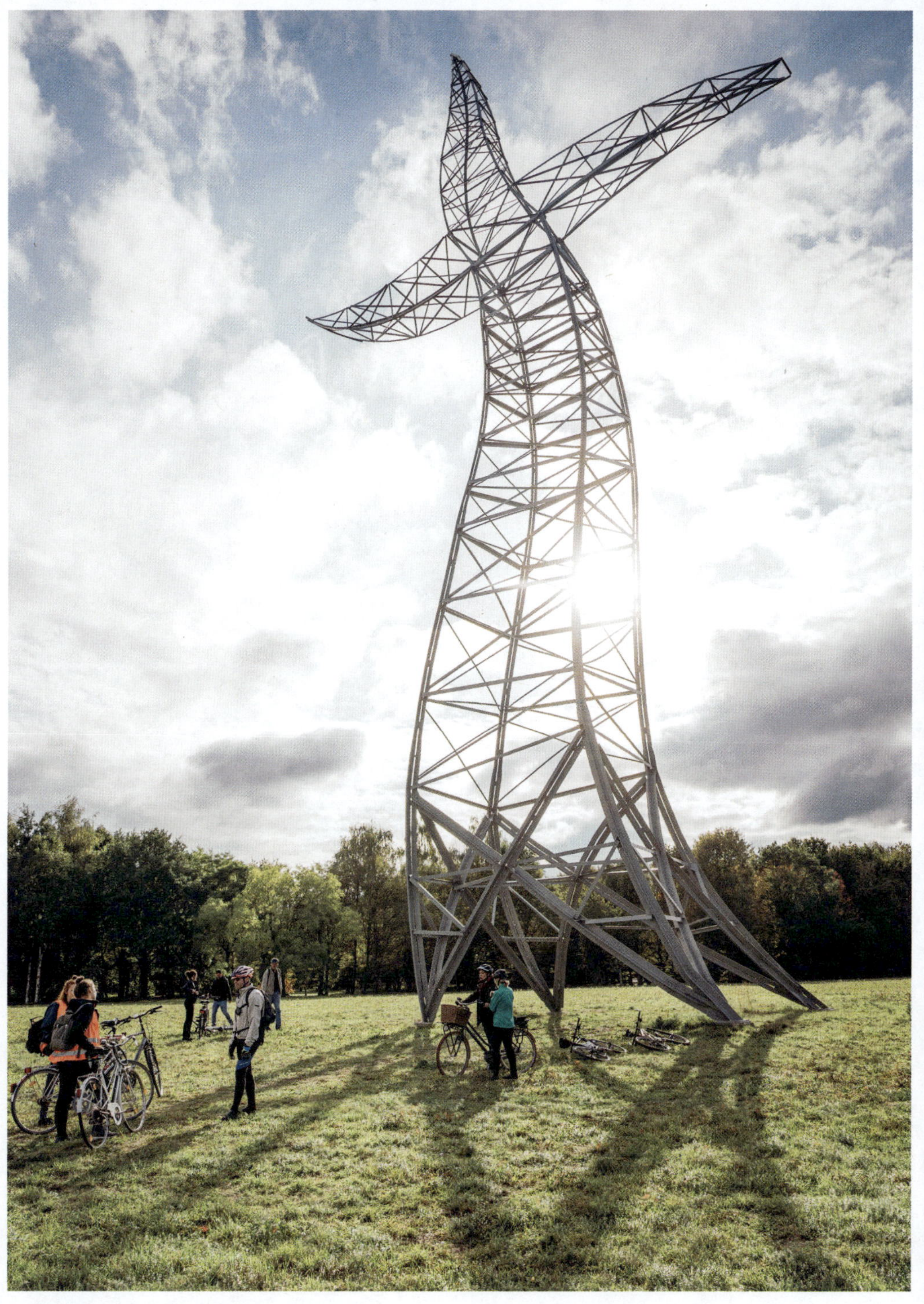

263

Jana Kerima Stolzer
wanders:

A2 NS IX A40 —
EMSCHER VALLEY

I'm on the northern side of the valley, at the lowest point, picking a few of the last grapes from the vine at the rusty fence. I can't see further than twenty metres, where the path ends. The majority of the fruit is already slightly brown, though I can find some edible grapes while standing there and looking around. It is an afternoon in late autumn, a dead end, a small field path; the sun has already disappeared behind the horizon. I'm surrounded by the motorway (bridge), state roads, active and derelict train tracks on several levels and a few allotments. I stop and eat one grape after another. At the gate to the garden, two faded koalas laugh at me. There is a hum. The specific acoustics of the place. The dead end leads to an inaccessible hill, several metres high and steep. Overgrown, brambles, ivy and thorny bushes. At the very top, the bridge overcomes the valley cut and finds its way back to the lowlands. From down here, I can only perceive the noise protection wall, illuminated orange red by the last rays of the sun. I assume the constant low noise is caused by the passing cars behind it. Already, I miss the broad view of the landscape. I think I can hear conversation from a garden hut somewhere. It's difficult to guess distances down here in the valley; the acoustics change as soon as I linger in the bridge's shadow. Reverberating and dull at the same time. The Autobahn cuts through the landscape and habitats and it remains shadowy underneath it.

I get to this valley through a single road, the Hahnmühlenweg. I must cross a train track; a small passage opens to a view of the development of almost sixty residential units. Three streets of buildings, erected almost one hundred years ago. A housing estate formerly for mine workers built at the beginning of the twentieth century with new building materials, originally meant for just ten years. They seriously called the estate N****dorf [n**** village]. I researched that on the internet. There is no concrete pointer as to where the name came from. The neighbouring coal mine Tremonia had washing facilities for the workers, who, contrary to what might easily be assumed, did not come home with coal-coloured faces anymore. The U-shaped structure of an African tribe settlement might be another explanation.

In its elongated shape, the housing estate follows along the Emscher, a narrow river that over the course of industrialisation had to swallow the waste-water of humans and machines, and is now slowly finding its natural form now after the mines were closed. Residential buildings, oscillating between sand colour and a washed-out yellow, appear uniform, behind them a garden, next to them a parking space, and after the last house of the residential street, a small sports ground. With a car, there is only one way of accessing this — some cars are parked on the street. I don't see anybody.

I follow the main path leading into the estate, on my right is the Emscher, on the left driveways, one like the next. Sometimes a fake marble lion laughs at me from the steps to an entrance; a few houses down, a wind chime moves in the gentle breeze and makes me listen for a moment. After a few hundred metres, I reach a small river crossing and the adjacent sports ground, behind it, wasteland. On the other riverbank, an allotment association. Wet leaves obscure the individually designed plantings of the allotments, which by now are in the shade of the afternoon sun. I walk along the wasteland until the prong of the bridge rises up before me.

The area seems abandoned, gone to seed; on the ground I can barely make out the outlines of former plots. Cut-down, rotten remnants of a fence are there. Sometimes I step on building materials, cricks, bramble grows over individual heaps of rubble. There is a humming sound above me. It is cool down here — in the shadow of the massive bridge construction, hoarfrost gently covers the blades of grass on the ground. This makes me think of the novel *Concrete Island* (James Graham Ballard, 1974): because he is too fast, a man veers off the road and breaks through the guardrail so that he finally lands on a traffic island below. When he comes to, he realises that he is at a place that has always been forgotten, traffic flowing around it on all sides, sometimes ten metres higher, sometimes bordered off by sound insulation walls, sometimes indirectly visible. His first attempts to get back into civilisation are foiled by the speed of the surrounding traffic mass. He keeps finding himself back on the island, where — in addition to the will to survive — initially only his own speed exists. Surrounded by traces of past accidents, car wrecks and nature, he slowly begins to appropriate the space.

I look back to the wasteland behind me. A few years ago, there were still small dwellings here: each had its garden, its small field, a house number, build decades ago. On around thirty plots, structures were built that were officially on a park area. According to the city, the inhabitants never had permission to build on so-called *Grabeland* [digging land]. This is where people lived. Twelve years ago, the courts decided that the dwellings had to be removed, and for almost five years now the area has been a complete wasteland. What remains are derelict garden and plot gates that point the way to the past.

The seemingly indestructible motorway bridge crossing the valley (called Schnettkerbrücke), constructed shortly after World War I to save travellers from having to go through the valley, has existed in its current form only for six years. Before, it was not nearly as massive. The new construction is now 41.6 metres wide; everyday, 100,000 vehicles pass over it. The common driver, because of the high noise protection walls to the right and left of the road, doesn't even notice that this might be a bridge. Just look ahead.

Under the massive steel and concrete construction, to the east of the development, there is a railway embankment bordering the estate. Further back, the thorny bushes are denser, and the Emscher disappears under a deeper underpass, crosses the disused train tracks. All attempts to find a path here fail. Only through a narrow inconspicuous footpath on the opposite river bank are the two sides of the valley connected.

It seems as if life had withdrawn from this site, as if the shadow of the bridge had made a piece of history disappear — a hundred years ago, the Emscher meadows had been a popular recreational area. A boat ride to the Schnettkerbrücke was jokingly called «a trip to America». The estate was idyllically located in the meadows near the river, on the one side the coal mine, on the other the river, fields and nature. East and west, connected by a street. Small paths along the Emscher and the train tracks provided access to the valley.

Five years ago, the construction of a bypass road linking two Autobahns was finished — the Dornfelder Allee links the A40 running across the Schnettkerbrücke

with the A2 and surrounds the Emscher
valley on the western side with a several-
metres-high noise protection wall. In this
way, the wide valley became an island
in the middle of the speed of everyday
life, in the middle of thousands of people
who pass through the area in motorised
vehicles.

I pass under the bridge on the
narrow path, which leads me closely
along the concrete mass. Above me in
this moment: umpteen drivers. Behind
the next allotment association, a path
leads me to the next dead end before the
bridge. The gardens seem winterly and
abandoned. On the left is the gate, on it,
two koalas made of wood. The vine at the
fence bears a few last fruits. I pick them
and listen to the hum (autumn 2019). ←

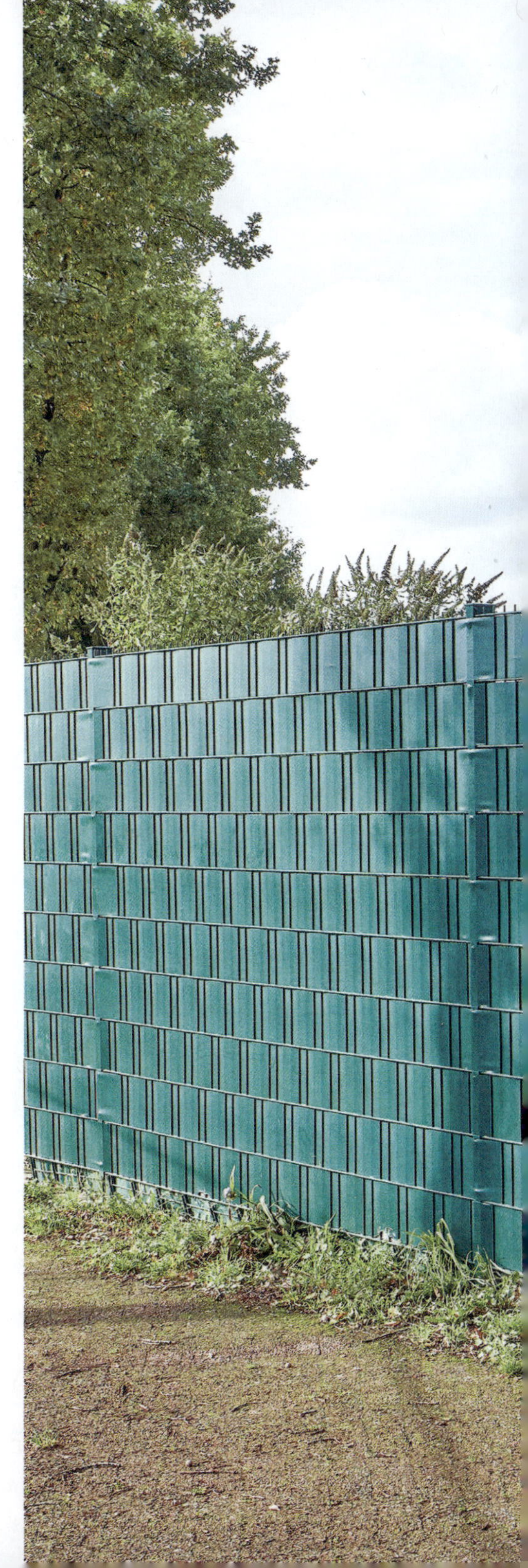

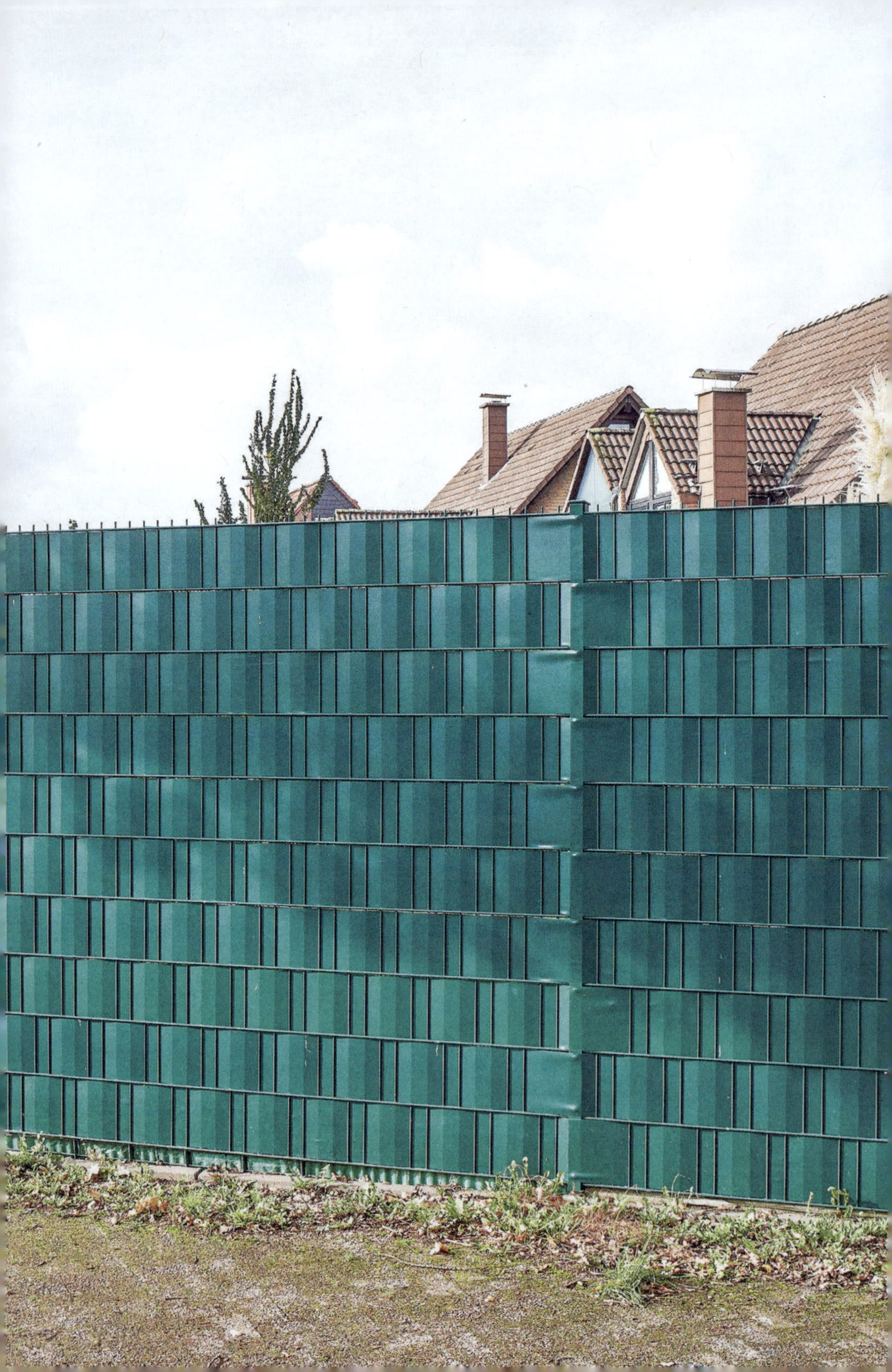

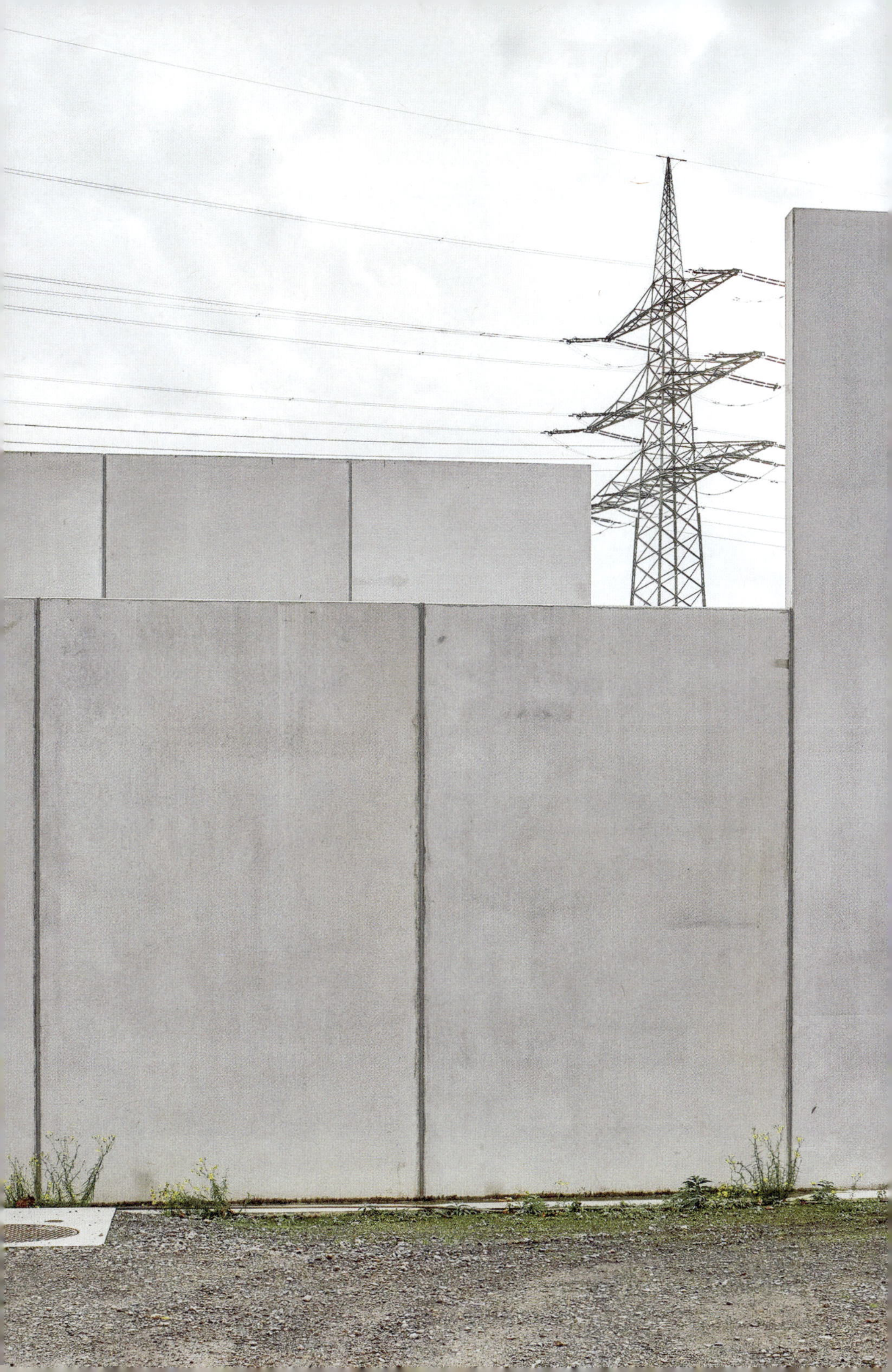

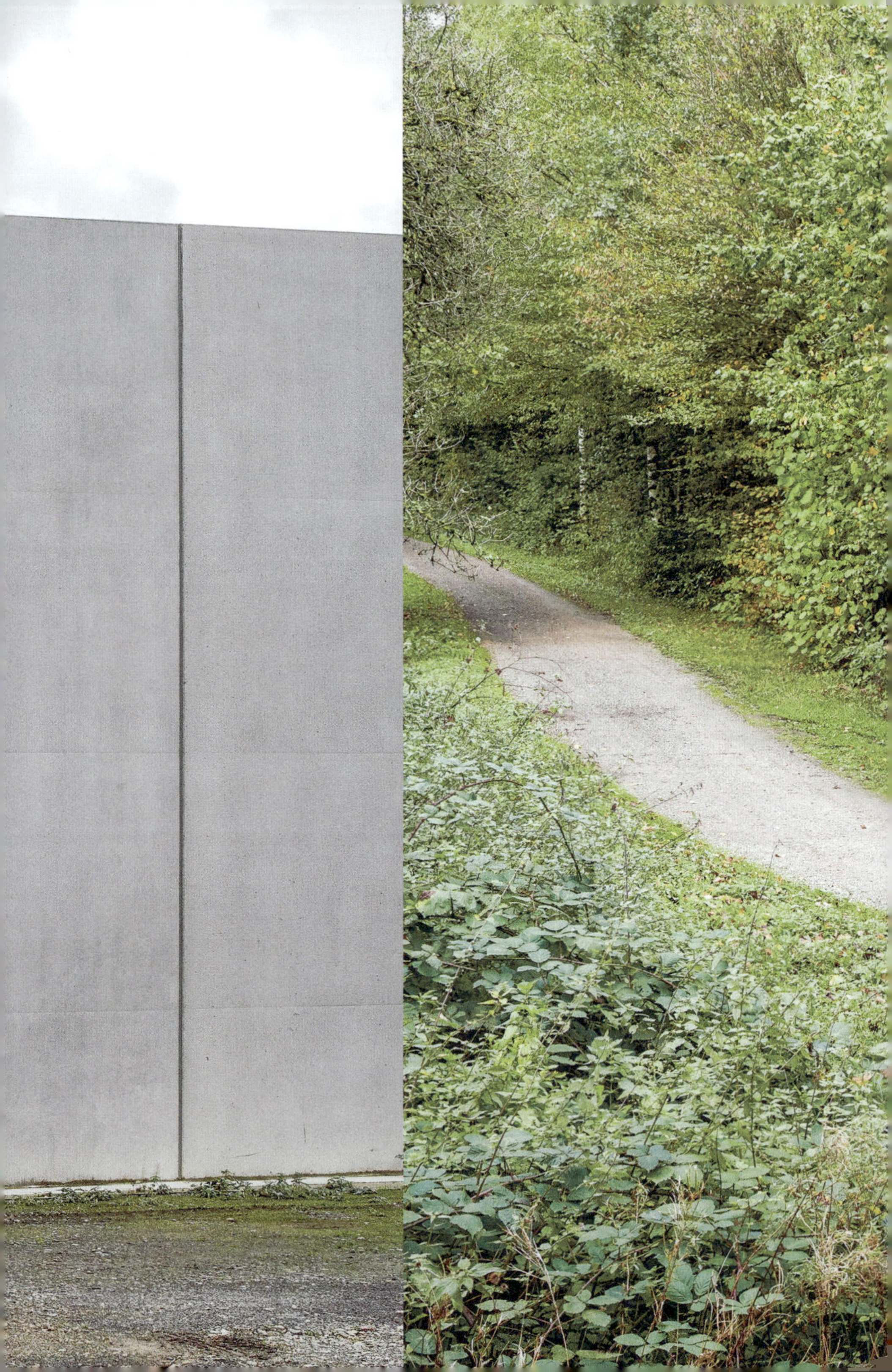

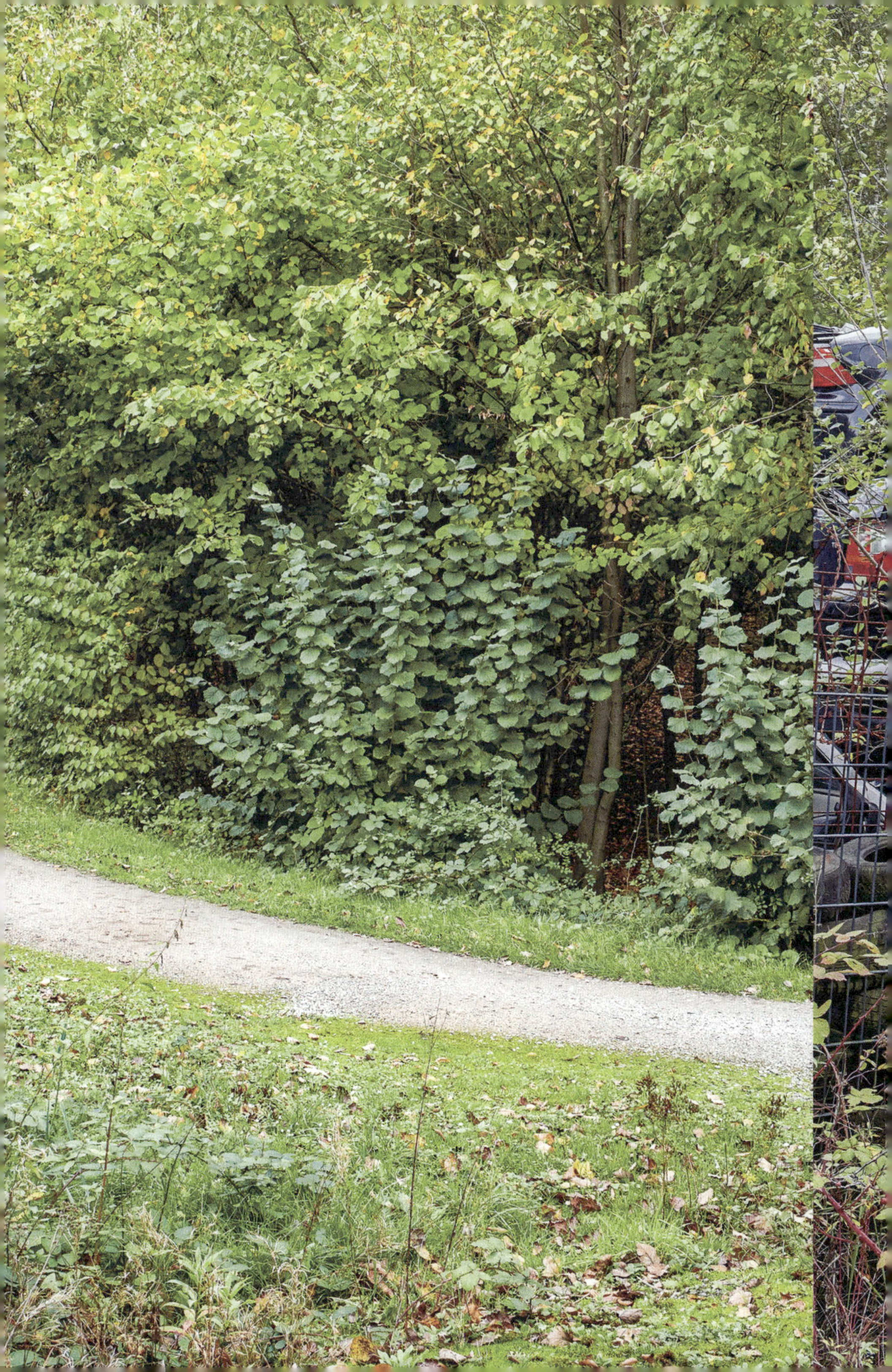

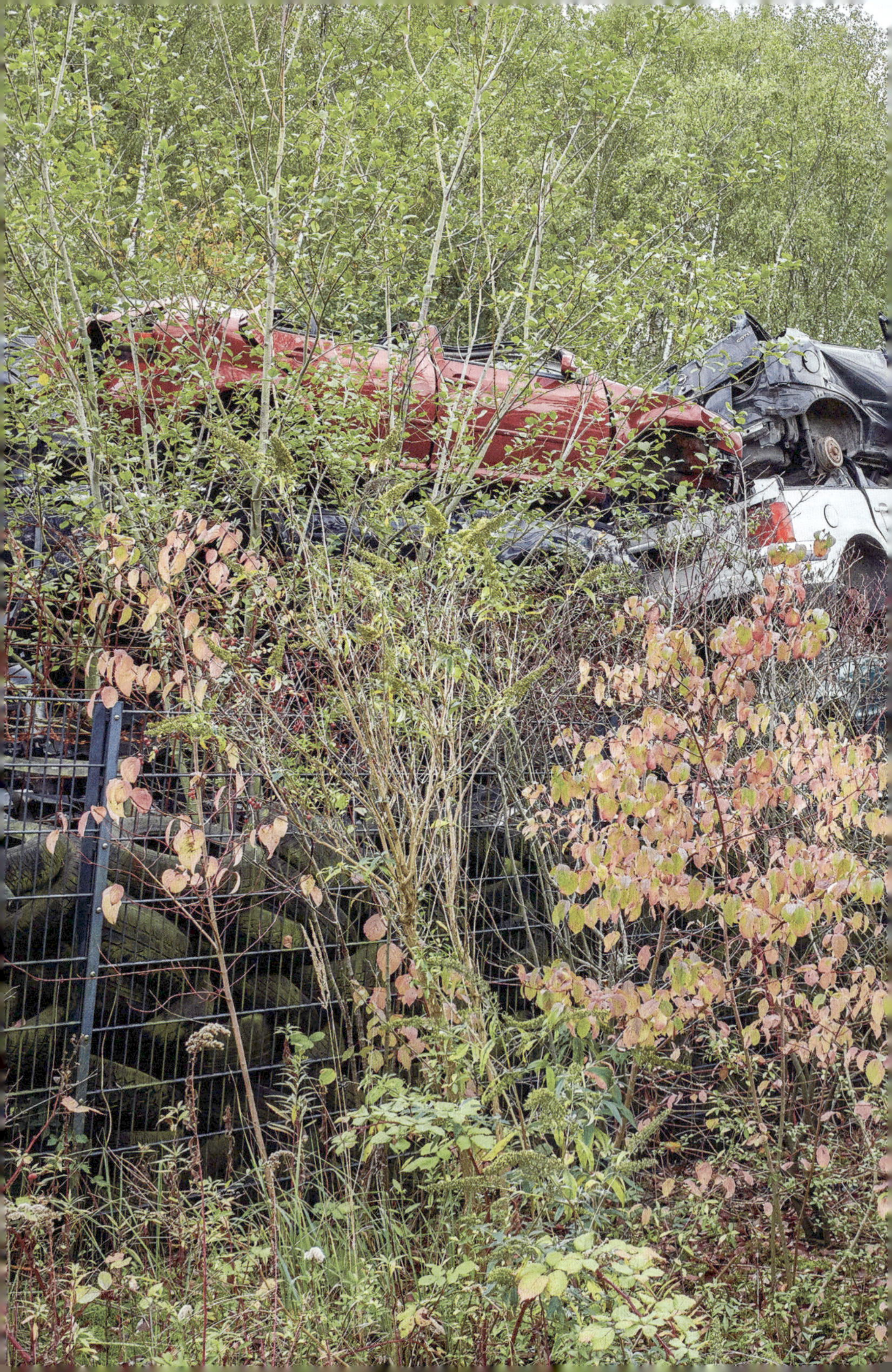

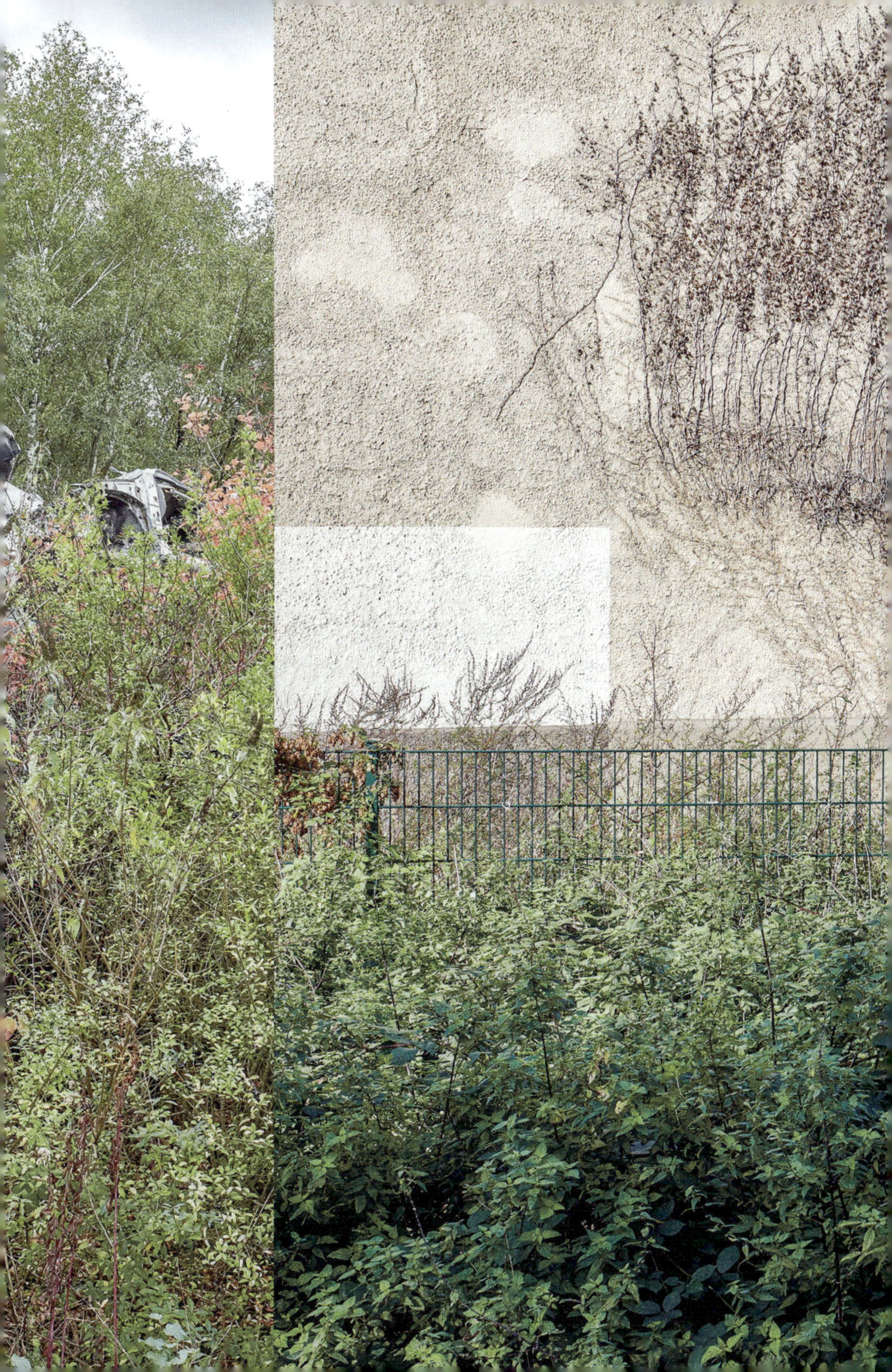

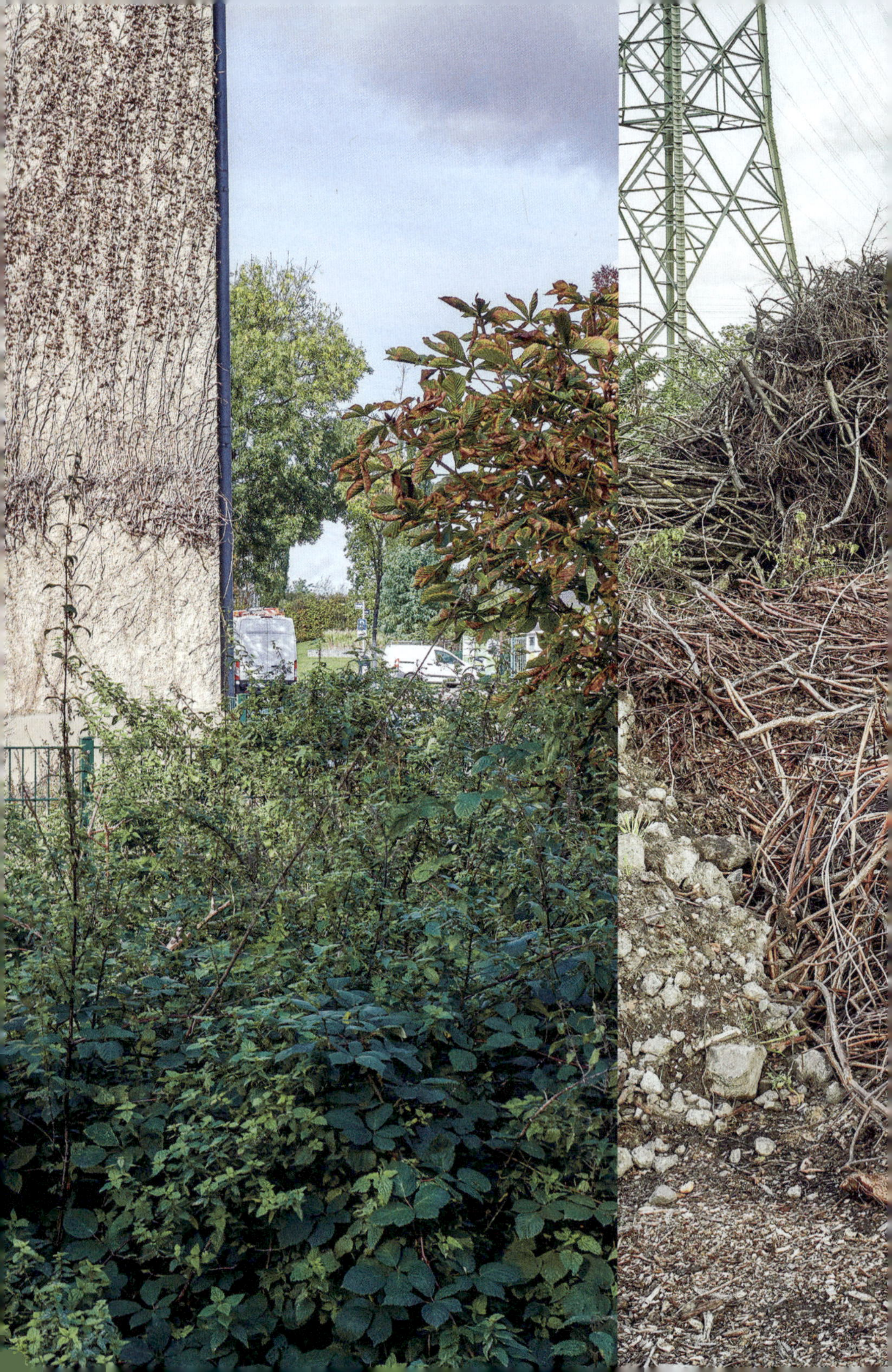

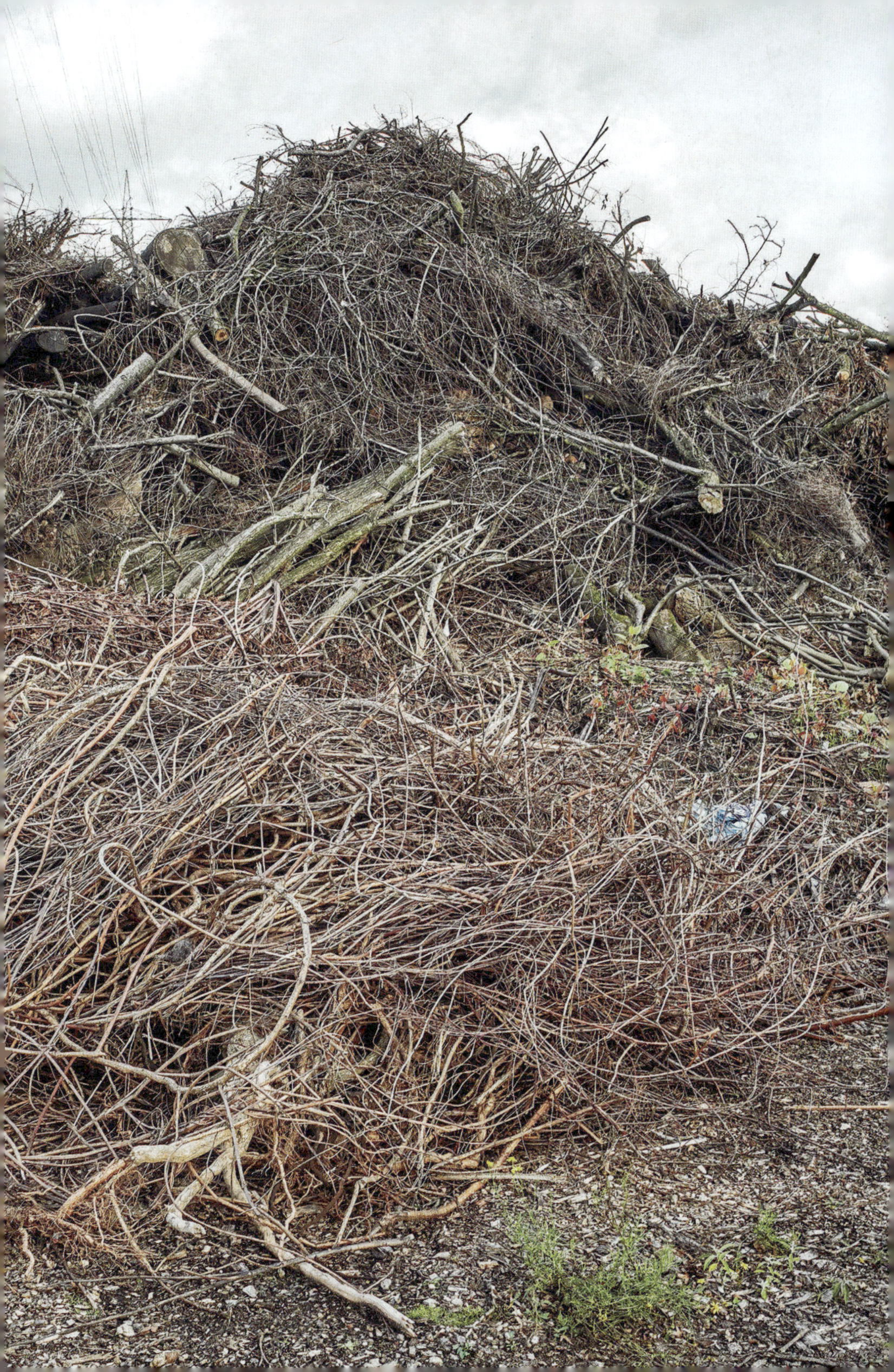

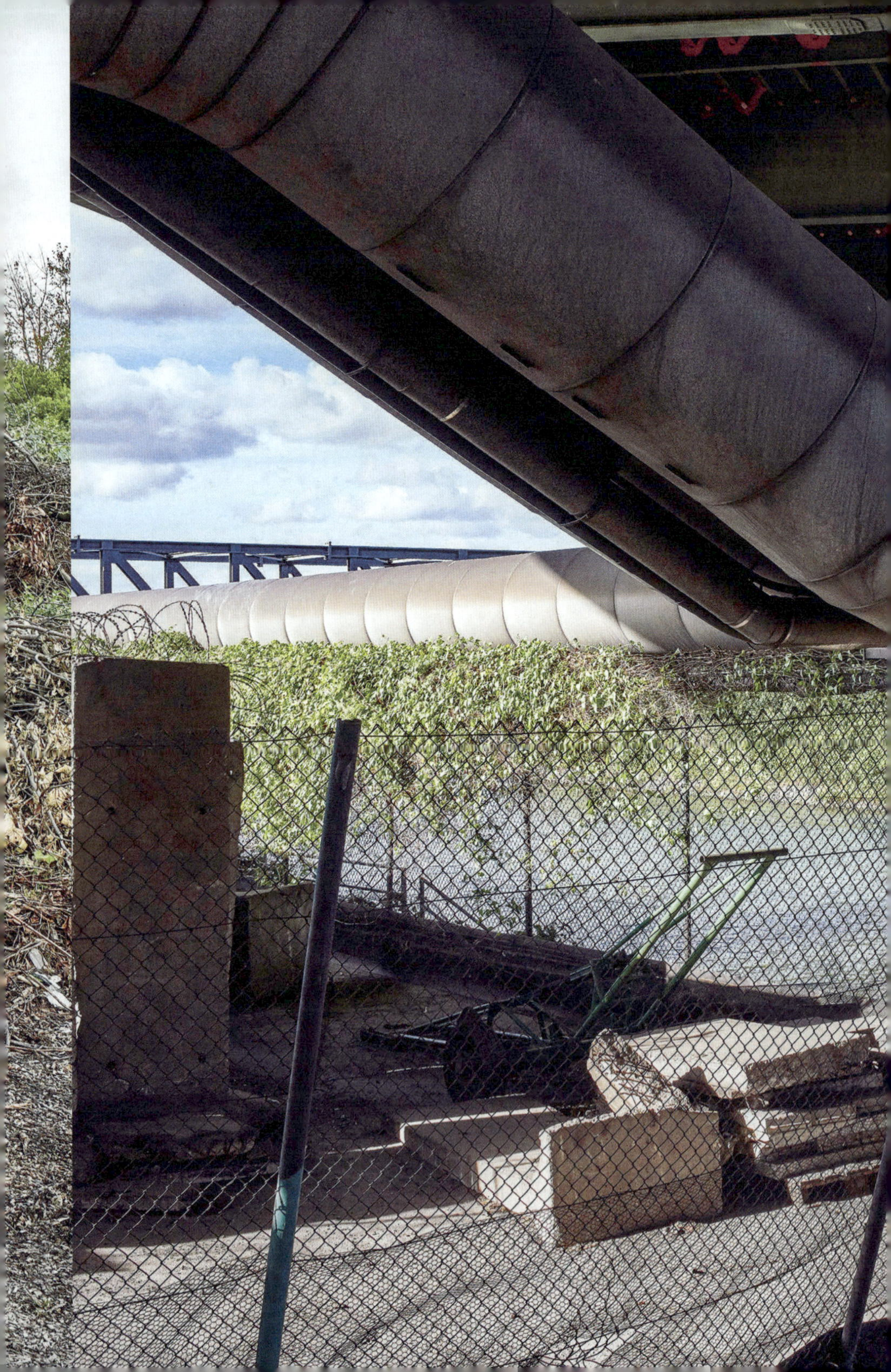

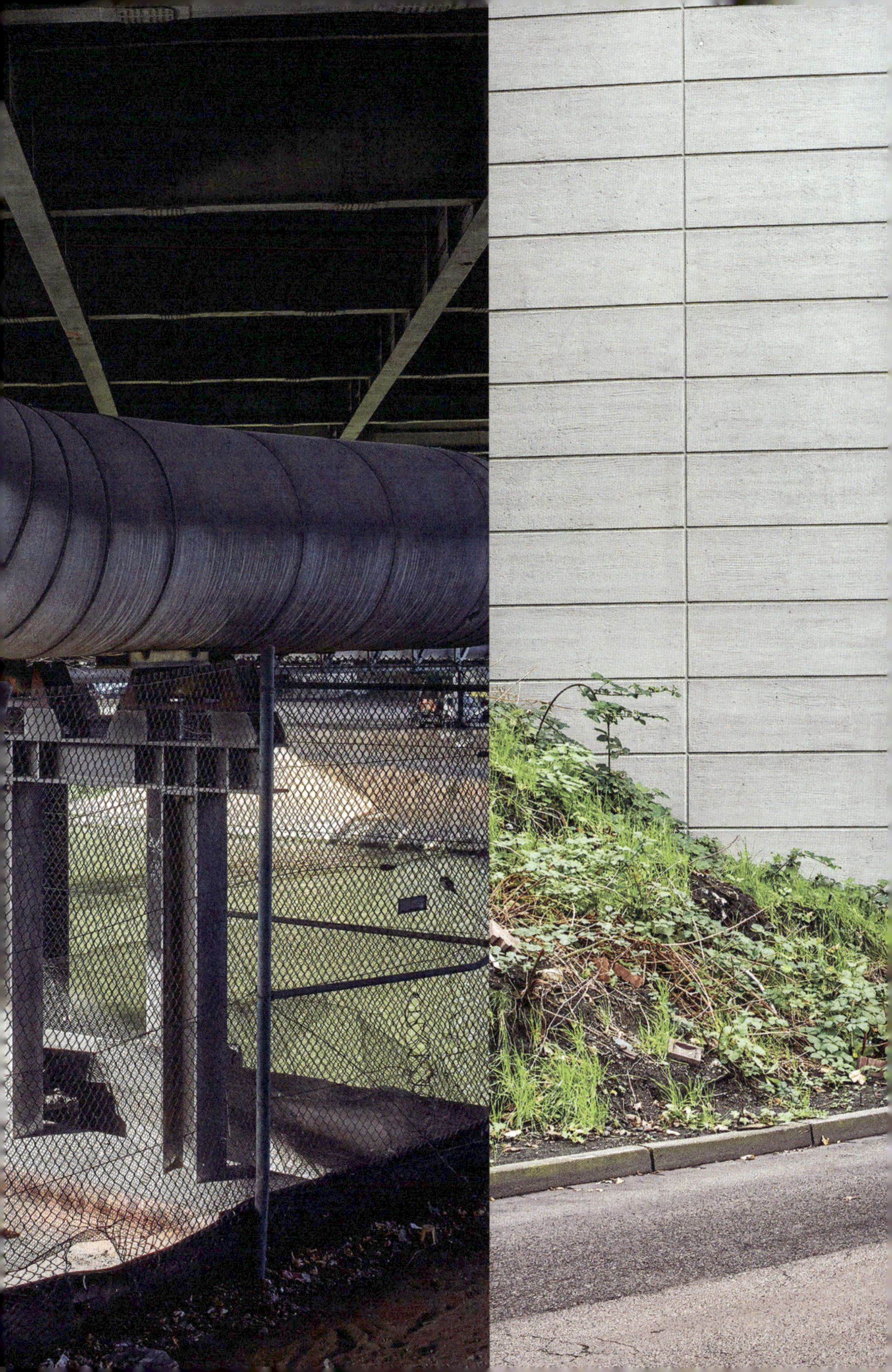

ABC

280

The first entries in this glossary were published in Urbane Künste Ruhr's magazine in 2019: since then, the glossary has grown with each new issue. Everyone on the team joins in writing them; the collective of authors now consists of twenty-one former and current colleagues. The collection of texts from the magazines one to nine presented here is incomplete, illogical and largely unsystematic; instead, it illuminates interesting aspects about the works, sites, materials and circumstances that a sculpture trail along the Emscher involves from the various perspectives of those participating.

A

ABWASSER [SEWAGE]
As a result of industrialisation in the nineteenth century, ever-growing quantities of domestic and industrial wastewater were channelled into the meandering Emscher river and its tributaries, generating unhygienic conditions in populated areas. This prompted the founding in 1899 of the first-ever German water board association, the Emschergenossenschaft; one of its preeminent tasks was to regulate the disposal of waste-water. By 1920 the public water board was running thirty sewage plants. Today, the former sewage treatment plant Bernemündung in Bottrop-Ebel is the industrial monument and park BernePark. On view inside this listed building complex is a group work titled *CATCH AS CATCH CAN* by Lawrence Weiner and Mischa Kuball. One of the two clarifying tanks harbours a work by Piet Oudolf in collaboration with the landscape architecture office GROSS.MAX, titled *Theater der Pflanzen* [Theatre of Plants], which consists of 21,000 shrubs and flowers. [JF, M2 2019]

ABWASSERFREIHEIT [ABSENCE OF SEWAGE]
Sewage in the Emscher? That will soon be history. At the end of 2021, the long-term Emscher Conversion project will be completed, and the Emscher river system will be free of sewage. For decades, wastewater has flowed through the Emscher region above ground, until the river's ecological conversion was decided upon as part of the *Emscher Park International Building Exhibition* (1989—99), and in 1992 the ceremonial ground-breaking ceremony took place for a project costing billions that is unique in the world. The added value of the Emscher Con-version can already be seen: in the Deusen district of Dortmund, part of the main watercourse has already been renaturalised, nature has returned and vines are even being grown by Lake Phoenix. [SW, M5 2021]

ALLE [EVERYONE]
Art in public space is there for everyone, 24/7. There is no threshold to cross, no admission fee, no opening times, no white walls. Instead you are outside in the fresh air but also in an unprotected space. The works are exposed to any adversities inflicted by people and nature. If we treat them well they have something to give us — new perspectives, an outlook, a way-marker, an encounter, pleasure, identification. Especially in uncertain times such as these, the Emscherkunstweg is an oppor-tunity to spend time outdoors while jointly — at a distance — experiencing art. Incorporated in the changing urban spaces of the Ruhr region, Emscherkunstweg promises art for everyone at all times. [JF, M4 2020]

B

BANKETT-SCHNITT [CLEARANCE OF VEGETATION FROM THE HARD SHOULDER]
The German word «Bankett» comes from French Banquet and is used in road construction to refer to the verge alongside the road used as an emergency stopping lane, parking and turning area for works services. Along the Emscher cycle route the hard shoulder is regularly maintained and mowed. This ensures that the cycle path remains usable and prevents obstruction from climb-ing plants, hedges or overgrown trees. While the Bankett-Schnitt is a necessary measure to maintain the cycle path, the German term resonates with the noble gesture of clearing the path for cyclists. [DK, M8 2022]

BERNEPARK
Originally commissioned in 1955 as the modern «Kläranlage Bernemündung» in an industrial suburb of Bottrop, this sewage treatment plant sank into a deep slumber between 1997 and 2010 after it was decommissioned. In the autumn of 2010, it was declared an industrial monument and thus became a new cultural and recreational meeting point in the middle of the urban space of the Ruhr region. Twelve years later, this «neighbourhood park» now represents more than just the transition from an industrial plant to a recreational area. It represents art in public spaces that can be experienced, recrea-tion for immediate neighbours, tourism along the Emscher river and a place of education that enables social participation. Works by the artists Piet Oudolf and GROSS.MAX, Mischa Kuball and Andreas Strauss have been restored and artistically revised. They offer opportunities for young and old to explore and stay overnight. Above all this, the slogan *CATCH AS CATCH CAN*

by the US artist Lawrence Weiner symbolises more than just an advertisement from the 1950s. It is a call to action, individual to the eye of each beholder: «Take it as it comes» [KK, M7 2022]

BESUCH [VISIT]
Cycling is the best way to explore the sculpture trail, which runs alongside a 101-kilometre cycle path. You will need plenty of stamina and a place to stay overnight and sometimes you have to stray off the path to discover the artworks. Guided cycle tours run on the first Sunday of every month, 2 p.m.—5 p.m., from April to October. It's free, fun and you get to discuss art in public spaces and anything else that makes the Emscher region interesting. [JF, M3 2020]

BEWEHRUNGSSTAHL [REINFORCING STEEL]
Reinforcing steel is used to strengthen steel concrete construction components and is cast after being installed in the formwork.
Art emerges from ideas and combinations; it is the joint impact of content and form. Form consists of material, which sometimes has to be quite strong. Reinforcing steel is thus used in concrete and becomes works like *Neustadt, Monument for a Forgotten Future, Black Circle Square* and many other sculptures along Emscherkunstweg. [MM, M9 2023]

BRUTOLOGY
Brutalist architecture: is that the epitome of progress, growth, social justice, or does it mean just the opposite: monotonous, ugly, inhuman dimensions? In their work from September 2022, *BRUTOLOGY. The Built, the Unbuilt and the Unbuildable* choreographers and performers Montserrat Gardò Castillo and Petr Hastik engaged with Brutalist architectures and infrastructures. For *Emscherkunstweg: Vor Ort* [Emscher Art Trail: On Site], they appeared together with other performers under the traffic hub Mallinckrodtbrücke, an interstitial space between a cycle path, highway feeder road, waterway and railway tracks. With silvery inflatables, guitar riffs, and synthesiser sounds, dance and performance, a poetic and multi-perspective engagement with modernist architecture and its attributions emerged. The term brutalism derives from the French term «béton brut» — raw concrete, exposed concrete. The link to the troughs and wastewater pipes at various points of the Emscher restoration is especially striking. [EW, M9 2023]

BRÜCKEN [BRIDGES]
There are countless bridges across the Emscher for traffic — pedestrians, bicycles, cars, trains or even ships — or infrastructure in whatever form — cable lines, gas lines, pipes for liquids of all kinds. Due to the ground subsidence at various levels that has resulted in several places from mining, some of these bridges and links run in a confusing way on top of one another or next to one another. Probably the most beautiful of its kind is part of the Emscherkunstweg — Tobias Rehberger's *Slinky Springs to Fame*. It does not bridge over the Emscher, but the Rhein-Herne Canal right nearby, and it adds a new category to the local collection of bridges. It is not only functional, but combines elegance and playful finesse for an experience of dream-like flânerie, so that one would prefer to never reach the other shore. [DK, M9 2023]

C

CATCH AS CATCH CAN
Mischa Kuball and Lawrence Weiner probably conceived of *CATCH AS CATCH CAN* when they first visited the former treatment plant in Bottrop-Ebel in preparation of the *Emscherkunst* exhibition in 2010. Kuball took on the clarification tanks. When it's dark, a white light surrounds the edges of the tanks; seemingly tangible, and yet gone again just as quickly. Weiner's phrase *CATCH AS CATCH CAN* on the roof of the building captures the whole premises, echoes the rounded forms of Kuball's light installation and provides an ironic take on the BernePark plant. Quite unexpectedly, the former treatment plant has become a popular destination for art and leisure and has been fully restored in the process, with curators keeping a careful eye on the artists' works. [ML, M3 2020]

CHOLERA
Fortunately, this gastrointestinal disease only occurs these days in Germany in the proverb, «die Wahl zwischen Pest und Cholera», meaning a choice between equally unpleasant tasks. In the late nineteenth century, however, outbreaks of cholera occurred when the Emscher river, which carried effluent and had a weak incline, burst its banks. When the Emschergenossenschaft was set up in 1899, wastewater disposal and treatment, drainage and flood protection were regulated in towns and municipalities. The current COVID-19 pandemic can be measured in wastewater, but it is luckily not transmitted via this route. The research on measurable virus concentration in wastewater even adds to the information we have about this disease and its occurrence. [EW, M8 2022]

D

DREIKANTSCHLÜSSEL [TRIANGLE SPANNER KEY]
Along the Emscher, various barrier measures were and are necessary — game fencing, metal and barbed wire — that might seem somewhat excessive and

exaggerated. For many locals, the areas located behind the barriers are often used for daily activities such as walking the dog, so the enclosures are not taken seriously and regularly crossed since the necessary points of access and gates are accessible with a standard triangle spanner key. Due to the dangers that lurk there — potential sudden flooding, poison still in the water and the risk of slipping into the river and drowning, but also due to newly emerging biotopes that need protection, this should be rigorously avoided to protect oneself and others. [DK, M9 2023]

DÜKER [CULVERT]
A culvert is a pressure pipe through which, for example, water or wastewater can be channelled underneath an obstacle without recourse to additional energy. This method works on the principle of communicating pipes. The siphon under the bathroom sink is a culvert everyone is familiar with. Water flows through this U-shaped, water-filled pipe into main drainage, thus preventing any unpleasant smells coming back out of the sink into the bathroom. Up until a few years ago the Emscher river was also channelled beneath the Rhine-Herne Canal through a culvert in the vicinity of the *Walkway and Tower* by Tadashi Kawamata. But since the Emscher's course was relocated it now flows quite normally under the canal — the Emscher culvert was turned into an Emscher passage. Incidentally, Kawamata is currently working on a new concept for the walkway beneath the viewing tower since for conservational reasons this had to be dismantled in summer 2019. [MP, M2 2019]

E

EMSCHER
The river runs from Holzwickede along a course of some eighty-four kilometres through the central Ruhr region — through Dortmund, Castrop-Rauxel, Recklinghausen, Herten, Herne, Gelsenkirchen, Essen, Bottrop and Oberhausen — before finally converging with the Rhine at Dinslaken. In the nineteenth century the population of the originally sparsely settled meadow landscape rapidly expanded. Since then, the areas of Emscher valley and Emscherbruch (the flood plain of the Emscher, a marshy landscape) have radically changed. After being used for decades as an above-ground sewage canal system, thus precipitating the ecological death of the Emscher river and its tributaries, these are now being transformed back into a close-to-natural, albeit still artificial condition by the Emschergenossenschaft water board.
[JF, M2 2019]

EMSCHERBRÜCHER DICKKOPP [WILD HORSE BREED]
Almost two centuries ago, Emscherbrücher Dickkopp horses galloped along the route of today's Emscherkunstweg. This wild breed grew to a height of up to 135 centimetres and was first mentioned in records in 1369. They lived in the Emscher region — known as the Emscherbruch owing to its topographical features — between Waltrop and Bottrop and were used on battlefields and in underground mining due to their small, robust stature. Their free existence abruptly came to an end in 1840 when Duke Alfred von Croÿ captured herds over large areas and sold them to the town of Dülmen in the first step towards targeted pony-breeding. If you look closely, you will still find the Emscherbrücher Dickkopp in many places in the Ruhr. For instance, it is the central element on the coat of arms of the city of Herne, and the Cranger Fair is said to have developed along the tradition of horse market. [JLA, M8 2022]

EMSCHER FOLLY
In English and French eighteenth-century landscape gardening, the term follies refers to often eccentric architectural structures that seem to have a function, but in fact have none at all. Nicole Wermer's sculpture of the same name, which is planned to be one of the first new productions for the Emscherkunstweg, will be a surprising addition to the fallow land by the Steelworks Bruckhausen; a movement arrested in the form of a mystical triangle. A large number of bikes seem to have been randomly left there, but in fact they were painstakingly positioned and welded together with a specially designed stainless steel frame. The unexpected absence of urban space and its occupants from the scene creates a moment of confusion and estrangement. The sculptural qualities of the installation come to the fore and suddenly the apparently familiar material references its own design, forms of concentration, elements of construction, colour tones and stasis. [BP, M3 2020]

EMSCHERGRAM
We love a diversity of voices and changes in perspective! Which is why you can find Emschergram on the Emscherkunstweg website. On Emschergram, you can store, show and share your own photos of the works of art along the Emscher river. Simply go to emscherkunstweg.de/emschergram to do so. With just a few clicks, you can upload your image and your name. After they have been accepted, your pictures will play a long-term role on the artwork pages. We look forward to receiving your entries and are excited to see what you have experienced on the

Emscherkunstweg and how you have captured the works of art through photography!
[NL, M7 2022]

EMSCHER HÖFE [FARMS]
The Emscher Höfe is a series of three farmsteads and a park situated along the Emscher river between its source and its mouth. In an idyllic setting in Holzwick-ende is the historic timber-frame farmstead Emscherquellhof. Located in Castrop-Rauxel, the Hof Emscher-Auen lies very close to the area's largest flood retention basin. Hof Emschermündung is in Dinslaken near the Rhine. The fourth of these attractions is BernePark in Bottrop, a former sewage treatment facility that symbolises the structural change that has taken place in the Ruhr region. The Emscher Höfe serve as a platform for a wide variety of participants and projects, opening up new spaces for action, such as educational events, the arts, leisure and local recreation activities. As places of encounter and rendezvous they are easy to reach by bike along the Emscher-Weg, a cycle path.
[KK, M4 2020]

EWIGKEITSAUFGABE [ETERNITY TASK]
Eternity tasks, or eternity costs, burdens, promises or debts. Does that make you dizzy? Well, it should. If we look at the Ruhr region, these are primarily the consequences of hard coal mining that remain with us, well, for a very long time. Mining has caused the ground to sink up to twenty-five metres and ground-water needs to be constantly pumped out to keep the cities from going under. Groundwater purification and landfill measures, that is, ever-increasing dykes for the lower lying regions, come on top of that. Responsibility for these costs is delegated in a so-called «eternity clause», another such term. Without constant pumping, one-fifth of

the Ruhr region would be beneath a lake landscape. The Emscher would not flow into the Rhine, but into a lake north of Oberhausen, from the waters of which the upper half of the sculpture *Zauberlehrling* [Sorcerer's Apprentice] would tower.

Sometimes the final storage of atomic waste is referred to as an eternal burden. But it isn't: a permanent disposal site deep underground is according to German law «passive and free of maintenance», so without any eternity costs. Well, isn't that wonderful? [MM, M9 2023]

F

FAULBEHÄLTER [DIGESTION TANKS]
For her installation *Glückauf. Bergarbeiterproteste im Ruhrge-biet* [Good Luck. Miners' Protests in the Ruhr Region], created for *Emscherkunst* in 2010, the artist Silke Wagner used the digestion tank in the Emschergenossen-schaft's decommissioned sewage plant in Herne located between the Emscher river and the Rhine-Herne-Canal. Having been constructed originally as a vessel for the sludge resulting from wastewater treatment, Wagner converted the tank into a pictorial surface. In a vast wall mosaic she tells the history of miners' protests in the Ruhr region, thereby focussing attention on the imbalance between increased economic prosperity through industrialisation and the working conditions of the workforce.
[ML, M2 2019]

FISCHE [FISH]
Fish life is returning to the Emscher river. After the central river of the Ruhr region was used for over a century as an open wastewater course, the renatured sections of the waterway system now offer increasing evidence of the impressive success of the

transgenerational Emscher con-version project. In the Emscher river itself, but also in its tribu-taries such as the Deininghauser stream in Castrop-Rauxel, the Borbecker Mühlenbach stream in Essen and the Läppkes Mühlen-bach stream in Oberhausen, the Emscher bullhead has been successfully reintroduced after 150 years of absence. But this is not the only type of fish to return to the Emscher waterways: in Dortmund trout have already been sighted, while in other areas the Emschergenossenschaft has confirmed the presence, among others, of the ninespine and threespine stickleback.
[IA, M4 2020]

FLUSSREGENPFEIFER [LITTLE RINGED PLOVER]
The little ringed plover, which has returned to the Emscher, is easy to overlook, because its brown feathers make it virtually invisible along the banks of the river. Special caution is thus required when walking in your rubbers during the breeding season from April to May, for the little ringed plover lays its small dotted eggs in a ditch dug by the males of the species in the mud near the water. The fifteen-centimetre-long bird prefers to spend its winters in warmer climates and flies to the Sahara as a long-distance migrant. Whether it will still have to fly so far in future is something that remains to be seen. Climate change already threatens the species today, because its breed-ing sites are being washed away by strong rains and wet spring days. [JLA, M9, 2023]

FUSSBALL [FOOTBALL]
Because the rules and equipment were simple, this bourgeois club activity, which was initially considered a «gentleman's sport», gradually developed into a street sport for working families around the turn of the century and is closely linked to the history of industrialisation in the Ruhr region. During the German

Empire, mining and factory workers were politically and socially isolated. As a result, football took on a symbolic political dimension when «bourgeois» and «working» clubs competed, and the lower-class population tried to liberate itself from enduring social devaluation. As a result, many football clubs were set up, especially in the industrial areas along the Emscher river — most notably the first factory team in the German football league: FC Schalke 04. [AJ, M8 2022]

G

GENERATIONENPROJEKT [GENERATIONAL PROJECT]
The Emschergenossenschaft's most well-known project is the generational Emscher conversion project. The land subsidence caused by the mining industry in the Ruhr region meant that underground tunnels could not be built in earlier years as they would have been damaged. As a result, wastewater was dumped in the Emscher — the area's central river — and in its side streams. When the mining moved northwards, the risk of subsidence vanished and underground tunnels could finally be built. The Emschergenossenschaft has been planning and implementing the Emscher conversion project since 1992. Every body of water gets an underground tunnel that transports the wastewater to treatment plants; thus, the streams are clean and restored to their natural state. The Emschergenossenschaft has invested more than five billion euros in this project over the last three decades. [IA, M3 2020]

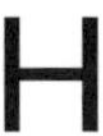

H

HEALING COMPLEX
Since 2022, the encounter site Healing Complex initiated by artist Irena Haiduk in Gelsenkirchen-Erle — near Emscher river — has been inviting guests in collaboration with Urbane Künste Ruhr to the former church St. Bonifatius to participate in a wide variety of joint activities and processes of design, be it collective baking and subsequent coming together at a table, creating artworks, regenerating from everyday stress by way of sauna rituals (as in the mobile sauna at the event «Summit») or the theoretical and practical engagement with the magical facets of fungi cultures. In close collaboration with the residents and other interested parties, at the centre of encounter the potential of networking is tested out and room is opened to invent the use of the space anew over and over. [AJ, M9 2023]

HERNER MEER [HERNE SEA]
The collaborative work by sculptor Bogomir Ecker and composer Bülent Kullucu that juts out of the water between the lock and the yacht harbour makes a strange and fragile appearance. As if assembled by a child, yellow and silver building blocks are stacked to create two towers that are lit up at night by a sixteen-metre-high streetlamp. The wind catching in the apertures of the individual blocks produces tones, and the sculpture begins to resonate. In *reemrenreh (kaum Gesang)* — read backwards, the title states the work's location at the «Herner Meer» — art and nature are brought into harmony; the object's seeming instability and its «uncertain» presence in the water heighten the ephemeral quality of the moment.
[TH, M4 2020]

HOCHWASSER-RÜCKHALTEBECKEN [FLOOD DETENTION BASIN]
A flood detention basin is a water-retaining structure that regulates the amount of water in rivers and streams. If too much water flows, it is stored in a basin and released at a delay. In this way, flooding can be avoided. The largest flood detention basin for the Emscher is located right next to the project by Andreas Strauss *dasparkhotel_inside-outsite* at Hof Emscher-Auen in Castrop-Rauxel, where you can spend the night in three renovated sewage pipes. The terrain is home to many birds that can be wonderfully observed from the pavilion erected explicitly for this purpose. [MM, M9 2023]

I

IGA 2027 [INTERNATIONAL GARDEN EXHIBITION 2027]
After the *International Building Exhibition Emscher Park* and the European Capital of Culture year RUHR.2010, the project of the next decade in the Ruhr area will be the *International Garden Exhibition (IGA)* in 2027. It will connect the entire region on different levels. The new «Zukunftsgärten» [future gardens] in Gelsenkirchen, Duisburg, Dortmund, Castrop-Rauxel/Recklinghausen and Bergkamen/Lünen form the five main locations. Under the rubric *Unsere Gärten* [Our Gardens], the focus will be on existing gardens and parks, and the section *Mein Garten* [My Garden] will showcase the horticultural talents of individuals, initiatives and associations. The Ruhr is on its way to becoming the greenest industrial region in the world. For example, a tree will be planted for every resident in the Ruhr area by 2027 — a total of five million new trees! [TH, M8 2022]

J

JÖCKELN [JAUNT]

You can take a pleasant jaunt on bike or on foot along the banks of the Emscher over a stretch of 101 kilometres. From the historical half-timber house «Emscherquellhof» at the source of the Emscher to its mouth, a variety of green industrial plants, historical parks, water technology, artificial tips and a wide range of natural landscapes along the Emscher-Weg, all maintained by the Emschergenossenschaft, illustrate the charged history of the river and the region. Most of the eighteen works of art on the Emscherkunstweg are located in immediate proximity to the cycle trail. For further details:
→ emscher-weg.de
[JF, M2 2019]

K

KLIMA [CLIMATE]

After *Ruhr Ding: Territories,* held in early summer 2019 in the cities of Bochum, Dortmund, Essen and Oberhausen, the temporary exhibition format will migrate in May/June 2020 to the north of the region as *Ruhr Ding: Climate.* As with the preceding theme «Territories», the «Climate» edition will draw on regional issues with global significance. For historical reasons — mining was first undertaken in the south and from there gradually expanded northwards — and because of the general direction of the wind, the northern part of the region suffered the most and the longest from industrial pollution. Animated testimony of this is offered by the chequered history of the Emscher, which together with the Emscherkunstweg is an important element of the forthcoming project. [BP, M2 2019]

KOOPERATION [COLLABORATION]

Collaboration? Collaborations! From the outset, collaborations have been inscribed on the institutional DNA of Urbane Künste Ruhr, whose task is to develop projects and networks within the region. Collaborations between regional, supra-regional and international institutions, cultural practitioners and artists have resulted in many art projects that take up the region as a theme. The Emschergenossenschaft, a water management association, is one of the oldest partners of the Urbane Künste Ruhr with whom there was an initial collaboration on the temporary *Emscherkunst* project, as well as the permanent Emscherkunstweg since 2019, during which it also pursued its own interests. This unusual partnership grew from the Ruhr Capital of Culture in 2010. Along around eighty kilometres of the Emscher river, the region is presented with international artistic appeal. Collaborations like this underline how powerful the belief in the transformational power of art is, and how barriers can be overcome as a result.
[CK, M8 2022]

L

LANDMARKEN [LANDMARKS]

Over the past seventy years a wide variety of artworks in surprising density have been created for public spaces within the region. If you drive up the A40 you will spot, above all, the large format «landmarks» on the waste tips of former industrial sites. Although these landmarks are spread over the entire coal mining district, as elements of the Emscherkunstweg these works are all located very close to the river, running like a gold thread from East to West through the Ruhr region. The works themselves specifically relate to their immediate surroundings. They reflect the conversion of the Emscher and the newly created landscape and allow for individual engagement with the agitated history and dynamic present of the region. [ML, M2 2019]

M

MONUMENT FOR A FORGOTTEN FUTURE

With this lovely title, a large concrete sculpture was created by Olaf Nicolai and Douglas Gordon, a steel scaffolding with sprayed concrete on a surface area of 150 square metres, to be precise in 2010 on Emscher Island near the sluices in Gelsenkirchen. From the inside, a composition by the Scottish band Mogwai plays quietly in a loop.

In this work, everything is just right: the true-to-original replica of a rock from Joshua Tree National Park near Los Angeles has been brought to the Ruhr region. To claim it's the logical future of the «close-to-nature» Emscher restoration and at the same time to mourn that restoration could have multiple consequences. On the one hand, aesthetically it will not take on the extreme dimensions that had been planned (because the plans lie in a drawer somewhere). On the other hand, at a point in time that lies behind the future, nobody will remember that the copy of a boulder from an American national park once metaphorically referred to the future: it is a humorous-sculptural-linguistic stroke of genius. And on top of this, the Mogwai endless loop in the concrete bed as a reference to the artificiality, but also as a notable example of how an almost indestructible audio installation can be realised in public space.
[BP, M9 2023]

N

NATURNAH [CLOSE TO NATURE]
As the Emscher turned into a wastewater canal, from the end of the nineteenth century, it became confined to the watercourse itself and lost any real relationship to its surroundings. And in the twentieth century the surroundings also underwent profound changes characterised by intensive land use: housing developments were built, along with pipeline and transport infrastructure. The more land that can be returned to the river in the course of the current Emscher conversion, the greater the opportunities for self-starting development involving minimal maintenance and maximum sustainability. But the necessary space is often lacking, which means that the river has to be integrated into its current environment. The Emscher-genossenschaft's landscape ecologists know the processes and cause-and-effect sequences of river ecosystems and develop complex, detailed solutions for achieving watercourse and structural development that are as typical as possible.
[MS, M5 2021]

NEUPRODUKTIONEN [NEW PRODUCTIONS]
The curatorial team is currently engaged in discussions with the artists Wermers and Julius von Bismarck about possible new productions. For her sculptural works Nicole Wermers often uses everyday objects that have lost their original utility and are deployed in new contexts, thereby exploring both formal and socio-cultural issues. In his mostly technically complex works von Bismarck is concerned with scientific as well as politically pressing questions. Both artists were invited to travel widely throughout the Emscher region and to develop concepts for new permanent works by the Emscher river based on their accumulated impressions. [ML M2 2019]

NEUSTADT [NEW TOWN]
Julius von Bismarck's miniature landscape is planned on open land close to the Landschaftspark Duisburg-Nord. The installation will consist of toy-sized sculptures modelled on some twenty buildings that have been demolished in the Ruhr region since the turn of the twenty-first century. The extensive installation consists of various architectural topoi, from detached family homes to housing estate buildings, from swimming pools and schools to abandoned factories, and in terms of visual axes and fictitious street layouts has the look of an urban planning structure. Almost as an ex negativo mirror image of that which no longer exists, the installation brings together buildings from different regions and periods to form an urban entity of manageable proportions. The shift in scale lends new emphasis to the relationship between nature and architecture: prominent edifices awaken memories yet at the same time are overrun by shrubs and thickets. The overall ensemble is an invitation to stroll and dwell. It calls into question already executed urban planning decisions as evidence of ongoing social change — including the future possibility of adding further demolished buildings, analogous to real measures of urban transformation. [BP, M4 2020]

O

ONLINE
Since 2020, in addition to the physical sculptures along the Emscher river, digital works of art have also been created for the Emscherkunstweg. The artist duo thisisinternet opened the digital collection *Emscherkunstweg: online* with the short film *Pawāaraibu — filling the vacuum* (2020). Beginning with the pumping stations and landscapes along the Emscher river, they came up with a scenario in the film in which the earth has been abandoned by humans but is available to other living beings as a museum learning centre. In her video *Suffusion of Yellow* (2021), the artist Ani Schulze relates the Emscher reconstruction to cleansing rituals, healing and technological extensions of the body, such as high-tech prosthetics. This year, Alina Schmuch will be using the technical image archive of the Emschergenossenschaft to create another film-based work, in which she will be examining both the topic of water infrastructures as well as the role of photography as a method for producing images. The release is scheduled for October 2022. All the works of art in the series *Emscherkunstweg: online* are available on the Emscherkunstweg website and YouTube channel. [CN, M7 2022]

ORNITHOLOGIE [ORNITHOLOGY]
It is not only ornithologists who will feel at home in the former gas tank that has been converted into a birdwatchers' hide. Mark Dion's installation *Gesellschaft der Amateur-Ornithologen* [Society of Amateur Ornithologists] at the Bottrop sewage treatment plant blends seamlessly into its surroundings, with only a «crow's nest» lookout post on the roof standing out. But anyone stepping through the large, round glass door feels transported to a bygone era: the red walls are adorned with the names of great naturalists; an antique sofa invites you to linger; hats and walking sticks hang on the clothes rack; and bird sightings are catalogued on the desk. A truly charming work of art — and not just for birdwatchers. [NR, M5 2021]

P

PARKHOTEL
Austrian artist Andreas Strauss' wonderfully simple hotel is probably the most unusual place to spend a night in the Emscher valley. Established in BernePark in 2010 and called the «hospitality tool» by the artist, *dasparkhotel* consists of five concrete tubes — three metres in length and 2.5 metres in diameter — in which visitors and people passing through can spend a night from May to September. The hotel offers a unique natural setting, an exciting encounter with art and a shift in perception and is designed to host people exploring the Emscherkunstweg by bike. More locations in the Emscher area will be added to *dasparkhotel* to form a network of hospitality on the Emscherkunstweg. [TV, M3 2020]

PAWĀARAIBU
The Dortmund-based artist duo called thisisinternet.de has a lot of empathy, for machines too. Since 2020 they have been developing *Pawāaraibu — filling the vacuum,* a video series set in a post-human future about the inner life of a small drone. The first episode follows the flying body over the landscapes and works its way along the Emscherkunstweg. In the musical-like clip, carried by a cute and beguiling song in a kind of fantasy Japanese with subtitles, the drone introduces us to the earth as an organism kept alive by all kinds of apparatuses. Looking ahead, the last humans had set it up as a museum. The surroundings of the Emscher river, complete with pumping stations and sewage treatment plants, prove to be the perfect setting: the film marks the prelude to a series of digital or performative art projects, all of which subject the real sculpture path to an astonishing change of perspective via their different imaginings. [BP, M5 2021]

PFEIL [ARROW]
It's the journey that counts, not the destination. That's how you might describe the new corporate design of the Emscherkunstweg. nodesign from Essen found a logo that suits this public art project, where an arrow next to the name is the main event. This graphic element is playfully rendered in different forms depending on the medium; sometimes it fills the space around it, sometimes it's scaled right back, sometimes it follows a train of thought or has twists and turns, but invariably the arrow leads the way. Let's go! [JF, M3 2020]

PHOENIX-SEE [PHOENIX LAKE]
Until the turn of the millennium they continued to toil there, the workers at the steel plant Phoenix-Ost in Dortmund-Hörde who so profoundly shaped the Ruhr region. But in 2001, the plant was purchased by ThyssenKrupp, closed, demolished and shipped to China to be rebuilt there, a measure that changed the area forever. The grounds of the plant, polluted with toxins, were «restored» with a half-metre of new topsoil and transformed in the shortest period time from a working-class neighbourhood to a leisure area. Only few of the former residents still live here today, the lake as a destination and panorama has improved the quality of life, but simultaneously made the cost of housing shoot up and led to gentrification. The memories of the steel workers are today maintained in the artwork *Spirits of the Emscher Valley* and have a fixed place on today's Phoenix Lake. [JLA, M9 2023]

PROJEKT [PROJECT]
The Emscherkunstweg is a permanent sculpture trail whose collection has been secured for the next ten years — so it's more than just a short project. Nevertheless, the term «project» is often used in this context, but what does it actually mean? Generally speaking, a «project» is a temporary period in which a wide range of people work together actively and in a process to engage with a given topic. The topic can be chosen freely. «Projects» are not only professional, but can also be private or social undertakings. The term rose to prominence in management contexts in the 1990s. From there, its use extended into all areas of life. From a management point of view, one of the characteristics of a «project» is that the staff involved are employed on fixed-term contracts and can either continue to be employed on other «projects» or dismissed after the «project» has been completed. [CN, M7 2022]

PROMENADOLOGIE [PROMENADOLOGY]
Promenadology, or the science of strolling, is a method of conscious aesthetic perception of the environment and was introduced by the Swiss sociologist and economist Lucius Burckhardt (under the term «Promenadologie»). During strolls, one should closely monitor that which is seen and, in particular, the behaviour of the people in the respective location. This allows one to draw relevant conclusions about planning problems in architecture and the city and landscape planning. Burckhardt proposes that since an aesthetic experience no longer occurs automatically, the landscape design must be able to justify itself in how it contrasts with the urban environment in terms of its properties. In line with this, the Emscher Promenade offers exciting views and makes the river space a new experience. It invites you to go for a stroll as well as to spend time there and to relax, combining nature and culture. In terms of promenadology, this represents successful planning. [NL, M7 2022]

PUBLIC HYBRID
Since 26 November 2021, the multi-piece sculptural

installation *Public Hybrid* by David Jablonowski has enriched the Emscherkunstweg in Dortmund-Schüren — at a transit location that was initially unspectacular, as is so often found along the Emscher river. The artist combined the contrasting materials of sandstone and plastic in a surprisingly harmonious manner. The 3D-printed elements and the Ruhr sandstone from nearby Sprockhövel are layered and seem to penetrate each other. At the same time, a gradient of colour in the plastic components creates associations with rock layers — from the future? — and gives an impression of the depth of the landscape. The contrast between the materials in Jablonowski's work also brings with it a new understanding of raw materials and extraction. While the sandstone is a natural, biodegradable product, the 3D elements are made of recycled plastic, using digital technology to layer plastic waste in a printing process. [CN, M7 2022]

PUMPWERK [PUMPING STATION]
In winter 2021, walkers along the Emscherkunstweg were invited to breathe deeply. Only a few months prior, such a request would have been unthinkable. Since the Köttelbecke [literally «droppings basin»] and its tributaries were relocated underground, the air along the path has been breathable again. Today, the sewage flows odourlessly along a fifty-one-kilometre-long subterranean canal system with a gradient of 1.5 metres per kilometre. The slope ensures that the wastewater of more than 1.8 million people can be transported from the Emscherquelle in Holzwickede via the sewage treatment plants to the estuary at Dinslaken/Voerde. The three pumping stations in Gelsenkirchen, Bottrop and Oberhausen compensate for the incline of the underground sewer system. Without them, the wastewater would become too deep at the Emscher estuary seventy-five metres below the surface. These stations pump up the wastewater from a depth of up to forty metres. Finally, the former wastewater is treated and discharged into the Rhine. [AJ, M8 2022]

Q

QUELLE [SOURCE]
Rivers and their sources are often steeped in sagas and fairy tales, including the Emscher. One of the most imaginative is of the spring nymph who dwells in the Emscher's source on the Emscherquellhof estate in Holzwickede. It is said to be the spirit of the Emrizza Amberhus. Emrizza was an unmarried woman whose parents bequeathed her a grocery store in the village. As a successful businesswoman, she accumulated abundant wealth. However, she was miserly and ungenerous towards the poor and sick. Shortly before she died, a celestial apparition is said to have appeared to her, who prophesied that she would make up for her lifetime failures when she died. In terror, at the end of her life, she bequeathed all her belongings to the Church. Since then, her young face has always appeared as a warning over the Emscher's source when disasters, such as fires, are imminent. [ML, M8 2022]

R

REVISION [OVERHAUL]
At present a total of 18 works of art are situated along the banks of the Emscher river. Most of them were created for the *Emscherkunst* exhibition in 2010. Further works were added during the following editions in 2013 and 2016. As part of the overhaul both the condition and the underlying concept of the works will be reviewed. For example, in the course of almost ten years the spatial conditions at a few of the sites have changed so much that it might be appropriate to make adjustments to some works. [ML, M2 2019]

ROUTE
The works of art along the Emscherkunstweg are strung together like a thread of pearls — one might say. In reality, they stand quite far apart and are not as easy to visit in sequence as, say, in a sculpture park. Clearly, the Emscherkunstweg is best explored by bike! But finding the ideal route is not that simple over a distance of almost one hundred kilometres. From Holzwickede to Oberhausen the Emscherkunstweg does not tally exactly with the already existing network of cycle paths. Located somewhat off the track are, for example, *Reemrenreh* by the Herne Sea or the *Monument for a Forgotten Future* on Wild Island in Gelsenkirchen. On our website — soon online! — we propose various possible routes, available as downloads. And of course, you can trace these routes on a map — a printed version is also in the pipeline — and simply set off. Alternatively, you can use your smartphones for navigation, and later on post your snapshots from the trip on our website — as Emschergram! [JF, M4 2020]

RUHRLAUB [RUHR VACATIONS]
Holidays in the angle of the Rhine and the Ruhr are always an experience. Where coal and steel once set the tone, urban life now combines with nature, culture and industrial history. The first thing to do is to get an overview — ideally from one of the numerous slag heaps, the «mountains» of the Ruhr region. They shape the face of the region and are the sites of unique works of art by, for example Augustín Ibarrola, Otto Piene, or Richard Serra. The fifteen towns and districts of

the Ruhr region are also easy to explore by bike. Pedalling along the streams and rivers, over former railway lines and past important industrial monuments, you can feel the heartbeat of the Ruhr metropolitan region in a very special way. [TH, M5 2021]

S

SCHWARZERLE
[BLACK ALDER TREE]
The black alder tree is a mid-sized deciduous tree from the birch family widespread across Europe. It is easy to recognise with its cone-shape infructescence, serrated leaves rounded at the tip, the bare shoots and the black brown bark. Alders do best on wet or flooded grounds (Venice is built on alder and oak piles) and are thus of interest for our last new production at the Emscher-kunstweg. Markus Jeschaunig's sculptural installation is located on a former pumping station; in the middle of the installation a damp biotope — a quarry forest — is planted. The preference for marshy, often quite murky and uncanny areas brought the alder the reputation of offering natural spirits or even the devil a home. On top of that, alders «bleed»: when they are freshly cut; red fluids flow out and seem to attest to black magic. Goethe's Erlkönig [Alder King] is from this realm. Our black alders were pre-grown at a nursery (they are now already thirty-six years old) and develop a magic all their own in the *Königs-grube,* or «King's Pit».
[MM, M9 2023]

SLINKY SPRINGS TO FAME
For *Emscherkunst* 2010, Tobias Rehberger designed this unusual stress ribbon bridge in Oberhausen, 460 metres long, which spans the Rhine-Herne Canal in 496 spirals. Unique in engineering terms, it connects the Kaisergarten, where there is an old arm of the Emscher, with the Emscher Island. After fifteen months of construction, *Slinky Springs to Fame* (the name relates to the spirally shaped children's toy, Slinky), was opened in 2011 and has since delighted children's hearts with its colourful, swinging surface ten metres above the canal. Not only that, but the night-time illumination of this sculptural bridge creates a downright surreal atmosphere. It is probably one of the most photographed works on the Emscherkunstweg and has become one of Oberhausen's landmarks. [JF, M5 2021]

SOCIETIES
Swedish artist Henrik Håkansson's works often explore the relationship between humans and nature, and his work *The Insect Societies,* created for the exhibition in 2016, is no exception. Installed in a large meadow of wildflowers at Emscherquellhof in Holzwickede, it consists of two dice-like structures and acts as a refuge for wild bees. The work reflects both modern housing development and the decline of wild bees, which has been increasingly discussed in recent years and addresses an issue that is of great importance to the Emschergenossenschaft. The water board is an active member of various projects to fight the decline in wild bees and insects and produces its own honey at its farms in cooperation with local beekeepers. [AS, M3 2020]

SPAGHETTIEIS
[SPAGHETTI ICE CREAM]
There is nothing that better captures the essence of West German taste in the 1960s and 1970s than spaghetti ice cream. Even if the inventors are unknown, one thing is sure: the ice cream dish was invented by Italian immigrants in reminiscence of the typical Italian pasta. In the meantime, spaghetti ice cream has arrived in Italy, just like the döner, a variant of Turkish cuisine that was invented in West Germany, can now be found in Turkey. Foods like these are testimony to the labour migration to the old West Germany, without which the Ruhr region would not have secured the economic upswing of Western Europe, without which today's industrial history of the twentieth century would have taken a different course and perhaps the Emscher would also have had a different history. With these and other questions of temporality, the artist Inga Krüger engages with her performance *Perspektivisch gesehen, Spaghettieis* [Spaghetti Ice Cream Seen in Perspective] at the new mouth of the Emscher in the summer of 2023.
[ML, M9 2023]

T

TOLLE PERFORMANCE:
MEINE WUNSCHDOMAIN
[A WONDERFUL PERFORMANCE: MY DESIRED DOMAIN]
It's a warm August afternoon in 2022: a blue tent is placed next to the artwork *Zur kleinen Weile* [For a Short Spell] with a sign in front of it reading: *Poetry for Future — Fortlaufend Orakel-Performances* [Ongoing Oracle Performances]. In the tent: two women wearing splendid headdresses surrounded by magical objects, books, tea. The oracle duo Meine Wunschdomain, with Julia Nietzsche and Ruth Schultz, invite passers-by on foot or bike to stop and see their theatre of illusion to jointly create a personal «poem for the future». Then things move over to the golden interior of the accessible sculpture *Zur kleinen Weile,* and the poems for the future are performed as a kind of mantra in the impressive acoustics of the artwork. Several works of art were activated before in the series *Emscherkunstweg: Vor Ort* [Emscherkunstweg: On Site], but never as poetically as here.
[MM, M9 2023]

U

UMBAU [ALTERATIONS]

«Köttelbecke» [literally «droppings basin»] is a local term for a wastewater channel straightened by concrete shells. With the conversion of the Emscher river and its tributaries by the Emschergenossenschaft, wastewater can now be separated from clean water and fed via new conduits to the large sewage treatment plants. Streams are rid of their concrete shell channels and between the still needed embankments they are once more afforded, wherever possible, ample space to revert back into close-to-nature streams with new green banks. Over a period of some thirty years the Emschergenossenschaft will have invested more than five billion euros in this centennial project. [TV, M2 2019]

V

VANDALISMUS [VANDALISM]

Wilful damage to works of art in public space is a heavy blow to all involved. It almost feels as though not only the art has been attacked, but also those who are committed to its creation and its significance. More distanced observers manage to see the situation abstractly; they consider the destruction of an artistic work to be a special form of communication. In the long term, this is certainly the right approach, because it is rare that an examination ends with an act of concrete violence. Ideally, this instead releases new ideas and energies on how to deal with destruction. The true disaster would be for the fear of vandalism to succeed in preventing art projects in public spaces before they even begin — or just creating art projects from concrete and steel. Then the examination of public space is abandoned, and not because vandalism has won, but because of the desire for control. [BP, M7 2022]

VERKUNSTUNG [ARTIFICATION]

«Artification» is a nice term. It requires no explanation and immediately conjures up what it implies: a scattering of more or less decorative sculptures or artistic marks with no context on an urban or rural environment. Karl Ganser, CEO and mastermind of the *International Building Exhibition Emscher Park* from 1989 to 1999, uses the term in his 2007 essay when discussing the relationship between art and landscape architecture. Even his essay title refers to it: «Landscape art between the poles of design quality and artification». With refreshing fury, he opposes the damage done to landscapes by marketing events in particular. In contrast, *IBA Emscher Park,* which preceded the temporary *Emscherkunst* exhibition and the permanent Emscherkunstweg, placed great value on the freedom of artistic perspectives and ideas. But it did so with high-quality design, an equally nice term. [BP, M8 2022]

VISION

The Emscherkunstweg is developed from a growing number of permanently installed artworks along the Emscher. The art does not complement the beauty of its natural setting, as in a traditional sculpture park, but instead reflects the historical repression of nature in favour of industry and more recent efforts to restore the landscape. New works are progressively added to the trail to broaden the scope, showcase underrepresented voices in the international art scene and to open up the contemporary idea of sculpture. The Emscherkunstweg is also a living generational project that will grow and change over time. [BP, M3 2020]

VÖGEL [BIRDS]

A small street in Dortmund. A vacant store with unlit shopwindows and the broken, incomplete lettering of the store's name, Ö and L, the remaining letters are missing and here nothing has glowed for quite some time. This must have been how Samuel Treindl found the location where one of the most urban, lightest art works of the entire Emscherkunstweg is located.

Treindl added the letters V, G, and E to the letters Ö und L, the remains of the word *Möbel* [furniture], to spell *Vögel,* or birds. From then on, there was once again a sign aglow on Rheinische Straße, without advertising purposes, indeed entirely without a purpose at all, except of turning our gaze towards the sky to let fantasy take flight. [JLA, M9 2023]

VOR ORT [ON SITE]

Setting up new works of art in public space is preceded by numerous on-site meetings with the artists and construction engineers: first of all, to find a suitable place for a work's installation, then to take account of all the local conditions affecting planning and carrying out the work. The series of events *Vor Ort* reflects on this process. Through a combination of artists' talks, performances or musical commentaries visitors have the chance to find new approaches to and engage with the artworks along the Emscherkunstweg. The series kicked off in 2020 with a conversation between the artist Silke Wagner and the historian Holger Heith from the Archiv für Soziale Bewegungen [Archive of Social Movements] at the Ruhr University Bochum. In early August 2020, Nicola Gördes and Stella Rossié activated the work *Kunstpause* by atelier le balto with a live performance. For more information on forthcoming events, see: → emscherkunstweg. de. [ML, M4 2020]

WALKWAY AND TOWER

As a means of observing the progressive changes in the landscape caused by the Emscher Conversion project the Japanese artist Tadashi Kawamata created his work *Walkway and Tower* in 2010, situated in close proximity to the waterway junction of the Emscher river and the Rhine-Herne Canal near Castrop-Rauxel. Via a walkway that zigzags up to higher ground the visitor reaches a wooden observation platform that offers an all-round panoramic view. Strolling along the walkway — which in the course of the project's overall artistic restoration in spring 2020 underwent a technical and aesthetic overhaul — the visitor can enjoy a variety of different perspectives of the work's setting. This contemplative immersion in the landscape is often an integral element in Kawamata's works in public space. By guiding visitors along a fixed route that entails ostensible detours he encourages them to consciously perceive their surroundings.
[ML, M4 2020]

WASSERSTRASSE [WATERWAY]

Waterways are rivers and canals that are navigable, that is, they are part of the networks for transporting people and goods by ship. As industrialisation progressed in the late nineteenth and early twentieth centuries, Germany's waterway network was expanded to include numerous canals. The Emscher, a sluggish and shallow river, was never suitable as an industrial inland waterway, although consideration was indeed given to expanding it for this purpose in the course of straightening it. Instead, today's Rhine-Herne Canal was built, which partly follows the former course of the Emscher and was initially also called the Emscher-Seitenkanal [Emscher Lateral Canal]. This is still one of the most important freight transport routes in the Ruhr region, connecting it to the port of Duisburg on the Rhine. Today, however, it is also a special attraction for culture and sports enthusiasts with well-planned cycle paths along its banks and numerous works of art on the Emscherkunstweg, such as the *Zauberlehrling* by the group called Inges Idee, or Tobias Rehberger's *Slinky Springs to Fame.*
[ML, M5 2021]

WESTDEUTSCHLAND [WEST GERMANY]

In many ways, the Ruhr region is the epitome of the old Federal Republic of Germany, if only because of the importance of local industry for the post-war economic boom. Michael Holzach, who hiked through West Germany penniless in 1980, penned a loving portrait of the landscapes and people along the Emscher. Unfortunately, he was renowned not only for his book *Deutschland umsonst* [Germany for Free] but also because of his tragic accidental death. While filming the book's film adaptation, he drowned trying to rescue his German Shepherd Feldmann from the Emscher. This was reason enough for the writer Pascal Richmann, born in 1987 and raised in Dortmund, to recently dedicate an essay to Holzach, the Emscher itself and his youth with the title «Oh Mengede, dass du an der Emscher liegst», in which he recounts vivid stories — in the olfactory sense too — about everyday life in the West at the time when the river was still filthy.
[BP, M8 2022]

WETTER [WEATHER]

Germany, it is frequently observed that everyone talks about the weather. The worse — metaphorically speaking — the general weather situation, the more absurd it seems to have an extensive conversation about the current temperatures. Nevertheless, it remains a connecting element: nice weather outside improves the mood. Either way, the relationship between weather and climate can be compared to the discrepancy between moods and emotions. Sometimes one's mood is good, even if global warming is driving us into despair in the long run, or vice versa: an emotional thunderstorm can be brewing, even though there is a deep basic trust in one other. The Emscherkunstweg isn't just worth visiting in good weather; it can also be wonderfully melancholic, especially in a bad mood and drizzle. [BP, M7 2022]

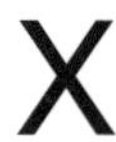

X

WASSERKREUZ CASTROP-RAUXEL [CASTROP-RAUXEL WATERWAY CROSSING]

Like the two legs that make up the letter X, two different waterways cross in Castrop-Rauxel, the industrial Rhine-Herne Canal and the renatured Emscher river, which flows through an underground conduit beneath the Rhine-Herne Canal. With a spectacular bridge structure, the *Sprung über die Emscher* [Jump over the Emscher] the cities Castrop-Rauxel and Recklinghausen are also linked via the two regional cycle paths Emscher-Park-Radweg and Emscher-Weg across the aquatic intersection. The twelve-metre-high sculptural viewing platform *Walkway and Tower* by the artist Tadashi Kawamata is located on an elevation along Emscher-Weg and offers an especially good view of the new landmark in the northern Ruhr region and the nature and water park Emscherland, which also opened recently.
[AJ, M9 2023]

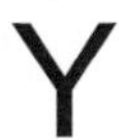

Y

YACHTHAFEN [MARINA]
When we hear the word marina, most of us think first of the Côte d'Azur or Miami, but there's also a marina in the Ruhr region along the Rhine-Herne Canal. There's even one on the «sea», Herner Meer. It has existed there since 1920 and is operated by WasserSportVerein Herne 1920 e. V. It even has the quality seal «maritime». One can dream, listening to the wind that blows through the sculpture *reemrenreh* by Bogomir Ecker far off in the distance. Towards the Rhine, the next waterway to the sea, there are at least two more marinas. Stoelting Marina Gelsenkirchen near Graf Bismarck since 2018 and the Marina in Oberhausen since 2004. Harbours make clear the global water network: everything is connected, and why not travel to the Côte d'Azur by boat from Herne? [ML, M9 2023]

Z

ZAUBERLEHRLING [SORCERER'S APPRENTICE]
Densely populated landscapes such as the Emscher valley are marked not only by motorways and railway lines, but also by pylons. These supply electricity to the almost 5.5 million people living in the Ruhr region. The Berlin-based artists' group Inges Idee adopted a humorous approach to this phenomenon as its contribution to the *Emscherkunst* exhibition in 2016. Inspired by Goethe's «Zauberlehrling», a poem about a sorcerer's apprentice who brings objects to life using magic but ultimately loses control over them, the artists developed a seemingly living electricity pylon that dances. Owing to its caricature-like appearance this work could also be read as a critical commentary on the ever-increasing electrification of our daily lives. The sculptural work *Zauberlehrling* is currently being overhauled: due to certain structural problems its steel frame has had to be restored. The work is scheduled to be completed by autumn 2019. [ML, M2 2019]

ZEIT [TIME]
Permanent outdoor projects have a generous relationship with time. They patiently allow their artistic concept to be reassessed with every new encounter. Incomprehension gives way to love, spontaneous inclination morphs into routine, dismissal prompts interest, familiarity shifts to enthusiasm — or the other way round, and in ever-changing variations. Neither short-term opening times nor a fixed exhibition duration prescribes the time frame of the relationship. A long-term work in public space asserts its existence around the clock and in varying individual or social moods. It bundles the energy that was required for its making — but even if this power cannot be stored for all eternity it nonetheless outlives any day-to-day events.
[BP, M4 2020]

ZUFLÜSSE [TRIBUTARIES]
On its way from its source in Holzwickede to its mouth at Dinslaken, the Emscher river encounters various tributaries. These tributaries will also be rebuilt as part of the restoration measures. The result is greener tributaries, where flora and fauna can continue to spread. This allows new habitats to evolve, not only directly by the river, but also again in its former riverbed and smaller streams. In addition to the numerous positive effects for humans and nature, the reconstruction measures have a less obvious practical benefit. The floodplains of the Emscher tributaries that are now green and thriving also help reduce flood risk. [NL, M7 2022]

ZWANZIGEINUNDZWANZIG [YEAR'S TURNING]
Subject to the logic of whatever COVID-19 protection measures are necessary, the turn of the year from 2020 to 2021 marks, above all, a promise — but not a completely new beginning. (Strictly speaking, it does not do so even in pandemic-free times, but then one's fate seems to be more in one's own hands.) Nevertheless, 2021 promises to be an action-packed year for the Emscherkunstweg. We are looking forward to several openings, on-site functions and other events, joint cycling tours and everyday life. Because that's the beauty of the project: the Emscherkunstweg grows and flourishes! [BP, M5 2021]

IA   Ilias Abawi
Head of Communication
Emschergenossenschaft

JLA Jana Luisa Aufderheide,
Assistant Press
and Marketing
Emscherkunstweg,
Urbane Künste Ruhr

JD Juliane Duft
Project Coordinator
Emscherkunstweg,
Urbane Künste Ruhr
(2019—20)

JF Judith Frey
Press and Public Relations
Emscherkunstweg,
Urbane Künste Ruhr
(2019—22)

TH Thomas Hensolt
Culture, Sport and
Industrial Culture
Regionalverband Ruhr

AJ Alicia Jütte
Project Coordinator
Emscherkunstweg,
Urbane Künste Ruhr

CK Carola Kemme
Project Manager
Urbane Künste Ruhr
(2016—21)

DK Daniel Klemm
Project Manager
Urbane Künste Ruhr

KK Kai Kolodziej
Director of Operative
Coordination Farms
Emschergenossenschaft

NL Nora Lobe
Assistant Press
and Marketing
Emscherkunstweg,
Urbane Künste Ruhr
(2021—22)

ML Marijke Lukowicz
Curator
Emscherkunstweg,
Urbane Künste Ruhr

MM Monika Madert
Press and Marketing
Emscherkunstweg,
Urbane Künste Ruhr

CN Clara Niermann
Project Coordinator
Emscherkunstweg,
Urbane Künste Ruhr
(2021—22)

BP Britta Peters
Artistic Director
Urbane Künste Ruhr

MP Markus Pohl
Project Manager,
Head of Planning
and Construction
Emschergenossenschaft

NR Nicole Reidick
Events and Outreach
Projects
Emschergenossenschaft

AS Agnes Sawer
Curatorial Director at
Emschergenossenschaft
and Lippeverband
and Project Director
Emscherkunstweg,
Emschergenossenschaft

MS Mechthild Semrau
Group Leader Landscape
and Water Structure
Emschergenossenschaft

TV Thomas Voßmerbäumer
Projects Art and Culture
Emschergenossenschaft

SW Silke Wilts
Head of Infrastructure
and Events
Emschergenossenschaft

EW Elgin Wolf
Project Director
Emscherkunstweg,
Urbane Künste Ruhr

ATELIER LE BALTO
    VÉRONIQUE FAUCHEUR
    MARC POUZOL
Véronique Faucheur (*1963 in
Oran, French Algeria) and Marc
Pouzol (*1966 in Bourg-la-Ceine,
France) are the two members of
atelier le balto. *Kunstpause* was
realised in collaboration with Marc
Vatinel (*1967 in Lille, France). The
key focus of the Berlin-based
collective is the transformation
of public spaces. Their work
is characterised by minimal
architectural and horticultural
interventions in the respective
found setting. In this way they
open up frequently isolated,
overgrown or abandoned, fallow
inner-city green spaces, but also
gardens and parks, invest them
with new aesthetic appeal and
make them accessible (or return
them) to public use.

MASSIMO BARTOLINI
Massimo Bartolini (*1962, in
Cecina, Italy) works in various
media, ranging from sculpture,
performance, photography to
large-scale and/or site-specific
installations. In his work he often
makes subtle changes to a space
or manipulates the sound, smell
or lighting conditions to disrupt
expectations and create sensations that prompt or unsettle
sensual perception. His work was
represented, for example, in 2012
at documenta 13 in Kassel.

JULIUS VON BISMARCK
Julius von Bismarck (*1983 in
Breisach am Rhein, Germany)
studied visual communication
at Universität der Künste
Berlin, participated in the MFA
Programme at Hunter College
New York and studied at Ólafur
Elíasson's Institute for Spatial
Experiments. Among the awards
he has received are the IBB
Photography Award (Berlin),
the Golden Nica des Prix Ars
Electronica (Linz, Austria), the
Prix Ars Electronica

Collide@CERN (Linz) and the
«Junge Stadt sieht junge Kunst»
[A young city sees young art].
Julius von Bismarck works on the
boundaries between art, science
and technology. He investigates
the perception, manipulation
and documentation of natural .
phenomena, but also issues of
urban space.

MARK DION
Mark Dion (*1961 in New Bedford,
Massachusetts, United States)
worked as an art restorer prior
to studying art. His keen passion
for collecting is reflected in
his frequently richly elaborate
and multipartite objects and
installations. One focus of his
work is nature, our relationship
to it and how it is represented in
exhibitions and other contexts.
Again and again, ecological, philosophical and political issues play
an important role in his approach.

MARTA DYACHENKO
Marta Dyachenko (*1990 in Kyiv,
Ukraine) studied architecture
and fine arts, specialising in
sculpture at the Universität der
Künste Berlin, among others
under Arno Brandlhuber and
Manfred Pernice. Her installations
frequently involve interventions
in landscape settings with
model-like sculptures. In her
artistic work a predominant role is
played by her preoccupation with
the relationship between nature
and human activity, particularly
our socially constructed view of
landscape.

BOGOMIR ECKER
Bogomir Ecker (*1950 in Maribor,
Slovenia) followed his training
as a typesetter by studying at
the Staatliche Akademie der
Bildenden Künste Karlsruhe,
then at the Kunstakademie
Düsseldorf. At the Academy of
Fine Arts Hamburg he held a chair
for sculpture. From 2002 until
his retirement in 2016, he was
professor at the Hochschule für
Bildende Künste Braunschweig.

The point of departure for his
artistic explorations are social
motors such as communication
and technology; in particular,
seeing and hearing as forms of
sensorial perception play a major
role.

Bogomir Ecker was invited in
1987 to show work at Documenta 8
in Kassel and is represented in
numerous collections.

DOUGLAS GORDON
Douglas Gordon (*1966 in
Glasgow, UK) studied at the
Glasgow School of Art and the
Slade School of Art in London.
In 1996 he won the prestigious
Turner Prize. He works on inter-
disciplinary and trans-medial
projects, frequently with film and
sound. He achieved acclaim with
his installation *24 Hour Psycho,* in
which he extended Hitchcock's
classic to last an entire day. Playing
with perception — especially with
the deceleration of time — has
become, as it were, a hallmark of
the Scottish artist's work.

GROSS.MAX
    EELCO HOFTMANN
    BRIDGET BAINES
The landscape architecture
office GROSS.MAX was founded
in 1995 by Eelco Hoftmann and
Bridget Baines in Edinburgh. Their
practice develops strategies for
urban design and regional and
landscape planning, as well as
developing design projects for
public parks and squares.

HENRIK HÅKANSSON

A central focus of Henrik Håkansson's (*1968 in Helsingborg, Sweden) artistic work is his exploration of our conceptions of nature, culture and science. He investigates how they interrelate and the kinds of images and realities they evoke. He couches his artistic questions and process-oriented research in various media such as film, photography, text, sound and cross-media installations. He was shown at the 2003 Venice Biennale and has had numerous solo exhibitions, such as in the Palais de Tokyo in Paris (2006) and in the Taipei Fine Arts Museum (2018/2019).

INGES IDEE
HANS HEMMERT
AXEL LIEBER
THOMAS SCHMIDT
GEORG ZEY

The artists' group Inges Idee was founded in 1992 by Hans Hemmert (*1960 in Hollstadt, Germany), Axel Lieber (*1960 in Düsseldorf, Germany), Thomas Schmidt (*1960 in Nuremberg, Germany) and Georg Zey (*1962 in Limburg an der Lahn, Germany). Since then, the four artists have realised numerous, mostly large-scale works as art in public space and «art for buildings». Their most humorous works are always related to their location and evolve from an intense exchange of ideas between the artists, each of whom is also independently active as an artist.

DAVID JABLONOWSKI

David Jablonowski (*1982 in Bochum, Germany) studied at the Gerrit Rietveld Academie, Amsterdam and the Kunstakademie Düsseldorf. In his artistic work he deals with communication, its codes and formats and examines how media transport and change content. As a sculptor, he translates the diverse interconnections into mostly multimedia sculptures. Having grown up in the Ruhr area and being influenced by industrial change, he is particularly interested in industrial materials, their creation and infrastructures. Thus the formal language in his work has developed in recent years along the lines of the latest technological achievements, including those in the materials industry. *Public Hybrid* at Emscherkunstweg is his first permanent work in public space.

MARKUS JESCHAUNIG

Markus Jeschaunig (*1982 in Graz, Austria), studied at the Universität für künstlerische und industrielle Gestaltung Linz, the Mimar Sinan Fine Arts University Istanbul and the Technische Universität Wien. In 2012, he founded his own artistic practice under the title «Agency in Biosphere». In 2012, he participated in the Change Course Conference organised by the Club of Rome in Winterthur. As a member of team.breathe.austria, he is co-author of *Breathe.Austria — Austrian Pavilion at Expo 2015 in Milan*. Inspired by the forces and dynamics of the lithosphere, hydrosphere, atmosphere and biosphere, Jeschaunig's works unfold in the field of tension between art, ecology, landscape, urbanism, technology as well as public space and activism.

TADASHI KAWAMATA

Tadashi Kawamata (*1953 in Hokkaido, Japan) has created numerous works for public spaces throughout the world. One of his largest installations was the work *L'Observatoire* (2007) in Lavau-sur-Loire in France. Kawamata has also presented work at the 1982 Venice Biennale and at the 1987 documenta in Kassel. Between 2007 and 2019 he was professor at the École nationale supérieure des Beaux-Arts in Paris.

MISCHA KUBALL

Mischa Kuball (*1959 in Düsseldorf, Germany) works as a conceptual media artist, mostly using light as material. In his works he frequently examines historically or architecturally significant sites in urban contexts. He is represented with numerous works in public spaces throughout the Emscher region, among them *Yellow Marker* (2000) in Bönen and Kamp-Lintfort, *Blaues Lichtoval* (1999) in Herne and the neon sign *Kunstsammlungen Uni Bochum* (2003).

RITA MCBRIDE

As a sculptor, Rita McBride (*1960 in Des Moines, Iowa, United States) is concerned with the mechanisms of urban fabrics and their structures of communication, frequently adopting a reduced, almost minimalist formal language. She has created several large-scale sculptures for public space, among them *Mae West*, one of Europe's tallest works: a fifty-two-metre-high, carbon-fibre sculpture standing in Munich. McBride has held a chair for sculpture at the Kunstakademie Düsseldorf since 2003, where she was also director from 2013 until 2017.

MOGWAI

Mogwai is a Scottish band from Glasgow, formed in 1995. Members are Stuart Braithwaite, John Cummings (guitar), Dominic Aitchison (bass) and Martin Bulloch (drums).

OLAF NICOLAI

Olaf Nicolai (*1962 in Halle/Saale, Germany) studied German philology in Leipzig; following German reunification and his completed doctorate in 1992, he started working as an artist. Adopting a conceptual artistic approach, he works in various media and collaborates in many projects with different artists. His contribution to the 2010 *Emscherkunst* exhibition evolved in cooperation with Douglas Gordon.

PIET OUDOLF

The garden artist Piet Oudolf (*1944 in Haarlem, Netherlands) turned his attention to gardening and landscape architecture at the age of twenty-five. Up until 2010 he and his wife Anja ran a centre for ornamental garden design in Hummelo near Arnhem. Initially influenced by the austere style of the Dutch garden designer, Mien Ruys, he gradually developed a more naturalistic, painterly style and established a garden design closely tuned to nature. One of his most prominent works is the *Garden of Remembrance* in Battery Park and the garden design of the High Line, both in New York. In Germany he is known for projects such as the gardens in Maximilianpark in Hamm and in Bad Driburg.

RAUMLABOR

Founded in 1999, raumlabor is a collective of architects that operates at the interface of architecture, city planning, art and intervention. For each project the group assembles a bespoke team of experts. Participants might be artists, musicians, scientists or urban residents. Its experimental spatial practice is characterised by a fundamentally process-oriented, research-based approach. Among the projects the group has realised are monumental temporary architectures for public space or artistic interventions. These focus often on transforming difficult places, as for example in the project *Eichbaumoper* [Oak Tree Opera] for the Eichbaum underground railway station close to the A 40 motorway between Essen and Mülheim an der Ruhr.

TOBIAS REHBERGER

Tobias Rehberger (*1966 in Esslingen, Germany) is known as a boundary-crosser between art, architecture and design. Currently based in Frankfurt am Main, the artist studied there at the Städelschule under Martin Kippenberger and Thomas Bayrle. He has also been teaching at the school as professor for visual art since 2001. He has executed numerous installations in public space. In 2009 he was awarded a Golden Lion for his design of the cafeteria in the Giardini, the central hub of the Venice Biennale. Since May 2015, the sculptural path *24 Stops* featuring his works connects the Fondation Beyeler in Basel with the Vitra Design Museum in Weil am Rhein.

ANDREAS STRAUSS

Andreas Strauss (*1968 in Wels, Austria) works mostly in public space. His concepts intentionally create fluid boundaries between art and design and defy pigeon-holing into strict definitions. Instead, his artistic works are concerned with forms of social coexistence that call economic and cultural conventions into question and enable new possibilities to be explored.

STUDIO ORTA
LUCY ORTA
JORGE ORTA

Lucy Orta (*1966 in Sutton Coldfield, UK) and Jorge Orta (*1953 in Rosario, Argentina) have been working together as an artists' collective since the 1990s. Their work focusses on social and ecological issues, and their artistic practice frequently assumes a collaborative form. They work with a wide variety of technologies and media ranging from drawing, painting, sculpture and photography to fashion design and film. Their Paris studio «Les Moulins» also serves as a kind of arts centre where they have built up a collective entourage dedicated to artistic research and the production of contemporary art.

APOLONIJA ŠUŠTERŠIČ

Apolonija Šušteršič (*1965 in Ljubljana, Slovenia) first studied architecture in Ljubliana, then completed a postgraduate programme at the Rijksakademie in Amsterdam. She subsequently took a doctoral degree at Lund University in Malmö, Sweden, since which she has held various lectureships. She currently lives and works in Oslo, Norway. In her projects for public space a central aspect of her artistic strategy is the participatory dimension, as shown in her 2011 community pavilion on Brunnenplatz in the Hustadt district of Bochum.

SOFÍA TÁBOAS

Sofía Táboas (*1968 in Mexico City, Mexico) studied fine arts at the Universidad Nacional Autónoma de México. She is a founding member of the alternative art space: Temístocles 44 in Mexico City. In her work, the artist explores both natural and man-made space; how it is built and reshaped, thought and perceived. This interest extends to the materials she uses in her sculptures and installations, such as artificial and living plants, mosaics, swimming pool equipment, building materials and plastic. Her artistic approach testifies to a great awareness of materials that seeks to make the space that is passed through more complex from a different or rarefied perspective.

SAMUEL TREINDL

Samuel Treindl (*1980 in Beuron-Hausen, Germany) is concerned with materials research, process-oriented projects in public space and a constant scrutiny of aesthetic and social constructions. After training as a lathe worker, he studied product design at the Fachhochschule Münster [Münster University of Applied Sciences], and then sculpture at the Kunstakademie Münster under Ayşe Erkmen and Mariana Castillo Deball. Through his project «Forschungsstelle für anarchistische Produktion»

[Research centre for anarchistic production] he campaigns for the equality of all design and fabrication systems and produces art and design objects. He has already participated in numerous group and solo exhibitions.

SILKE WAGNER
Silke Wagner (*1968 in Göppingen, Germany) creates conceptual works exploring social, political or ecological issues. Her works are always preceded by extensive research, for which she frequently collaborates with different social groups or actors. Another of her works for public space is located in the centre of Münster: *Münsters GESCHICHTE VON UNTEN* [Münster's HISTORY FROM BELOW] was created in 2007 for *Skulptur Projekte Münster.*

LAWRENCE WEINER
Lawrence Weiner (1942—2021 in New York, United States) was one of the leading exponents of US American concept art which emerged in the 1960s. Often formally tending towards Minimalism, Weiner's works for public space consist primarily of text and characters that always make reference to their location. Another of his works in the vicinity is situated on the campus of the Ruhr University Bochum: *&so weiter* (2010).

NICOLE WERMERS
Nicole Wermers (*1971 in Emsdetten, Germany) lives and works in London and Emsdetten. Since 2017 she has been a professor at the Akademie der Bildenden Künste in Munich. Among other things, she was a fellow of the German Academy Villa Massimo in Rome in 2012 and was nominated for the Turner Prize in 2015. In her sculptures, photographs and collages, the artist combines formal questions with investigations of urban space and its social, economic and psychological inscriptions. The artist's work reveals a reference to the design of everyday objects, renegotiating their purposeful use within recompositions, often in combination with other materials, forms and contexts.

AUTHORS AND EDITORS

DR. VERA BATTIS-REESE

Dr. Vera Battis-Reese has been the managing director of Kultur Ruhr GmbH in Bochum since July 2017. She is also a lecturer at the Dresden International University for cultural management at Dresden International University.

After studying law at the at the Universität Köln, she wrote her doctoral thesis on stage labour law. Dr. Vera Battis-Reese worked from 2000 to 2004 at the Frankfurt Ballet (Städtische Bühnen Frankfurt am Main) as deputy artistic director of William Forsythe. In 2005 she became managing director of the newly founded The Forsythe Company GmbH.

From 2015 she also held this position together with the artistic artistic director Jacopo Godani for the Dresden Frankfurt Dance Company.

JULIANE DUFT

Juliane Duft studied art and film studies at Johannes Gutenberg-Universität Mainz. Her curatorial work focusses on space in art since the onset of modernism and expanded artistic practices since the 1960s that engage with the psychological and social dimensions of design and art. She has prepared exhibitions and programs at Museum Angewandte Kunst, Frankfurt am Main (*SUR/FACE. Spiegel,* 2017), Kunsthalle Darmstadt (*Planet 9: Projections,* 2017), Kölnischer Kunstverein (*Aus- und Vortragen,* 2017–2019; *Cut-Up,* 2019), Pik Deutz, Cologne (Access, 2019), and Museum Ludwig (*Original und Fälschung,* 2020) and published widely. Curator at Kunstmuseen Krefeld since 2019, recent work includes Andrea Zittel's solo exhibition and her contribution for the sculpture garden at Haus Lange & Haus Esters.

BRIGITTE FELDERER

Based in Vienna, Brigitte Felderer teaches cultural studies at Universität für angewandte Kunst Wien [University of Applied Arts] where she is director of the master's programme Social Design/Arts as Urban Innovation. As a curator, she has realised numerous exhibition projects and publications.

JES FERNIE

Jes Fernie is an independent curator, writer and lecturer based in the UK. Many of her projects are situated in the public realm beyond gallery walls. She is interested in the social, political and environmental context in which art is made, situated and viewed. In 2021 she launched the Archive of Destruction, a research project that brings together narratives around public sculpture that has been destroyed by rage, boredom, fear, greed and love.

KAROLA GEISS-NETTHÖFEL

Karola Geiß-Netthöfel, born in Lünen, North Rhine-Westphalia in 1958, has been regional director of Regionalverband Ruhr since 2011 while also serving as department head. In 1986, she began her professional career as a government official for the Land North Rhine-Westphalia. From July 2008 to July 2011, she held the position of district vice-president in Arnsberg. Before that, she had worked as division head responsible for areas such as regional development, the promotion of business, and municipal and construction inspection.

JANA GOLOMBEK

Jana Golombek is head curator at Dortmund's LWL-Industriemuseum. She has curated exhibitions on the cultural history of the Ruhr with emphases on migration, the impacts of deindustrialisation and working-class social history. She was an assistant at Institut für Soziale Bewegungen, Ruhr-Universität Bochum and held a position at

Deutschen Bergbau-Museum. She has published widely on the history of migration in the Ruhr region, deindustrialisation and industrial culture. She is currently completing her dissertation on industrial culture and the construction of landscapes of memory in the Ruhr region and Pittsburgh.

THOMAS HENSOLT

Thomas Hensolt is an art historian at StiftsMuseum in Xanten and is responsible for committee work at Regionalverband Ruhr. He studied art history and modern Japan at Heinrich-Heine-Universität in Düsseldorf and then held a position at Kunsthalle Recklinghausen. He then worked for various museums in the Ruhr region and Cologne as a curator, art educator and author for medieval and contemporary art. Most recently, he was in charge of Netzwerk der RuhrKunstMuseen for several years.

GEORG IMDAHL

Based in Düsseldorf, Georg Imdahl, born in Münster in 1961, is an art critic and has held a professorship for art and publicity at Kunstakademie Münster since 2011, where he initiated the Münster Lectures. He completed his dissertation in philosophy at Universität Witten/Herdecke on Heidegger. Imdahl writes primarily for the *Frankfurter Allgemeine Zeitung* and Deutschlandfunk and has been a member of Association Internationale des Critiques d'Art since 1993. His most recent publication: *Ausbeute: Santiago Sierra und die Historizität der zeitgenössischen Kunst* (Hamburg, 2019).

MARTINE VAN KAMPEN
Martine van Kampen is curator for Land Art Flevoland, a flexible organisation taking care of the interests of ten large-scale land art works in the province of Flevoland, centrally located in The Netherlands. This collection has been realised since 1977, when the *Observatory* by Robert Morris was placed in the bare landscape of this new Dutch polder being constructed at the time. *Land Art Flevoland* started from the *Land Art Live* programme, which invited younger artists to make interventions at the land art sites, eventually bringing them together in an exhibition and a catalogue: *Land Art Live: The Flevoland Collection* (Rotterdam, 2020). Currently Land Art Flevoland is working on realising two new works in the region. Before 2013, Martine worked as a curator for Museum De Paviljoens in Almere, did a residency at AIR Berlin Alexanderplatz (funded by the Mondriaan Foundation) and worked for the Dutch Foundation for Art and Public Space.

MARIJKE LUKOWICZ
Marijke Lukowicz is an art historian with a focus on twentieth- and twenty-first-century art. Since December 2018, she has been working at Urbane Künste Ruhr as curator for the Emscherkunstweg project under the artistic direction of Britta Peters. From 2013 to 2017, she worked at the LWL Museum of Art and Culture in Münster. There she curated, among others, the exhibition *Unerwartete Begegnungen* together with Dr. Tanja Pirsig-Marshall as well as the exhibition series *RADAR* in cooperation with the Westfälischer Kunstverein. As deputy curator for contemporary art, she was in particular in charge of the public collection of the Museum in the city of Münster during the *Skulptur Projekte* 2017.

She has already participated in numerous juries and competitions in the field of art-in-building and publishes on contemporary art, especially on issues of art in public space.

GLENDA MENSE
Glenda Mense, born in Holzminden in 1983, studied musicology and the history of modern and contemporary art in Regensburg, Berlin and Bochum. As a student, she already held a position at the art collections of the Ruhr-Universität Bochum and as a freelance art educator at Skulpturenmuseum Glaskasten Marl, Bundeskunsthalle and various projects of Urbane Künste Ruhr. She has served as co-curator and assistant for several exhibitions in the Rhine and Ruhr region. At the moment she is working primarily at Zentrum für internationale Lichtkunst in Unna and at Duisburg's Museum Küppersmühle.

NOOR MERTENS
Noor Mertens, born in 1984, studied art history and curating in Utrecht and Amsterdam. In 2017, she took a position as managing director and chief curator at Kunstvereins Langenhagen. Previously, she worked in galleries and private collections and, from 2011, was museum curator in charge of the Modern and Contemporary Art Collection and the City Collection at the Museum Boijmans Van Beuningen in Rotterdam. In 2021 she was named director of Kunstmuseum Bochum.

DR. VANESSA JOAN MÜLLER
Dr. Vanessa Joan Müller is an art historian and curator. She is the author and editor of numerous publications on contemporary art. She has held positions as curator at Frankfurter Kunstverein, research director at European Kunsthalle in Cologne, director of Kunstverein für die Rheinlande und Westfalen in Düsseldorf, and director of the division for dramaturgy at Kunsthalle Wien. In 2017, she served as curator of the Albanian pavilion at the Venice Biennale.

PROF. DR. ULI PAETZEL
Born in 1971 in Gelsenkrichen, Germany, Prof. Dr. Uli Paetzel has been Chairman of the Emschergenossenschaft and Lippeverband since 2016. He studied sociology and French at the Ruhr-Universität in Bochum and at François Rabelais University in Tours, France. In 2001 he completed his doctorate in sociology at the Ruhr Universität Bochum, where he's also been an adjunct instructor in sociology since 1999. He spent three years as the head of publicity and marketing for a software company before becoming mayor of the city of Herten, Germany, in 2004 — an office he retained until 2016. Since the beginning of 2019, Paetzel has also been President of the German Association for Water, Wastewater and Waste e. V.

BRITTA PETERS
Britta Peters has been the artistic director of Urbane Künste Ruhr since January 2018. Previously, she was the curator of *Skulptur Projekte Münster* 2017 in a team with Kasper König and Marianne Wagner. With a background in cultural studies, she has curated various major exhibition projects in Hamburg, including as director of Kunstverein Harburger Bahnhof from 2008 to 2011. After the exhibition *Demonstrations. Vom Werden normativer Ordnungen* 2012 at the Frankfurter Kunstverein, in 2014 she curated the

project *Krankheit als Metapher: Das Irre im Garten der Arten* at various locations in Hamburg. Peters has participated internationally in numerous committees, events and publications on the topic of art in public space and has taught as a visiting professor at the Kunstakademie Münster.

STEFANIE REICHART
Since December 2018, Stefanie Reichart has been head of the department for culture, sport and industrial culture at Regionalverband Ruhr. The task of her department is to position the Ruhr metropolitan area as an important site for culture and sport and to shape the region as an attractive, worldly, urban region. In addition, the department is responsible for the sustainability concept agreed upon between the RVR and the Ministry for Culture and Science of the State of North Rhine-Westphalia for the European Capital of Culture 2010. Since 2022, Stefanie Reichart has also served as managing director of Manifesta 16 RUHR gGmbH.

AGNES SAWER
Agnes Sawer is an art historian and since 2023 has been curatorial director at Essen's Emschergenossenschaft. She studied art history and Spanish Philology in Bochum, Pamplona and Paris. Her research emphases are on French painting of the eighteenth and nineteenth centuries, fashion research, contemporary art and art and ecology. From 2019 to 2023 she served a project director the Emscherkunstweg at the Emschergenossenschaft.

JANA KERIMA STOLZER
Since 2016, Jana Kerima Stolzer has worked as a freelance artist together with Lex Rütten. Their works move at the intersection of installation, performance and research. In 2020 she was named a fellow at the Akademie für Theater und Digitalität [Academy for Theatre and Digitality], from 2018 to 2020 she worked as a curatorial assistant at Urbane Künste Ruhr, before which she studied at Folkwang Universität der Künste [Folkwang University of the Arts] and Kunstakademie Münster, where she completed a class with Aernout Mik.
  In March 2023, the artists opened their first joint exhibition at Dortmund's Hartware MedienKunstVerein.

THOMAS VOSSMERBÄUMER
Thomas Voßmerbäumer is a trained engineer for water management and has held a position at the Emschergenossenschaft and Lippeverband since 1989.
  He was initially responsible for the planning and maintenance of engineering structures and has been responsible for the maintenance management of the public art of the Emschergenossenschaft and the Lippeverband since 2019.

URBANE KÜNSTE RUHR/
KULTUR RUHR GMBH

ARTISTIC DIRECTOR
URBANE KÜNSTE RUHR
Britta Peters

CURATOR
EMSCHERKUNSTWEG
Marijke Lukowicz

PROJECT DIRECTOR
EMSCHERKUNSTWEG
Carola Kemme (until 2021)
Elgin Wolf

PROJECT COORDINATOR
EMSCHERKUNSTWEG
Alicia Jütte
Clara Niermann (until 2022)
Elgin Wolf (until 2021)

PRESS AND MARKETING
EMSCHERKUNSTWEG
Judith Frey (until 2022)
Monika Madert

ASSISTANT
PRESS AND MARKETING
EMSCHERKUNSTWEG
Jana Luisa Aufderheide
Nora Lobe (until 2022)

TECHNICAL DIRECTOR
URBANE KÜNSTE RUHR
Stefan Goebel

HEAD OF MARKETING AND
SALES DEPARTEMENT
KULTUR RUHR GMBH
Franca Lohmann

HEAD OF PRESS DEPARTMENT
KULTUR RUHR GMBH
Angela Vucko

LEGAL DEPARTMENT
Annika Trockel

HEAD OF ADMINISTRATION
Vanessa San Román Domínguez

REGIONALVERBAND RUHR

HEAD OF DEPARTMENT
CULTURE, SPORT AND
INDUSTRIAL CULTURE
Stefanie Reichart

TEAM CULTURE
Maria Baumeister (until 2019)
Thomas Hensolt

EMSCHERGENOSSENSCHAFT

HEAD OF STAFF
PUBLIC RELATIONS
Friedhelm Pothoff

HEAD OF INFRASTRUCTURE
AND EVENTS
Silke Wilts

PROJECT DIRECTOR
EMSCHERKUNSTWEG
Agnes Sawer

PROJECT MANAGER,
HEAD OF PLANNING AND
CONSTRUCTION
Markus Pohl

PROJECTS ART
AND CULTURE
Thomas Voßmerbäumer

ASSISTANT PROJECT
MANAGER
SOCIAL MEDIA MANAGER
Björn Herting
Alejandra Quintero (until 2022)

EVENTS AND MEDIATION
PROJECTS
Nicole Reidick

ADMINISTRATIVE
ASSISTANCE
Stephanie Eul (until 2022)
Julia Nitsch (until 2022)
Sonia Schnitzler

LEGAL ADVICE
Sven Schubert

IMPRINT

EDITED BY
Vera Battis-Reese
Karola Geiß-Netthöfel
Uli Paetzel
Britta Peters

EDITORIAL
Marijke Lukowicz
Britta Peters

PROJECT MANAGEMENT HATJE CANTZ
Angelika Thill

PROJECT MANAGEMENT URBANE KÜNSTE RUHR
Monika Madert

TEXTS
Juliane Duft
Brigitte Felderer
Jes Fernie
Jana Golombek
Thomas Hensolt
Georg Imdahl
Martine van Kampen
Marijke Lukowicz
Glenda Mense
Noor Mertens
Vanessa Joan Müller
Britta Peters
Stefanie Reichart
Agnes Sawer
Jana Kerima Stolzer
Thomas Voßmerbäumer
Silke Wilts

TRANSLATION
Brian Currid
61—67, 219—224, 280—295,
302—305

Michelle Miles
23—29, 233—237

Matthew Partridge
14—16, 18—21, 53—59, 80—147,
152—207, 257—262,

David Tushingham
31—41, 249—254

Wilhelm von Werthern
148—151, 265—268

PROOFREADING
Aaron Bogart

PHOTOGRAPHY
Arwed Messmer
2—10, 42—51, 68—77, 208—17,
238—47, 269—79, 310—19
The photographs are part of
the work *Emscher Walk* (2019),
arranged from the source to the
mouth of the Emscher.

Roland Baege
138—39, 159

Volker Beushausen
41

Julius von Bismarck
188

Heinrich Holtgreve
189, 202, 254—55

David Jablonowski
98

Roman Mensing
162

Henning Rogge
80—97, 99, 105—36, 141—57,
161, 164—87, 195—201

Daniel Sadrowski
34—35, 37, 84—89, 174, 252—53,
258—59, 261—63

Caroline Seidel
32, 38—39

Thomas Voßmerbäumer
250

EGLV/Archiv
54—55

EGLV/Stefan Tuschy
56 above

EGLV/Rupert Oberhauser
56 below

RVR/Staudinger
62—67

DRAWING
Markus Jeschaunig
143

PUBLISHING PRODUCTION
Kati Klaeske

REPRODUCTIONS
Schwabenrepro GmbH,
Fellbach

LAYOUT
nodesign

PRINT AND BINDING
Westermann
Druck Zwickau GmbH

PAPER
Circle Offset Premium White

PUBLISHED BY
Hatje Cantz Verlag GmbH
Mommsenstraße 27
10629 Berlin

→ hatjecantz.com

A Ganske Publishing
Group Company

ISBN 978-3-7757-5569-6
(German)

ISBN 978-3-7757-5571-9
(English)

Printed in Germany

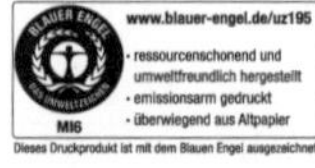

FUNDED BY

Ministry of Culture and Science
of the State of
North Rhine-Westphalia

A COLLABORATION OF

Urbane Künste
Ruhr

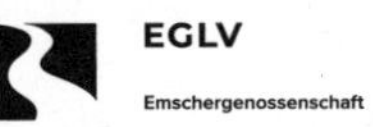

EGLV

Emschergenossenschaft

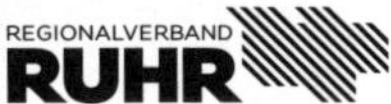

REGIONALVERBAND
RUHR

309

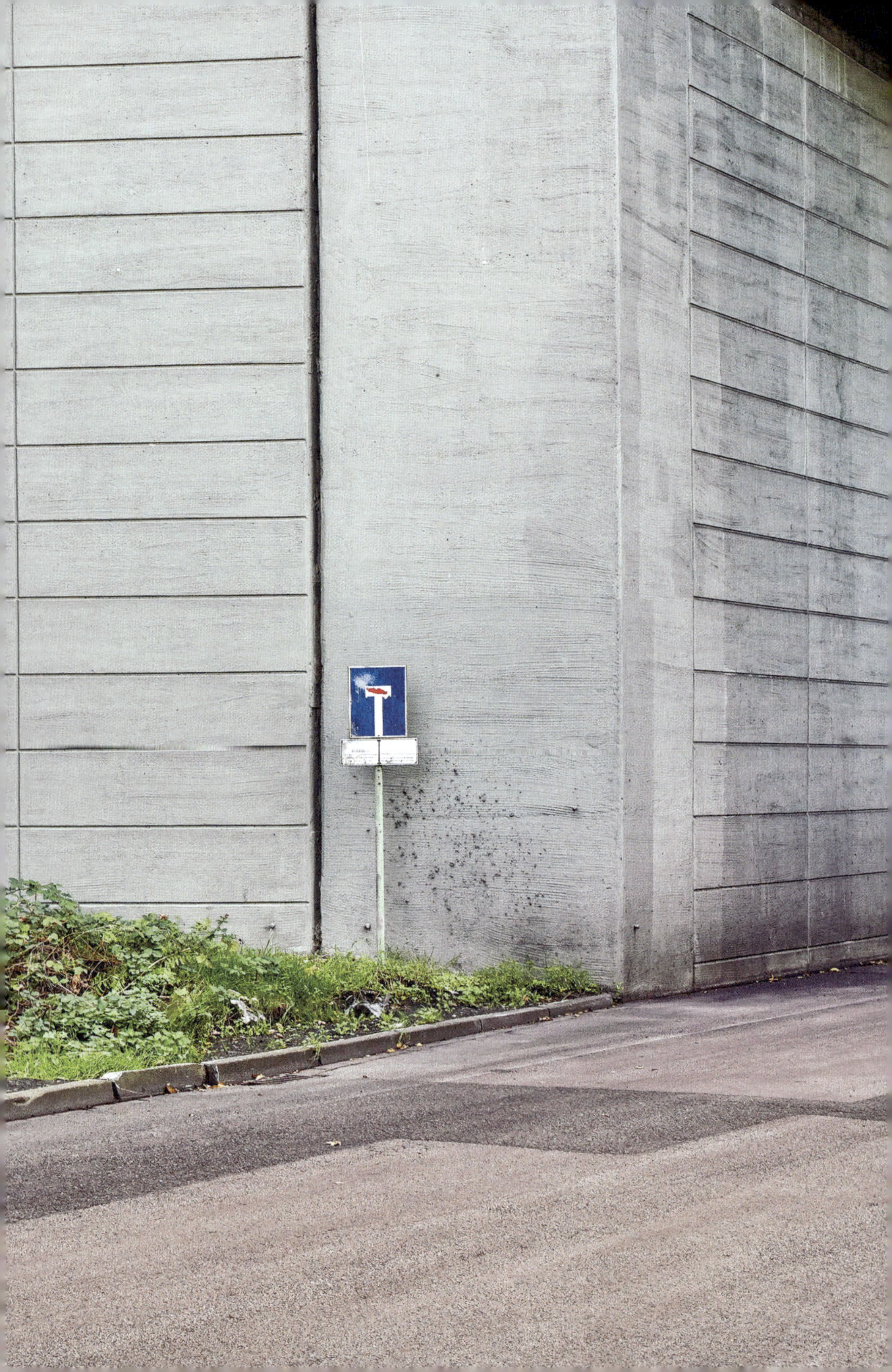

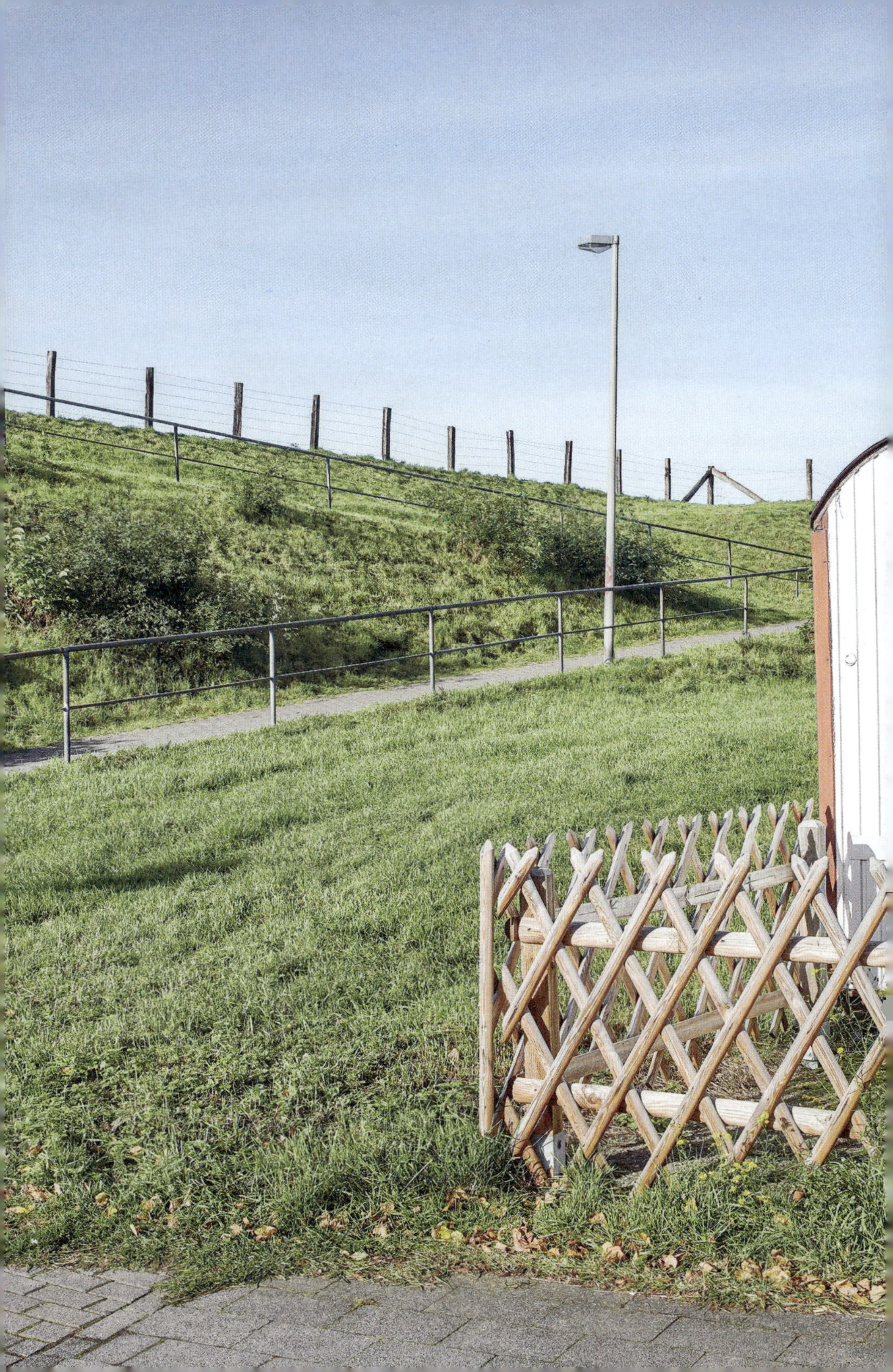

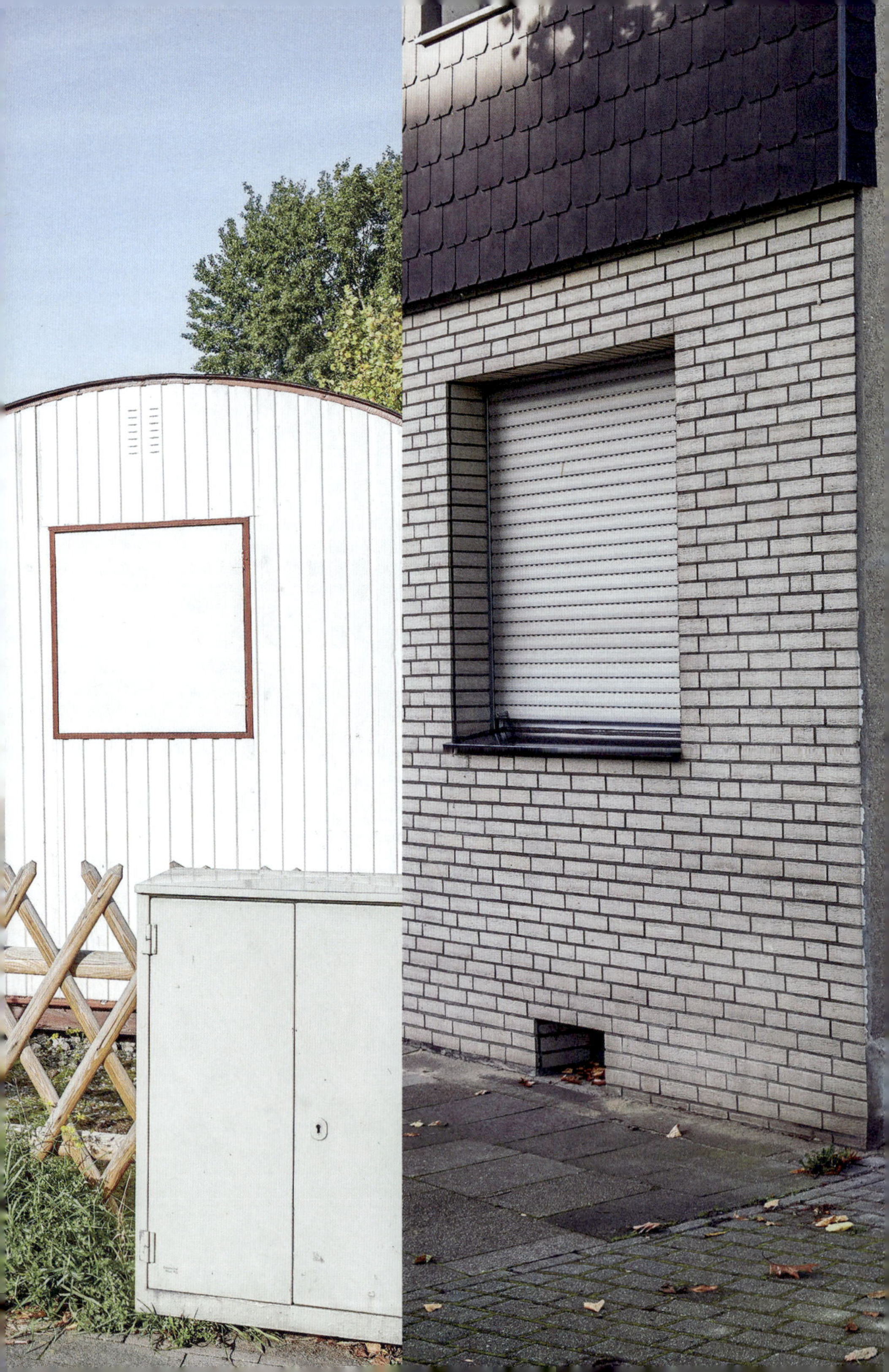

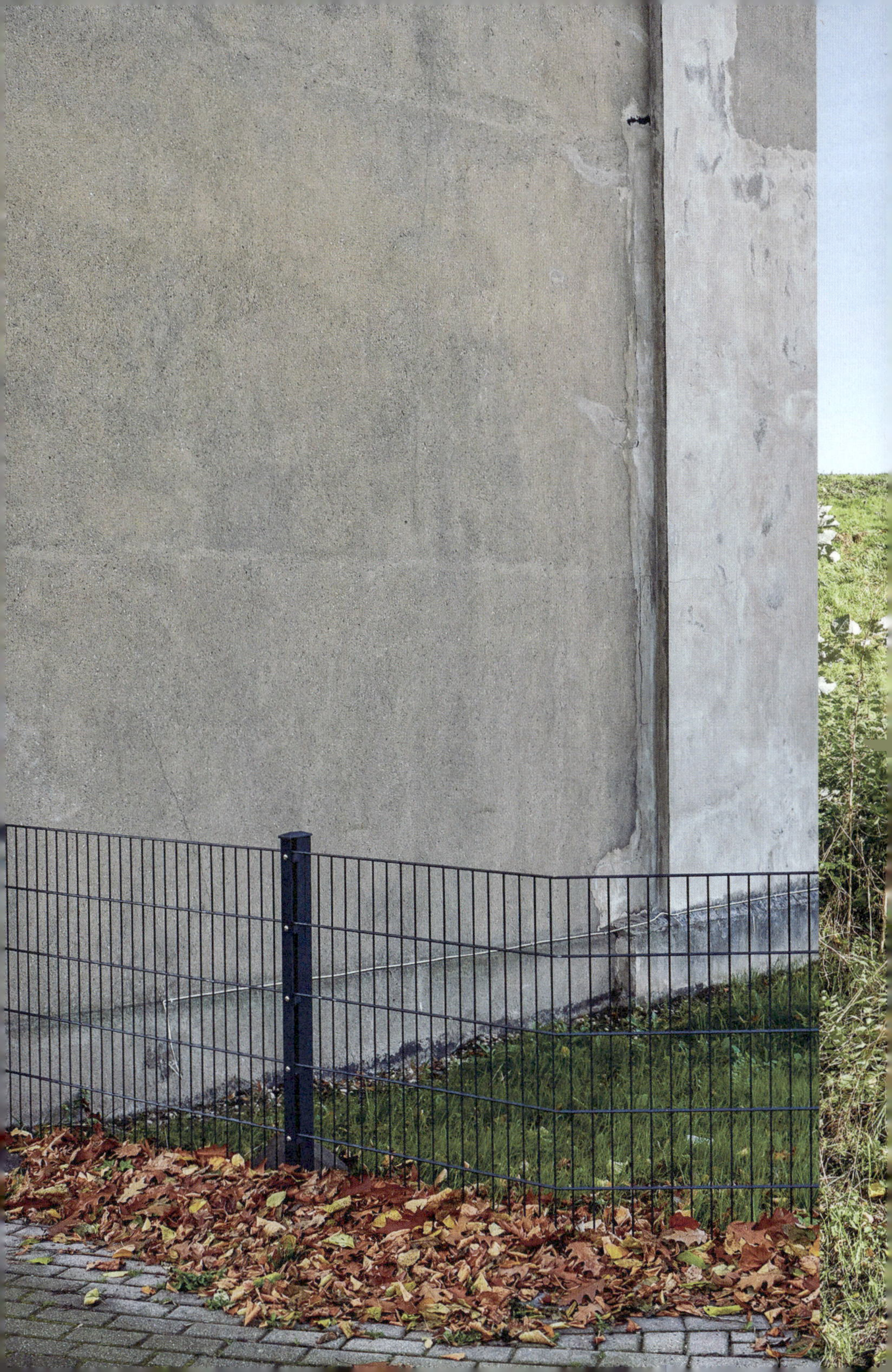

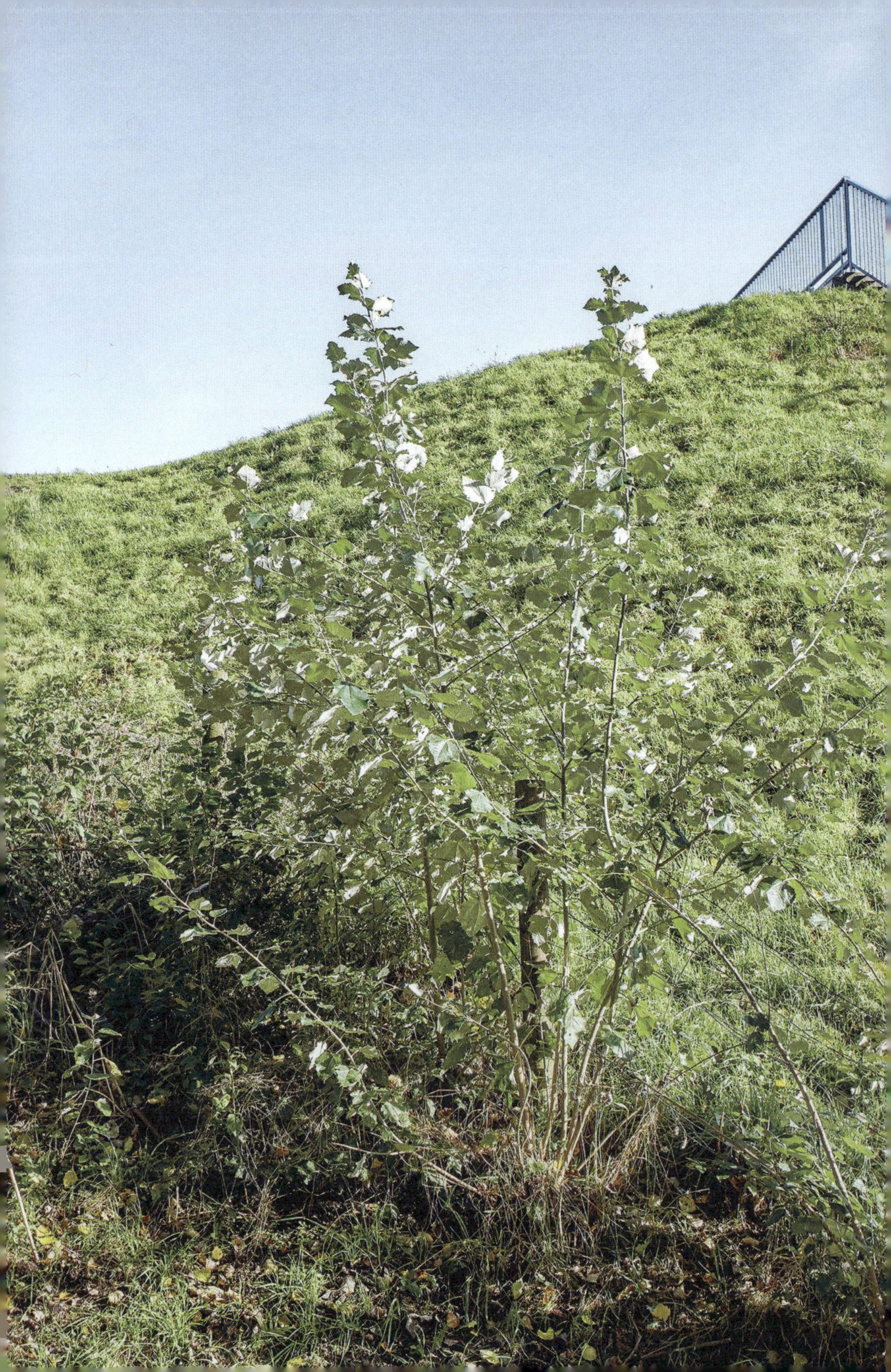

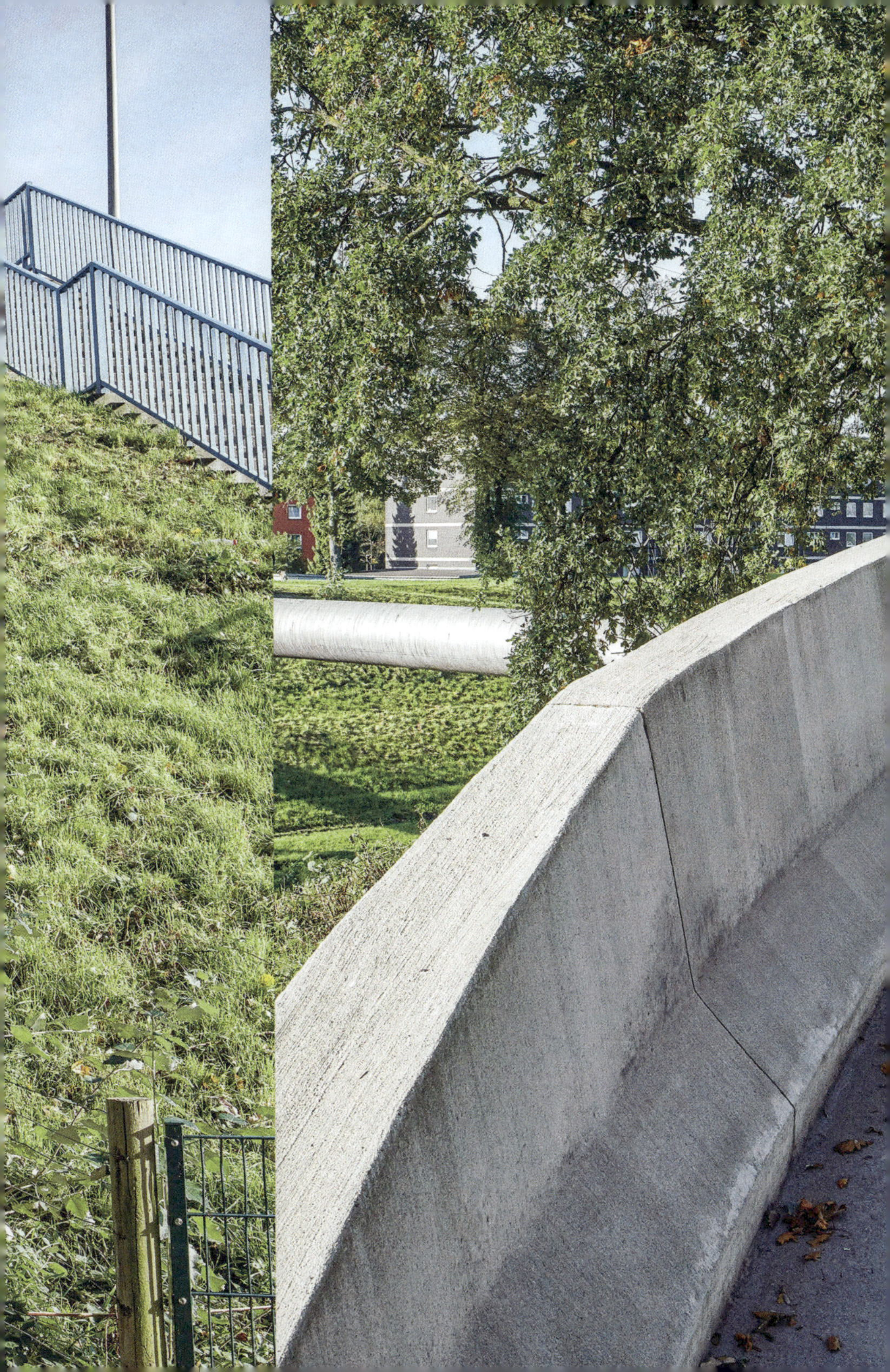

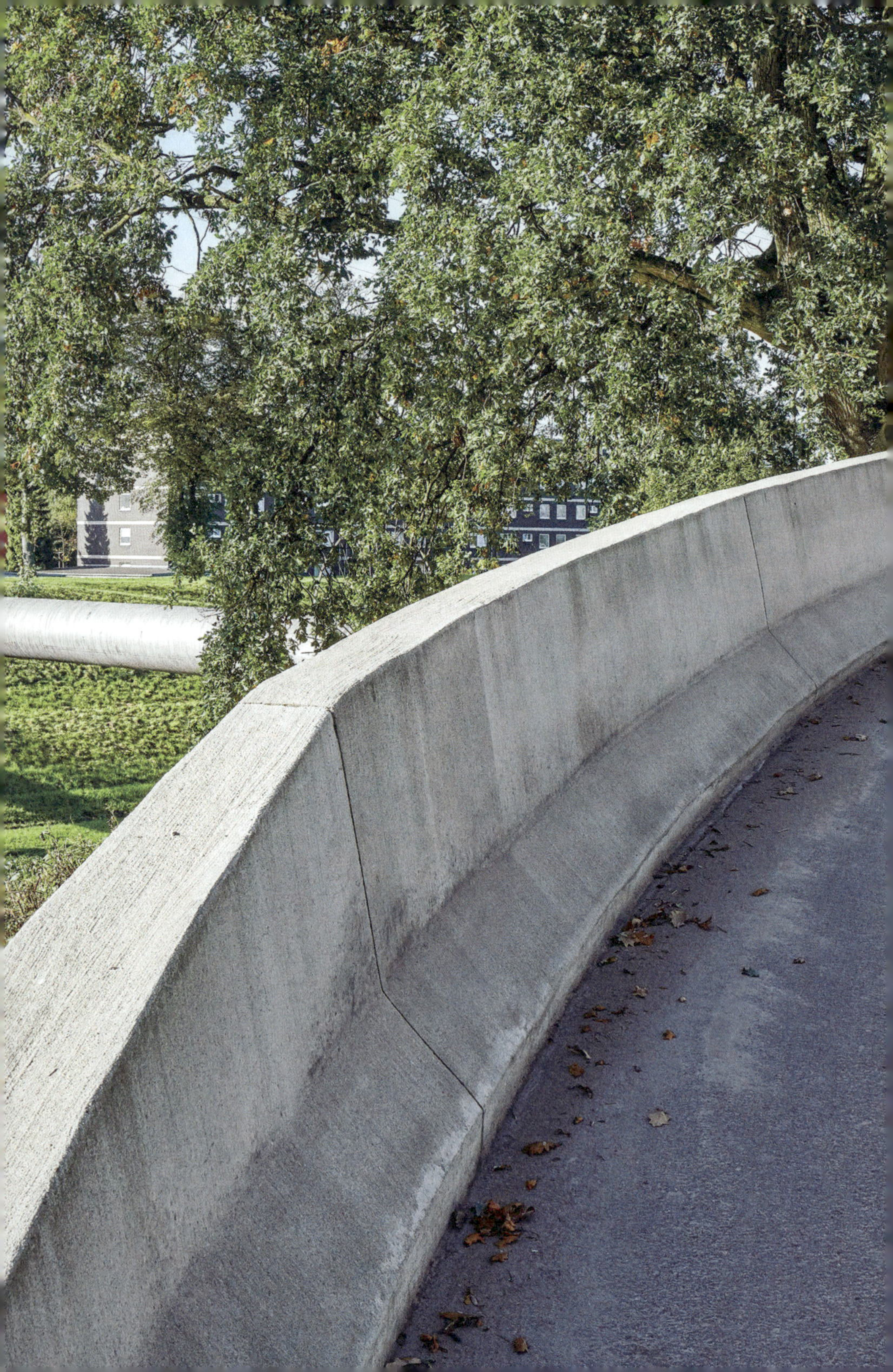

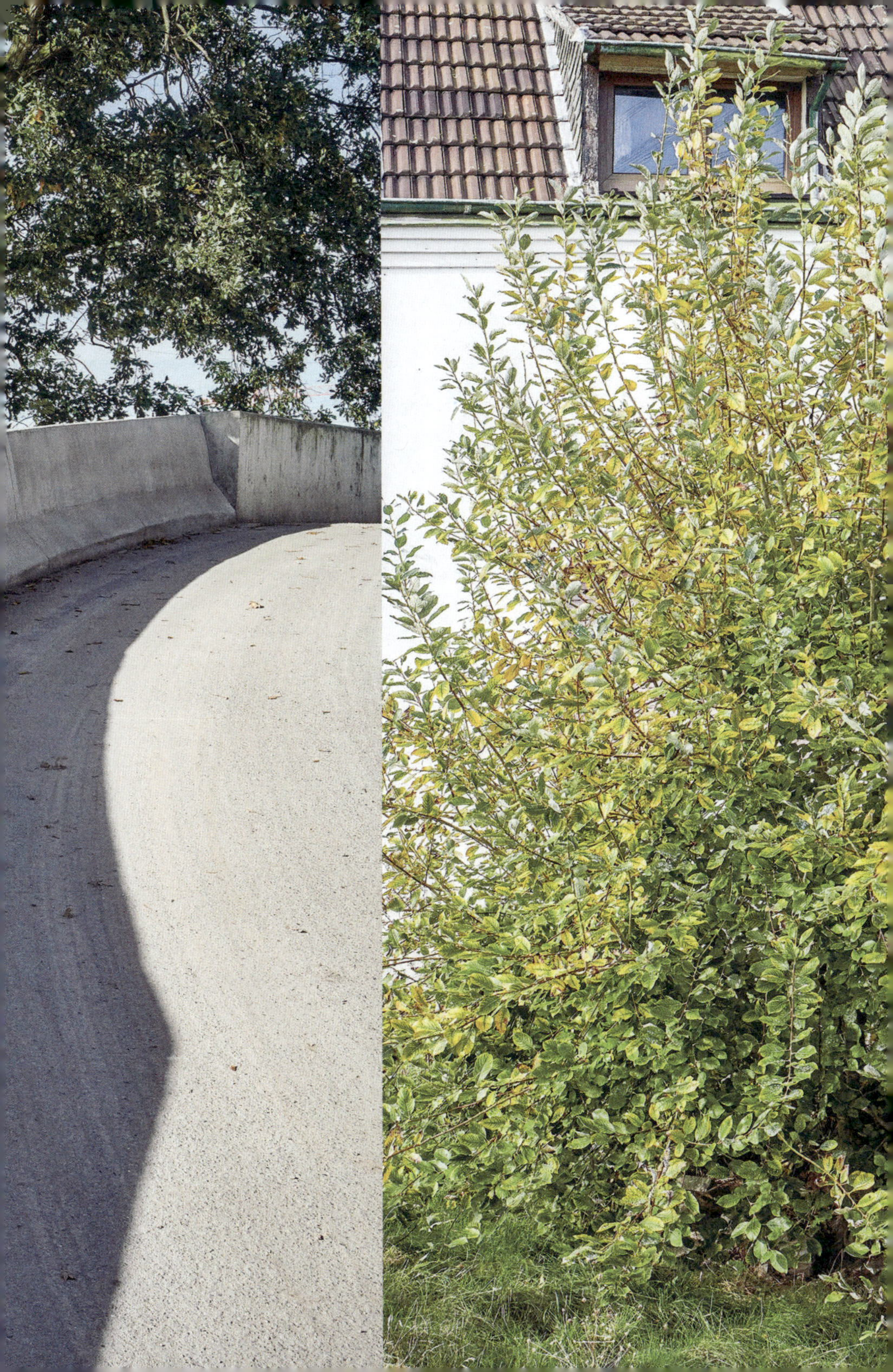

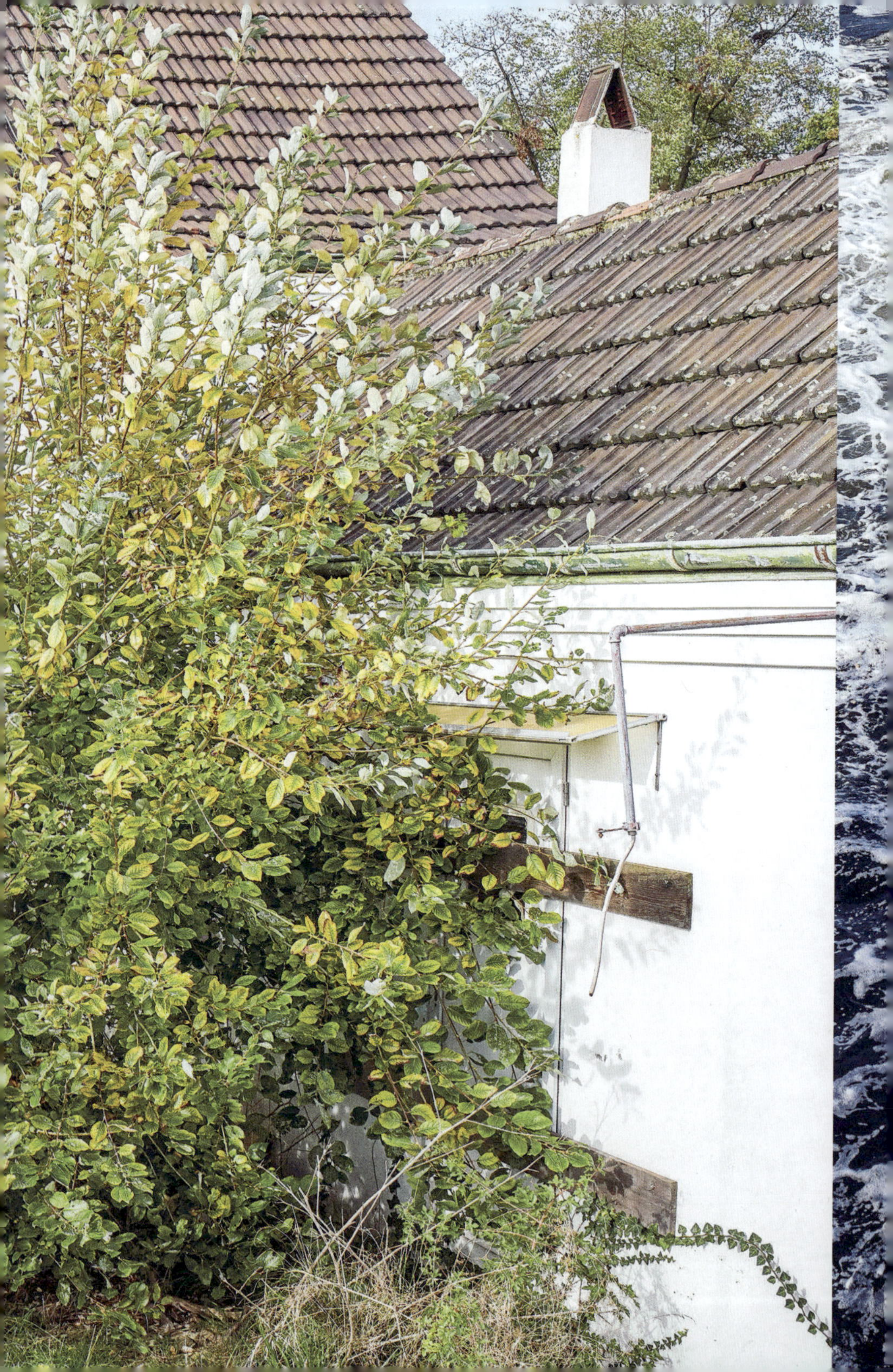

GLADBECK
BOTTROP
RHINE
DUISBURG
OBERHAUSEN
MÜLHEIM
75
77
74
67
65
59
58
60
56

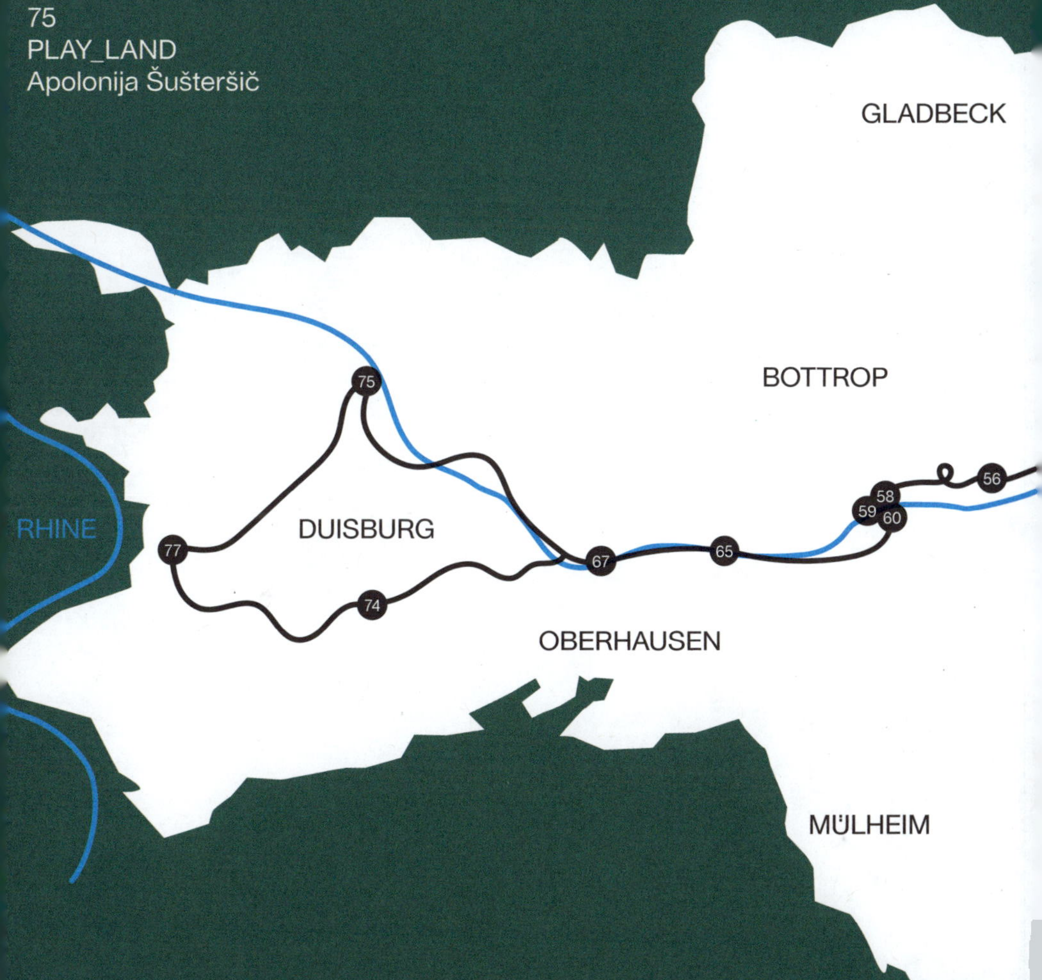

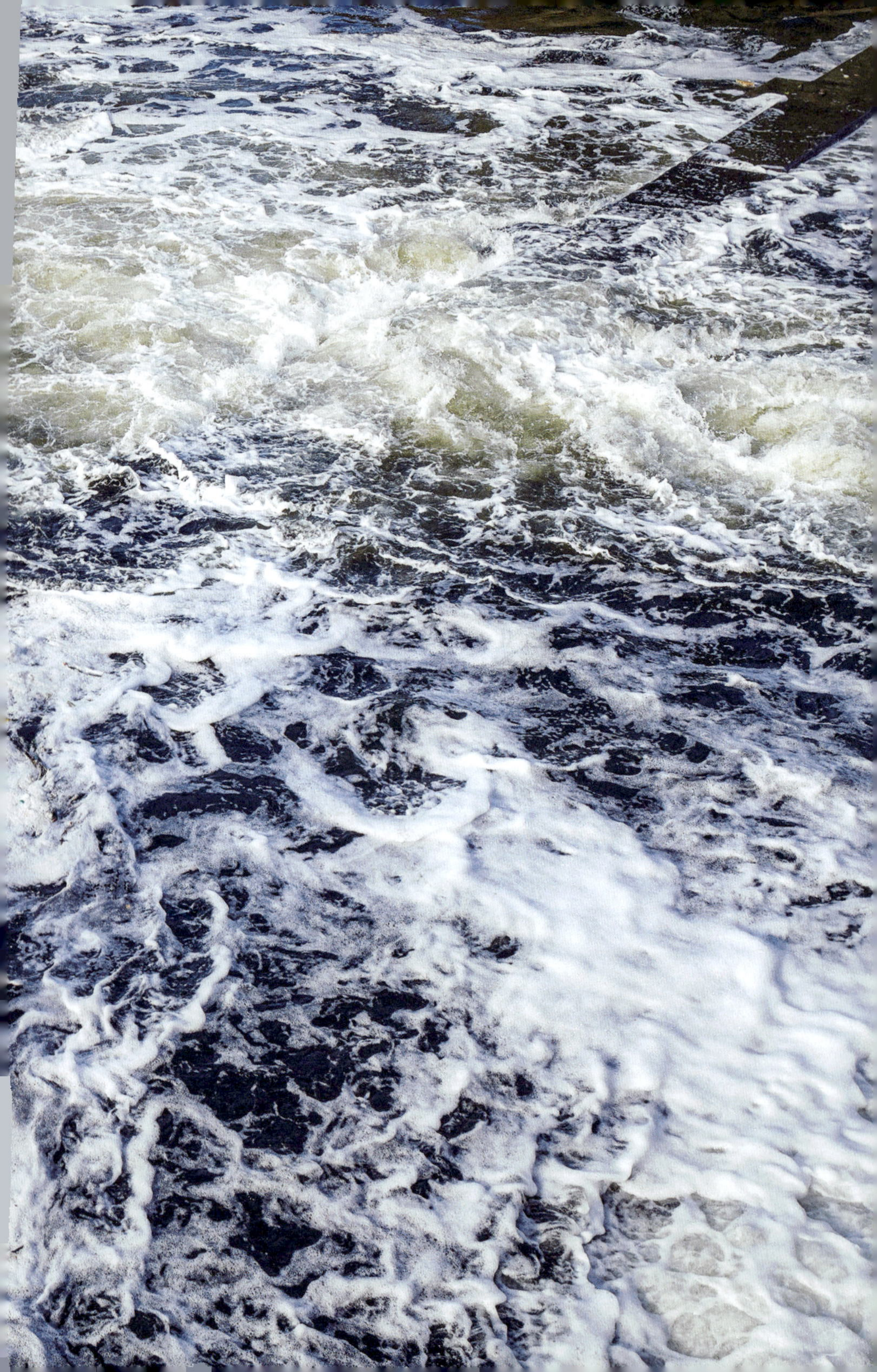